Thinking Geographically

Thinking Geographically

Space, Theory and Contemporary Human Geography

Phil Hubbard
Rob Kitchin
Brendan Bartley
Duncan Fuller

continuum
LONDON • NEW YORK

Continuum

The Tower Building, 11 York Road, London SE1 7NX
370 Lexington Avenue, New York, NY 10017-6503
www.continuumbooks.com

First published 2002

British Library Cataloguing-in-Publication Data
A catalogue record for this book is available from the British Library.
ISBN 0–8264–5624–3 (hardback)
       0–8264–5625–1 (paperback)

Library of Congress Cataloging in Publication Data
Thinking geographically : space, theory, and contemporary human geography / Phil
Hubbard . . . [et al.].
       p. cm.
   Includes bibliographical references and index.
   ISBN 0–8264–5624–3 — ISBN 0–8264–5625–1 (pb.)
   1. Human geography.   I. Hubbard, Phil.

   GF49 .T47 2002
   304.2—dc21   2002025925

Typeset by RefineCatch Limited, Bungay, Suffolk
Printed and bound in Great Britain by Bookcraft (Bath) Ltd

Contents

Thinker Profile Boxes

Preface

Our experiences as university teachers have revealed two shared observations. First, the majority of undergraduate geography students have an aversion to studying theory and do not understand or appreciate its importance. 'Facts' about the world, it seems, are fine, but ideas about the way the world works are less approachable, more slippery and more difficult to comprehend. As such, students often claim to prefer the empirical to the theoretical, the observable world to an abstract world of ideas and propositions. Second, and related to this, encouraging students to 'think geographically' can be a difficult and often thankless task, made all the more arduous by the lack of accessible texts that spell out clearly to students the *value* of theory and *why* they should (and need to) engage with it. A more common approach is for texts to write of theory only in the abstract, fastidiously cataloguing the history of different schools of thought but rarely showing how such ideas impinge on the practice of creating geographical knowledge.

Thinking Geographically has been written to address both of these observations. Simply stated, our aim is to demonstrate *why* addressing theory is important by showing *how* it shapes the production of geographical knowledge. In a wider sense, we want to enthuse and encourage students to engage with different ways of 'thinking geographically', and for them to recognize the importance of theory in the 'doing' of geography. Consequently, our prime objective has *not* been to write a text describing a 'history of geographic thought' or to provide an expansive overview of contemporary philosophical traditions in human geography – it is not an attempt to provide a comprehensive and authoritative 'God's-eye' view of the entire spectrum of contemporary geographic thought; nor is it a biography of the discipline's evolution, noting the collaborations and confrontations between different individuals that have characterized its chequered history. Instead, it seeks to explain why an understanding of theory and its history is an important, necessary and stimulating part of being a geographer. Consequently, we have adopted a different structure from other texts that aim to communicate geographic theory to students, one that is not primarily organized around abstract discussions of the philosophical nuances of schools of thought (what Gregory, 1997, terms the 'ologies' and 'isms' approach). Rather, we have divided the book into two key sections, each written to be accessible to undergraduate students.

In the first section, *Theorizing Human Geographies*, we seek to provide a general overview of the role of theory and the different theoretical traditions in human geography. In the first chapter we introduce theory and the production of knowledge, discuss its value in a geographic context and provide initial illustration of the ways in which different concepts – space, place and nature – can be thought about in radically different ways. Taking a broadly historic perspective, Chapter 2 provides a *concise* introduction to the different theoretical traditions that have shaped *Anglo-American* human geography in the post-war period, exploring how different theories of space have been developed at different times, and demonstrating how these theories have been informed by wider academic ideas and fashions. By outlining the changing lineaments of human geography we show that the way geographers think has always been evolving (and contested), but that certain ways of thinking have become associated with particular types of geography (as well as particular geographers). This is followed in Chapter 3 by an introduction to some of the emerging concepts that are shaping the discipline today and are likely to inform the production of geographical knowledges at the start of the twenty-first century. In combination, the chapters show geography to be a discipline that is ever-evolving and derivative in its borrowing of theoretical constructs from other sciences, social sciences and humanities.

In the second section, *Practising Theoretical Geographies*, we illustrate how different theoretical approaches have informed the study of five concepts – the body, text, money, governance and globalization – which are at the heart of economic, social, cultural and political geography. While far from an exhaustive list of key geographic concepts, each of the five chapters is intended to show how the theories and ideas introduced in the first half of the book have been *practised* by geographers as they study particular concepts and write particular geographies. While the focus is primarily on geographical scholarship, the chapters endeavour to show how concepts derived from other disciplines have been invoked and developed by geographers, using appropriate case studies and examples to clarify the distinctive contribution of particular ideas in producing geographical knowledge. Individually, each of our chapters thus demonstrates that key issues in economic, social, cultural or political geography can be theorized from a variety of radically different and competing approaches, while, collectively, they demonstrate that to 'think geographically' is inevitably to take theory seriously. This means that, although the first section and second section can be read independently, they are designed to 'talk' to one another, to create a dialogue between theory and practice and (ultimately) to problematize that distinction.

In order to illustrate our arguments and provide entry points to particular literatures, we have included brief profiles of a number of theorists and their work throughout the book (highlighted in **Profile** boxes). We acknowledge that our choice of thinkers is selective, especially if it is accepted that ideas cannot be solely attributed or reduced to one thinker since they emerge from complex academic and institutional networks of interaction. Given the limitations of space, however, we have restricted our choice of profiles to people whose ideas are exemplary in relation to our case studies and who are acknowledged to have expanded the theoretical horizons of human geography in some way. Some may feel that these boxes do scant justice to the complexity and scope of the work completed by these thinkers, yet that was not our intention. Rather, it is simply to introduce readers to these thinkers, providing brief biographical details, a summary of their theoretical influence on geography and (crucially) a guide to some accessible (English-language) readings that might lead to a more nuanced understanding of their ideas. This introductory tone is one we seek to maintain throughout the book, with references used sparingly so that readers may be steered towards some of the more widely available, accessible and recent texts that explore ways of thinking geographically. We can only hope that the book inspires people to do this further reading.

ACKNOWLEDGEMENTS

This book was a genuinely multi-authored book from initial proposal to finished product. Whilst each of us took primary responsibility for individual chapters, each chapter was ultimately co-authored, with all of us editing and revising the finished manuscript. It has been an enjoyable experience that has led, we feel, to a text that is more than the sum of its parts and one which could not have been completed by any of us individually.

As with any book there are a number of people who, despite their names not appearing on the front cover, contributed to it in various ways. In particular, we would like to thank Cora Collins, Una Crowley, Marcus Doel, Paddy Duffy, Mike Gane, the Globalization and World Cities group (Loughborough), Jamie Gough, Lewis Holloway, Sarah Holloway, Keith Lilley, James Monagle, Kasey Treadwell Shine and Rob Wilton. In addition, we would like to thank the geography students of National University of Ireland, Maynooth, who provided valuable guidance on the accessibility of the text. We also wish to thank Ray Tomlinson, the inventor of distributed e-mail. Although we met on four separate occasions, without his efforts this book would have taken a lot longer to write.

Finally, we would particularly like to thank Tristan Palmer at Continuum Publishing and to acknowledge that writing a book on contemporary theory in human geography was largely his idea (although we are fully responsible for the structuring and content). We are glad he put us on the path to writing it.

Theorizing Human Geographies

Chapter 1   Introducing Theory

1.1 INTRODUCTION

Just fifty years ago, geography was frequently characterized as an atheoretical endeavour. Now, such criticisms are rare, and the pendulum has swung the other way, with some suggesting it is overly theoretical at the expense of empirical study. This is a charge expressed by many undergraduate geography students, who often claim not only to dislike theory but also to challenge its value and relevance, particularly that which might be termed abstract or conceptual theory. This book has been written to illustrate to sceptical students the value and utility of geographic theory. As such, it aims to illustrate how the world around us is theorized from a geographic perspective; why there are different, competing theories; and how and why theories, and their popularity, change over time.

Put simply, a *theory* is a set of ideas about how the world works. As such, it is the means by which geographers seek to describe, explain or predict aspects of the world. Harvey (1969; 1972) likens theory to a map. A map, he details, provides a range of useful functions. It acts as a store of knowledge about a landscape, it reveals basic patterns and relationships between features in a landscape and it acts as a communication device, allowing users to navigate the terrain. Theory performs similar functions, detailing knowledge about the world, revealing relationships between data and communicating such knowledge. Both maps and theory are selective portrayals designed to detail with clarity a richer and more complex landscape. Both use specific 'languages' to construct, store and communicate knowledge. For example, a map uses symbols made intelligible through a legend, a projection, a scale and an orientation. And just as there are different kinds of maps (e.g., contour, choropleth and so on) displaying data at different scales, so also there are different kinds of theory. In all cases of map and theory, a consistent set of rules is used in their creation, designed to create internal consistency whereby contradictions and fallacies are minimized. Just as the art of creating, using and interpreting maps is not easily acquired but is learnt over time and developed with experience, so it is the same with theory. Consequently, theory can be difficult to comprehend and interpret because its construction and use is not always intuitive and its central tenets and underlying constructs have to be learnt.

Like a map, however, once it is appreciated how theory is constructed, interpreted and used, theory becomes a valuable tool for understanding and engaging with the world: 'a practical means for getting on' (Thrift, 1999, p. 334). Hence, there is an important link between theory and *praxis*. Praxis concerns how theoretical ideas are translated into practice through research, teaching, discussion and debate. As such, our central argument in this book is that, while it is tempting to dismiss theory, or to try to avoid it because it seems difficult, the reality of doing geography is that we *cannot avoid* theory. In short, theory infuses the practices of academic geography. In trying to understand the world about us, even in common-sense and non-academic ways (e.g. trying to predict who might win a political election or knowing where to shop for particular products), we are constantly employing theoretical tools and making claims or judgements about how the world works and our position within it. As Harvey (1969, p. 87) notes, 'any speculative fantasy may thus be regarded as a theory of some sort'. In many ways, academics seek to develop and deepen our understanding of the world by extending everyday and intuitive theory-making. They do this by constructing, testing and refining theoretical tools which seek to describe and explain phenomena and situations. Often, this theorizing involves adapting theories developed in other disciplines, such as social theory, economic theory or political theory. Ultimately, this 'borrowing' of ideas from other disciplines serves to make the strange familiar, and helps geographers to conceive of the world in new ways (Culler, 1997).

Unsurprisingly, there are many different opinions concerning how one should go about the tasks of thinking and researching particular phenomena, actions, ideas and concepts. This brings us to questions of *philosophy*. Put at its simplest, philosophy can be described as theories about theory. It promotes a fundamental and general analysis of the world and attempts to know it:

> Philosophy aims at the logical clarification of thoughts. ... Without philosophy thoughts are, as it were, cloudy and indistinct: its task is to make them clear and to give them sharp boundaries. (Wittgenstein, 1921)

Just as there are many theories in geography, so there are also many definitions of, and approaches to, philosophy. Philosophical questions are about the most fundamental aspects of life: reality, the nature of knowing, the mind, matter, truth and so on. However, it is not the subject matter alone that defines philosophy, so much as the style of questioning and the extent to which it interrogates the deep-rooted assumptions of both the issues in question and the questions themselves. Philosophy, then, is about the rigorous interrogation of the definitions and assumptions employed in all thinking, including those of everyday life and the academy. As such, it is more a method of analysis than the study of any particular substantive issue or empirical subject matter.

One of the perennial foci of philosophical analysis is questions about the nature of knowledge or the ways in which the world may be known. In other words, it is concerned with defining and delimiting the nature and focus of theories and how they are constructed and operate. Consequently, every theory sits within a philosophical framework. One useful way to think about philosophy, the differences between philosophic traditions and the ways in which they underpin particular theories is to identify their qualities in relation to four key characteristics: ontology, epistemology, ideology, and methodology. These four components essentially define the parameters of each philosophical approach to study, as several different positions can be adopted in relation to each component.

Ontology is part of metaphysics, the branch of philosophy that studies the nature and operation of reality or being. It concerns the set of specific assumptions about the nature of *existence* underlying a theory or system of ideas; beliefs about what exists and can be observed, and therefore known. For example, we can believe that the world exists and is organized as part of an ordered universe, or, conversely, that the universe and its contents are inherently chaotic and must be understood in those terms. Science as practised in disciplines such as biology, chemistry and physics generally accepts the former and posits that we can only truly know what can be observed and measured in quantitative terms. These disciplines generally ignore questions such as 'Is there a God?', regarding them as essentially unknowable questions of faith. Such an ontological position means that those geographers who subscribe to such a belief put verifiable, measurable facts at the core of their theories, rejecting values, opinions and beliefs as unverifiable, and therefore unknowable in any kind of strict sense (or at least unacceptable as evidence). Others posit that values and opinions can be known, either through scientific measurement or other means, and are therefore legitimate constituents of knowledge production. Different ontologies informing geographical theory therefore set out a number of positions such as: the things we experience are the things that exist; the things we agree amongst ourselves to exist, exist; what exists is what is perceived to exist; and so on (Johnston, 1986).

Epistemology concerns how knowledge is derived or arrived at; assumptions about *how* we can know the world. Essentially it concerns how we can validly come to know something. As we will see in Chapter 2, epistemologies in physical geography have tended to draw on a set of foundational beliefs that underpin science more generally. These beliefs contend that the world can only be truly known and understood through the application of a rigorous and systematic scientific method that is logical and rational. In this framework, physical geographers come to know the 'truth' about the world through systematic, scientific measurement and analysis of collected data. However, science's 'claims to know' have been challenged on a number of fronts. For example, foundational beliefs concerning truth, objectivity and value-free practice have been deconstructed and shown to be open to contestation. Moreover, it has been argued that traditional geography privileges particular Western and masculine ways of viewing the world, overvaluing Cartesian geometry and visual data whilst dismissing other forms of knowledge as unscientific and therefore less valid and worthy (Rose, 1993; Gregory, 1997). For these reasons, and others, human geographers have often embraced other epistemologies of knowledge, and struggled to reconcile their own studies with those of physical geography and the 'natural sciences'. Hence, epistemology in human geography is often predicated on *interpretative* frameworks adapted from the humanities rather than the natural sciences.

Ideology concerns the underlying social/political reasons or purpose for seeking knowledge, and like many other fundamental concerns in theory it straddles all of the main branches of philosophy: ontology, epistemology and ethics. Some philosophies posit that the production of knowledge should be an ideologically neutral activity. This view implies that it is the job of a theorist to develop ideas about how the world works and it is for others to decide how to use the ideas they uncover. Others posit that it is impossible to be ideologically neutral, and that, whether we like it or not, it is impossible to isolate personal social and political beliefs from wider theorization. On this basis, they argue that academics should use their theories to try and change the world for the better rather than leave it to others to interpret their ideas (see Section 3.2). This debate is well illustrated by the exchange between Reg Golledge (1993, 1996; see Box 2.2), Brendan Gleeson (1996) and Rob Imrie (1996) about how research concerning the geographies of disability should be framed ideologically. Golledge, for example, argued that geographers need to map out the spaces of disability from a scientific and ideologically neutral perspective, effectively mapping the geographies *of* disabled people. In response, Gleeson and Imrie contended that geographers should seek to create ideologically infused, transformative geographies *for* and *with* disabled people, aiming to alter the social and political conditions that serve to oppress people with disabilities.

Methodology is the set of procedures used to develop or test a theory; it is the means by which data are generated and analysed. To be consistent, these procedures must not deviate from the ontological and epistemological assumptions of the overall philosophy of investigation. So, for example, someone who believes that metaphysical questions are impossible for science to answer will not normally attempt to pose such questions. Such a researcher will instead seek measurable, quantifiable facts that can be analysed and modelled using scientific techniques. For others, metaphysical questions can be known and therefore such questions can usefully be asked. Whatever the beliefs, the upshot is that there is a variety of qualitative and quantitative methods that enable inherently different questions to be answered about what exists and what is important in the world. Like theory, these methods derive from different disciplines, with healthy debate existing about the merits of particular methods in relation to particular epistemologies, ontologies and ideologies (see Flowerdew and Martin, 1997; Robinson, 1998; Kitchin and Tate, 2000).

Geographers' recent sustained engagement with different philosophical traditions means that there is now a number of competing schools of thought on how best to think geographically and how most effectively to research geographical questions (see Chapter 2). Consequently, contemporary human geography has been characterized as being extremely diverse in the range of approaches and methods of enquiry it employs (Cloke *et al.*, 1991). It is this high degree of theoretical plurality that can make geography confusing for students new to the discipline. However, as Hill (1981, p. 38) notes, it is important to engage with philosophy as it underpins *all* geographic thought:

> Many geographers doubt that philosophical issues are actually relevant to geographic research. [However] no research (geographic or otherwise) takes place in a philosophical vacuum. Even if it is not explicitly articulated all research is guided by a set of philosophical beliefs. These beliefs influence or motivate the selection of topics for research, the selection of methods for research, and the manner in which completed projects are subjected to evaluation. In short, philosophical issues permeate every decision in geography.

As might be imagined, developing a theoretical position that is coherent and internally consistent in relation to a particular philosophical tradition (and its underpinning ideology, ontology, epistemology and methodology) is no easy task. Consequently, the arguments developed are quite complex, using carefully selected and, it often seems, ambiguous and overly complicated language. The net effect of this for the reader is 'often a lot of apprehension, disenchantment and an uneasy feeling of being lost in a philosophical wilderness' (Ragurman, 1994, p. 244). Theory, whether conceptual (abstract) or quite grounded (concrete), can often be very difficult to comprehend. This applies as much to academics as it does to students. We would be the first to acknowledge that we struggle with many theoretical constructs and we certainly do not claim to have detailed knowledge of all the theories currently employed in geography or their philosophical bases. It is, however, important to try to grasp why *thinking* geographically is a vital part of becoming a geographer. The central purpose of this book is to help you to explore different approaches to geographical theory and philosophy. Sometimes this will prove a difficult journey, but hopefully a stimulating and rewarding one. Certainly, on completion of this journey, you will have a fuller understanding of what it means to think 'geographically', and you will be able to:

1. understand how geographers have approached a particular issue and why they have studied the world in the way that they have;
2. appreciate why geography is so wide-ranging in the type of theories it has developed, and appreciate the arguments for and against different theories;
3. understand how theoretical ideas are diffused through and across disciplinary boundaries, being adapted for particular ends by geographers and others;
4. develop your own understanding of the practice of geography and be able to justify and defend your own thinking;
5. think through issues you encounter outside the remit of your academic studies and make beneficial links back to these.

1.2 THE PRODUCTION OF KNOWLEDGE

Before we turn to examine how theory has shaped the discipline of geography, it is worth exploring the nature of knowledge production. This discussion is useful, we feel, for two reasons. First, it provides an illustration of competing theories of the same endeavour (knowledge production), and second, it helps to explain how we have approached the writing of this book. The two theories we examine here can be characterized as a *scientific* approach and a *situated* approach.

A 'scientific' understanding of knowledge production is that it is a rational, objective, and neutral pursuit. That is, the role of scientists is to gather data which they then analyse using standardized and non-biasing procedures (e.g., using statistical tests). All analysis and interpretation is carried out in a detached manner to provide a set of value-free results. This scientific approach thus supposes that the world consists of data that can be collected or 'harvested' unproblematically when using carefully constructed methodologies that conform to scientific standards and that knowledge can be gained simply by analysing these data in a particular fashion. Until recently, nearly all geographical analyses, regardless of philosophical differences in ideology, ontology, epistemology and methodology, claimed to adopt such an approach. That is, regardless of what were considered to be valid sources of data, all data were collected and analysed rigorously from an 'objective' position. This scientific approach meant that regardless of how the results were used, the findings from one study could be validly compared with another, so a body of knowledge could develop and accumulate in a logical manner.

This scientific account of knowledge production has been challenged by those who believe that knowledge is not simply 'out there' waiting to be collected and processed, but rather knowledge is made by actors who are *situated* within particular contexts. As such, knowledge production is not a neutral or objective activity but is constructed, partial, situated and positioned. Here, the work of Donna Haraway (1991; see Box 1.3) has been important. She contends that objectivity is a parable which fails to describe how scientific research is actually undertaken. She suggests that all forms of knowledge are social constructions. That is, theorization, and its operationalization through research, is shaped by a host of influences ranging from personal beliefs to the conditions of funding to individual relationships between researcher and researched. Academic work then is recognized as being situated (e.g., shaped by the culture of academia, institutional pressures, individual lifestyles) and political (e.g., developed for particular ideological purposes) (Bourdieu, 1988). As a consequence, Haraway argues for the development of 'situated knowledges' where theorization and empirical research are framed within the context within which they were formulated. She thus posits that a view from an acknowledged (situated) position may be more truthful than one from nowhere (i.e., a supposed objective, neutral one). The Women and Geography Study Group (WGSG) (1997, p. 14; see Box 2.5) elaborate: '[k]nowledge is never pure but is always situated in the complex and sometimes contradictory social locations of its producers and audiences'.

This situated approach to the production of knowledge also recognizes that what constitutes 'academic knowledge' is shaped by silences and exclusions. Feminist theorists in particular have argued that the academy, including geography (see Domosh, 1991; Rose, 1993), is masculinist in nature (see also Section 2.4). The suggestion here is that men have dominated the academy and what constitutes 'legitimate' and scientific knowledge has largely been decided by men:

> It is important to realise how much geography as we know it today is the product of a series of decisions, some considered and others more impulsive, some prompted by idealism and others more pragmatic, but all of them taken in particular historical situations by a relatively small number of men occupying positions of authority and prestige in the discipline. (Gregory, 1978, p. 18)

Accordingly, the contributions of women have largely been written out of the history of geography, and, even when female academics have been recognized for their academic achievements, this is often because they have adopted a masculine or 'malestream' way of looking at the world (Blunt and Wills, 2000). Moreover, the geographies and histories of other groups, such as black people, those in developing countries, disabled people, gay, lesbian, bisexual and trans-gender individuals, have largely been written from certain dominant positions, thereby silencing other voices and providing selective and partial geographical accounts (see Sibley, 1995). A significant part of contemporary human geography has been directed at uncovering these silences and exclusions and challenging traditional epistemologies of what are considered valid forms of knowledge and how such knowledge should be generated or constructed (see Chapter 3).

Geography's contribution to the study of how knowledge is produced, beyond many geographers adopting a more *reflexive* approach to their work (see Chapter 3), has been a recognition that knowledge is socially and spatially situated (see, for example, Livingstone, 1992a; Sibley, 1995; Sidaway, 1997). In essence, this suggests that the form and content of knowledge is dependent on the location in which it is formulated:

> Your context – your location in the world – shapes your view of the world and therefore what you see as important, as worth knowing; context shapes the theories/stories you concoct of the world to describe and explain it. (Hanson, 1992, p. 573)

As such, there has been a recent concern with exploring the 'sites, places or media in and through which geographical knowledge is produced, transmitted and consumed' by both 'expert' and 'lay' people (Desforges and Jones, 2001, p. 334). This has led to the development of approaches to human geography informed by work in feminist, post-colonial and postmodern geography that 'acknowledges that the nature of geography has always been contested and negotiated . . . recognises that geography has meant different things for different people in different places; and . . . focuses on accounting for how and why particular practices of geography get to be legitimated at different times and in different places' (Women and Geography Study Group, 1997, p. 14).

We are broadly in agreement with the argument that knowledge production is not a neutral and objective pursuit, but is rather embedded in the practices and ideologies of its creators and the contexts within which they operate. Accordingly, this book seeks to describe the situatedness of different geographical theories, (partially) charting, from our own situated positions (as white, male, heterosexual, middle-class academics schooled in England and Ireland, with particular research interests), the changing nature of geographical thinking in both general (Chapters 2 and 3) and specific terms (Chapters 4 to 7). As such, we do *not* claim to be geography's 'umpires', charting a definitive guide to contemporary theoretical understanding or dictating which theory is 'right' or 'better' than others. Rather, we acknowledge that the 'stories' we tell are partial, selective and shaped by our own views and histories and the pedagogic purpose of the text – the book is merely one account which we are sure will be contested by others. Moreover, while we do hold personal preferences for which approaches have more salience for us in our own work, we acknowledge that they are not necessarily 'right' or 'better'. They do however have salience for us, allowing us to theorize the world in ways which seem to make sense. We start this exercise by exploring the varying ways in which human geography is defined.

1.3 THEORIZING HUMAN GEOGRAPHY

In this section, we start to think about how geography has been variously theorized over time, beginning by considering how the discipline itself is conceived. Given the discussion so far, it should be of little surprise to learn that the definition of human geography as a disciplinary endeavour is constantly changing, as the focus, content and praxis of geography are continually rethought. Over the past forty years, in particular, as geography has entered into a sustained engagement with philosophy, questioning its ideology, epistemology, ontology and methodology (see Chapter 2), the question of how geographers conceive their disciplinary focus has diversified. This is because there is a recursive relationship between theoretical approach and the object (and objectives) of study, with each affecting the other. Indeed, the different theories and philosophies of geography provide a distinctive view of the *nature* of geography (Harvey, 1969). Consequently, for decades contemporary human geography has been struggling with its identity, with no clear consensus as to what geographers *are*, what geographers *do*, or *how* they should study the world. This means that a number of different definitions of geography can be found (see Figure 1.1).

Figure 1.1 Defining geography

Hartshorne (1959, p. 21):
'Geography is concerned to provide accurate, orderly, and rational description and interpretation of the variable character of the Earth's surface.'

The Concise Oxford Dictionary (1964, p. 511):
'Geography, n. Science of the earth's surface, form, physical features, natural and political divisions, climate, productions, population, etc. (*mathematical, physical* and *political*, ~, the science in these aspects); subject matter of ~; features, arrangement, *of* place; treatise or manual of ~.'

Yeates (1968, p. 1):
'Geography can be regarded as a science concerned with the rational development, and testing, of theories that explain and predict the spatial distribution and location of various characteristics on the surface of the earth.'

Dunford (1981, p. 85):
'Geography is the study of spatial forms and structures produced historically and specified by modes of production.'

Haggett (1981, p. 133):
'[Geography is] the study of the Earth's surface as the space within which the human population lives.'

Johnston (1986, p. 6):
'Literally defined as "earth description", geography is widely accepted as a discipline that provides "knowledge about the earth as the home of humankind".'

Haggett (1990):
'Geographers are concerned with three kinds of analysis:

- Spatial (location): numbers, characteristics, activities and distributions.
- Ecological: the relationship between humans and environment.
- Regional: the combination of the first two themes in areal differentiation.'

Geography Working Group's Interim Report (1990: Department of Education and Science and the Welsh Office):

'• Geography explores the relationship between the Earth and its peoples through the study of place, space, and environment. Geographers ask questions where and what; also how and why.
- The study of place seeks to describe and understand not only the location of the physical and human features of the Earth, but also the processes, systems, and interrelationships that create or influence those features.
- The study of space seeks to explore the relationships between places and patterns of activity arising from the use people make of the physical settings where they live and work.
- The study of the environment embraces both its physical and human dimensions. Thus it addresses the resources, sometimes scarce and fragile, that the Earth provides and on which all life depends; the impact on those resources of human activities; and wider social, economic, political and cultural consequences of the interrelationship between the two.'

Gale (1992, p. 21):
'Geography, for me, is about how we view the world, how we see people in places.'

Peet (1998, p. 1):
'Geography is the study of relations between society and the natural environment. Geography looks at how society shapes, alters, and increasingly transforms the natural environment, creating humanised forms from stretches of pristine nature, and then sedimenting layers of socialisation one within the other, on top of the other, until a complex natural-social landscape results. Geography also looks at how nature conditions society, in some original sense of creating the people and raw materials which social forces "work up" into culture, and in an ongoing sense of placing limits and offering material potentials for social processes like economic development.'

Source: Updated from Kitchin and Tate (2000, p. 4)

As Tim Unwin (1992) notes, part of the problem is that definitions can change depending on whether we try to define geography as simply 'what geographers do' (academic), 'what geographers study' (vernacular) or in terms of its distinctive contribution to teaching and learning (pedagogic). However, the problem is more deep-rooted than how we decide to define a subject. As Peter Haggett (1990) details, geography has a long history and its development as an area of study contributes to the difficulty in assigning an agreed definition. He reports that geography occupies a puzzling position within the organization of knowledge, straddling both the social and natural sciences. This he attributes to the development of geography as a distinct form of knowledge by classical Greek scholars who viewed humanity as an integral part of nature. By the time geography became an established university subject in the late nineteenth century, academic studies had already been divided into the natural and physical sciences on the one hand, and the humanities and social sciences on the other. Geography, with its natural and social constituents, had to be slotted into this existing inappropriate structure. This uneasy positioning, at the intersection of natural and social science, he suggests, has led contemporary human geographers to constantly refine and redefine their discipline in order to demonstrate its intellectual worth. David Livingstone (1992b), in contrast, argues that this process of refinement and redefinition is not a recent phenomenon. He details how geography as a practice has constantly changed throughout history, with different people attaching salience to different interpretations in particular contexts:

Geography . . . has meant different things to different people at different times and in different places. (Livingstone, 1992b, p. x)

This continual contest over the definitions of geography, then, is due to the way in which different scholars conceptualize and rework the content and focus of the subject. In other words, there are many different geographies, some new, some old. All have slightly different philosophical bases, different emphases, and some are more widely practised than others. For example, Hartshorne (1959) saw geography as an *idiographic* science (that is, its main emphasis being description), whereas Yeates (1968) saw geography as a *nomothetic* science (that is, its main emphasis being explanation and law-giving). Some scholars still agree with Hartshorne or Yeates, but others have a different vision, seeing potential in approaches which transcend both description and science. In the rest of this section, we illustrate the ways in which the definition of geography continues to be contested by briefly detailing how three of geography's core concepts – space, place and nature – are persistently being rethought in relation to geographical theories.

1.3.1 Space

How geographers and others understand space is always changing. As we detail more fully in Chapter 2, most geographical analyses up until the 1970s adopted (implicitly, if not explicitly) an *absolute* understanding of space (Shields, 1997). In this view, space is understood as a system of organization, a geometry, 'a kind of absolute grid, within which objects are located and events occur' (Curry, 1995, p. 5). In geographic terms, absolute space is defined and understood through Euclidean geometry (with x, y and z dimensions) and, for analytical purposes, treated as an objective, empirical space: 'an absolute container of static, though movable, objects and dynamic flows of behaviour' (Gleeson, 1996, p. 390). Here, an essentialist view, where space is effectively reduced to the essence of geometry, is adopted so that dimensions and contents of space are unquestionably understood as being natural and given; there is a belief that there are pre-existing physical laws that can be scientifically measured. This conception of space largely underpins the work of positivistic and quantitative geographers. They seek to delimit general spatial laws that can be used to explain the interrelationship between people and place, and identify the logic in patterns of human settlement and endeavour (see Chapter 2). For many, the key text here was David Harvey's *Explanation in Geography* (1969), which detailed a comprehensive theoretical and empirical basis for 'scientific geography' (see Box 6.2).

More recently there has been sustained criticism of these absolute and essentialized conceptions of space. Indeed, some have argued that 'reducing the world to a spaceless abstraction . . . [has] very limited utility' (Crang and Thrift, 2000a, p. 2), suggesting that this take on space does not pay sufficient attention to the spatial problematic (and, hence, does not consider space at all). Instead, a relational view of space has been forwarded that seeks both to critique absolute theorizations and representations of space and to provide an alternative position. A *relative* understanding of space prioritizes analyses of how space is constituted and given meaning through human endeavour. Here, space is not a given neutral and passive geometry but rather is continuously produced through socio-spatial relations; the relationship between space, spatial forms and spatial behaviour is not contingent upon 'natural' spatial laws, but is rather a product of cultural, social, political and economic relations; space is not essential in nature but is constructed and produced; space is not an objective structure but is a social experience. As such, space is 'constituted through social relations and material social practices' (Massey, 1994, p. 254). Against this, Ed Soja (1985) takes a more restricted view of space when he defines socially produced space as 'spatiality', suggesting that not all space is socially produced, but all spatiality is. Similarly, Shields (1991, p. 31) takes as his object of study 'social spatialization', a term which captures both the symbolic construction of space at the level of the social imaginary as well as its more concrete articulation in the landscape. Conceived of in these terms, an everyday space like a football stadium can be seen to be both a physical form constructed by certain agents and institutions as well as a space given meaning through myth, language and ritual: its use and occupation is shaped both by its material form and the immaterial meanings that coalesce around it.

The notion of treating space as socially produced is perhaps most clearly advocated in the work of **Henri Lefebvre** (1991; see Box 1.1). He detailed how the production of space (i.e., the process of spatialization) is premised on three, complementary levels. First, he identified a set of *spatial practices*; 'concrete' processes, flows and movements that can be perceived in the realm of the everyday, manifest as movements, migrations, routines and other journeys through and in space that influence the 'where' of human endeavours. In relation to urban space, for example, it is these spatial practices that serve to (re)produce the city, making and unmaking it as a functioning urban system. Second, he identified a set of *representations of space* (e.g., images, books, films and so on) which serve to represent and make sense of space. These conceptions of space have their own power to reproduce space, working ideologically to legitimate or contest particular spatial practices. Urban representations like plans or maps are

---

Box 1.1 Henri Lefebvre (1901–91)

Henri Lefebvre, a French sociologist-philosopher, has had a significant impact on how academics theorize space, especially since his book *The Production of Space* was translated into English in 1991 (Ed Soja, 1996, suggests that it is arguably the most important book ever written about human spatiality and spatial imagination – a point echoed by Merrifield, 2000b). In *The Production of Space*, Lefebvre developed a 'unitary theory of space' that sought 'rapprochement between *physical* space (nature), *mental* space (formal abstractions about space), and *social* space (the space of human action and conflict and "sensory phenomena")' (Merrifield, 2000b, p. 171). He suggested that these different types of space are of the same substance and same force, each being socially produced. Seeking to decode the production of space, he emphasized the entwining of the three elements that make up space: spatial practices, representations of space and spaces of representation (or representational space). In turn, these equate to the routine spatial behaviours that can be perceived in the world, the conceptions of space which order our notion of what is possible, and the spaces that are produced by the body in everyday practice. The relations between these are complex, so that representations of space are held in tension with spaces of representation, producing spatial practice. Moreover, it is apparent that spatial practice provides the basis for both

thus recognized as social productions, commonly produced by professionals such as engineers, architects and planners who purport to offer an objective view of the way the city works. Third, Lefebvre identified the existence of *spaces of representation*. In contrast to perceived or represented space, this is the space that is lived and felt by people as they weave their way through everyday life. Lefebvre saw that these spaces too were imbued with ideological and political content, claiming that it is in such spaces that the dehumanizing tendencies wrought by capitalist processes could be overcome (i.e., proclaiming the power of people to produce their own space and create new forms of urban life). Together, these three forms of space combine to produce a complex spatiality, the relationship between them varying over time. Crucially, all three make up 'space'; analytical priority cannot automatically be given to one over any of the others.

As Crang and Thrift (2000a and b) note, one of the consequences of non-absolute understandings of space is that space has come to mean different things to many people, especially those outside the discipline of geography, taking on metaphorical qualities that seem far removed from 'space as container'. One can take space to exist separate from social conceptions of space, or take space to be always social. Equally, one may see spaces as fixed outside time, or always in a 'state of becoming', known only in, and through time (Unwin, 2000). In short, then, space is a highly complex term that is used and understood in a variety of ways. We return to many of these understandings later in the book.

representations of space and spatial representations. Transforming Marx's periodization of capitalism into a history of space, Lefebvre accordingly showed how different relations between those elements produced different forms of space, from the historical space of classical times to the abstract and contradictory spaces of late capitalism. In the latter epoch, for example, he argued that the abstract space of cold capitalism had overpowered the lived space of sensuous and warm bodies, and that a rational bureaucratic form of space had become dominant. Shields (1998), however, argues strongly against these periodizing concepts, suggesting that different forms of space can coexist. Lefebvre's work implies that the main struggle in society is not class struggle, but spatial conflict. Although his ultimate faith in the ability of human beings to create revolutionary forms of space (differential space) through bodily practice is somewhat at odds with much post-structuralist thinking, Lefebvre's work has been widely cited and celebrated by geographers, who emphasize that it represents a thoroughly geographical analysis of social life (Soja, 1996).

Further reading: Lefebvre (1991); Merrifield (2000b); Shields (1998); Unwin (2000)

1.3.2 Place

As with space, place, until relatively recently, was theorized purely in absolute terms. Within this tradition (as adopted by regional and quantitative geography), place was understood merely as a gathering of people in a bounded locale (territory) – literally a portion of geographic space (Duncan, 2000). Place was thus conceived as a unique site that, while connected to other places, could be understood as a largely self-contained unit. This unit, because of its salience to the people living there, gave rise to a 'sense of place' which itself could be studied as a phenomenon unique to that locale. For example, during the 1970s, geographers adopting humanistic approaches (see Section 2.3) began to undermine the absolute conception of place in two ways. First, these humanist approaches saw place as more subjectively defined. As such, what constituted a place was seen to be largely individualistic, although attachments and meanings were often shared. A place meant different things to different people. This led Agnew (1987) and Entrikin (1991) to provide working definitions that mediated between objective and subjective understandings of place. Entrikin (1991), for example, argued that place is both the external context of our actions and a centre of meaning; there is a tension between subjective and objective conceptions of place that has to be accommodated in theorizing and researching geographic questions. Agnew (1987) identifies three main elements of place, the first two objective, the last subjective:

1. *Locale* – the settings in which social relations are constituted;
2. *Location* – the objective geographical area encompassing the setting for social interaction as defined by social and economic processes operating at a wider scale.
3. *Sense of place* – the local structure of subjective feeling associated with an area.

Second, humanist approaches, along with Marxist geographers, began to adopt a critical approach questioning the uniqueness of places within a globalizing world. For example, Edward Relph (1976), in his book *Place and Placelessness*, critiqued the uniqueness and 'sense of place' of traditional conceptions of place.

Relph's thesis was that a combination of economic and cultural globalization (see Chapter 8) and large-scale mobility is transforming the relationship between people and place, and thus how place and place-making should be theorized. Through a sustained analysis he discussed experiences of 'outsiderness' and 'insiderness' in places. Peet (1998, p. 50) summarized these experiences as: '*existential outsiderness*, in which all places assume the same meaningless identity; *objective outsiderness*', in which places are viewed scientifically and passively; '*incidental outsiderness*, in which places are experienced as little more than backgrounds for activities; *vicarious insiderness*, in which places are experienced in a second-hand way' (e.g., through paintings); '*behavioural insiderness*, which involves more emotional and empathetic involvement in a place; and finally *existential insiderness*, when a place is experienced without deliberate and unselfconscious reflection, yet is full of significance'. Relph (1976) used these concepts to examine the notion of 'authentic' place-making and inauthentic place-making (placelessness). To Relph, an authentic 'sense of place' involved a sense of belonging, with an inauthentic being the converse. Inauthentic places, he contended, are the prevalent mode of industrialized, mass societies and stem from an acceptance of mass values (Peet, 1998). Place-lessness, then, is 'a weakening of the identity of places to the point where they not only look alike, but feel alike and offer the same bland possibilities for experience' (Relph, 1976, p. 90).

Relph's analysis leads towards a more *relational* understanding that views place as contingent and tied into a broader context. A relational understanding of place argues that places do not just exist as bounded territorial units but that they are created, and are situated in social, political, economic and historical contexts, which in turn they help to shape. Developing from the work of geographers adopting structuralist (e.g., Pred, 1984), critical (e.g., Harvey, 1989a) and feminist (e.g., Rose, 1993) approaches (see Chapter 2), places are thus theorized as very complex entities that are situated within and shaped by forces from well beyond their own notional boundaries. Here, there is a recognition that places should not be romanticized as pre-political entities but that they are shaped by often oppressive institutional forces and social relationships.

Doreen Massey's (1991, 1994, 1997) writing has been particularly influential in reshaping how we conceptualize place (see Box 1.2). She views places as the complex intersections and outcomes of *power geometries* that operate across many spatial scales from the body to the global (see Chapters 4 and 8). To her, places are thus constituted of, and the outcome of, multiple, intersecting social, political and economic relations, giving rise to a myriad of spatialities. Places and the social relations within and between them, then, are the results of particular arrangements of power, whether it is individual and institutional, or imaginative and material. As such, places are not defined by their unique and

Box 1.2 Doreen Massey (1944–)
Doreen Massey, Professor of Geography at the Open University (UK), has been a key influence on the discipline of geography for more than two decades. Her earlier work combined Marxist and feminist theories to examine the spatial and gendered division of labour (1984). Here, we consider her recent work on understanding the concept of place. Starting with an article in *Marxism Today* (1991), she has through a number of publications (e.g., 1994, 1995, 1997) developed a 'progressive sense of place', formulated as a reaction to the charge by some theorists that the significance of place(s) was being eroded by large-scale 'space-time compression' due to globalization (see Chapter 8). To Massey, places are produced by the complex intersection of processes that operate across spatial scales from the local to the global. Places then are made up of flows and movements, rather than rootedness and tradition. So, for example, in her example of Kilburn, a district of London, she notes that its residents' sense of place is defined by a number of factors ranging from in-migration from Ireland, Pakistan and other nations; local, national and international employers; its range of employment types; its diversity of shops,

distinctive location, but rather by 'the intersections of sets of social relations stretched out over particular spaces' (WGSG 1997, p. 8). These relations exist at a variety of interlocking scales.

Massey's '*progressive concept of place* recognises the open and porous boundaries of place as well as the myriad interlinkages and interdependencies among places. It also acknowledges that the lives of some people are highly interconnected into a global network . . . while others lead severely circumscribed lives' (Duncan, 2000, p. 583). Places are thus relational and contingent, experienced and understood differently by different people; they are multiple, contested, fluid and uncertain (rather than fixed territorial units). As Linda McDowell (1999, p. 4) writes, 'It is socio-spatial practices that define places and these practices result in overlapping and intersecting places with multiple and changing boundaries, constituted and maintained by social relations of power and exclusion. Places are made through power relations which construct the rules which define boundaries. These boundaries are both social and spatial – they define who belongs to a place and who may be excluded, as well as the location or site of the experience.'

1.3.3 Nature

Like space and place, nature is a contested term meaning different things to different people. Indeed, the cultural critic Raymond Williams (1976, p. 184; see Box 5.1) proposed that is it 'perhaps the most complex word in the language'. Castree (2000, p. 537) suggests that this complexity can be boiled down into three main meanings: firstly, the essence of something (as in 'it's in his nature'); secondly, areas unaltered by human actions (i.e., nature as a realm external to humanity and society); and thirdly, the physical world in its entirety, perhaps including humans (i.e., nature as a universal realm of which humans, as a species, are part). All three meanings can be understood differently, with

restaurants and services; and so on. Kilburn is simultaneously local and global, its social, cultural and economic relations stretched out across the globe in a myriad of ways. She goes on to argue that the socio-spatial processes that operate within and across, and which help to shape, a place, are knitted within complex power geometries. In other words, socio-spatial processes that help shape and define places do not operate evenly, with different social groups and individuals relatively positioned as a consequence. Places then are not mere bounded locales where people gather, nor are they being unproblematically eroded and rendered placeless by processes of globalization, but rather they are complex entities shaped by particular power geometries that operate across spatial scales. This progressive understanding of place thus unifies the tensions between local and global, while recognizing uniqueness and difference, and acknowledging the unevenness of processes shaping places.

Further reading: Massey (1991, 1995); Duncan (2000)

alternative conceptualization dependent on whether nature is perceived to be essential or constructed.

Traditional, essentialist understandings of nature accept it as a fixed, stable concept. Here, the idea of what constitutes nature is accepted unproblematic-ally and uncritically. Such conceptualizations often underlie research concerned with resource management and some environmentalism. Here, there are def-inite understandings of what nature and natural resources are, and the focus of attention is on how people use and misuse them. Within such understanding, nature and human 'culture' are often positioned as separate, although symbiotic (mutually supporting) domains.

In contrast, other theorists question both the essentialized notion of nature and the separation between nature and humanity. They posit that 'nature is as much an idea or concept as it is material reality' (Castree, 2000, p. 539). Consequently, they argue that nature is a social construction and an instrument of social power (that is, it is employed politically). Far from being separate from, or subordinate to, humanity, these theorists argue, nature is discursively con-structed to particular discourses and representations that are ideologically charged (i.e., designed to portray certain messages). In other words, they suggest that there is 'nothing natural about nature at all' (Barnes and Gregory, 1996, p. 174). Drawing on an historical analysis of ideas and science, they demonstrate that how nature has been conceived has changed over time, for example from a God-given landscape to an evolutionary one. Moreover, they highlight how nature is produced and remade by humans, blurring the dualisms between culture and nature, and technology and nature (e.g., through farming practices, wildlife television programmes, genetic engineering, biotechnology, medical science and so on).

The conflict over the definition of the term has led to many different contested positions. Here, we detail just a few, following Barnes and Gregory (1996). The first two adopt largely essentialist positions and the latter two employ constructivist positions (although note, this not always the case). *Technocentrism* is founded on the view that nature is malleable and easily manipu-lated, something to dominate and use, and can be improved through human intervention. This view is underlain by the assumptions that nature is separate from humanity, that it exists to satisfy human purposes and that it is best managed through science. *Deep Ecology* and *Ecocentrism* seek a less exploitative approach, suggesting that humans need to live in harmony with nature. Deep Ecology, in particular, argues that all life is valuable and that it is immoral not to seek some kind of coexistence. *Ecofeminism* is a reaction to the androcentric bias of much Deep Ecology and Marxism, arguing that these approaches reproduce the subordinate position of women by conceiving of nature through masculinist reasoning. Finally, *Marxists* suggest that Ecocentrism is politically naïve, contending that humanity's relationship with nature has been driven by capitalist social relations. They suggest that how nature is thought about and represented is shaped by how it is exploited and used economically and politically.

The adoption of non-essentialist and politicized conceptions of nature has led many human geographers to reconsider the relationship between people and nature. Much of this work has studied what has been termed the 'production of nature', that is, how people have shaped nature for capital gain (see N. Smith, 1984); for example, examining how farmers use selection and breeding methods to alter farm livestock and crops in order to increase productivity. More recent work has taken a more 'cultural' perspective (see Section 3.1), and has explored people's relationship with animals from a non-economic perspective. Work here has investigated how animals are represented in the media (e.g., wildlife films and books), how we treat 'wild' animals (e.g., hunting versus preservation) and how we allocate 'nature' a place in the city through the design of zoos, parks and urban gardens (see Wolch and Emel, 1997; Philo and Wilbert, 2000). This research highlights the ways in which ideas about nature, in this case animals, are mediated and how nature is understood and has changed over time.

Other culturally orientated geographers have focused on our relationship to, and consumption of, 'nature'. For example, there is much research exploring the moral panics accompanying the advent of genetically modified and 'contaminated' food products (Whatmore and Thorne, 1997), while others have examined the management and conservation of natural landscapes and vistas. As we discuss more fully in Chapter 4, another growing area of interest is in the geography of the body. Here, geographers are starting to examine how the 'natural' body is a socially inscribed concept, with our understanding of it as something that is biologically given being disrupted by changing notions of health, beauty, fitness and appearance. In particular, technological enhancements (e.g., cosmetic surgery) and replacements (e.g., pacemakers) are problematizing the idea that bodies are only medically and biologically defined. Here the work of **Donna Haraway** has been important (see Box 1.3).

Box 1.3 Donna Haraway (1944–)

Donna Haraway is Professor of History of Consciousness and Women's Studies at the University of California, Santa Cruz. As detailed in the text, her wide-ranging critique of modern science has been important in at least two respects. First, her attack on the supposed objectivity of modern science has gained widespread support amongst many geographers (see Section 1.2). Consequently, her concept of 'situated knowledges' has been widely adopted, reshaping the praxis of much contemporary human geography. Second, her critiques of essentialist understandings of nature have helped to reconfigure how human geographers understand the concept of nature. Haraway's work seeks to disrupt the binaries of culture/nature and technology/nature which underlie scientific thinking. She does this through an exploration of the concept of the cyborg, illustrating the ways in which the human body is not solely a biological entity but is increasingly replaced, reshaped and supplemented by technology. Developing the motif of the cyborg body,

1.4 CONCLUSION

In this chapter, we have sought to detail what theory is, to explain why engaging with theoretical ideas is important, and started to illustrate the ways in which different theoretical ideas lead to different understandings of the world. It should hopefully be clear that you cannot avoid theory in the study of geography; theory is an inherent part of geographical praxis shaping how we conceptualize, approach, analyse and interpret the world we inhabit. Given this, it seems eminently sensible to try to understand different theoretical ideas, how they relate to one another and how they can be employed to create different geographical knowledges. In this way, you can start to understand and appreciate the role of theory in how you understand geographical phenomena. The rest of the book is designed to help you to start to think geographically from a more informed position, illustrating how the same geographical concepts have been conceptualized in alternative ways according to different theoretical frameworks. Hence, in the following chapter we provide a brief history of geographic thought, documenting key theoretical traditions in human geography, followed in Chapter 3 by a survey of some of the emerging theoretical ideas that are shaping contemporary human geography.

Haraway contends that human embodiment is fluid, partial and dynamic, ascribed meaning through social practices, norms and expectations. Using these ideas, Haraway has developed what she terms a 'cyborg politics' which aims to undermine the naturalization of women's subjugation to men (e.g., that it is natural that women occupy certain roles such as the main child carer) by undermining the systems of binary thought that underlie such assertions. In effect, Haraway is seeking to create a new body politics of gender that is not reliant on the so-called natural attributes of bodies, thus subverting patriarchy. Given the focus on gender, her work in relation to rethinking the naturalness of the human body has been widely used by feminist geographers seeking to explain the ways in which women are socio-spatially marginalized and oppressed (see Section 2.4).

Further Reading: Haraway (1985, 1991)

Chapter 2   A Brief History of Geographic Thought

<table>
<tr><td>**This chapter covers**</td><td>2.1 Histories of geographies
2.2 Geography as (spatial) science
2.3 Developing 'human-centred' theories
2.4 Structural theories and radical responses
2.5 Conclusion: an intellectual battleground?</td></tr>
</table>

2.1 HISTORIES OF GEOGRAPHIES

In the first chapter, we began to explore the importance of theory in geography by demonstrating that all geographical enquiry is, to a lesser or greater extent, informed by ideas and theories about how the world works. In particular, we emphasized the fact that theory informs what geographers study and how they study it. We began to show this by looking at definitions of geography (in terms of its preoccupation with the related concepts of space, place and nature) and how they have been informed by particular packages of theoretical and conceptual thought. However, so far we have not explored how such theories have impinged on what academic geographers have actually done (i.e., how they have gone about studying and writing 'geography'). But in many ways, theory cannot exist without praxis; for Harvey (1999, p. 576) the acid test of new thinking comes with the active transformation of geographical thought into practice. It is impossible – or at least very difficult – to assess the utility of geographic theory without exploring how it has helped (or hindered) geographers in their research, discussion and debate. Consequently, we cannot hope to understand the practice of geography without understanding something of the theories that inform that practice. Equally, it is extremely difficult to understand why certain theories enjoy popularity unless we are aware of how they are sustained, reproduced and modified through practice.

The aim of this chapter is, therefore, to identify how different philosophical and theoretical impulses have served to influence the practices and procedures of academic geography (and vice versa) at different times. First and foremost, the intention is to show that human geographers have imagined and conceptualized the relationships between people and their surroundings in varying ways, developing different theories to account for the 'realities' of everyday life. As we shall see, these theories, which are informed and sustained by distinct philosophies of knowledge, are often antithetical, in the sense that some theories contradict and undermine other theories. This has led to innumerable intellectual confrontations and skirmishes as geographers seek to prove that 'their' theory is the correct one for explaining the nature of the relationship between people and place. In turn, it will be demonstrated that different geographers have adopted very different approaches for exploring these relationships. Here, the links between high-level 'abstract' thinking and the nitty-gritty business of actually studying the world are brought into sharper focus; the history of geography tells us that what geographers have studied, and the way they have studied it, have been explicitly and implicitly informed by philosophical and theoretical concerns (Martin and James, 1993). As we stressed in Chapter 1, geographers have not been able to avoid theory any less than they have been able to avoid engaging with the messiness of the real world!

What will become evident in our brief history of geographical theory is that, at certain times, particular packages of theoretical and philosophical thought have enjoyed wide currency in the discipline, so that distinctive ways of 'doing' geography have become widespread. This has led several commentators to highlight geography's propensity to move through successive phases of intel-lectual and theoretical development where particular ideas about what is the 'correct' way of doing geography have become dominant (Mair, 1986; Unwin,1992; Haggett, 2001). In the work of Ron Johnston, in particular, this has led to the descriptions of different geographic *paradigms* (Johnston, 1986, 1991, 2000). This concept was introduced by Thomas Kuhn in his key work *The Structure of Scientific Revolutions* (1970). In essence, paradigms refer to the idea that academic disciplines move through phases of development characterized by different assumptions about how work should proceed. By way of example, Kuhn referred to the development of chemistry from an embryonic and pre-paradigmatic endeavour (associated with random experiments in alchemy) to a scientific paradigm underpinned by atomic theory, standardized chemical classifications and experimental procedures. In turn, he stressed that each para-digm is associated with the development of particular forms of notation, jargon and language – often incomprehensible to those working outside the paradigm. In Kuhn's estimation, each paradigm becomes an accepted way of gathering and synthesizing knowledge until the weight of 'anomalies' which cannot be explained using existing theories demands the formulation of new ideas. It is at this point that an apparently superior paradigm may emerge, with existing theories and ideas rejected in favour of this new paradigm. Often, the influence of one academic or one key text has been sufficient to dramatically change the trajectory of a discipline, instigating such a paradigm shift. In chemistry, for instance, Dalton's work on atomic theory is cited as a key influence in the development of scientific chemistry, while the replacement of Newtonian physics by Einstein's theory of relativity is often cited as the quintessential paradigm shift in the history of physics.

What Kuhn's ideas suggest is that every academic discipline goes through distinct episodes where different assumptions about what exists and how to study it predominate. Moving from one paradigm to another demands a fun-damental re-conceptualization of the world by academics – they need to look at the world in a new way and learn a new language for talking about it. What Kuhn thus documents is a situation where disputes over fundamentals mean that meaningful debates between the proponents of different paradigms are impossible – they simply 'argue past each other'. As we shall see, this assertion resonates with some of the episodes in the history of geography, as many thinkers in geography have argued (at various times) that their way of looking at the world represents the most meaningful, progressive and correct way of doing geography, rejecting existing modes of exploration and explanation out of hand. Exploring this contention, Johnston identifies three separate paradigms that became dominant within academic geography in the period up to 1950. These can be summarized briefly as follows:

- *Exploration*: An arguably pre-paradigmatic phase of geography where the growth of knowledge about the globe was the principal aim. This was characterized by efforts to accumulate and map information about the world, implicating geography in the wider process whereby the colonial powers sought to expand their global reach through the accumulation of knowledge. Here, the dominant motif was one of integrating knowledge acquired on 'voyages of discovery' into coherent and logically presented taxonomies, encyclopaedias and gazetteers. This paradigm can be loosely traced from the beginnings of European maritime trade and exploration in the fourteenth and fifteenth centuries to the late nineteenth century. At this stage, geography was also closely associated with cartography, so that charting the 'unknown' lands and 'empty spaces' beyond the European heartland was a key objective (Harley, 1992). Gradually, however, dissatisfaction set in with this accumulation of knowledge for accumulation's sake, leading some to advocate that this knowledge ought to be used to test certain assumptions about the links between people and their surroundings.
- *Environmental determinism*: Associated with the institutionalization of geography in the nineteenth century (e.g., the formation of the Royal Geographical Society in Britain in 1830), this was a paradigm characterized by attempts to theorize the types of human activity documented in different parts of the world with reference to characteristics of the environment. Influenced by Darwinian and evolutionary thinking, this proposed that human activities were influenced by their environment. In the view of its most forthright proponents (American geographers Ellen Semple and Ellsworth Huntingdon), climate and physical conditions were bequeathed causal powers, able to determine human development, physiology and culture. In turn, this led to explanations of national development based on accounts of environmental physical characteristics. For example, late nineteenth- and early twentieth-century texts on Australia described a dangerous and hostile environment that was consequently populated by Aboriginal races that were deemed inferior to white European races (see Ploszajska, 2000). It has been subsequently argued that this 'new geography' was therefore connected to the impulses of colonialism, albeit in the guise of 'new imperialism' (see especially Livingstone, 1992a). So, while this paradigm shift witnessed geographers beginning to engage with the ideas of inductive and logical reasoning in the development of theory (particularly in the work of

Fredrich Ratzel), cumulative evidence suggested that environmental determinism was too simplistic to explain the variations in human activity and
culture, leading to spurious (and often racist) theories of environmental caus-
ation. Ultimately, and retrospectively, this led many to begin to question the
usefulness of this paradigm.

- *Regionalism*: Associated primarily with the work of French geographer Vidal
  de la Blache at the turn of the nineteenth and twentieth centuries, this
  paradigm argued that the region should become the primary focus of geographical enquiry. This took inspiration from preceding paradigms in the
  sense that it involved taxonomic classification of different regions in terms of
  the *genres de vie* (or ways of life) that characterized them, as well as postulating
  a relationship between physical environment and human activity (see also
  Sauer, 1925). Yet, unlike determinist accounts, a premium was placed on rich
  descriptions of the intimate and varied relationship of culture, physical landscape and region, with the interconnection of these three resulting in the
  distinctive identities of (for example) specific counties, regions and nations.
  Hartshorne (1939) was later to codify this concern with areal differentiation
  in his text *The Nature of Geography*, which provided an erudite theoretical
  framework for regional geography based on the identification of regional
  differences and similarities.

In passing, we should note that Johnston's description of paradigm shifts has
been widely disputed, with Mayhew (2001), for example, suggesting that it
imposes too much order on the 'geography' carried out in the early modern
period (i.e., pre-nineteenth century). None the less, this threefold description of
geography's theoretical influences has been often repeated (e.g., Bird, 1989;
Cloke *et al.*, 1991), and provides the basis of human geography's 'institutional
memory' (Barnes, 2001a).

However, after 1950, Johnston (and others) have recognized a much more
rapid set of paradigm shifts as geographers have become increasingly preoccupied with the purpose, direction and relevance of their discipline (and
increasingly dissatisfied with the theory and practice of regional geography).
Thus, writing in 1991, Johnston identified a 'quantitative revolution' leading to
the establishment of a spatial science paradigm in the 1950s and 1960s, a
behavioural and humanistic paradigm emerging in the 1960s and 1970s and a
radical/structural paradigm becoming dominant in the 1970s and 1980s (see
also Bird, 1989; Peet, 1998; Haggett, 2001). It is these apparently distinctive
episodes that provide the context for contemporary geographical thinking, and,
as such, they provide the focus of our chapter.

What this historiography will hopefully show is that contemporary theoretical
approaches to human geography need to be understood contextually, in relation
to at least three things (see Castree and Sparke, 2000):

1. The *history* of geography – how geography has actually developed in terms of
   what geographers have studied (and how).
2. The *sociology* of geography – how institutions, social networks, journals and

educational structures (particularly universities) have shaped the development of geography.
3. The *psychology* of geography – how individual geographers have adopted
   ways of thinking about and interpreting the world, whether conformist or
   confrontational.

Here, we must therefore balance our focus on the first of these with an understanding that geography has not developed in a vacuum, but has been
developed by individuals (and individuals collaborating) within particular institutional and social structures. A key argument running through this chapter
(and, by implication, the book) is that it is impossible to understand what geographers do without reference to the way that individual theories have been
promoted (or quashed) by particular practitioners at particular moments in the
development of a discipline which, in turn, is subject to a series of social,
professional and institutional influences. In relation to the latter, we need to be
mindful of the geographers' accountability to the university or college in which
he or she works, the wider geographical community that he or she represents
and the wider society which he or she often claims to serve. For instance, Castree
and Sparke (2000) argue that in recent years geographers have been subject to a
series of corporatist accounting pressures which have forced them to focus on
the quantity rather than quality of their work, and that the changing nature of
their work can only be understood in relation to these institutional imperatives
(see also Sidaway, 1997).

As the chapter unfolds, the difficulty of writing geography's histories will
become apparent. In particular, any attempt to write the recent history of
geographical thought in terms of distinct paradigms will be seen to be highly
problematic, not to say dubious. As Johnston's (1991) own attempts to use
Kuhn's paradigm concept have demonstrated, the danger of adopting the
paradigm idea is that it imposes an artificial constancy on what Livingstone
(1992a) memorably termed the 'situated messiness' of geographical endeavour.
In particular, the idea that geography has moved through unified (and gener-
ational) paradigms glosses over the ideas and practices associated with those
who did not conform to the dominant or fashionable way of doing things. The
consensus among geographers at any one time that there is a best way of doing
things has seldom been complete or stable, and to pretend that it has been so is
to obliterate the voices of many researchers. In relation to recent histories of
Anglo-American human geography, we therefore need to be mindful of the fact
that it is often white, English-speaking, middle-class, heterosexual, able-bodied
male academics who seek to define the *Zeitgeist* and identify which ideas are most
useful to progress. The net result of this is that dissenting voices – and alternative traditions within geography – are often marginalised or obliterated in the
pages of geographic history (Greed, 1993; Sibley, 1995). At the same time, we
should be wary of an account that presents a linear, developmental account of
geography as the summation of its history rather than its *histories*; the enterprise
of geography takes many forms, and it is only relatively recently that geographers have began to acknowledge the existence of different knowledges

(Bell *et al.*, 1995; Driver, 1995). Mindful of this, as you read our account of the recent histories of geographic thought, you might want to reflect on the gender, age, class and *positionality* of the most forthright proponents of particular world-views (something evident in our thinker profiles). You will probably begin to discern that certain types of academics are represented as having had most influence on the discipline's trajectory, with others apparently conforming to their ideas in order to get published. In later chapters, we will perhaps see this trend is beginning to change, as geography opens up to a plurality of voices and ideas, but for now you should be wary that most histories of geography can serve to legitimate the careers of an academic elite while obliterating the views of others regarded as insignificant.

2.2 GEOGRAPHY AS (SPATIAL) SCIENCE

The relationship between human geography and science has always been complex, and although many human geographers have identified strongly with the methods and ideas of science, the relationship between them has been marked by periods of mutual distrust and antagonism (Gregory, 1994b; Massey, 1999b). In part, this is a consequence of geography's uniquely broad focus, which encompasses the exploration of both physical and human phenomena (see Chapter 1). While this twin focus lends geography much of its distinctiveness as a discipline, the net result of this is that something of a schism has emerged between those physical geographers who identify with the natural sciences and those human geographers who feel an affinity with the arts and humanities. This is mirrored in many geography departments in the United Kingdom and Ireland, where students specializing in physical geography are often awarded a Bachelor of Sciences degree and those mainly studying human geography receive a Bachelor of Arts. In this sense, it could be argued that, historically, most human geographers have felt distanced from debates concerning the philosophies and methods of science, preferring to subscribe to a version of geography which concerns itself with scholarly interpretation rather than scientific explanation. Certainly, this could be described as the dominant feeling among human geographers in the pre-war era, where an emphasis on the careful description of people and place was deemed the cornerstone of a discipline based on areal differentiation (Gregory, 1978). Yet to argue that pre-war human geography was not at all influenced by the ideas and theories of science would be quite incorrect. Regional geography was in fact implicitly rooted in long-standing ideas about the procedures and philosophies of science, particularly induction. This is a process which led geographers to make generalizations on the basis of repeated observations, so that conclusions about the nature of different spaces and places could be made on the basis of particular premises. This implied the adoption of scientific notions of causality, where certain things were deemed to be associated with other things. For instance, in many accounts, regularities in human behaviour in different regions of the world were deemed to be related to certain environmental characteristics of that region. By extension, this led geographers to make certain universal conclusions.

However, it was in the 1950s that human geographers apparently became more concerned with adopting the principles and practices of scientific investigation (Rogers, 1996). In part, this appeared to be related to concerns that geography was unsystematic in its explorations. We can perhaps discern two underlying anxieties here: firstly, that geographers were simply accumulating facts (about regional geography, for example), without integrating them into an overarching theoretical framework, and, secondly, that they lacked the ability to distinguish between causal correlations and accidental or spurious associations. An example of the latter may be found in the environmentally determinist (and *possibilist*) accounts that suggested that a factor such as high ambient temperature, for example, caused a lack of development in a region because of its tendency to induce sloth and idleness among local residents. While such an assertion might appear correct on the basis of observation, by the standards of scientific method, such thinking represents 'bad' science as it fails to distinguish between causal and non-causal relationships. Moreover, it was apparent to some that much geographical thinking was guilty of committing what, by scientific standards, were obvious ecological fallacies – i.e., believing that the characteristics of people could be inferred from the aggregate data that described the general character of the area in which they reside. For instance, to infer that a person living in a country where average educational attainment is low will have a poor standard of education is an example of how inductive thinking can lead to overgeneralized and false conclusions. In logical terms, this represents a process whereby the truth of a universal conclusion cannot be guaranteed even if particular premises are true (Werlen, 1993).

When coupled with a general institutional desire to establish human geography on more systematic grounds, the problems of such fallacious thinking were identified as a serious hindrance to the development of the discipline by a number of practitioners (Hill, 1981). Different histories of geography have thus identified particular individuals (and publications) that encouraged geographers to establish their studies on more scientific (and apparently *firmer*) ground. Notably, these included a posthumous paper published in 1953 by Fredrich Schaefer on 'Exceptionalism in Geography'. Herein, he rejected the argument that there was anything particularly unique about geography's focus on a disparate range of natural and human phenomena, arguing that it could profitably engage with ideas from mainstream science about the possibility (and desirability) of constructing general laws through systematic study. This suggested that there could be an essential unity of method between the natural and social sciences (i.e., *naturalism*), making possible a conversation between physical and human geography. Schaefer identified the essence of synthetic, *nomothetic* science as being a process of inference and observation leading to the deduction of causal relations. More broadly, this begins to indicate the principal features of positivist science, a form of scientific thinking which can trace its roots to the Enlightenment of the eighteenth century, and later to the writings of Auguste Comte (1798–1857). Rejecting the imprecise and poorly specified thinking that characterized science at the time, Comte argued that the objective collection of data was a prerequisite to the discovery of cause and effect relationships. The characteristic features of contemporary positivism may be catalogued as follows (see Johnston, 1986):

— Positivist science is based on the collection of data through observation and measurement of things that are known to exist and can be directly experienced (Comte's notion of *le réel*);
— Positivist science assumes that the development of generalizations and deduced laws can only follow on the basis of repeated observations and the testing of hypotheses about the causal relationships that exist between phenomena (Comte's notion of *la certitude*);
— Positivist science aims to combine accepted generalizations and hypotheses into theories and laws that explain how the world works (Comte's precept of *le précis*);
— Positivist science argues that these theories can never be completely validated (i.e., verified) in the sense of proved absolutely correct, but can be provisionally accepted until contrary evidence or data are collected (hence, Comte's notion of *l'utile* – knowledge as a means to an end).

In relation to the latter, it is significant that falsification has been identified as one of the important distinctions between science and non-science (Kitchin and Tate, 2000). However, it has also been argued that this is the distinction between two forms of post-Comte positivistic science, *logical positivism* and critical rationalism, the former emphasizing verification, the latter stressing the importance of falsification (Werlen, 1993). Falsification suggests that science should not seek confirmatory evidence for its theories, but should concern itself with identifying contradictory evidence that would lead to the rejection of hypotheses and ideas. In short, falsification involves checking a theory against evidence that could disprove it rather than collecting and accumulating supporting evidence for the theory. Thus, to use an often-cited example of the difference between the two approaches, the continual collection of examples of white swans as evidence for the hypothesis that 'all swans are white' would never completely verify the claim until every single swan was demonstrated to be white. Falsification, on the other hand, involves searching for evidence of black (or non-white) swans so that a failure to find them would permit the conclusion that the opposite must apply (i.e., 'all swans are white'). This theory is then upheld provisionally, unless and until evidence to the contrary is produced (for example, a black swan). In practice, rational criteria for falsification are generally established so that one anomaly or single disconfirmation would not result in the rejection of a theory, but a certain weight of evidence would (Gregory, 1978). In this light, the goal of scientific process is to strive for better theories through a progressive process of measurement, hypothesis testing and rejection of theories. Through the influential work of Popper and Lakatos, logical positivism also stressed that certain mathematical and scientific statements were axiomatic, and required no empirical validation (hence departing from Comte's assumption that all statements were to be grounded in direct experience of the world).

Rooted in (logical) positivist philosophy, scientific method appeared to offer systematization and rigour. Within human geography, this appeared attractive to many of those geographers who regarded regional geography as banal and descriptive. Hence, Schaefer was drawn to logical positivism (via the work of Gustav Bergamann and the Vienna Circle) because he saw the regionalism pursued by Hartshorne and Sauer *et al.* as simply uncovering patterns, not producing laws. Significantly, it also seemed to offer a way for geographers to harness the potential offered by new technologies of computation and data handling, with one of the pioneers of quantification in geography, William Garrison (1956, p. 428), proclaiming the virtues of 'the universal language of mathematics'. The turn to positivist packages of thought was thus closely associated with geographers' use of quantitative methodologies. This was manifest in the adoption of statistical and computational procedures which allowed the processing of increasingly large data sets. These were accordingly analysed so that significant regularities and patterns in the data could be distinguished from insignificant (and hence spurious) regularities. Adapting the ideas of Bayesian probability, this often resulted in theories being built on the basis of reasonable probability (a variant of critical rationalism that holds to the concept of degrees of truth rather than verification or falsification of the truth). In the 1950s and 1960s this encouraged some far-reaching attempts to restyle geography as a spatial science, seeking to construct theory on the basis of statistical analysis (Robinson, 1998). This was reflected in the publication of texts presenting the principles of statistical analysis to geographers (e.g., S. Gregory, 1963), and, later, those that sketched out the principles of spatial statistics based on regression, clustering and autocorrelation (Abler *et al.*, 1971). For many, the ultimate promise of this progressive and processional process of statistical

---

Box 2.1 Peter Haggett (1933–   )

In many accounts, Peter Haggett's paper at the Royal Geographical Society in 1963 is depicted as a pivotal moment in the rejection of an 'old style' regional geography and its replacement by a 'new', scientific geography (Robinson, 1998). This paper used statistical methods (such as probability sampling) to describe patterns of forestry in Brazil, challenging the dominant mode of interpretative description. Provoking disquiet in some quarters, this none the less paved the way for Haggett's first text, the well-received *Locational Analysis in Human Geography* (1965). Combining the 'new' geography's interest in quantification with an awareness of the potentiality of a new way of thinking about space, this volume was particularly significant in terms of its emphasis on the formal geometries of space. Characterizing geography as a search for order, this – and his later work with Richard Chorley, *Network Analysis in Geography* (1969) – offered a tool kit for scientific geography comprising (new) techniques of autocorrelation, regression and spatial analysis. More importantly, perhaps, it sought to stress the analytical breakthroughs that might be possible by considering the arrangement of space in terms of networks, movements and flows, proposing that this taxonomy could be used effectively to model and predict patterns in space. In later work, he added a

testing and theory-building was the construction of predictive models (Chorley and Haggett, 1967).

Retrospectively, this period is described as representing a pivotal era in the history of the discipline – geography's 'Quantitative Revolution' (Bird, 1989; Barnes, 2001a). In fact, it is apparent that many geographers were not swept up in the enthusiasms for quantification, hypothesis-testing and statistical analysis. None the less, this new 'scientific' paradigm was responsible for ushering in a new conceptualization of space which became widespread among even those geographers resistant to the notion of quantification. In effect, this was to conceive of space as a surface on which the relationships between (measurable) things were played out. Looking towards other disciplines, notably neoclassical economics and physics, this placed emphasis on the importance of three related concepts – direction, distance and connection. In short, it became axiomatic that the relationships between things on the earth's surface could be explained in terms of these key concepts, and that it was possible to discern regular patterns which could be (geometrically) mapped and modelled (Wilson, 1999). This heralded a new language of spatial physics where human activities and phenomena could be reduced to movements, networks, nodes or hierarchies played out on the earth's surface. This effectively reduced the earth's surface to an isotropic plane – a blank canvas on which human relationships were played out. This empirico-physical conception of space thus lies at the extreme of the scale we examined in Chapter 1, imagining space as presocial and absolute as opposed to social and relational (see also Soja, 1996).

The promise of spatial science was to suggest that both human and physical geographers alike could enact a rigorous exploration of spatial structure – an argument emphasized in **Peter Haggett**'s *Geography: A Modern Synthesis* (1975) (see also Box 2.1). By adapting and rewriting classical locational theory (especially the models of land use proposed by Von Thünen, Christaller, Weber

consideration of the effects of time to his analysis of spatial patterns, heightening geographers' awareness of writing on spatial diffusion being undertaken by those in other disciplines (notably, epidemiology). These ideas were combined in his book *Geography: A Modern Synthesis* (1975) – which remained the standard introductory text for human geography over the next decade. Though such ideas of locational analysis have subsequently been subject to vehement critique, Haggett's work (including studies of the diffusion of HIV) continues to follow the principles of scientific explanation upheld in his early work, though his overview of the discipline, *The Geographer's Art* (1990), suggests that he is aware of the limitations, as well as considerable merits, of a geography founded on positivist principles and practices. The reissue of his key work in 2001 as *Geography: A Global Synthesis* shows his willingness to engage with one of the key concepts in contemporary geography (i.e., globalization), but a critical reading suggests an unwillingness to engage with many others. He is currently Emeritus Professor at the University of Bristol.

Further reading: Haggett (1990, 2001)

and Lösch), Haggett and others proposed that there could be an integrative and comprehensive foundation for modelling geographical pattern and process (i.e., a belief in *naturalism* – the equivalence of the natural and social sciences). This suggested that the place of things could be mapped, explained and predicted through the identification of underlying laws – often mathematically derived – of interaction and movement, with friction of distance regarded as a key factor explaining patterns of human behaviour. For such reasons, many spatial inter-action models were referred to as gravity models because of the way that they utilized Newtonian theories (of gravitational attraction) to model flows between (nodal) points. Thus, where a 'natural' science like physics tried to create gen-eral laws and rules about things like molecular structure, geography sought to create models of spatial structure which could, for example, generalize settle-ment patterns, urban growth or agricultural land use (e.g., Berry, 1967). The analogous use of scientific theory even led some to propose that human geog-raphy could be described as spatial physics (Hill, 1981), bequeathing it the status of a 'hard' scientific discipline rather than a 'soft' artistic pursuit. This seductive type of argument was typical of the case made for scientific human geography, with the standards of precision, rigour and accuracy evident in mainstream science proposed as the only genuinely explanatory framework available for the generation of valid and reliable knowledge (Wilson, 1972). This was also a key factor encouraging the adoption of the ideas and language (if not always the method) of science among those preoccupied with the status of the discipline and the links between physical and human geography. Add-itionally, for those believing that geography should be engaging with policy debates, scientific geography appeared to have considerable potential to become 'applied' geography, offering an objective and value-free perspective on the success of, for example, environmental management and planning policies (Pacione, 1999).

Within Johnston's (1991) disputed description of geography's paradigmatic progression, the move from a 'dominant' mode of regional geography was one that occurred in the late 1950s and 1960s. What is perhaps obscured here is that the positivist underpinnings of scientific method were not widely understood or discussed until somewhat later. Specifically, Harvey's *Explanation in Geography* (1969) was perhaps the first book-length treatise examining the theoretical basis of spatial science (see also Box 6.2). Essentially, summarizing developments in the discipline, this sought to review the scientific principles and methods which had been adopted by those seeking to transform geography into a fully-fledged spatial science. None the less, even Harvey was more concerned to offer a rigor-ous epistemological framework for future geographic research rather than explore the intricacies – and assumptions – of scientific thought (Cloke *et al.*, 1991). However, the publication of this book was to provoke widespread discus-sion of such issues, including much critical reflection on the philosophical basis of spatial science. Crucially, much of this was to focus on the assumed 'value-neutrality' of positivist inquiry, which was increasingly shown to be based on an idealized and unachievable notion of scientific objectivity (Barnes and Duncan, 1992; Rose, 1993).

Accordingly, by the time that the principles and methodologies of spatial science had been codified and widely disseminated, something of a backlash had developed, with critiques being articulated by a number of geographers (ironically, including Harvey) who felt that positivism offered an inadequate philosophical and political basis for the development of theory in human geography. As we shall see, these criticisms concerned both the ontological and epistemological basis of spatial science, characterizing quantification variously as arid, simplistic, irrelevant and exclusive. While many of these critiques were misplaced, and only applied to caricatured versions of logical positivism (Sheppard, 2001), their cumulative impact was to fuel the search for alternative theoretical frameworks in human geography. None the less, positivism in its various guises continues to underpin much research in human geography, particularly (but not all) research involving quantification. Similarly, the search for 'ground truth' and the principles of spatial science have continued to inform the development of Geographic Information Systems (Pickles, 1995). Hence, Barnes (2001b, p. 416) has insisted that 'the quantitative revolution was a pivotal moment for human geography, shaping it theoretically, methodologically and sociologically for years afterwards'.

2.3 DEVELOPING 'HUMAN-CENTRED' THEORIES

As described above, the proponents of spatial science argued that an understanding of spatial structures through quantitative analysis and modelling would lead to an enhanced understanding of spatial organization and human activity. Yet criticisms of this approach became increasingly widespread in the 1960s and 1970s as the assumptions of spatial science and (logical) positivism were bought into question. One of the most obvious critiques was that the isotropic and featureless landscapes assumed by spatial science simply did not exist (Cloke *et al.*, 1991). More fundamental, perhaps, was the emerging criticism that spatial science worked with a very limited view of what it is to be human. In many of the models developed by spatial scientists, people were frequently represented as vectors or movements (making up aggregated flows). Rejecting this idea, many geographers began to propose alternative models of human subjectivity in an attempt to articulate a more 'human' human geography. As Plummer (1983, pp. 77–8) explains, 'many sociologists or geographers begin with a view of the person as an active, creative world-builder, but before they have finished their theoretical endeavours, they have enchained, dehumanized, rendered passive and lost that same person' (see also Holloway and Hubbard, 2001, pp. 8–12). Two important (and related) traditions that emerged as a result of this critique were behavioural and humanistic geography.

2.3.1 *The behavioural critique*

Like those who attempted to restyle geography as a spatial science, behavioural geographers largely took their inspiration from the sciences, particularly psychology. In broad terms, psychology is the 'science of the mind'. Many people's image of psychology is that of a laboratory-based discipline, of scientists in white coats monitoring the behaviour of rats in mazes; for others, it might be of the psychoanalyst asking the patients to lie back on the couch and to tell them about their childhood. Either way, it might seem a little surprising that some geographers looked to psychology to provide them with clues as to how people related to their surroundings. However, the engagement between geography and psychology remains a very important one, albeit one that has become somewhat ghettoized since its heyday in the 1970s. Attempting to identify when this interest in psychology first became apparent is by no means straightforward (Goodey and Gold, 1985), although certain figures have been cited as particularly influential in expanding the horizons of geography beyond the realms of locational analysis by exploring psychological ideas. Gilbert White, William Kirk, John Wright and David Lowenthal have all been credited with bringing such ideas into the geographical fold, although further archival analysis reveals less obvious lines of intellectual heritage from the Berkeley School (a North American group of historical-cultural geographers led by Carl Sauer and interested in the relationships between humans and environments as manifest in specific landscapes). Although many of these individuals and groups were writing in the 1940s and 1950s at a time when descriptive regional analysis was still predominant, their influence was primarily felt in the late 1960s as dissatisfaction with the mechanistic and deterministic nature of the models prominent in the discipline began to take hold (Gold, 1992).

One of the most important ideas that these geographers began to introduce to the discipline is that space is not a real (or objective) phenomenon which is experienced and understood in a similar manner by all individuals. Instead, behavioural perspectives alerted geographers to the fact that each individual potentially possesses a unique understanding of his or her surroundings, and that this understanding is shaped by mental processes of information gathering and organization (Porteous, 1977; Gold, 1980). Here, the key psychological concepts of *perception* and *cognition* became widely utilized by geographers in their anxiety to explain why human behaviour did not fit the patterns sometimes anticipated in the models of spatial science. Simply put, these concepts propose that people do not have complete or perfect understanding of their environment, but have only partial knowledge because of the way that the senses (touch, taste, smell, sight and hearing) acquire information from the surroundings (Rodaway, 1994). This perceived information is then organized through mental processes of cognition to construct selective, partial and distorted images of the world which vary from person to person. Thus an important precept underlying behavioural geography is that it is misleading to analyse human spatial behaviour in relation to the objective, 'real' environment, as people do not conceive of (and experience) space in this way. Instead, it is suggested that the focus should be on the way that people act in relation to the images of space that they construct, shifting the focus from the way people dwell in 'concrete' empirico-physical space to the geographies of the mind (Holloway and Hubbard, 2001).

Therefore, fundamental to a behavioural perspective is the idea that people's knowledge of their surroundings is perceived through the senses and mediated by processes of the human mind. The idea that people's behaviour in the world might best be understood by focusing on their perception of the world is often claimed to have been introduced to geography by William Kirk (1963, p. 361), who sought to make a distinction between the objective (or real) and behavioural environment. In his view, while the former consisted of the physical world around us, the latter consisted of the 'psycho-physical field in which phenomenal facts are arranged into patterns or structures that acquire values in cultural contexts'. Kirk thus believed it was the behavioural, not the objective, environment that provided the basis for human behaviour and decision-making. In effect, this idea challenged the idea that human responses to environmental stimuli are based on the environment as it 'really' is, and instead proposed that these responses are based on the environment as it is perceived to be. The implication here was that human beings do not make decisions based on full, accurate and objective information about what exists in the world, but on what our senses tell us exists and what our brain is capable of dealing with. According to Kirk, our daily interactions with our surroundings could only be understood in relation to the partial, distorted and simplified understanding that we have of our surroundings (see Walmsley and Lewis, 1993).

Methodologically, behavioural geography continued within the traditions of quantitative and scientific analysis, leading some to depict it as an outgrowth, rather than a reaction to, spatial science (Harvey, 1970). Foremost in this endeavour was the utilization of questionnaires, perceptual tests and rating scales to explore the images of the environment that informed individuals' decision-making processes. This included methods designed to measure people's ability to remember, process and evaluate spatial information. Acknowledging a dichotomy between fact/value and objective/subjective space, much of this was designed to identify differences between (for example) real and perceived distance/orientation (see Walmsley and Lewis, 1993). One of the more innovative techniques adopted for these ends was the mental map technique (devised by an architect-planner, Kevin Lynch, 1960). This technique simply required that individuals completed a basic sketch map of a town or area, marking those features that were most important to them. Examining these maps became a means by which geographers could see how people mentally simplified their surroundings and how images of place varied according to a person's gender, age, class, place of residence and so on (Kitchin, 1996). In part, such knowledge allowed geographers to explain why certain individuals adopted behaviour which might, in relation to the decision-making assumptions of neoclassical theory, be described as suboptimal or satisficing. In the work of **Reg Golledge** (Box 2.2), this notion of mental mapping was extended into a wider project of understanding spatial memory, cognitive ability and wayfinding. This seemingly promised a full integration of psychological theory and ideas into an understanding of spatial behaviour, and hence the development of better models of spatial decision-making.

By the 1970s, behavioural geography was increasingly being adopted by

36   Theorizing Human Geographies

researchers to study a number of different themes, influencing studies of migration, retailing, housing, tourism, industrial location, town planning and so on. By focusing on the complex ways that people obtain sensory information from, make sense of and remember their surroundings, behavioural geography promised the construction of more realistic and human-centred models of the world. While this led to some research collaborations between (environmental) psychologists and geographers, in the main this led to geographers adapting concepts from psychology in a fairly loose and imprecise way. For some, this meant that behavioural geography was as reductive and simplistic as the spatial science it sought to critique (Ley, 1983). Indeed, some accounts of behavioural geography describe it as proposing a stimulus-response model of behaviour, whereby people's behaviour is seen to be a response to particular environmental characteristics or stimuli (Cox, 1981). In psychology, behaviouralism was none the less conceived as a reaction against the determinism of the logically positivist behaviourist theories that dominated in that discipline. Specifically, behaviouralism recognized the capacity of humans to think creatively, in stark contrast to the rigidity of Watsonian stimulus-response models that dismissed the notion of subjectivity (Gold, 1992). In geography, the distinction between behaviouralism and logical positivism was perhaps less marked, with many behaviouralists refusing to explore those aspects of the world that could not be observed and measured (cf. Golledge, 1981, on the more general and epistemologically less constraining philosophy of positivism underpinning his version of behavioural geography). Importantly, most behavioural theories continued to explore the differences between people's understandings of the world and a 'real' world that was still regarded as knowable and mappable. Simultaneously, behavioural theories in geography were developed inductively according to scientific principles of measurement, statistical testing and generalization (Gregory, 1978). This led to criticisms from those, particularly geographers subscribing to humanistic theories, who felt that the value-free and objective principles of scientific explanation espoused by behavioural geographers were overly simplistic. In

---

Box 2.2 Reginald Golledge (1937–)

Many of those strongly associated with behavioural geography in its heyday have subsequently rejected its theories and practices. Reginald Golledge is a notable exception to this. Working out of the University of California, Santa Barbara, his work over three decades has sought to develop a behaviourally based understanding of human spatial behaviour and decision-making. This has involved attempts to examine individuals' way-finding abilities through psychological investigations and computational analysis of 'place utility' and spatial choice. An important idea underlying these explorations is that the complexity of the world is reduced through cognitive processes that serve to summarize spatial relations in terms of key routes between anchor points. This marks an important elaboration of Lynch's (1960) basic ideas that the world is understood in terms of nodes, landmarks, neighbourhoods, edges and paths. On the basis of this, Golledge has been able to suggest the possibility of information systems and algorithms that can approximate human decision-making and spatial way-finding abilities (Golledge, 1991). Latterly, this

short, many saw behavioural geography as an inevitable appendage of spatial science, and depicted it as offering an inadequate (and mechanistic) understanding of human behaviour (see Golledge, 1981).

2.3.2 Humanistic thought and poetic geographies

Like behavioural theory, humanistic theory is concerned with articulating a human-centred understanding of the relations between people and their surroundings. In contrast to behavioural geography, however, the intention was to develop models of humanity based on different philosophies of meaning such as phenomenology, existentialism and idealism. Though very different in some ways, these ideas share the assumption that the reality of the world is, in fact, a human construct. Humanistic philosophies are strongly opposed to the naturalist assumption that social phenomena could be studied in the same way as physical phenomena – by looking for general laws or rules and causal explanations. Clearly, quantitative (positivist) geography, with its laws of spatial science, could be seen as adopting this naturalist perspective. The same criticisms were also extended to behavioural geography, especially in relation to the ideas of 'rationality' underpinning decision-making and cognitive processing of environmental information. According to Kevin Cox (1981, p. 3), behaviouralism remained firmly embedded in the presuppositions of naturalistic science, guilty of separating subject and object. Humanistic thinking rejects this separation, instead questioning 'being in the world' through a consideration of human agency and people's ability to experience and create their own (subjective) worlds. From a humanistic perspective, there can be no world of 'facts' unaffected by the personal values of the investigator (Olsson, 1980): the search for scientific laws is replaced by an interpretive and reflective search for meaning.

This type of *eidetic* reflection on the relationship between the self and the space which is brought into being through consciousness drew strength from a

has involved Golledge seeking to harness the potential of behavioural theory to provide a basis for helping those with physical disability. This has led to something of a robust exchange between Golledge and those who think that such theories ignore the wider social context in which disabled people live (particularly the processes of disablism that serve to discriminate against them). In this sense, Golledge (1993) takes a view of human bodily capabilities that is essentialist and biological when compared with more widespread ideas that emphasize the social construction of the body (see Chapter 4). None the less, Golledge remains one of the most forthright proponents of behavioural theory, and his co-authored book, *Spatial Behaviour: A Geographic Perspective* (1997), represents an impressive and voluminous overview of work carried out in the behavioural tradition.

Further reading: Golledge (1981); Golledge and Stimson (1997)

number of long-established philosophical movements. Important here were existential ideas that reality is created through the free acts of human agents. Associated with, for example, the French philosopher and novelist Jean-Paul Sartre, the German philosopher Martin Heidegger (see Chapter 4) and the Danish writer Søren Kierkegaard, this was a reaction to rational thinking. In sum, it is a philosophy which focuses on the subjective meaning of existence for the individual by stressing the specificity and uniqueness of each individual's experience of the world. Peet (1998, p. 35) explains that 'existence for existentialists is characterized by concrete particularity and sheer "givenness", as compared with the abstract and universal concepts of humanity and life common to positivist thought'. Translated into geographical practice, this was read as an argument for a human-centred interpretation of the world as opposed to the abstract, 'high-level' theorization that had turned diverse landscapes into isotropic surfaces populated by decision-making machines. Instead, existentialism demands a locally specific view from 'below'; a grounded view exploring the concrete and particular perspectives of individual people in specific places. Heidegger (1927) used the German word *dasein* to emphasize that what is important to human existence is being in the world (where 'being in' is opposed to rationally reflecting upon). For existentialists, this is a key to understanding the relationship between people and the world. 'Being' is characterized by existing physically in the world – taking up physical space and existing in relation to other physical objects (including other people).

In essence, then, existential ideas propose that humans create the world through the (mental) projection of meaning onto the physical phenomena – other people, places and objects – they encounter as they move through geographical space (Mugerauer, 1994). For thinkers like Sartre, this projection of meaning onto the world was related to our sense of separation, estrangement or alienation from the world (described as an essential part of the human condition). An *existential dread* results from the feeling that we are completely different from everything else we experience, so that we attempt to make the world of objects comprehensible to ourselves by giving these objects status and meaning.

Box 2.3 Yi-Fu Tuan (1930–   )

Perhaps more than any other geographer, Yi-Fu Tuan defies easy categorization. Tuan's work often transcends and ties together ideas from the seemingly unrelated scholastic worlds of philosophy, psychology, urban planning, landscape architecture and anthropology. If it is possible to identify a unifying theme in his work, it is a concern with how individuals fashion personal and cultural realities from their surroundings, and how those processes reflect collective and personal ideas of appropriate human–nature relations. In turn, this has lead Tuan to theorize place as humanized space – that is, a locality that has been transformed to place from space through human inhabitation and nurturing. In much of his work, he has been concerned with eliciting the rich and diverse meanings associated with particular places, contrasting these with the placeless qualities associated with space (particularly its modern articulations). This experiential framework gave rise to the concept of *topophilia* – a term that has

Objects, people and places thus become meaningful to us, while the systems of meaning that develop through this process become an essential part of the world we experience. The legacy of this type of thinking for human geography was a focus on the social construction of place – that is to say, an examination of the way abstract space was made into meaningful place through the thought and action of human agents. The work of both **Yi-Fu Tuan** (see Box 2.3) and Ted Relph (1976, 1987; see also Chapter 1) on the creation of place (and placelessness) can therefore be seen to be key examples of how existential philosophies inspired the development of 'new' human geographies in the 1970s. Both rejected the geometries and quantification of spatial science in favour of a more expansive and literate interpretation of the capabilities of human agency, indicating an awareness of the importance of critical reflection on questions of being in the world. In short, existentialism takes the view that each individual must provide his or her own meaning for life.

Alongside existentialism, *phenomenology* was to be another key influence on humanistic geography. Phenomenology is a philosophy based on the notion that we bring our own attitudes with us wherever we perceive things. It is related to existentialism, and can be seen as a methodology (way of studying) as well as an interpretative framework (way of knowing). This is an approach that suggests that the best way to find out about human relationships with the world is to use intensive forms of description. As with existentialism, individual human experience is central to this description. Phenomenology thus rejects scientific, quantitative methods of explanation in favour of understanding or appreciation. This reiterates the existential insistence that the external world does not consist of objects that can be observed and measured objectively. Instead, it suggests that experience is itself an essential part of reality, and there is no separate 'real' world external to human experience. In saying this, the founders of phenomenological thought, such as Edmund Husserl (1859–1938), sought to overcome the often assumed dualism between mind and matter (subject and object). This dualism, firstly, separated the human consciousness from a supposed 'real' world and, secondly, implied that this 'reality' could be studied independently of

---

subsequently come to be widespread as a definition of the type of close relationship that exists between richly symbolic places and the humans that use and inhabit them. In *Landscapes of Fear* (1978) he explored the inverse – the *topophobia* that makes individuals avoid specific spaces. Many of his ideas about the humanistic encounter of people and place were summarized in *Space and Place* (1977), while his later writing has continued to pursue an individualistic path through issues to do with the experience of place, language and culture. His last book before retiring from the University of Wisconsin in 1998 was *Escapism*, a wide-ranging text that explores the cultural and human histories of escapism as a practice (a theme that overlaps with contemporary geographic preoccupations with transgression and resistance – see Chapter 3).

Further reading: Tuan (1974, 1998b)

human experience. Instead, phenomenology seeks to appreciate the world in terms of the phenomena that are bought into existence through human experience of them. This is associated with the human subject's *lifeworld* – a concept used to describe the totality of a person's involvement with the places and environments experienced in everyday life. This is described by Peet (1998: 39) as the 'moving historical field of lived experience', implying that our experience is constantly changing as we live and do things in the world. This incorporates an appreciation of the *intentionality* that informs the relationship between a human body and the external world (see Chapter 4); Husserl insisted that intentionality links what we think about and the manner in which we think. He says that objects can only be understood as objects that human beings are conscious of and as objects that humans *intend* to use or interact with (Rojek, 1995). This happens spontaneously all the time, as we live and exist in the world, with phenomenologists aiming to recover the moment of intentionality (and hence the moment of objectification) by stripping away the accumulated layers of conscious meaning and conceptualization that hide the truth of human encounter and being. This suggests that things are created consciously and phenomenology is concerned with revealing the 'true essence' of the objects (and places) that people imagine or perceive to exist – irrespective of whether there really is a non-mental reality.

From this perspective, humanistic geography can be described as being concerned with eliciting the *relational* encounter that brings the world into existence for each person (Prince, 1980). In contrast to the view that reality and awareness are separate, phenomenology urges us to pay closer attention to our experiences of the world and to be prepared to think about it in new and different ways. This phenomenological perspective is distinct from the *epiphenomenalism* of behaviouralism that regards mental processes as effects of physical events rather than having any causal properties. Humanistic perspectives thus see mental processes as having physical effects, bringing the world into being through consciousness. This means that our knowledge of the world can, firstly, be said to be *created* by us (rather than something we simply discover) and, secondly, come about through mental and bodily *encounters* with things (which are, for example, perceived to be in front or behind, above or below, bigger or smaller than our bodies). This latter focus on encounter was to prove influential in geographic work on movement, space and dwelling – as, for example, in the work of David Seamon (1979) on bodies in space and Anne Buttimer (1976) on the lifeworld. When coupled with widely cited and acclaimed work on social geographies of place (Tuan, 1974; Ley, 1983), this began to suggest a more human-centred foundation for studies of human geography than was offered by behavioural theories:

> The purpose of the humanistic critique was to put man [*sic*], in all his reflective capacities, back into the centre of things as both a producer and product of his social world and also to augment the human experience by a more intensive, hence self-conscious reflection upon the meaning of being human. (Ley and Samuels, 1978, p. 7)

Methodologically, however, humanistic ideas of phenomenology and existentialism did not translate easily into practice. For example, describing the true essences of the objects and places bought into existence through human creativity and imagination involves being able to 'see' (as well as smell, hear, feel and touch) from the perspective of another human being. Given the impossibility of this (we are all unique, after all), humanistic geography thus developed by adopting qualitative methodologies that relied upon the ability of people to articulate the feelings and meanings that they associated with particular places. The 'truth' of such accounts was not brought into question: rather, they were used to create a faithful representation of people's world-view and engagement with place (see Eyles and Smith, 1988).

In practice, therefore, humanistic theories fuelled a geography in which qualitative methodologies were regarded as superior in the production of meaningful knowledge. Interviews, interpretative analysis and analysis of human texts (see Chapter 5) were all seen as viable ways of teasing out the emotional, aesthetic and symbolic ties that bound people and place. More controversially, perhaps, forms of covert and overt observational work were used to construct ethnographies of the particular and peculiar ways of life played out in different settings. Taking inspiration from the Chicago School of urban sociology, this involved researchers becoming observant participants (or participant observers) in social worlds that could be very different from their own (see Jackson, 1985; Herbert, 2000). Though this was an obvious reaction to the high-level abstractions of spatial science, the claim that this enabled the researcher to empathize with others' experience of being in the world remained contested (see Chapter 3). In sum, doubts were raised that geographers could develop appropriate methodological procedures for eliciting true meanings (see Pile, 1991). One fundamental critique, which has been raised in the context of post-structural debates surrounding the autonomy of the subject, is that people cannot easily articulate what they think (or even what they do!) because language relies on social conventions and traditions. In effect, it might be suggested that it is impossible to elicit people's true (inner) feelings because this relies on them using a set of social conventions, categories and descriptions that do not enable them to express or explain their world-view (see Olsson, 1980). In short, people are often unaware of the impulses and constraints shaping their decisions and behaviour and it is up to the researcher/analysts to identify these unrecognized/invisible aspects of behaviour. More widely, this points to the obvious methodological difficulty of a theorization that, in contrast to the natural sciences, takes consciousness and being (as opposed to observable action and practice, for example) as its object of study.

2.4 STRUCTURAL THEORIES AND RADICAL RESPONSES

In a variety of ways, both humanistic and behavioural geography articulated a people-centred geography that became widespread – if not paradigmatic – in the early 1970s. Yet, despite their many commonalities (particularly their focus on individual behaviour and agency rather than aggregate patterns and flows of human activity), their emphases on quantification and qualitative research respectively meant that co-operation between humanistic and behavioural geographers was rare (Golledge, 1981). Latterly, strong ontological connections between these apparently different geographical traditions have been identified (see Aitken, 1992), but these remained overshadowed by epistemological differences (and some vituperative confrontations) in the 1970s. The fact that the dialogue between these two 'camps' was strained is perhaps due to the fact that new developments in the discipline began to challenge the orthodoxy of any approach that held to the primacy of human agency.

One of the most fundamental criticisms of both approaches was articulated by those who claimed that a focus on the minutiae of individuals' lives fundamentally failed to take account of the material context in which human action took place. This critique was grounded in specific structural ideas about the workings of society. In general, *structuralism* is an interdisciplinary movement that holds that it is possible to understand the workings of society only with reference to the logic of the relational connections (or structures) that bind people together. Using an analogy from linguistics (see Chapter 5), it was suggested that individual acts of speaking can only be understood with reference to the rules of language, grammar and syntax. In the same way, it was proposed that understanding human behaviour required a keen theoretical sensibility whereby the rules and logic of social structures were theorized and exposed. What renders such an endeavour problematic is that the structures of society – like the rules of language – cannot be discerned by observing the things that exist in the world (or for that matter, the things that are said). Instead, structuralism proposes an approach to science that explores the relations that exist between observable things and the 'hidden' structures whose existence can only be theorized (Kitchin and Tate, 2000).

In some ways, it is helpful to think of structural theories using metaphors of depth. Structuralists generally hold that (positivist) science is good at describing and explaining surface appearances. For instance, it is apparent that the models and theories developed by spatial scientists are (within their own terms) very elegant and convincing explanations of the social, economic and political processes that result in specific patterns. Equally, both behavioural and humanistic geography allow the geographer to appreciate the human creativity and intentionality that informs these processes. Yet from a structural perspective, these theories potentially ignore (and obscure) the real processes that cause things to happen in the ways that they do. Stucturalism thus concerns itself with discovering the things that are real and important in social life by looking 'beneath' the taken-for-granted categories of things that are seen to exist in the world to explore the importance of things that are real but hidden. Within any structuralist framework, we can therefore identify three levels of existence (see Johnston, 1986):

1. The level of appearances (superstructure) – the realm of things (defined as any item whose existence can be acknowledged by a system of ontology, be it a mental construct or measurable object);

2. The level of processes (infrastructure) – the social, economic and political relationships between things that cause certain transformations and effects to become apparent in the superstructure;
3. The level of imperatives (deep structure or base) – the overarching conditions that structure and condition social relationships.

The net implication of this is that there are complex relationships (theorized differently by particular thinkers) between base, infrastructure and super-structure, and that studies grounded in the analysis of superstructure cannot adequately be used to account for its existence. Instead, structuralism argues that the key to understanding a social system is to expose the structural relation-ships of its parts and to explore the way these parts are related by regulative mechanisms (hence, structure is more than the sum of its parts, and cannot be reduced to those parts).

In practice, geography has taken influence from a wide variety of structural thinkers – from linguistics, politics, economics, anthropology and sociology. Foremost perhaps have been those historical materialist thinkers – Marx, Althusser, Habermas and Lefebvre (see Box 1.1) in particular – who have pro-posed that the reality of the world can only be understood with reference to the historically unfolding political and economic relations that structure social life. Here, Marx's idea that the world has been shaped by deep structures of capital-ism has proved particularly influential on a legion of geographers, suggesting there is a complex two-way *dialectic* between people's action and structure, where people's actions reproduce unobservable but real structures, and these political-economic structures reproduce and sustain people's behaviour. Central to such interpretations have been questions of the class relations played out in capitalist society. Latterly, however, this political-economy perspective has been critiqued by those who suggest that other structures and power relations are important in contemporary society, turning attention to other social structures such as racism, ageism and sexism. Both Marxist and feminist geography can be seen as offering significant insights into the structures that reproduce inequal-ities in society, and it is in this sense that they are often bracketed together as critical and radical theories of the relations of society and space (see Stoddart, 1986).

2.4.1 Marxist geographies

Though **Karl Marx**'s (Box 2.4) writings comprise a series of often dense and incomplete works on the history of political economy, written in the mid-nineteenth century, it is impossible to overestimate his influence on both aca-demic and popular thought. In short, his materialist theories on the formation of society in distinct historical epochs (i.e., slavery, feudalism, capitalism, social-ism and communism) provided a rich description of the inequalities and injustices that are associated with different modes of production. For example, in contrast to accounts which suggested that people and ideas shaped history (such as those associated with Max Weber or Emile Durkheim), Marx argued that material economic circumstances and their associated social (class) relations are the driving force of history. According to Marx, people's beliefs, along with other aspects of their behaviour, are determined by the prevailing economic and social arrangements. Philosophy, religion and popular ideas reflect the power structure of a society while simultaneously compelling people to fit in with that structure. His materialist conception of history asserts, therefore, that the political economy of a society shapes its superstructure. Thus, for Marx the prevailing mode of production of material life determines the general character of the social, cultural, political and other processes of life. Marx's view that it is not people's consciousness that determines their being but, on the contrary, their social being that determines their consciousness, places him in direct opposition to the phenomenological approach outlined above. For Marx, there is no such thing as an individual human nature – the kind of person one is and the kind of things one does are determined by the kind of society in which one lives. This theory is inherently *teleological*, in the sense that it sees events as stages in the movement towards a preordained (and socially just) future, and *functional* in the sense that it subsumes the individual to the logic of the capitalist system.

Marx argued that this totality of social relations could be best explicated by reference to the competing social classes which are themselves defined in terms of their standing relative to the mode of production or wealth creation. Marx's focus on the workings of capitalism, the latest and most 'efficient' mode of production, offered a damning description of the way that it exploits class divisions forged through 'blood and fire'. His articulation of the capitalist labour process as being based on unequal relations between the bourgeois owners of the means of production and an exploited proletariat (the class of labourers)

Box 2.4 Karl Marx (1818–83)

Karl Marx remains one of the most widely discussed and written about figures in academia over the one hundred and fifty years since his major works – the unfinished volumes of *Das Kapital, The Communist Manifesto* and *Grundrisse* ('Outline of a Critique of Political Economy') – were published. For some, his ideas remain inspirational, offering both an accurate description of the processes that drive capitalist economies and a set of prescriptions for the injustices and inequalities associated with that system. For others, he serves as a 'straw man' whose thinking on political change failed to predict the injustices that could be served in the name of socialist progress and class revolution (as witnessed, for example, in Stalinist Russia) and whose major legacy is to have perpetuated a dogmatic and inflexible way of thinking about the social world. It is difficult to reject either set of arguments; Marx's ideas were a product of their times and his focus on class relations was an obvious response to the changes occurring in industrialized capitalist societies (particularly Britain) in the nineteenth century. These were to inspire his ostensible transition from an idealist perspective on social life (based on belief in the powers of people to overcome the alienation that they felt) to his materialist interpretations which focused on the social and economic conditions which shaped human consciousness. In his estimation, capitalist society had developed to a stage where people could overcome alienation by seizing the social form of their

therefore placed labour power at the centre of the capitalist mode of production, suggesting that the proletariat was responsible for creating the added wealth, or surplus value, that drove processes of capital accumulation. This identified the proletariat (working classes) as exploited but also stressed that they had the potential to organize collectively to bring down the capitalist system (Marx, 1977). Writing with his colleague, Friedrich Engels, Marx thus identified capitalism as an inherently unstable system that was threatened with being overthrown at any time by working-class revolt. Additionally, he identified the instability introduced to the capitalist system by market forces that thrived on the invention of new products, competitive innovation and (concurrently) the identification of particular technologies and products as obsolete.

Though Marx's ideas became widely cited and influential among political thinkers around the world – in part, inspiring the working-class revolt in Russia – their influence on geography was to prove negligible until the 1970s. This is perhaps surprising given that Marx (and many in the 'classical' Marxist tradition such as Rosa Luxemburg and Lenin) began to write of capitalism in geographical terms. In particular, their writing stressed that capital accumulation – the process by which capital was deployed to create new (and surplus) capital – was an inherently spatialized process, relying on the annihilation of political boundaries. This was to conceive of capitalism as an imperial enterprise involving the spreading of capitalist infrastructure across the earth's surface, bequeathing an uneven geography of industrial districts, rural backwaters and urbanized centres segregated between the elite and the proletariat. While this offered a good description of the unfolding geographies associated with the parallel process of modernization and urbanization, in the English-speaking geographical community these ideas seemed to make little headway. In other

own production (i.e., redefining themselves and their subjectivity). The fact that they did not do so, he argued, was a result of capitalist class relations which frustrated this collective self-determination. In this way, his materialist interpretation of society, based on a structural theorization, was to prompt his work as a social agitator and revolutionary figure. Marx's ideas thus became a source of inspiration for those arguing for class revolt, with the subsequent failure of the communist states serving to discredit his ideas in the eyes of many (see Callinicos, 1991). Ironically, it is the failure of this classless 'self-determined' society to have materialized that actually inspires many geographers to continue to explore his ideas; to paraphrase Lefebvre (1991), we do not know why capitalism continues to survive, but we know how: by occupying space and producing place. Marx's legacy for geographers is his insistence on a structural reading of society and his careful articulation of the capitalist process; even in the present, when the reductionism of his ideas is derided by many, questions of class remain prominent in radical and critical geographical writing (albeit often considered alongside age, gender, sex and race relations – see Chapter 3).

Further reading: Harvey (1982); Castree (1999); Blunt and Wills (2000)

fields, however, Marxist ideas were to prompt the formation of new labour organizations, trade unions, and protest groups, united in a process of class struggle. In this struggle, they were joined by a range of Western thinkers who sought to update and adapt Marxist theory to develop critical theories of society that were as much about changing society as explaining it. The Frankfurt Institute of Social Research (founded in 1923) became particularly associated with this project, its director Max Horkheimer arguing that only a radical change in theory could cure the ills of society.

Geographers' turn to Marxist theory was then, in comparison to its uptake in other disciplines, strangely belated. In part, this can be explained with reference to geography's development in the twentieth century, particularly its preoccupation with regional geography and, later, spatial science. Both of these were viewed as inherently dispassionate and objective exercises in the construction of knowledge (see Stoddart, 1986). Within this framework, Marx's politicized ideas appeared to have little relevance. This was a view that was not really to be challenged until the early 1970s, prompted by changes outside the discipline as much as by changes within. Here, it is important to acknowledge the political and social changes that were occurring at this time – 1968 had witnessed student riots in Paris; there was a growing awareness of environmental problems; famine was rife in the Third World; war raged in Vietnam, and incidences of racial intimidation and violence were widespread. Against this backdrop, a number of geographers began to question the relevance of geography (particularly in its spatial science guise) to social problems (e.g., Harvey, 1973; Smith, 1977; Stoddart, 1986). For these writers, geography at the time appeared to be populated by practitioners who were constructing models and theories in splendid ignorance of the problems of those living in the world beyond the 'ivory towers' of academia. This critique was also extended to behavioural and humanistic geography, which was accused by some of the new breed of 'radical' geographers of pursuing a pointless trajectory that said nothing of the real processes causing inequality in society. Ironically, it was one of the most forthright proponents of quantitative geography – David Harvey (Box 6.2) – who now sought to propose a radical Marxist geography. In his oft-cited words:

> There is a clear disparity between the sophisticated theoretical and methodological frameworks which we have developed and our ability to say anything really meaningful about events as they unfold around us . . . There is an ecological problem, an urban problem, a debt problem, yet we seem incapable of saying anything in-depth or profound about any of them. (Harvey, 1973, p. 129)

It is perhaps wrong to suggest that all those who argued for geography's increased involvement in solving problems were convinced of the need for a Marxist geography. Indeed, some felt that spatial science and its positivist assumptions continued to provide a firm foundation for the production of useful and relevant knowledge. Against this, and informed by the ideas of the German philosopher Jürgen Habermas, others argued that positivist science simply reinforced the status quo, producing knowledge that could be used as an instrument of oppression (an idea we explore in more depth in Chapter 4 when we describe Foucault's ideas of how the state *disciplines* through knowledge). This implied that positivism simply described things as they appeared, rather than identifying real sources of power (Peet, 1998).

Geography's engagement with Marxism was thus the outcome of a variety of factors. In turn, this inspired a number of innovative and radical attempts to re-theorize space in terms quite different from those used by positivists. A key feature here was the idea that space was not a neutral given, but was *socially* produced (i.e., could only be understood in relation to material events and structures). This also represented a radical departure from humanistic ideas which gave primacy to human consciousness; materialism holds to the primacy of matter. In Marxist thinking, consciousness can only be understood in relation to what exists; it is the material world translated into forms of thought. At the same time, this epistemological argument – that matter has primacy over con-sciousness – stresses that there is a determinant relationship between matter and thought that can never be understood through positivist science (which simply endorses scientific method). This complex philosophical assertion implies that it is impossible to create laws about the working of society and space through positivist or humanistic procedures. Laws can only be established through a method of *dialectics* where space is treated as a something which is given shape through material processes, flows and relationships (see Soja, 1985). Dialectical thought has a long history in Western philosophy reaching back to the work of Aristotle and Plato, with Marx's own adoption of dialectical materialism inspired by Hegel (Jones, 1999). Unlike principles of deductive and inductive thinking, dialectics does not aim to test theory, but to work with it, adapting it and transforming it appropriately. For example, theories about the social-spatial dialectic (i.e., the relationships between society and space) seek to use data about what exists in the superstructure to identify underlying economic and political processes. This 'data' may entail observations, figures, thoughts and words about 'things' that exist; discerning opposition among these things (e.g., wealth and poverty) allows internal contradictions in the processes and systems to become apparent. Analytically, the identification of such contradictions and oppositions allows the identification of the processes by which such contradic-tions are resolved (but see Lefebvre, 1991, on spatial trialectics and the way organic and spontaneous bodily spaces can transcend the dialectic of spatial practice and representations of space).

In classic Marxist endeavour, dialectical thinking was used to identify the forms of contradiction and tension in capitalist societies that needed to be resolved by transformations and adjustments to the mode of production. For instance, coming to recognize the fact that exploitation of labour power by the capitalist classes threatened to instigate class revolt, Marx wrote of the perpetual modernization and agitation employed by the bourgeoisie to ensure that the relations of production were maintained. In capitalist societies where 'all that is solid melts into air . . . ', Marx thus argued that new forms of social relation were being constantly brought into being, reproducing capitalism (see also

Berman, 1982). In the writing of those geographers and urban theorists who first engaged with Marxist theory – David Harvey, Richard Peet, Doreen Massey and Manuel Castells – this type of reasoning was transformed into explications of the role of space in this process of legitimation and crisis avoidance. Simply put, geographers emphasized the importance of capitalism's spatial fix – the way that spatial differentiation and de-differentiation were implicated in capitalist relations. In Harvey's (1982) account, the contradictions of capitalism were thus scrutinized to come to an understanding of urbanization processes. Herein, the division of urban space into upper-class and working-class residential areas was seen as a key means by which working-class agitation could be suppressed, at the same time serving to create an urban landscape characterized by high and low land values. In Harvey's numerous works on the urbanization of capital, this form of uneven development was theorized as a crucial means by which capitalism could create for itself new opportunities for capitalist accumulation. In effect, by placing the poorer classes (particularly surplus labour) in marginal urban spaces with inadequate social infrastructure, capitalism denied an adequate quality of life to these people, excluded them from participation in political life and thus prevented them usurping the bourgeoisie. At the same time, the association of these areas with this 'underclass' drove down land prices, meaning that subsequent development could realize the difference between actual ground rent and the potential rent offered by that site (the so-called 'rent gap' – Smith, 1996). Such theories thus explained phenomena of 'blockbusting' and gentrification by developers as part of the process by which capital sought the most profitable locations for its realization (see Section 3.2).

Coupled with Castells's (1977; see Box 8.4) theories of the role of collective consumption in capitalist society (the importance of state support for the capitalist system through the provision of non-commercial public services such as schools, hospitals, community centres and so on), Harvey's writing on capitalism provided a remarkable structural interpretation of urban process theorized around the idea of circuits of capital. This emphasis on the way that capital was perpetually transformed into different forms (money, labour, commodities) so as to maintain capital accumulation was to provide an important framework for geographical enquiry. As such, numerous geographers began to explore the way that the organization of space helped to maintain and enhance these circuits. Such explorations operated at different spatial scales, from critical analysis of the interdependencies of core and periphery played out at an international (e.g., Slater, 1977; Corbridge, 1986) and national level (e.g., Massey and Allen, 1984) to the processes of gentrification and working-class displacement evident in both urban and rural locales (e.g., Smith, 1984). The common thread in these explorations, however, was a concern with unevenness, whereby capitalism seeks creatively to destroy specific spatial arrangements at one point in time in order to create new, more profitable arrangements at the next. Conceived of in this way, capitalist structures can be seen to be supported and maintained by the arrangement of things in space to create a profit surface characterized by peaks and troughs of high and low value. Capitalism tends to bring about the development of those spaces which are most profitable, and the underdevelopment of those that are least profitable (Smith, 1996). In some geographical accounts, this has been linked to processes of governance via an exploration of the way that politicians and policy intervene in the 'free' market, whether through 'entrepreneurial' regeneration and welfare policies in the urban West or aid programmes in the Third World (see Chapters 7 and 8). In relation to the latter, geographers working in the Marxist tradition have developed a radical critique of development, exposing aid and 'structural adjustment programmes' as neo-liberal strategies of Westernization implicated in the making of unequal and exploitative geopolitical orders (Crush, 1995; Slater, 1999).

The continuing range and vitality of political-economy approaches in geography thus put Neil Smith's (1996) wry observation that 'Marxism is dead' in context. Certainly, some have questioned the primacy of class as an analytical category, suggesting this has led Marxism into a theoretical cul-de-sac (see Laclau and Mouffe, 1985). For others, the decline of the Communist bloc signifies the inherent weaknesses of Marx's teleological thinking (Smart, 1996). Yet for Merrifield (2000a, p. 139), Marxism 'can still provide zest for life, can still be a veritable adventure of the mind and body, can still define the breadth and depth of the radical battlefield, dialectically highlighting the inner connections and contradictions between the economy and politics, between thought and action.' For him, the key to the continuing relevance of Marxism is the way that it turns these contradictions to its own advantage, using dialectical thinking to criticize and transform rapidly changing social structures from the level of the city street upwards. Merrifield thus cites the work of Lefebvre and Marxist urbanists as engaging flexibly with the concrete realities of space while being open to the abstract processes which, as Marx (1977, pp. 77–8) suggested, are often 'imperceptible to the senses'. This 'street Marxism' thus offers a revised take on Marxism, a neo-Marxism which is open to the changing rules of the capitalist game (an argument we return to in Chapter 3).

What is obvious here is that, while both the methods and subject matter of Marxist geography are diverse and eclectic, the presiding spirit is that of a radical endeavour determined to identify (and *change*) the processes, flows and relations that structure the lives of individuals. In contrast to humanism (or behaviouralism), structuralism rejects the autonomy of human agents (with Marx famously claiming that people make history, but not under conditions of their own choosing). Viewed from a humanistic perspective, this type of account appears highly deterministic, with people's endless capacity for creativity obfuscated by a perspective that sees humans as 'called upon' to fulfil structural (and functional) imperatives (Guelke, 1974). Against this, Marxists have tended to argue that notions of free will are similarly misguided, and that it is necessary to locate sequences of human action within wider contexts of social reproduction and transformation. To do otherwise, they argue, is to disengage from the real, structural processes that shape the world (see Gregory, 1978). This ongoing debate about structure and agency mirrors a more widespread debate in the social sciences about the merits of particular forms of explanation, where proponents of structural philosophies (both Marxist and neo-Marxist political economy) have clashed with those subscribing to idealist, phenomenological and, latterly, psychoanalytical accounts of the ongoing construction of the self (Pile, 1993).

Attempts to reconcile the structure/agency dichotomy (regarded as futile by some) have thus been widespread in the social sciences. Some of these (e.g., symbolic interactionism, social representation theory) have made little impression on geography, though the sociologist Anthony Giddens has proposed a theory of *structuration* that has been widely cited (see Cloke *et al.*, 1991; Giddens, 1991). This contends that there is a need to elucidate the relations between individual actions and social structures in a much more flexible and iterative way than articulated by proponents of Marxism, arguing for a duality of structure and agency where structure does not 'exist' beneath the superstructure but is created by and implicated in each and every human action. This framework was influential for several economic geographers in the 1980s (particularly those working in the localities tradition – see Cooke, 1989), as was *realism*. This is an approach to science that uses abstraction to identify specific causal powers of specific structures under specific causal conditions. Realists argue – *contra* humanists – that there is a world of material things and events which can be observed and measured. But for realists, the world is also made up of intangible mechanisms and structures, and it is these that are seen as allowing certain things to happen in particular circumstances (Bhaskar, 1978; Sayer, 2001). A key assumption in realism is that there are certain structures – such as capitalist labour processes – that have the necessary power to cause something to happen, but do not do so everywhere and anywhere. Outcomes depend upon contingent factors – such as the presence of particular welfare systems or the existence of certain planning policies at a local level. Realist research is concerned with teasing out the real chain of causality that makes events and things occur in particular circumstances. According to Sayer (1992), this involves a threefold research enterprise:

- *abstract research* – developing a theory of how structures and mechanisms might result in events – this is about identifying and naming the structural conditions that enable something to happen, the mechanisms that actually cause it to happen.
- *intensive research* – examining concrete or specific instances to see if the theory holds.
- *extensive research* – examining whether this explanation holds in different cases, to isolate causal processes.

The difference between this and the traditional science approach is that it recognizes there can be no general law, just specific explanations which are contingent on the existence of certain circumstances; what we can at least do is identify the processes that cause something to occur within a certain set of circumstances. For many, including Marxist geographers, this sort of approach appeared to offer a rigorous method for elucidating the dialectic between society and space (A. Pratt, 1995). For others, however, realism merely reinstated the scientific conceit of positivism (though with less methodological specificity), and geographers' enthusiasm for it (and, indeed, structural theories) appeared to wane in the 1990s in the face of 'post-structural' critiques that problematized the relationship between 'knowing' subjects and invisible social logics. It is these post-structural ideas, and the movement 'beyond' structuralism, that we shall explore in more detail in our next chapter.

2.4.2 Feminist geographies

If Marxist geography proposed a geography where class relations were seen as fundamental in understanding the dialectic of society and space, feminist geography can be characterized by its emphasis on the structures that reproduce gender inequality. Crucial here is the notion of patriarchy, a system whereby women are assumed to be generally subordinate to men and become subject to the control of men. According to Walby (1990), patriarchy is a system constituted by six interrelated but distinct structures in which men dominate women. The six 'spheres' she identifies are as follows:

1. *Waged work*: where women's average hourly pay tends to be two-thirds of that of men and where women are segregated into specific tasks and occupations.
2. *Household reproduction*: where women are charged with responsibility for domestic tasks, cleaning and childcare, even in situations where both they and their partner work on a full-time basis.
3. *State politics*: where women's participation in politics is discouraged by masculinist practices and institutions that devalue the opinions and rights of women.
4. *Fear of crime*: where women are constantly fearful of male violence, particularly rape and violent attacks perpetrated by strangers (which conversely encourages them to seek the protection of men).
5. *Culture and leisure*: where women's sports and leisure pursuits are marginalised and devalued by the media and politicians, who devote more airtime, expenditure and facilities towards 'proper' male pursuits such as football and baseball (simultaneously denigrating women's participation in these same sports).
6. *Sexuality*: where women's bodies are commodified (i.e. turned into something that can be bought and sold) through processes of representation that depict women as sex objects whose natural role is to be subordinate to sexually aggressive males.

In sum, it can be seen that patriarchy represents an ingrained system of assumptions, practices and mechanisms that collectively serve to subjugate women and make them susceptible to male social control. In accordance with structural ideas, this does not imply that all men are sexist, or that all women are subordinate to men, but that, generally, we are all caught up in structures that perpetuate gender inequality. This also stresses that feminist geography is not simply a geography of women, rather a geography that seeks to explore the way space is implicated in the perpetuation of unequal gender relations (Monk and Hanson, 1982). Latterly, this has meant that geographers have devoted considerable energy to examining the place of men in the world, both within and without the academy (e.g., Sparke, 1996).

The relationship between feminist and Marxist perspectives has subsequently provoked much debate (Rojek, 1995). In the eyes of some, patriarchy needs to be theorized as part and parcel of a capitalist system that thrives on inequality; in such interpretations, sexism and patriarchy are seen as crucial systems that ensure the reproduction of the household, a social unit that is central to the capitalist labour process (see Watson, 1986). In other interpretations, patriarchy and capitalism are seen as dual systems; writers have pointed to the fact that forms of gender inequality existed in pre-capitalist societies too (Foord and Gregson, 1986). Irrespective of this, feminist writing in geography – particularly as it became established in the discipline in the 1970s – was fiercely critical of gender inequality, serving to ally feminist geographers with the wider feminist movement that was campaigning for women's rights and gender equality. At this time, work by Doreen Massey (Box 1.2), Jackie Tivers, Linda McDowell (Box 6.4), Sophie Bowlby and other founders of the **Women and Geography Study Group** (Box 2.5) began to highlight the forms of gender inequality played out in the spaces of the home and the city, placing particular emphasis on the role that women's segregation (and virtual imprisonment in the suburban home) played in constraining their employment and leisure opportunities (see also MacKenzie, 1989; Pratt, 1992). At this time, the focus was squarely on the experiences and geographies of women rather than exploring the relations between men and women manifest in different spaces. In part, this focus was deemed necessary by feminist geographers in the light of the innate masculinism of the discipline. Not only were most academic geographers male, they argued, but they conceived of space in male terms, marginalizing the

---

Box 2.5 Women and Geography Study Group

Though there have been allied groups in other countries, the Women and Geography Study Group of the Institute of British Geographers has been a key influence on the trajectory of feminist theory in geography since its formation in 1980. The group's aims since that time have been to encourage geographic study of the implications of gender differentiation as well as to promote research and teaching from a feminist standpoint. This intention was mapped out through the publication of the well-received undergraduate text *Geography and Gender* (1984), which indicated the potential of feminist theory at a time when such ideas were still largely unexplored in the discipline. Highlighting the distinctive contribution that geographers could make to the study of gender issues, it was this book that did much to consolidate feminist geography as a key component of many degree courses. This text was written through collaboration between a group of authors, emphasizing the possibilities of a feminist praxis that was supportive and collective rather than individual and competitive. Importantly, royalties from this book, as well as the follow-up *Feminist Geographies: Explorations in Diversity and Difference* (1997), were donated to the group, providing support for a vigorous programme of conference sessions, symposia and study weekends. Both books offered state-of-the-art

experiences and opinions of women in the process. In this sense, feminist geography was conceived as a reaction to the models of 'man' that dominated in positivist, behavioural and humanistic geography, and an attempt to address key silences in the discipline (Jones *et al.*, 1997).

Here we should note that feminism in geography was never a monolithic undertaking, and drew upon different strands of feminism with different priorities concerning the emancipation of women. 'First-wave' French feminism, for example, was always a key influence, closely associated with the work of Simone de Beauvoir (who employed existentialism to demonstrate the ways in which women through history have been defined by patriarchal society as inferior to men). De Beauvoir also used literary analysis to explore why and how women have accepted their socially constructed second-class position against their best interests. Similarly, Hélène Cixous, a member of the 'second wave' of French feminism, sought to work past the limitations placed on women's writing by challenging male ideals of 'reason' via a playful and thought-provoking writing style. Presaging post-structural ideas (see Chapter 3), she argues that the way something is said can be as revealing as what is being said, and that feminists need to think and write in different ways to men. This approach, known as *écriture feminine*, proposed that women should use their creativity and turn the tables on men by either rejecting traditional male approaches to writing or using them in new ways (Cixous, 1981). In many ways, this poetic celebration of the feminine and the maternal jarred with the type of socialist feminism more widespread in the United Kingdom in the 1970s and 1980s. This underlines the fact that feminism does not imply a unified political stance, let alone a unified field of theory.

But even if feminism (and hence feminist geography) has always been multifaceted, important generalizations can be made about the links between feminist theory and practice. Mainstream geography has invariably been depicted

---

summaries of the scope and range of feminist geography, highlighting the particular way feminists work with notions of difference, methodology and representation (Jones *et al.*, 1997). Reading the books together, however, it is possible to discern crucial changes in approaches to feminist geography, with the initial commitment to improving women's position in the labour market tempered by the awareness that gender identities are simultaneously shaped by nationalism, imperialism, heterosexism, racism, ageism, disabilism and so on. Also evident is an increasing concern with contesting and appropriating masculinist ways of 'doing' geography to disrupt established hierarchies of quantitative/qualitative technique and hard/soft data (something emphasized in the diverse range of contributions to the journal *Gender, Place and Culture*, founded in 1994). Though the membership of the WGSG has changed considerably since its formation, with increasing numbers of men now working with feminist and queer theory (see Chapter 4), its agenda continues to be dominated by discussion of gender inequalities both within and outside the academy.

Further reading: WGSG (1984, 1997); Laurie *et al.* (1999); McDowell (1999)

by feminist geographers as 'malestream', utilizing methods and techniques that produce knowledge deemed real and important only from a male perspective. For example, Rose (1993) felt that the preoccupation of spatial science with abstract geometries was a reflection of a rational male urge to impose order on a natural world conceived of as feminine. Rejecting such reductive gender-biased impulses, feminist epistemology – in geography and elsewhere – has been primarily associated with 'softer' methods of enquiry (open-ended interviews, ethnography and storytelling in particular). By adopting such techniques, the intention was to elucidate and articulate the multiple perspectives of women while avoiding the use of methods that might potentially inflict harm on research respondents (Dyck, 1997). The principle that research should be with women, rather than on them, was (and remains) a key precept in feminist methodology:

> Feminist research is about the development and construction of knowledge founded upon the relationship between women's everyday experience, academic knowledge, political power and social action. This methodological approach facilitates the central involvement of the women, who are active participants in the social construction of knowledge, empowerment and social change. (O'Neill, 1996, p. 131)

As a theoretical framework, feminism is therefore grounded in an ontology and epistemology dedicated to producing knowledge that promotes social change (Blunt and Wills, 2000). This identified feminist geographers as *dissident* geographers, dissatisfied with the role that the discipline was playing in addressing women's issues and determined to develop new frameworks of theory and practice.

In the 1980s, feminist geography became a much more broad undertaking, and, as a theoretical framework, feminism has been employed by both female and male geographers to explore issues across the discipline (including physical geography). The fact that feminist theories about identity and difference became much more widely discussed in the social sciences in the 1980s and 1990s meant that those working in the feminist tradition were able to strike up a dialogue with those in other disciplines who were exploring the construction of gender difference. One important influence here was the work of those social theorists who proposed that the categories of men and women, far from being fixed through human biology, are social constructions (see Bondi, 1992; Greed, 1993). In effect, this conceptualization of gender and sex prompted geographers to explore how the category of women was mapped out of, and onto, specific spaces, so that (for example) the association of women with home served to perpetuate ideas that women are 'naturally' responsible for child-rearing and domestic reproduction (McDowell, 1983). In the 1990s, the influence of post-structural ideas (see Chapter 3) was to transform feminist theory yet again, so that the unified categories of 'women' and 'men' were subject to critical fragmentation. This type of deconstruction suggested that the notion of patriarchy was perhaps too simplistic to conceive of gender relations in all their variety, suggesting instead that performances of *masculinity* and *femininity* vary across space in complex ways (Longhurst, 2000a). In this sense, gender inequality is theorized as being produced through multiple axes of difference, with dominant constructions of masculinity and femininity varying according to age, class, ethnicity, nationality and sexuality (Laurie *et al.*, 1999). This concern for identity and difference mirrors some of the wider theoretical impulses that have driven human geography in recent years (see Chapter 3), meaning that feminist theory remains widely discussed and debated by those who do not necessarily hold to the central precepts of feminist thinking.

Feminist geography is now a broad framework, having extended its corpus from its preoccupation with women's geographies to a more wide-ranging consideration of the relations of gender, place and culture (Women and Geography Study Group, 1997). At the same time, its methods have become more diverse, with quantitative and archival analysis now complementing the qualitative techniques that have been the mainstay of much feminist enquiry. As such, feminist theory (like Marxist, positivist, humanistic or behavioural geography) is perhaps best described as offering a variety of theories, concepts and methods that have been utilized in different ways in particular research contexts. Certainly, the range of topics covered in *A Feminist Glossary of Human Geography* (1999) edited by Linda McDowell and Joanne Sharp shows that feminist theories of patriarchy and gender inequality have come to be very significant in many areas of the discipline.

2.5 CONCLUSION: AN INTELLECTUAL BATTLEGROUND?

As this chapter has unfolded, we have sought to describe some of the different theoretical impulses that have shaped the theory and practice of geography in the post-war era. In some ways, it is tempting to describe this as a period where different intellectual traditions and ideas have 'battled' for paradigmatic dominance, each imagining concepts of space, place and nature very differently. Certainly the way this history is narrated in some texts relies on a military language to describe a struggle between different groups; followers of different camps wage war on one another, advocates of particular approaches seeing their arguments shot down in flames, philosophies revealed as fatally flawed and so on. But, following Doel (1999), we should perhaps be suspicious of this narration. Far from being 'dead' or killed off, the theory and practice of spatial science, Marxism, humanism, feminism and behaviouralism are all alive and well. Of course, it is possible to argue that certain of these are less widely discussed or written of than they used to be, but to suggest that geography is a discipline where one way of thinking or one way of doing has become dominant at any one time is problematic. Instead, we perhaps need to think about the geographical tradition as being characterized by a singular diversity. Herein, different theories and ideas coexist, intermingling and cross-fertilizing to produce new offspring. Geography, then, is always evolving (though not necessarily improving), with attempts to assert order on it (by labelling specific ideas, geographies and writers as 'Marxist' or 'humanist', etc.) serving to reduce its difference to sameness.

Following Johnston's (2000) claim that there is no one geography, no predominant statement of where it has come from, what it knows and how it produces knowledge, we might then view this chapter not so much as the story of theoretical battles fought as geography edges nearer to a truly authoritative account of how the world works, but as an attempt to map out some of the different theoretical strands that contribute to the continual dynamic complexity of geographical thinking. The way some of these strands have been woven together, braided and unravelled in more recent times is the subject of our next chapter.

Chapter 3   New Theories, New Geographies?

3.1 INTRODUCTION

The previous chapter suggested that the theoretical landscape of human geography, like that of other disciplines, is ever-changing. New ideas and concepts are constantly being incorporated into the lexicon of the discipline, reshaping how academics examine, research and write 'geography'. In this chapter we explore some of the more recent ideas that are impinging on the production of geographical knowledge, detailing the theoretical frameworks that are currently most influential in shaping human geography. We begin this chapter by describing two related impulses encouraging geographers to engage with theoretical ideas from beyond the discipline. The first of these concerns the ways in which space has increasingly become a focus of analysis for scholars in other disciplines (the so-called 'spatial turn'). Conversely, the second relates to what has been termed geography's 'cultural turn' (i.e., the integration of social and cultural theory into geographical analyses). Following on from this, the remainder of the chapter outlines how such impulses are manifest in three (overlapping) theoretical engagements. The first of these is represented by geographers' interest in 'critical' theory, which involves a distinctive (and *engaged*) analysis of power and difference. The second involves the rise of what might be termed 'postmodern' geographies, examining how the ideas of postmodern scholars have challenged traditional notions of (geographic) knowledge production, opening up the academy to a diversity of Other voices (via a simultaneous dialogue with queer and post-colonial theory). The third engagement concerns the increasing geographic interest in post-structural theories, especially the work of a key group of European philosophers whose ideas about language, subjectivity and complexity have raised important questions about the way we seek to understand the world.

Before we start, however, it should be noted that the distinction between critical/postmodern/post-structural theory is problematic, with significant interrelationships existing between the themes and theories within each section. It should also be noted that the theoretical traditions discussed in the previous chapter, but largely ignored in this, are still very much part of the landscape of human geography. Few of those invoking the ideas discussed in this chapter dismiss the theoretical frameworks of positivism, behaviouralism or humanism, for example, as irrelevant or outdated aspects of contemporary human geography. Indeed, significant and important work is still being undertaken within all of these traditions, often bringing 'newer' concepts into dialogue with the 'old'. Consequently, our aim here is to explore emerging theoretical ideas, but *not* to privilege them as necessarily the way geographers should engage with geographical concepts. In other words, the chapter is not a survey of all the theoretical approaches currently being used in human geography and does not provide a popularity measure of current approaches – it merely seeks to document and reflect on some of the new ways in which geographers are thinking geographically.

3.2 NEW WORDS, NEW WORLDS

Taking our section title from the collection of the same name edited by Chris Philo (1991), here we outline some of the new words and new worlds emerging as geographers look beyond geography for theoretical inspiration. At the time that Philo edited this collection, one of the most significant new trends was the increased prominence given by geographers to *social* theory. Peet (1998) suggests that social theory occupies the middle ground between philosophy and theory and is a storage and bridging device, storing the findings of one field in a form of ideas that can be transferred across theoretical bridges to others. This storage and bridging allows for the development of general social theory – theory that transcends disciplines. Peet asserts that recently most disciplines have started to make social theory their primary focus, seeking to add, refine and develop it rather than focusing on their own disciplinary ends. Here, interchange (the cross-disciplinary comparison of ideas) is even extending into attempts at unification. It can thus be argued that disciplinary boundaries across the academy have started to become more blurred and less important. This has led to the suggestion that scholarly work in the twenty-first century will effectively be post-disciplinary, with the borders between subject areas becoming highly permeable and eventually disappearing altogether (M. Smith, 2000).

The growing importance of social theory across the social sciences during the 1980s and 1990s had its corollary in two key trends, both of which might be taken as partial evidence for the thesis that we are moving towards a post-disciplinary landscape. The first of these is a so-called 'spatial turn' in disciplines such as sociology, cultural studies and literary studies. This is certainly evident across the social sciences and humanities as researchers have come to appreciate the importance of space in understanding social and cultural phenomenon (especially, it seems, in the context of a globalizing world – see Chapter 8). For example, sociologists such as Anthony Giddens (1991), John Urry (1994) and Rob Shields (1991), political theorists such as Manuel Castells (1989, 1996) or Zygmunt Bauman (1998) and cultural commentators like Frederic Jameson (1991), Stuart Hall (1996), Richard Sennett (1994) and Frank Mort (1998) have all explicitly considered the role of space in their work (and there are many more). James Ryan (2000, p. 10) thus writes that 'geographical metaphors and techniques for "mapping" the "topographies" of culture have become incorporated into the language and practice of disciplines such as cultural studies', while Crang and Thrift (2000a, p. 1) suggest '[s]pace is the everywhere of modern thought'. The consequence of this is that academics outside the discipline have begun to theorize space in ways that have appeal for geographers. This means their work is being imported into geographical thought in a variety of ways. Conversely, work by geographers is increasingly being used and read by those in other social sciences and humanities. However, it has been argued that geography seems to borrow far more than it is borrowed from. In part, this explains why so many of the theorists we discuss in this and the following chapters would not necessarily consider themselves to be 'geographers', even though their work is inherently geographical.

The second major symptom of post-disciplinarity (and the focus of our discussion here) is then geographers' engagement with various strands of social theory, especially (but not only) those that are concerned with the importance of culture in the making of social relations. Dubbed geography's 'cultural turn' (Philo, 1991), this has entailed a recognition that questions of culture are inadequately addressed in geographical analysis. While the 'cultural turn' is perhaps better understood as a series of cultural insights, interventions and circuits (Cook *et al.*, 2000, p. xii), a unifying concern was that culture needed to be understood in very different ways than it had been in 'traditional' cultural geography, particularly that practised by Carl Sauer and the Berkeley School (see Chapter 2). This conceived of culture as something manifest in material artefacts, believing that studying cultural artefacts and their place in the landscape could reveal 'ways of life' or *genres de vie* (M. Crang, 1998). In contrast to this static view of culture, the 'new' cultural geography conceived of culture as a *process* – the shifting and unstable system of meanings through which people make sense of a world of material objects. Rooted in cultural history and literary theory (see Chapter 5), this is a conceptualization that focuses on the role of language and text in creating meaning, simultaneously exploring how this meaning is embodied and embedded in the material and social world (Hall, 1996; McEwan, 2001). Culture is thus recast as the principal means through which society and space are *constructed*, providing people with their sense of identity at the same time that it maps out power-laden social and spatial hierarchies (Hall, 1996).

Proponents of 'new' cultural geography, such as **Peter Jackson** (1989; see Box 3.1), argue that, by largely ignoring culture as a fundamental process in shaping societies, geographers had created sterile accounts of what were rich and complex human landscapes. Through his empirical research on the geographies of race and racism, Jackson argued that, in order to understand the socio-spatial inequalities and divisions inscribed on the urban landscape, it was important to unpack the ways in which categories of 'black' and 'white' were culturally constructed through language and the media. In turn, he suggested it was important to consider how these stereotyped representations were then mapped onto space (e.g., through pernicious myths of non-white 'ghetto' areas). Importantly, Jackson suggested that such representations could not be privileged in relation to the other factors that sustained ethnic segregation (such as the behaviour of housing agencies, employers or politicians) but entwined with these more material concerns to shape geographies of disadvantage and exclusion. He thus sought to marry the insights of the cultural Marxism developed by Raymond Williams (see Box 5.1) with a more humanistic concern for text and textuality, calling for the interrogation of what he termed 'maps of meaning' – the frameworks which give people and places meaning. His work thus emphasized that 'culture is not a residual category, the surface variation left unaccounted for by more powerful economic analyses: it is the very medium through which social change is experienced, contested and constituted' (Cosgrove and Jackson, 1987, p. 95).

At approximately the same time that Jackson was starting to examine the 'cultural politics of place', others were starting to use the reconceptualization of culture as a process to examine the way that places themselves encapsulate and communicate cultural identities. Discussed in Chapter 5, the work of Cosgrove (1984; see Box 5.3) and Duncan (1990) adopted a broadly cultural materialist position to argue that landscapes – like language – can be 'read'. This decoding of landscape imagery showed that highly ideological and political messages were often written into, and read from, specific landscapes, with notions of 'spectacle', iconography and symbolism central in many 'enculturated' accounts of the urban (e.g., Mills, 1993) and rural (e.g., Mordue, 1999). Such accounts suggest that the meaning of places – like representations – is constructed via language (interpreted in its broadest sense) and is thus beyond the 'author's'

Box 3.1 Peter Jackson (1955–)

A Professor of Human Geography at the University of Sheffield (UK) and an editor of the journal *Society and Space*, Peter Jackson has been a key figure in the development of 'new' cultural geography. This was initially articulated through his work on 'race' and racism in the UK (see Jackson, 1987 and Jackson and Penrose, 1993 for overviews). In this work, Jackson sought to expose the flaws in more 'traditional' studies of the geography of race which tended to adopt a spatial science perspective. Studies within this tradition concentrated upon mapping and describing patterns of ethnic segregation through positivist choice and constraint models. Jackson argued that such explanations of racial segregation were theoretically weak given that they failed to acknowledge the social and political dimensions of racism. Instead, he suggested that racism is structured through ideological practices aimed at maintaining a dominant (white) hegemony. Racism, from this perspective, is deemed to be inherently embedded in both material and representational practices (i.e., racist language, imagery and symbolism as well as racist practice). Along with others such as Susan Smith (1989a), he documented how cultural myths based upon animalization, naturalization and disease have been used to construct racial categories, exposing how these representations perpetuated the dominance of white, Western Europeans both in colonial and

control, being open to constant reinterpretation by differently situated audiences. Of course, this in itself undermines the authority of geographers to provide definitive interpretations of places or their representations (something very much at odds with the Berkeley School's conception of culture, in which cultural artefacts were subject to the interpretative authority of the academic).

Out of the work of Jackson, Cosgrove, Duncan and others, 'new' cultural geography has grown to become a popular and vibrant subdiscipline of human geography (see Anderson and Gale, 1992; Duncan and Ley, 1993; Crang, 1998; Mitchell, 2000). Perhaps more significantly, the importance of culture has been seized upon widely across the discipline, with social, political and economic geographers seeking to undertake culturally sensitive analyses. For example, many economic geographers have considered the role of culture in shaping the space economy, leading to what has been termed 'new economic geography' (see McDowell, 1997; Leyshon and Thrift, 1997; Lee and Wills, 1997 – and also Chapter 6). Illustrative here is the work of Erica Schoenberger (1996), which explores the 'cultural economy' of the firm, and Thrift's (2000b) analysis of the performance cultures of the 'fast' subjects who play a pivotal role in the articulation of Western capitalism. Additionally, interest in the representation of people and place has inspired some innovative work in political geography, especially (but not exclusively) that work concerned with the relation between 'developed' and 'developing' nations (e.g., Blunt and Rose, 1994; Slater, 1999; Gregory, 2000b). Marcus (2000, p. 14) thus states that 'what the cultural turn has meant for geography is a strong intervention of interpretative theories, methods and ideas in a field heavily influenced by tasks of mapping, describing societies spatially, and economistic theories'.

This is not to say that the cultural turn has been enthusiastically embraced by

post-colonial contexts. This careful attention to language and 'cultural politics' was similarly evident in his highly influential text *Maps of Meaning* (Jackson, 1989), which persuaded a large number of academic geographers to consider the merits of 'new' cultural geography. In this text, Jackson drew on social and cultural theory, and in particular the work of Raymond Williams, Clifford Geertz, Stuart Hall and Antonio Gramsci (see Box 3.3), to explore the ways in which culture sustains (spatialized) power relations. Jackson adopted a materialist view of culture which emphasized the 'cultural politics' shaping the geographies of Western societies. Subsequently, his work has concentrated on the geographies of consumption, shopping and fashion (see, for example, Miller *et al.*, 1998), with a particular emphasis on the cultural politics of masculinity. Like several other first-wave, 'new' cultural geographers he has recently warned of the dangers of focusing on the immaterial and discursive at the expense of the material, arguing that doing so neglects an important aspect of how cultures are grounded in material relations and the 'traffic in things' (Jackson, 2000).

Further reading: Jackson (1987, 1989, 2000).

all (see Barnett, 1998). For example, many geographers remain sceptical of the 'usefulness' of 'new' cultural geography in a world of growing social and economic inequalities (Barnes, 1995; Harvey, 1996; Sayer, 2001). Ironically, such has been the perceived pervasiveness of the cultural that one of its leading commentators and proponents recently stated that 'the cultural turn has been *too* successful, has become *too* hegemonic, and has led to the realms of (say) economic and political geography making too many accommodations with a cultural orientation' (Philo 2000b, p. 28). Here, Philo is concerned that, such has been the success of the cultural turn in focusing human geographers' attention on the role of culture, that other important aspects of human geography are being neglected. His specific worry is that an emphasis on the cultural, and in particular the immaterial ('the play of identity politics through the less-than-tangible, often-fleeting spaces of texts, signs, symbols, psyches, desires, fears and imagining', p. 33), is leading to dematerialized and desocialized human geographies – concerns echoed by Jackson (2000), McDowell (2000a) and N. Smith (2000).

   In conclusion to this section, it should be noted that, while the combination of the 'cultural turn' in geography and a wider 'spatial turn' across the social sciences and humanities might create the semblance of a more fluid, post-disciplinary landscape, disciplinary boundaries *do* continue to exist as administrative units within institutions and within the popular (academic) imagination (Sibley, 1995). Certainly, while the transfer of theoretical tools has become more evident, each discipline continues to contend that it has a unique identity and makes a distinctive contribution to knowledge production. Indeed, it can be argued that geography remains distinguished from the other social sciences by its *explicit* focus on space and place (see Massey and Allen, 1984; Johnston, 1991; and Unwin, 1992 for accounts of the disciplinary identity of geography). As such, there is a complex tension between the unifying forces of social theory and the unitary forces of disciplinary identity.

3.3 CRITICAL GEOGRAPHIES

Linked to the 'cultural turn', but also something of a reaction to it, has been the development of 'critical geography'. Though diverse in its epistemology, ontology and methodology, and hence lacking a distinctive theoretical identity, critical geography none the less brings together those working with different approaches (e.g., Marxist, feminist, post-colonial, post-structural – see below) through a shared commitment to expose the socio-spatial processes that (re)produce inequalities between people and places. In other words, critical geographers are united in general terms by their *ideological* stance and their desire to engender a more just world (see Section 1.1). This interest in studying and changing the social, cultural, economic or political relations that create unequal, uneven, unjust and exploitative geographies is manifest in engagements with questions of moral philosophy, social and environmental justice (see Harvey, 1996; Proctor and Smith, 1999; D. M. Smith, 2000) as well as attempts to bridge the divide between research and praxis. Joe Painter describes critical geography as:

> A diverse and rapidly changing set of ideas and practices within human geography linked by a shared commitment to emancipatory politics within and beyond the discipline, to the promotion of progressive social change and to the development of a broad range of critical theories and their application in geographical research and political practice. (Painter, 2000a, p. 126)

The diversity of theoretical frameworks adopted by critical geographers means that contemporary critical human geography is extremely diverse in its formulation and substantive foci (which include, *inter alia*, the geographies of poverty, international relations, the exploitation of nature, the cultural politics of identity, etc.). It also means that much contemporary critical human geography (though not all) is fundamentally different from the more homogeneous, radical geography practised in the late 1960s and 1970s (see Section 2.4). Most crucially, there has been a shift in emphasis from an examination of the role of capital in shaping society to a broader focus on the multiple axes of power and difference that create social and economic divides. As such, structural and materialist accounts have been complemented (and in many instances replaced) by positions more sensitive to human agency and questions of culture (Barnes, 1995). Further, an emphasis on studying the geographies experienced and created by the majority has been supplemented with a focus on those groups on the margins of contemporary society (see Section 3.4). By paying more attention to the voices of these marginal peoples, categories of analysis that were once conceived of as fixed (e.g., centres/margins) have themselves been recognized as more fluid, fragmented and socially constructed. This has involved geographers thinking about how they reach out to marginal groups, incorporating their voices in the writing of geography. As noted in Chapter 1, critical geographers have also turned their gaze inwards, recognizing that knowledge is produced and situated (and hence becoming more aware of their own *positionality*).

Not unsurprisingly, detailing even some of the key ideas in critical geography is beyond the scope of one section of a book like this. Therefore, here we only examine two aspects of critical geography in order to provide a flavour of some of the theoretical ideas that underlie such analyses. In the first section, we detail work that has sought to understand the unevenness of social well-being by extending 'traditional' Marxist interpretations of the nature of inequality in society to incorporate a concern with lifestyle and culture. In the second section, we focus on a rather different elucidation of power, exploring ideas that evoke a more diffuse notion of inequality (as well as highlighting the potential of people to negotiate a more equal society through resistance). In both sections, a key theme is how inequality is spatialized – 'always played out in, and through, the many spaces of the world' (Sharp *et al.*, 2000, p. 1). As Jackson (1994, p. 562) stresses, it is through its concern for human diversity and difference that geography has 'maintained its critical edge, emphasizing not just how differences are expressed in space, but how social inequalities are spatially structured'. It is this concern with elucidating the complex social differences and inequalities created through 'variable geometries of power' (Massey, 1993) that unites much critical geography.

3.3.1 Enculturating capital

As we described in Chapter 2, the Marxist geographies developed in the 1970s argued for the primacy of the political economy in accounts of social formation. More recently, these ideas have come under attack from those who argue for a more fluid account of the making of social inequalities (see Callinicos, 1990). This has resulted in some interesting confrontations and collaborations between those arguing for the analytical priority of capital and those arguing for the importance of culture. Put simply, for some, centring analysis on cultural agents, their lifestyles and the representations they make of place is the key to under-standing socio-spatial process, while others continue to hold to the logic of capital accumulation and the cycles of investment and disinvestment that drive social exploitation. In this latter account, all power relations (e.g., between men and women, blacks and whites, able-bodied and disabled, North and South) are deemed the structural product of capital relations (with, for example, patriarchy ensuring the division of household labour and supply of fresh workers; racial divisions ensuring a supply of cheap labour and so on). In the former version, social processes are seen to have cultural rather than capitalist roots, with gender divides, for example, emerging from social processes that can be conceived of independently from the realms of capitalist production.

An illustration of how these debates were played out is provided by the work on urban/rural gentrification that blossomed in the 1980s and 1990s. Broadly, gentrification may be described as the process whereby less affluent rentiers and homeowners are displaced from an area by more affluent owner-occupiers (Lees, 1996). Often associated with the improvement and aestheticization of housing stock, this is a process that can be observed in many Western cities, as well as in the many commuter villages experiencing repopulation by ex-urbanites. Seeking explanations for this process, a battle raged between those (Marxist) thinkers who claimed this was a redeployment of capital (and hence that gentrification was capital-supply or production-driven) and those who argued for user-orientated or consumption-side explanations, which focused on the lifestyles and demands of the gentrifiers themselves. Neil Smith (1996) para-phrases this battle as one about capital versus consumption, a back to the city move of people versus a back to the city move of capital. Gradually, it was realized that both could be correct interpretations, and that culture and capital entwined in very specific ways to create particular landscapes of gentrification (Mills, 1993). Eschewing narrowly conceived accounts that remained ideologic-ally wedded to the primacy of capital or culture, more nuanced accounts of gentrification emerged, exploring the values attached to different lifestyles and the way particular spaces and cultures were commodified (literally, made into a commodity to be bought and sold). Zukin's (1992) account of the emergence of 'loft-living' in Manhattan is an exemplary account, showing how the machinations of the real estate market and the social valuation of a bohemian, artistic lifestyle conspired to transform areas of Greenwich and Soho.

Out of these debates about the utility and relevance of Marxist ideas in explaining gentrification (as well as other key debates about the exploitation of nature, the nature of dependency and so on) emerged a more productive engagement with Marxist theories that, in essence, began to recognize the importance of culture within the overall framework of materialist enquiry. As Blunt and Wills (2000, p. 82) suggest, this acknowledged that 'aesthetic and cultural practices matter, and that their conditions of production deserve the closest possible attention'. Associated with this was the treatment of difference and Otherness not as something to be added to more fundamental Marxist categories of class but as something that should be considered as crucial in grasping the dialectics of social change. Categories of race, sexuality, gender and age were thus deemed as important as class within a framework of 'geographical-historical materialism' (Soja, 1996). None the less, many geographers continue to suggest that the 'fault lines' in the contemporary social world (e.g., between different ethnic groups) can inevitably be explained with reference to the changing regimes of capital accumulation that create fundamental class divides at one moment only to inflect these identities through different modalities of class, age and ethnicity in a different epoch. The project advocated by such thinkers is that it is necessary to interrogate the making of identities through consumption practices and lifestyle choices, but it is important to remain mindful of the rhythms of capital accumulation that enable and encourage such consumption practices (see Cloke, 1993; Murdoch, 1995; and Phillips, 1998, on the reconceptualization of class and lifestyle in rural studies).

This type of interpretation, which sees the cultural politics of identity as crucial but still subordinate to the political economy, is evident in the work of geographers such as **Neil Smith** (1984, 1996, 1998; see Box 3.2). Smith's work has focused on the uneven production of space, especially in urban environments. Through a variety of case studies, he has argued that social inequalities and political processes of inclusion and exclusion at the 'local' scale are grounded in the material socio-spatial processes operating up to the global scale. For him, inner-city riots, hate crimes, gentrification, suburbanization, processes of deindustrialization, regional decline, international divisions of labour, intensified nationalism and so on are intimately interconnected as key processes in the continual transformation of capitalism. Smith (1998) illustrates the potency of what he terms 'El Niño capitalism' by highlighting how, just as El Niño shapes global climate, economic crises create shock waves far beyond the locale within which they occur; for example, a devaluation of the Thai *baht* leads to a crash in other markets within hours and has knock-on consequences for businesses, jobs and local economies across the planet. This creates risks and opportunities for capitalism, and fuels the perpetual disinvestment and subsequent embedment of capital so crucial in late capitalism. This then is a capitalism that feeds on the perpetuation and reinvention of inequality at different scales. Within this scenario, representations are seen as essential in so much as they exploit and accentuate these inequalities. For example, historically the cultural representations of black people helped legitimate slavery and secure political and economic relations as Europe expanded and exploited its colonies. These representations have been reproduced over time because they remain useful for capital, for example by providing cheap manual labour.

Smith's aim, along with others such as Harvey (1989a) and Knox (1993), has been to try to unravel the socio-spatial logics of capitalism, developing a thesis which centres on the continuing importance of uneven development and a 'return to Marx' (Smith, 1998, p. 163) which is attuned to cultural politics. To illustrate how uneven development operates he has undertaken extensive studies of gentrification, particularly in New York City, showing how relatively poor, socially marginalized and stigmatised areas of cities are represented, policed and 'improved'. Coining the notion of a *revanchist* city (i.e., a city in which the middle class exercises revenge against concessions won by the working class in a previous regime), he shows how such processes encourage gentrification, displacement and homelessness. Here, his work has sought to identify the ways in which areas become devalued only to be 'reclaimed' by capital at a later time, assisted by neo-liberal policies, myths of the American frontier, and the aspirations of a newly affluent service class. In so doing, his work illustrates that an understanding of gentrification in New York needs to be grounded in its political economy, acknowledging its significance as a global city, the hub of major corporate, financial and political networks.

The way such ideas of uneven development can be used to theorize different types of social and spatial inequality is apparent in the work of Brendan Gleeson (1999). In contrast to Smith, Gleeson's analysis focused on the marginalization of one particular group in society: disabled people. Like Smith, Gleeson

---

Box 3.2 Neil Smith (1954–)

A Distinguished Professor of Anthropology and Geography at City University of New York, for the past twenty-five years Neil Smith has sought to bring space to the centre of Marxist analysis, arguing that uneven development and the production of space are central to the logic of capitalism. In his highly cited book, *Urban Development* (1984) Smith explored the role of capital in the production of space, nature and scale, culminating in his see-saw theory of uneven development. Capitalism, Smith surmised, has two opposing tendencies: a drive to create an equalisation of the levels and conditions of production, while at the same time a desire to exploit differences in levels and conditions of production. In effect, capital is continually being invested into places in order to produce surplus value and expand the basis of capital itself. Equally, however, it is continually being withdrawn from locales so that it can move elsewhere and take advantage of the differences in costs between locales to derive higher profits. This tension between use value and exchange value creates a constant cycle of investment and flight from places and drives social inequalities and tension between people. In other words, social conflict has its roots in capitalism's production of space. Smith illustrates his theory of uneven development by examining processes of gentrification. In his 1996 book, *The New Urban Frontier*, he argues that gentrification is far more than a reflection of middle-class tastes for urban living, but rather is expressive of capital being drawn

theorized their socio-spatial exclusion using an approach devoting attention to both the political economy and cultural politics of disability. Building on the work of Michael Oliver (1990), Gleeson argued that the role of disabled people in society was fundamentally altered with the transition from feudal to industrial society. Along with large-scale spatial transformations from rural- to urban-based production, this transition led to a division between home and work. He contended that, while disabled people had a productive role to play in feudal times, when the site of home and work were one and the same, they were viewed (and represented) as unproductive in relation to their non-disabled counterparts on the (capitalist) factory floor. Unable to work or contribute to the reproduction of the household, Gleeson argued that the way disabled people were positioned in society changed radically. This change has structured the social positioning of disabled people up until the present, leading to specific geographies of exclusion and institutionalization. In other words, Gleeson posited that it is impossible to understand the exclusion of disabled people in Western societies without considering the central role of capitalism in shaping the experiences of disabled people and how non-disabled people relate to them. In contrast, however, to a straight historical-materialist reading of disability and the production of space, Gleeson recognizes the value of an enculturated analysis, calling for an embodied reading that recognizes that capitalism relies on specific valuations of the body (see Chapter 4).

Other work by critical geographers has sought to extend Marxist analyses of nature–society relations by exploring the cultural construction of nature (see Section 1.3.3). This was manifest in the 1980s in an entwining of Marxism with cultural ecology to produce a *political ecology* that addressed the diverse ways in which nature was produced and exploited for capital gain in an era of flexible

---

to new sites of investment and being grounded in the built environment. As such, gentrification is the exploitation of social inequalities created by previous uneven development and is the result of historically rooted, interconnected patterns of investment and liberal urban policy. In turn, gentrification creates social tension, eviction, homelessness and displacement. The latter produces the flight of capital from another area thus creating a new site for gentrification in future years. For Smith, the most recent rounds of gentrification signal a strategy of capital reinvestment based on a reclaiming of the margins (manifest in acts of 'revenge' wrought by neo-liberal politicians against the 'excesses' of the post-1960s consensus). Some of his most incisive recent work has therefore exposed the 'zero tolerance' policies pursued by New York's former mayor Guiliani as tied into pernicious processes of uneven development. Sceptical of the rhetorical excesses of postmodern and post-structural thinking (see Smith, 2000), his work remains rooted in a Marxist tradition, suggesting that the fight against inequality and injustice can be best served by accounts that expose the material basis of these inequalities rather than just their expression in culture.

Further reading: Smith (1984, 1996, 1998)

accumulation. In other words, 'issues of how communities are integrated into a global economy' were wedded to issues of 'resource management and environmental regulation and stability' (Peet, 1998, pp. 95–6) to produce insights into the social exploitation of nature. For example, Piers Blaikie in *The Political Economy of Soil Erosion* (1985) detailed the complex ways in which pressure is bought to bear on ecosystems due to economic and political pressures on those who work the land. In doing so, he rejected previous models that blamed environmental constraints, mismanagement, overpopulation and market crises for environmental degradation, and instead posited that it was the political-economic system that facilitated soil erosion (Watts, 2000). In the developing countries of South Asia and Africa in particular, debt, poverty and imported discourses of development were forcing states to exploit natural resources, likewise placing pressure onto people and farmers. These problems were further exacerbated by systems of local decision-making, cultural values, political stability and so on. Similarly Watts (1983) examined the causes of famine in Northern Nigeria, noting how colonial development and the shift to export cropping had substantially altered the system and cultures of food production, and undermined the adaptive, flexible strategies to accommodate climatic risks traditionally used by farmers. As such, Watts highlighted that farmers' integration into capitalist modes of production and exploitation of nature had removed their response mechanisms to drought and left them vulnerable to famine. More recently, this political ecology has led to a broader engagement with social theory as (taken-for-granted) concepts such as nature are reconceptualized (see Section 1.3.3). Consequently, there has been a fragmentation of political ecology into many strands (Watts, 2000). Here there is a recognition of the crucial role of science in creating the environmental knowledges which underpin (culturally specific) understandings of nature, sustainability and exploitation (Bryant, 1992; Barnes and Gregory, 1996; Demeritt, 1998).

This enculturation of Marxist analysis has led Castree (1999) and Gibson-Graham (1996) to call for a revised Marxism which reveals the social relations at the heart of capitalism and which overcomes the 'impasse' of Marxist political economy that ignores complexity and diversity. Unlike Smith and Gleeson, both Castree and Gibson-Graham argue that Marxism is an approach that is too capital- and class-oriented. Gibson-Graham (the joint pen name of two authors) seek to rethink capitalism and class, suggesting that economic practice, for example, comprises a rich diversity of 'capitalist' and 'non-capitalist' activities, the latter being largely ignored in Marxist analysis (an argument that has also figured in debates concerning production/consumption – see Barnes, 1995). Moreover, they suggest that the formulation of a homogeneous bourgeoisie as *the* enemy and a homogeneous working class as *the* insurgent actor fails to recognize the diversity of social relations within the economic system. In an insightful essay Castree (1999) identifies a 'third way': a way to reconstruct Marxism in far less closed terms than traditional Marxist analysis. He thus reformulates capitalism as an open, heterogeneous system which, 'through abstract and concrete labour, is constantly infused by its putative "exteriors": differences of nationality, gender, sexuality, geographical location and so on are constantly gathered together in the domain of concrete labour and, through abstractions of social labour and labour time, are forcibly articulated into a global system with a structured coherence' (p. 153). Similarly, he reformulates class as an open category: ' "the" working class is not an "it" that is either exploited, dominated or able to "reclaim" its power under socialism. Rather, class is a certain structural position in relation to processes of capital accumulation' (p. 153). This open formulation recognizes the differences between people, and yet, Castree contends, still provides a focus on class (providing a common basis from which to fashion a global political movement against capitalism). In essence, then, Castree is seeking an enculturated Marxism; a critical approach that keeps the critique of political economy centre stage, whilst being more open to the concerns of other critical theorists, such as identity, difference and diversity.

3.3.2 Geographies of domination and resistance

While the interest in the cultural politics of identity has been seized upon in particular and productive ways by those working in Marxist traditions, questions of diversity and difference have been developed somewhat differently by those working within other theoretical frameworks. Accepting that space is a crucial means through which social identities and distinctions are created and maintained, here the focus is on the power relations that shape how space is claimed, occupied, used and regulated to the benefit of some and the detriment of others. Casting the analytical net somewhat wider than class-based, Marxist-inspired accounts, the outcome has been a spatialized politics of identity (examining the geographies of power as they relate to individuals and groups of people), and an identity politics of place (examining the geographies of power that operate in particular spatial arenas) (see Keith and Pile, 1993).

Many geographers have accordingly examined what might be termed the 'geographies of domination and resistance'. By and large these examinations have consisted of descriptions of the socio-spatial processes which serve to oppress particular groups socially, politically and economically. The flip side of such examinations, however, is a recognition that such processes are resisted through transgressive acts, activism, civil disobedience, the use of formal political systems and, following Michel de Certeau (1981), everyday practices (such as a single look, a movement or a spoken word). In both cases, there is a focus on how *power* creates and reproduces inequalities and how it is challenged. While we return to consider the forms of power enacted by the state in Chapter 7, here it is useful to consider what that term means. Certainly, the work of **Antonio Gramsci** (see Box 3.3) has been highly influential for theorists seeking to conceptualize power. Imprisoned by Mussolini's Fascist government in 1928 until his death, Gramsci sought to understand why an essentially repressive and undemocratic political party had acquired popular support. Although a committed Marxist and Italian Communist Party member (its leader between 1924 and 1926), Gramsci argued that conceiving of inequality and oppression purely in terms of capital relations was flawed, insisting on a more nuanced understanding of power. Gramsci favoured a focus on the power of persuasion, developing a non-economistic model of how ideology is grounded in material institutions and cultural practices (Forgacs, 1984). In explaining the rise of Fascism, he developed a concept of *hegemony*. Generally, hegemony refers to a situation of uncontested supremacy. Gramsci, however, reworked this definition, so that hegemony referred to the power of a dominant group to persuade subordinate groups to accept its moral, political and cultural values as the 'natural' order. Essentially, Gramsci was interested in the 'organization of consent', how particular sets of ideas, beliefs and values were accepted as desirable, inevitable and taken for granted and thus allowed a particular vision of society to become accepted as common sense. This humanizing shift away from capital to a wider notion of power has meant that Gramsci's notion of hegemony has been cited by a multiplicity of geographers (e.g., Jackson, 1989; Myers, 1998), many of whom would not consider themselves Marxists.

For example, drawing broadly on social theory and the 'new' cultural geography, Tim Cresswell has sought to document the ways in which hegemony is maintained and resisted through the production of space. In his book *In Place/Out of Place* (1996) he examines the ways in which cultural ideologies work to codify and regulate space, reproducing spatial hegemony, and how these place-inscribed ideologies are challenged. He posits that we are socialized into understanding what is acceptable in a particular space and when something or someone is 'out of place'. Here, spatial structures and places within the landscape provide a set of cultural signifiers that signify belonging. These can be explicit (e.g., place names) or implicit (e.g., the type and appearance of housing). Reading the symbolic meanings of landscape indicates how to act. For example, a church suggests reverence, a library the need to be silent. Cresswell describes how these places reproduce the meanings associated with them in natural, self-evident and common-sense ways: 'We are silent in a library because we believe it is appropriate to be silent in libraries, and by being silent in libraries we contribute to the continuation of silence' (p. 16). In other words, place-inscribed ideologies work to reproduce hegemony.

In his work, Cresswell details the ways in which marginalized groups use

---

Box 3.3 Antonio Gramsci (1891–1937)
Gramsci's writings (1971; first published in Italy between 1948 and 1951) have been widely explored across the social sciences, and acknowledged as significantly advancing Marxist thought. In his prison notebooks, written between 1929 and 1935, he sought to chart through an historical analysis the reasons why Fascism had gained political power and why it was ineffectively opposed by the Left. He concluded that military support and physical intimidation were only part of the answer. He posited that Mussolini, the pre-World War II Fascist dictator, had been able to forge a new hegemony through persuading the Italian people that Italy was the cradle of civilization and the spirit of the Roman Empire could be recaptured through adherence to a programme of state Fascism. Gramsci accounted for the rise of Fascism by tracing the historical development of Italy, contending that the fragmented nature of the state (with no modern state until the late nineteenth century), regional-cultural heterogeneity, the lack of a national language, the

multiple tactics of transgression (crossing geographical and social boundaries), seeking to disrupt taken-for-granted interpretations of what is appropriate in particular spaces. To do this, he uses three case studies: New York graffiti artists, New Age travellers and the Greenham Common peace women. All three groups, he contends, used transgressive acts that disrupted what was acceptable behaviour in a location. For example, graffiti artists 'tagged' the urban fabric, the New Age travellers ignored land rights and institutional directives and camped on 'private' land, and the Greenham Common women camped outside an American military base and disrupted deliveries of missiles to that base. Cresswell notes that the transgressive use of space by these groups is itself resisted by the dominant group as it seeks to maintain the spatial hegemony. For example, the work of graffiti artists was reappropriated as a mainstream art form through co-option into art galleries. In the case of the New Age travellers' attempted use of Stonehenge and English Heritage redefined who could legitimately use the site based on concepts of middle-class respectability, the nuclear family and traditional family values. In addition, new laws were enacted to try and police where New Age travellers could meet, thus marginalising and regulating their lifestyle (see also Sibley, 1995). The 'transgressive' acts of the Greenham Common peace women were widely vilified in the press, with the women portrayed as 'unfeminine', out of place in the 'rural idyll', endangering themselves and their children by undertaking an 'unnatural' course of action.

Notwithstanding Cresswell's careful reading of spatial conflicts and 'turf wars', work employing Gramsci's notion of hegemony often slips into juxtaposing society as the powerful versus the less powerful: domination and resistance are conceived as oppositional processes, where processes of domination seek to maintain the status quo and resistive processes seek to undermine it. This conceptualization of power has been challenged by those who posit that power relations are much more complex, consisting of circuits of power in which domination and resistance are not viewed simply as oppositional forces (something that Cresswell's later writing acknowledges – see Cresswell, 2000). The

---

separation between intellectuals and people and the small size of the Italian proletariat resulted in the people being divided and disorganized and had left the nation open to the uniting forces of Fascism and the alliance between the political Right, industrialists, landowners, and petty bourgeoisie. As Gramsci noted, however, hegemony is never total, always open to contestation. In his example, he noted that hegemonic Fascism could be overturned through counter-hegemonic ideas and resistive practices that sought to undermine the taken-for-granted assumptions of Mussolini's ideas. Gramsci argued that the development of a national-popular movement was needed, bringing proletariat and peasants, and north and south Italy, together and extending beyond class interests to form expansive and universalizing alliances capable of creating a new, more inclusive hegemony.

Further reading: Gramsci (1971); Forgacs (1984, 2000)

72 Theorizing Human Geographies

work of Michel Foucault (see Box 4.2) in particular has become highly influential for those seeking to theorize power. From the late 1960s until his death in 1984, Foucault examined the histories and geographies of power as expressed through institutional and government practices. He was particularly interested in the transition from early modern (1600s–1700s) to industrial society (1800s–   ), documenting the creation of new 'regulatory regimes' designed to shape and control society. He therefore examined the creation of new modes of regulation in a variety of contexts. In one strand of work (Foucault, 1977), he studied regimes of discipline and punishment, charting the shift from *ad hoc* systems of direct and often bloody retribution designed to bully the populace into obedience to apparently more subtle and uniform systems of punishment with their own 'apparatus of capture' (i.e., systems of surveillance) designed to punish, reform and maintain social order (Sharp *et al.*, 2000). This work focused on Victorian institutional settings and their designated role of creating healthy, respectable and moral individuals. Through examining the rationale, design and organization of prisons and mental asylums he argued that power was both repressive (e.g., by imprisoning people and stopping particular behaviours) and productive (e.g., reforming prisoners and encouraging normal modes of behaviour). Moreover, he argued that attention should be paid to the 'microphysics' of power, how power is operationalized and brought to bear on people across a range of contexts, and how agencies seek to effect changes in the conduct of others.

In a later strand of work on governmentality, Foucault examined how the practices of the state influence and shape individuals' self-regulation (Foucault, 1981). He did this chiefly through an exploration of the interconnections between an individual's sexuality and the genealogy (i.e., historically nuanced evolution) of morality. Referring to the representations of sexuality contained in national policy documents, medical guidebooks and religious treatises, he suggested that the state was able to produce a system of power/knowledge that encouraged all people to adopt national moral values through the cultivation of an 'ethics of the self' in which people were made highly aware of their own sexuality. Foucault proposed that this enticed people to participate in forms of self-surveillance, suggesting that there is an interiorization of power. As such, Foucaultian perspectives suggest that power is not simply 'objectifying, intrusive and imposing' (Robinson, 2000, p. 68), operating in a top-down fashion, but is seen to work in other, more subtle, ways. Power then is 'something that is exercised by everyone, is potentially productive and at the heart of all social relations' (Cresswell, 2000, p. 261). He continues, 'power is not something to be overthrown, but rather be used and transformed' (p. 264). This conceives of power not as a 'thing' held by certain affluent people and groups, but a process involving flows, movements and relations which can be diverted, worked with and mutated. Similarly, drawing on Foucault's work, Sharp *et al.* (2000) argue that power is not merely acts of domination countered by acts of resistance but is much more complex and messy, bound up in everyday practices of living. Here, domination and resistance are spoken of as a 'dyad', being so thoroughly entangled that they cannot be conceived of separately. As we detail further in

Chapter 4, several geographers have productively applied Foucault's approach to power, examining the micro-circuits of power played out in particular contexts (e.g., Philo, 1987; Ogborn, 1995; Lees, 1997).

This concern with geographies of power is also evident in the development of what has been termed 'moral geographies', which David Smith (2000) takes to be symptomatic of a broad re-engagement by geographers with moral philosophy (i.e., fundamental questions of what is right and wrong, good and bad in society). This engagement consists of a set of three overlapping projects. In the first instance, it refers to geographical studies that seek to provide a 'moral' reading of society and space (e.g., analysis of how different senses of 'right' and 'wrong' are inscribed in different locations; see Matless, 1995; Hubbard, 1999). Secondly, it includes studies that seek to determine what a 'spatially' just society would consist of – a 'moral' geography (see Harvey, 1996; D. M. Smith, 1994). Thirdly, it relates to work that considers the morality, ethics and moral responsibility of geographers themselves and the discipline of geography (e.g., how 'moral' is the practice of geography?; see Chouinard and Grant, 1996; Kitchin, 1999; Roberts, 2000). Taken together, the construction of 'moral geographies' can be seen as the binding that ties together the plurality of approaches employed by critical geography. Critical geography then is united by a concerted and engaged encounter with issues of inequality, one that is increasingly recognizing multiple axes of power, with a commitment to emancipatory politics and social change.

3.4 POSTMODERN GEOGRAPHIES

In this and the next section we consider the ideas and influence of postmodern and post-structural thinking on contemporary human geography. We have chosen to highlight these sets of theoretical approaches because, along with various versions of feminism (see Section 2.4), they have greatly influenced recent thinking and have prompted extensive debates about how geography should be conceptualized and practised (see Benko and Strohmayer, 1997; Peet, 1998). This is not to say, however, that there have not been (many) other significant theoretical developments. For example, there is a growing engagement with psychoanalytical theories (Pile, 1996; Nast, 2000; Sibley, 1995) which we elaborate on in Chapter 4. Equally, much work in economic, social and political geography in the 1990s was influenced by Bruno Latour, Michael Serres and the ideas of Actor Network Theory (see Chapter 7). Holding to the idea that the world is the constantly shifting product of networks of actants (people, animals, objects), this perspective is clearly important, but here we subsume both it and psychoanalytical ideas within our discussions of the ways geographers have used theory. In passing, however, we might note that there are some very important connections between the (fairly tightly defined) precepts of psychoanalytical or Actor Network theories and the (wider) philosophical concerns of postmodern and post-structural thought.

We begin by outlining the essence of postmodern ideas. This is no easy task.

Michael Dear (1988; see Box 3.4) suggests that postmodernism is a complex and contested term – something that many people have heard of, but no one can quite explain. Peet and Thrift (1989) suggest this is because postmodernism is a term which represents a combination of different ideas. At one level, post-modernism refers to a new *way of understanding* the world. It is a revolt against the rationality of modernism, and represents a fundamental attack on con-temporary philosophy (Dear, 1988). At another level, postmodernism refers to *an object of study*, whereby postmodernism is conceived as the study of the tem-poral and spatial organization of postmodernity (an epoch characterized by socio-spatial relations regarded as fundamentally different from the modern ones that preceded them). Hence, postmodernism has been written of both as an alternative to (flawed) modernist accounts of society (Poster, 1995) and as the latest phase of flexible, capital accumulation (Harvey, 1989a). Here, we are interested primarily in the former, considering postmodernism as a theoretical approach to understanding contemporary society (see Best and Kellner, 1991).

Most of the theoretical approaches discussed in the previous chapter, such as positivism and Marxism, are approaches that are fundamentally modernist in formulation. Modernism concerns the search for a unified 'grand' theory of society and social knowledge and seeks to reveal universal truths and meaning: the kind of theory that wants to build 'systematic accounts of the world which aspire to certain standards of exactness, and which wants to understand the totality of social life in terms of those accounts, as stories that add up' (Thrift, 1999, p. 297). At the heart of modernism there is a notion that it is possible to build up knowledge cumulatively into better and more accurate theories, and that it is possible to explain the world and reveal its true order by following certain rational procedures (Holloway and Hubbard, 2001). We could, there-fore, explain the development of competing theoretical traditions within geog-raphy (as outlined in the previous chapter) as an attempt to produce 'better', more 'truthful' understandings of society and space. Each tradition claims

---

Box 3.4 Michael Dear (1944–)

A key influence on the development of postmodern thought in geography has been Michael Dear, Professor of Geography at the University of Southern California and Director of the Southern California Studies Center. His initial research interest centred on the geography of mental health care facilities and the organization of health care delivery systems. This led to a concern with the political–economic dynamics of health care, and an engagement with broader questions of the welfare state and the nature of the state in general. Here, Dear drew on social theory to examine the situatedness of public policy. In turn, this led Dear to examine service provision in cities in general, and processes of urban change and development. In particular, he became interested in exploring the utility of postmodernism in theor-izing human geography. In his highly cited 1988 article, Dear argued that geog-raphy needed to engage with social theory, and in particular with the ideas of postmodernism, for three reasons: (1) it would reposition geography to a pivotal role in the social sciences and humanities; (2) it would recast the internal structure

authority by virtue of its modernism – it is *the* best way to make sense of the world because it is of the moment, happening and new. Dear (1988) argues that this modern conceit led Western academia to a variety of internally consistent but mutually exclusive approaches that failed to live up to the Enlightenment ideal. He, along with others (e.g., Soja, 1989), were arguing by the late 1980s (some years after other social sciences) that geographers needed to rethink how they theorized human geography, suggesting an alternative, postmodern approach.

Postmodernism is inimical to modernist thinking because it questions established 'truth claims' and knowledge accumulation strategies. In essence, postmodernism is based upon the notion that there is no one form of knowledge that is necessarily superior or dominant to another (no 'grand theory'), reasoning that no one's voice should therefore be excluded from dialogue (Dear, 1988). Postmodernists argue that there is no absolute truth and no truth outside of interpretation (Lyotard, 1984). In other words, it is posited that no one theory can be sufficient for explaining all occurrences of a phenomenon, and therefore no one theory should be privileged as 'better' than any other (hence Lyotard's suspicion of meta-narrative). Postmodern approaches represent a shift from ways of knowing and issues of truth, to recognizing the validity in a pluralistic approach to knowledge production and utilization. Postmodern thinking is thus concerned with developing an attitude towards knowledge, methods, theories and communication, and posits that we should move away from questions relating to 'things actually going on ... to questions about how we can find out about, interpret and then report upon these things' (Cloke *et al.*, 1991, p. 170). Here, 'the very possibility of acquiring knowledge or giving an account of the world is called into question' (Lyon, 1994, p. 11) and the transferability of theories evolved in specific contexts regarded with scepticism (Gregory, 1997). Within postmodern approaches, organized science is replaced by a post-science which acknowledges the position of scientist as agent and participant in the creation of knowledge rather than a neutral observer of given 'truths' (see

of the discipline; (3) it would reforge geography's links with mainstream philosophical debates. Whilst arguing against simple relativism (that all theories have equal worth), he contended that interpretative, non-universal theories needed to be developed within geography and the creative tensions between these theories explored. Given its unifying effects, Dear contended that if geography failed to engage with social theory it would become isolated within the social sciences and risked its own survival as a university subject (see Section 3.1). In subsequent work he has developed postmodern theories of urbanism (see text), with a particular focus on Los Angeles, culminating in his recent book, *The Postmodern Urban Condition* (2000). Because of this, he is often spoken of as a leading member of the 'LA School'.

Further reading: Dear (1988); Dear and Flusty (1998); Dear (2000)

Section 1.2). Postmodernism thus offers 'readings' not 'observations', 'interpretations' not 'findings', seeking intertextual relations rather than causality (Rosenau, 1992).

In relation to human geography, a postmodern approach encourages analysis of socio-spatial relations within a specific context without claims for universality or scientific rigour (in the traditional sense of positivism, for example). The ideas of postmodernism have had particular resonance in urban geography and the conceptualization of urban change and development. This is because the ideas and implications of postmodernism were largely introduced to human geography by urban geographers interested in theorizing the form and development of contemporary (postmodern) cities, particularly in North America. These geographers, notably Alan Scott, Michael Dear and Ed Soja (based in Los Angeles), began to contend that cities were changing in ways that could not be adequately explained by modernist theories such as Marxism or humanism. Related to this is the idea that cities – as sites of work, home and play – are brought into being through the naming and mapping practices of geographers as much as through material processes of capital accumulation. As we have seen, Zukin (1992) contended that how we see and organize the city changes as the consumption of space is abstracted from the logic of industrial production. This, she suggests, is part of a broad change as the city becomes a spectacle for consumption – an experience to be absorbed and responded to. City landscapes then take on new shifting meanings and forms, with geographic conceptions of urbanization often unable to keep up with, or make sense of, these new *structures of feeling*.

Exploring the connections between cultural politics and political economy in new ways (see Section 3.3.1), theorists such as Dear, Soja and Zukin suggest that a sensitivity to place is essential if one wishes to do justice to the complex interplay of capital and culture. For example, Soja (1986) argued that an examination of Los Angeles revealed a diverse and ever-changing landscape constantly being shaped in a myriad of ways through local politics, state and national policies and institutional directives, and the internationalization and globalization of trade and labour. These processes often work in contradictory and unique ways which mean that while modernist-framed urban theory will detect trends similar to other cities, it will also be inadequate in other ways, and will present a vision of the city at odds with that held by many of its residents. Dear and Flusty (1998) similarly explore the concept of postmodern urbanism, documenting that how cities are organized and run today is very different from in the early part of the twentieth century. Like Soja, they suggest that there has been a radical break in the way cities are developing. Again using Los Angeles as a case study, they detail how the logics of earlier urbanization (a single-centred city with growth out from the centre as exemplified by the models of the Chicago School, including Burgess's concentric ring theory or Hoyt's sector theory) have been replaced by a set of differentiated, competing urbanisms (they identify ten) created by cities having to adapt economically to the forces of flexible accumulation and globalisation. For them, postmodern urbanism has several fundamental characteristics, including a complex interplay between global and local, ubiquitous social polarisation, continuous reorganization and the centre being organized by the periphery. These characteristics produce centreless urban systems that are subject to a new spatial logic that they term 'keno capitalism'. Here, urbanization is seen to be occurring on a quasi-random basis, springing up where opportunity exists, ignoring concepts such as the centre and the margin to produce a highly differentiated and 'non-contiguous collage of parcelized and consumption-orientated landscapes' (p. 66). This all suggests a new era of postmodern urbanism:

> Driven by global restructuring that is permeated and balkanized by a series of interdictory networks; whose populations are socially and culturally heterogeneous, but politically and economically polarized; whose residents are educated and persuaded to the consumption of dreamscapes even as the poorest are consigned to carceral cities ['no-go' areas]; whose built environment, reflective of these processes, consists of edge cities, privatopias [gated communities], and the like; and whose natural environment, also reflective of these processes, is being erased to the point of unviability while, at the same time, providing a focus for political action. (Dear and Flusty, 1998, p. 66)

They contend that understanding the complex urban processes characteristic and formative of 'keno capitalism' necessitates the adoption of an approach that is itself postmodern, sensitive to difference and rapid change (see also Dear, 2000). This approach involves a detailed mapping of the variety of spaces within the city, how they are shaped by a variety of social forces operating at different scales, and how they are experienced by different populations.

Similarly, Chris Philo (1992) has argued for a postmodern approach to rural issues. He suggested that, up until the time he wrote his article, the rural had largely been theorized from the perspective of white, middle-class men using modernist narratives that prioritized the values and understandings of the dominant group in society (namely white, middle-class men). This had led, he contended, to a partial account of the rural – an account that failed to acknowledge the many ways in which the rural is understood and experienced. As such, he called for a 'postmodern sensitivity to difference' (1992, p. 200) recognizing that the plurality of people who make up the rural (women, children, the elderly, gays, lesbians, racial and ethnic minorities, the unemployed and poor, Gypsies, 'New Age travellers', alternative lifestyle communities) have varied understandings and experiences of living in the countryside – meaning there can be no universal account of the rural (see Cloke and Little, 1997). This has subsequently been followed by an analysis of what constitutes 'the rural', problematizing universal, fixed meanings of the term (see Halfacree, 1993; Milbourne, 1997).

This is not to say that postmodernism has been embraced by all urban or rural geographers, or those in other areas of geography (see, for example, Curry, 1991; Murdoch and Pratt, 1993; Cosgrove, 1994b). Indeed, postmodernism has been criticized as being little more than a form of critique – an intellectual, speculative, 'self-seeking cynicism' (Lyon, 1994, p. 77) with little substance. Critics argue that the dominant bases of the modernist agenda (i.e., enquiry, discovery, innovation, progress, internationalization, self-improvement) are still the principles underlying Western society and that modernist theories are still the most appropriate to make sense of them (Berman, 1982). Accordingly, it has been suggested by some that postmodern critiques should merely be used to improve modernist methods, to make them more robust and to widen their scope, not to replace them. Such a critical postmodernist approach has been put forward by Jürgen Habermas (1989), Anthony Giddens (1991) and David Harvey (1989a; see Box 6.2). They all treat modernity as an incomplete project, and like postmodernists challenge foundationalist approaches to science; although they insist that a critical, reflexive approach to social science can still yield useful distinctions between truth and falsity (Lyon, 1994). Harvey (1989a), for example, recognizes the postmodern fracturing and urbanism of the contemporary era as compatible with the latest phase of flexible accumulation of capital and hence does not see the need to abandon the search for fundamental theories. Other approaches, such as feminism, also largely try to reframe modernist thought within a more emancipatory or reflexive framework rather than move to a new postmodern position (although there are many feminists who would claim to be postmodernists).

3.4.1 Speaking from the margins

Despite disagreements about the nature of postmodernism, an important part of the postmodernist agenda is sensitivity to differences between people. As such, we have seen that postmodernism has opened up spaces in which to consider questions of Othering; that is how people are defined as being different from the norm, and how this is constructed in specific places at particular times. For instance, drawing on the important work of bell hooks (1992) and Gaytari Spivak (1990), a number of geographers have challenged dominant and universalistic analyses by providing accounts sensitive to the views of those oppressed in society. These accounts have political value, providing critical knowledges that can be used on the ground to confront spatial hegemonies (see Freire, 1970; hooks, 1991). Here, there is a distinction between the centre, generally conceived as white, male, heterosexual and abled, and the margins (their counter). In contrast to the centre, 'into which some are gathered and from which others are exiled' (Rose, 1995, p. 414), the margins thus provide critical 'locations' from which the relatively powerless can challenge dominant knowledges. In the first part of this section, we focus on how geographers' engagements with queer theory has led to powerful arguments about the sexing of space, providing a challenge to dominant heterosexist accounts. This is followed by a brief discussion of post-colonial theory and the way in which Eurocentric geography has popularly understood – and marginalized – the 'South'.

Over the past fifteen years, geographers have been increasingly concerned with the relations of sexuality and space, documenting many geographies of sexuality, particularly those of gay men and lesbians. Importantly, much of this has argued that what little past research had been conducted tended to essential-ize sexuality, failing to recognize the plurality of expressions of sexuality across space and time. These studies, it has been contended, 'exoticized' gay men and lesbians, often conceptualizing and treating them as if a separate species (e.g., Castells, 1983; Lyod and Rowntree, 1978). Furthermore, their analyses gener-ally suggested that the geographies of these groups were fixed, so that non-heterosexual identities and practices could be mapped on specific urban areas (see Bell and Valentine, 1995). This research often adopted an urban socio-logical perspective which could trace its origins to the Chicago School of the 1930s, using observation and secondary sources such as gay directories to map the distribution of gays and lesbians and to identify the existence of 'gay ghettos'. These so-called 'ghettos', it was hypothesized, existed for reasons of defence and security, and as a base for economic and cultural reproduction, and were the result of rational decision-making by their constituents (see Box 3.1 for similar arguments in relation to race). As detailed below, this neglects the complex structural and discursive practices that shape sexual relations. As a consequence these studies have been 'heavily criticised for their patronising, moralistic and "straight" approach to lesbian and gay social and sexual rela-tions' (Bell and Valentine, 1995, p. 5).

Influenced by postmodern theories accentuating diversity, this essentialist approach to sexuality has now been largely replaced by an approach that recog-nizes that sexuality is socio-spatially constructed (and hence, fluid). In this view, sexuality is a regulatory framework that is currently maintained by heterosexism and patriarchy, both of which are underlain by normative assumptions – that there are commonly agreed, 'natural' rules that govern sexual encounters. Such assumptions include the idea that in most Western societies 'normal' expressions of sexuality are centred on a specific form of heterosexuality. Those adopting sexual roles or seeking sexual experiences outside of these conventions are largely regarded as engaging in deviant, unnatural, abnormal and immoral acts. Such individuals include those seeking same-sex encounters – gay men, lesbians, bisexuals, but also those involved in 'marginal' heterosexual activities such as bondage, sadomasochism and commercial sex work (see Hubbard, 2000).

Hence, many geographers are involved in the development of 'queer' theory. Following **Judith Butler**'s influential ideas (see Box 3.5), queer theory seeks to undermine or denaturalize the 'naturalness' or 'normalness' of such ideas by examining the inconsistencies between chromosomal sex, gender and sexual desire (Jagose, 1996). Examples include questioning where transgendered indi-viduals fit into a supposedly 'natural' sexual order, exploring acts such as cross-dressing, and detailing how same-sex desire has had different cultural meanings at different times in different places. Exposing these inconsistencies, queer theo-rists argue that allegedly stable and fixed sexual relations are in fact unstable and fluid, with different meanings being attached to the same sexual acts by different people. Categories such as 'heterosexual' and 'gay', 'man' and 'woman' are thus viewed as (compulsory) fictions. Consequently, the normative assumptions of heterosexism are regarded as open to rewriting.

What has been of particular interest to geographers is the way in which heterosexist behaviours and assumptions feed into the production of spatial Othering and the contestation of what constitutes proper behaviour within a space. They have thus charted the various ways in which space is generally sexed as heterosexual – so that the practices and performances of heterosexuality, such as a man and woman holding hands or kissing, are accepted unproblematically, and yet a same-sex couple performing the same acts in the same space may be 'out of place' (Valentine, 1993). They have also explored the ways in which this heteronormatively coded space is resisted, subverted, parodied and challenged by those who might be termed 'sexual dissidents'. Research has thus examined how heteronormativity varies spatially and temporally (see Beemyn, 1997; Bell and Valentine, 1995), the spatial tactics used to create and sustain social networks (Valentine, 1993), the formation and nature of gay spaces (Knopp, 1995; Whittle, 1994), spatial strategies of resistance such as gay pride marches (Davis, 1995) and much more (see Binnie and Valentine, 1999 for an overview).

Using the margins as a site from which to rewrite sexual geographies has also had important implications for conceptualizing how geographical knowledge should be produced. 'Queer' geography promotes the use of situated knowledges (see Section 1.2) via a queer objectivity that acknowledges the diverse experiences of those with 'dissident' sexualities. Drawing from postmodern theory, this approach demands that the 'dispassionate' academic voice is replaced, introducing Other voices into writing, and that the geographer adopts the role of activist, seeking to undermine heterosexist assumptions. In practice this involves using research methods that challenge 'conventional' research techniques, allowing research participants to tell their own stories rather than have heterosexist assumptions foisted upon them. Often ethnographic work using interviews and observation is thus used strategically to undermine essentialist

Box 3.5 Judith Butler (1960–)
Professor of Comparative Literature at the University of California at Berkeley, Judith Butler has been a key thinker in the construction of queer theory. Articulated in a series of thought-provoking and widely cited studies, the key concept underpinning Butler's work has been that of performativity. Rejecting the idea that people have essential identities which can be read off from their bodies, or that the meaning of their bodies is wholly socially constructed, her work posits the idea that identities are *performed*. The implication here is that individuals construct seemingly coherent subject identities (e.g., male or female, old or young, black or white) through repetitive performances and practices. Here, she draws on both Foucaultian concepts (see Box 4.2) as well as psychoanalytical theory (see Chapter 4) to suggest that, while interior psychic identity is inscribed on the body through acts and gestures, 'true' identity rests neither in the (psychological) self of the actor nor in public and social discourse. Instead, Butler argues that socially intelligible identities are an illusion created by the acts and gestures that constitute the body. These stimulating and incisive ideas have recently proved extremely influential for those seeking to rethink the connections between sexual and gender identity (e.g., Smart, 1996; Bondi, 1997), as well as geographers seeking to explore the main-

and heterosexist accounts of dissident sexuality and to reveal a more nuanced sexual landscape.

While geographers interested in sexuality have explored the Othering of dissident sexualities, those theorizing post-colonialism have likewise examined the ways in which people and places outside the developed 'West' are Othered. Originally used as a chronological marker, referring to the 'post-independence' era of many former European colonial countries after the Second World War, post-colonialism is now widely used to refer to the political, linguistic and cultural experience of such societies (Blunt and Wills, 2000). As such, post-colonial theory is 'centrally concerned with the impact of colonialism and its contestation on the cultures of both colonising and colonised peoples in the past, and the reproduction and transformations of colonial relations, representations and practices in the present' (Gregory, 2000b, p. 612). It thus seeks to examine the ways in which Western metropolitan centres and their colonies were bound together in an unequal system of power, the ways in which colonial power was exercised, legitimated and resisted, and the manner in which these past relations shape the present (Blunt and Wills, 2000).

According to post-colonial theory, it is important to consider the way that the 'West' has represented the 'non-West' using its own terms of reference to comprehend both the material and discursive basis of neo-colonialism. For many, this stresses that there are many continuities between the way 'non-West' nations were represented in the colonial era and the way they are represented today. Exploring this proposition, post-colonialism seeks to question the origin of the Western terms and theories which label certain parts of the world as 'less developed', and which perpetuated Western power and knowledge as taken for granted and natural. Inspired by the work of **Edward Said** (see Box 3.6), post-colonial analysis has shown that the representation of the colonial as Other to

---

tenance of spatialized order (e.g., Bell *et al.*, 1994; Valentine, 1996). Focusing on the performativity and citationality of gender, Butler has sought to interrupt any neat mimetic correspondence between sexuality, biology and corporeality, or, for that matter, insides and outsides (Cream, 1995). Arguing that both sex and gender are regulatory fictions, maintained through repeated and stylized performance, Butler (1990b, p. 115) seeks to *denaturalize* what she refers to as the 'heterosexual matrix' – 'that grid of cultural intelligibility through which bodies, genders and desires are naturalized'. In doing so, she stresses that the apparent coherence of heterosex, where the binary structure of gender finds its complement in opposite-sex attraction, is the product of the discursive-chaining of gender to sexuality (Woodward, 1997), a linkage that can be broken, Butler argues, through queer parody of heterosexual performance. Butler continues to develop ideas at the cutting edge of philosophy, feminism and queer theory, including recent work exploring the connections between bodies and pleasure (Butler, 1999).

Further reading: Butler (1990a, 1993, 1999); McDowell (1999)

the apparent sophistication and modernity of Western Europe has shaped international relations for many centuries. In the colonial era, for example, this Othering was used to justify the establishment of a heavily militarised and centralised administrative system, which in turn served to impose Western ideas of democracy and civility on a population generally too weak to resist (Blaut, 1993; Corbridge, 1993a). Latterly, this Othering has bequeathed projects of development and aid that have been read as neo-liberal projects of cultural imperialism and oppression (Bell, 1994; Straussfogel, 1997). For example, Watts (1999) suggests that the development policy of Western nations represents an arrangement of power/knowledge (see Section 3.3.2) that is difficult to challenge. Presenting development in normative ways – as a technical achievement rather than a politicized project – such policies reinforce the idea that Western notions of progress, forged on rationalism and science, remain the only route to development.

Bhabha (1994, p. 70), in his arguments for a focus on the creation of colonial subjects, has remarked on the importance of racial stereotyping in this process, arguing that 'the object of colonial discourse was to construe the colonized as a population of degenerate types on the basis of racial origin, in order to justify conquest and to establish systems of administration and instruction'. Yet at the same time that this process of Othering relied upon pejorative and offensive stereotyping, it also included more affirmative and positive aspects. Myths of primitiveness, backwardness and incivility thus produced countervailing expressions of desire for the natural and noble lifestyles pursued by the 'savage' (see Sibley, 1995). Moreover, Bhabha (1994) also notes that these stereotypes were subverted and resisted through mimicry and parody, created by the partial adoption by the colonized of the colonizers' habits, lifestyle and values. Here, Bhabha illustrates that the supposedly fixed division between colonizer and colonized, Self and Other, is in fact much more unstable and hybrid.

Much post-colonial theory thus seeks to highlight the difficulties and inherent

---

Box 3.6 Edward Said (1935–   )

The Palestinian cultural and political commentator Edward Said is acclaimed as a formative influence on post-colonial studies, as well as an astute commentator on international political relations. His reputation was established with *Orientalism* (1978), a pioneering and adventurous work which combined Foucaultian notions of knowledge/power with a critical analysis of Western representations of the East ('the Orient'). Recognizing that the identity of colonized and colonizer are relational, and constructed through a process of Othering, this analysis traced the origins of contemporary Orientalist discourse back to nineteenth- and early twentieth-century representations of the East (primarily in art and literature). Here, Said identified myths of barbarism, despotism, mystery and sensuality as contributing to the imagining of the Arab world as essentially Other to the rational civility of the West. In later accounts (1994), he sought to show how the persistence of these myths shaped international political relations (e.g., legitimating Western intervention in the Gulf War). Being based in the United States, his work has attracted both critical praise and political consternation for its insistence on challenging established

dangers in the representation of Other cultures and traditions, and to destabilize the taken for granted and assumed of one's own culture and traditions
(Blunt and Wills, 2000). Given this, Gregory (2000b) argues that a post-colonial
analysis involves a close and critical reading of colonial discourse, an appreciation of the complicated histories through which colonialism passes from the
past into the present, a deconstruction of the ways in which metropolitan and
colonial societies are intertwined and interdependent and an awareness of the
politics of research. In relation to post-colonial geography, part of this awareness concerns the ways in which 'geographical imaginations have underpinned
colonial power and knowledge' and how the discipline itself has been complicit
in colonial discourses (Blunt and Wills, 2000, p. 167). With respect to the latter,
unpacking and unlearning established Western representations of the former
colonial world has shown the value of exploring the textual Othering of people
and place (see Chapter 5). Simultaneously, it has invigorated geographers to
interrogate the role of geography, past and present. Noting the discourses of
misogyny, implicit racism and developmentalist thinking that have coloured
many geographical explorations of marginal populations (see Jarosz, 1992;
Gregory, 1994a; Kearns, 1997), uneasy parallels may be drawn between traditions of travel writing, heroic accounts of expedition and geographic writing.
Often, it appears, geographers have been complicit in reinforcing distinctions
between what is regarded as exotic and what is regarded as normal – something
that has not been lost on those geographers seeking to create texts that better
bridge the divides between academia and the messy worlds of everyday life (see
especially Barnes and Gregory, 1996). On these grounds, many call for the
'decolonizing' of geography, a multifaceted task that includes a reassessment of
geography as a discipline past and present and the creation of post-colonial
geographies of people and places marginalized through colonial and neo-
colonial discourses (Blunt and Wills, 2000). As Spivak (1990) notes, however,
this latter project of creating *subaltern* geographies – geographies written and

myths of the Arab world. At the same time, he has become something of a spokes-
person for the dispossessed Palestinian Diaspora. Often explicitly spatial, Said's
work has been widely cited and reworked by geographers, some of whom have
sought to balance his obviously selective analysis of Western representations of
the East with consideration of those produced by those living in the East itself (e.g.,
Watts, 1997). While such work has to some extent highlighted the simplicity of
Said's account (after all, there have been many discourses of the East), this by
no means diminishes the pertinence of his arguments for those excavating
the connections of language, power and space. As he has argued in the light
of the 11 September 2001 attacks on America: '"Islam" and "the West" are simply
inadequate as banners to follow blindly . . . Demonisation of the Other is not a
sufficient basis for any kind of decent politics' (Said, 2001, p. 26).

Further reading: Driver (1992); Rogers (1992); Gregory (2000a).

recovered from marginalized, colonial subjects – is difficult, given that the
subaltern continues to be silenced, by imperialist and nationalist discourses.

Geographers' engagements with post-colonial theory has been used not only
to think about the legacy of colonial and imperial projects and the relationship
between the North and the South, but also to retheorize studies of 'race' and
racism within Western societies. In particular, the epistemological challenge of
post-colonialism has helped to open up racial categories to deconstruction, thus
enabling traditional, essentialist understandings of race to be challenged. Here,
most significantly, there has been a decoupling of the deterministic links
between biology and social status, accompanied by a recognition that such links
constitute a process of racialization that underpins racism. Most recently, most
notably in the work of Alistair Bonnett (2000b), this has led to a critical
engagement with whiteness as a racialized identity that seeks to destabilize its
social meaning and valorization, and opens up the 'centre' for critique (much
like queer theory requires reflection upon and analysis of heterosexuality – see
Hubbard, 2000). These reformulations have led to a new generation of
geographical studies of 'race' that are radically different from those practised
during the 1970s that mapped out patterns of segregation and mobility, labour-
market participation and poverty and political voting (Peake and Schein, 2000).
For example, Kay Anderson (1988) has traced the evolution of Chinatown in
Vancouver and how it was shaped through discursive constructions of the Chi-
nese community by White Canadians. Laura Pulido (1996) has used the lens of
subaltern studies to examine two cases of environmental racism (the siting of
environmental hazards in ethnic areas due to their weaker political power to
intervene and prevent such siting) in California. Both studies, and many others
like them, provide powerful insights into the mutual construction of racialized
identities and place, viewed in relation to the specificities of time and place.

3.5 POST-STRUCTURAL GEOGRAPHIES

In one sense (as the name implies) post-structuralism refers to those forms of
analysis that were developed in response to the principles of structural analysis
(particularly those which suggested that categories of identity and subjectivity
are created through systems of language which work to perpetuate capitalist
structures – see Chapter 5). Rejecting the idea of an underlying structure on
which language can rest secure and guaranteed, post-structuralism works with
a much more slippery notion of language and subjectivity, where neither is
given or fixed but where each is constantly *becoming*. Here, 'what we call the
"meaning" of a text is only ever a momentary stop in a continuing flow of
interpretations following interpretations' (Storey, 2001, p. 71). In other words,
post-structuralism argues that the meaning of a text is always unstable, as it
always relies on its relationship with other texts to communicate meaning. Such
perspectives raise important questions about the seeming solidity of established
categories of knowledge (as well as objects of study), exposing taken-for-granted
understandings of identity and difference as the outcome of linguistic practices.

Post-structuralist thinking thus suggests that the world comes to take on the illusion of solidity through acts of enunciation (i.e., speaking acts), even though it is infinitely complex, fractured and becoming. In this light, post-structuralism has important links to postmodernism (e.g., its suspicion towards grand theories), but differs in some quite important respects (Peet, 1998). In essence, while postmodernism may be described as a broad epistemological move-ment/attitude, rejecting the 'truth' of grand theories in favour of more local, grounded accounts which open geography to Other voices, post-structuralism is essentially a form of analysis that raises more profound questions about on-tology and claims to truth (whether universal or particular). Methodologically, this is manifest in attempts to deconstruct, disturb and interrupt existing accounts of the world and experiment with forms of academic enquiry based not so much on re-representing the 'real' but living it in different ways.

Proponents of more traditional philosophies of knowledge (e.g., positivism, humanism, structuralism, etc.) contend that post-structuralist accounts fail to address substantive, real-world problems in meaningful ways that can be grounded outside the academy (see Dixon and Jones, 1996). Moreover, post-structuralist writing is critiqued as being excessively playful and evasive, and in many cases obtuse to the point of being impenetrable and thus limited in readership and scope (Ellis, 1989; Eagleton, 1996). It is also accused of being a nihilistic and morally bankrupt 'anti-science' (although many post-structuralist thinkers would dispute this equation). But, in many ways, this is the point of post-structuralism: it holds to a different logic and cannot be judged in terms of established tenets of 'good' social science. None the less, this evasiveness makes it difficult to identify shared concerns and ideas at the heart of post-structuralism, leaving many unclear as to exactly why it claims to offer a better way of under-standing (and living in) the world. Certainly, the writing of key post-structuralist thinkers (who include Foucault, Deleuze, Iragaray, Žižec, Bataille and Nietzsche) is not easily summarized.

However, and following Dillon (2000, p. 2), we can tentatively identify a number of positions to which post-structuralist thinkers generally subscribe. Foremost here is a hostility to the acquisition of 'representational-calculative' knowledge (i.e., knowledge that claims to describe and explain the world as it is). It is in this sense that post-structuralism privileges ontological questions of being and living over epistemological issues of explanation. This means post-structuralism is more concerned with how we live and how we might live rather than questions of what we know (and better ways of knowing). This perhaps presents academics as artists rather than social scientists – unguided by concerns about what is fashionable, or what might constitute grand theory, there is an implicit idea that academics should simply get on with what they do, and immerse themselves in the world. Certainly, most post-structural thinkers regard established ways of knowing as inadequate for dealing with the *complexity* of the world, feeling that this inflicts violence upon it by dividing it into categories and identities that are repressive and 'ill-mannered' (Doel, 1999). A notable example of this for many post-structuralist thinkers is the description of society offered by Marxist theory. Based on a classification of society into the bourgeoisie and the proletariat, this offers a very convincing account of the way the world is organized according to the logic of capital (see Section 2.4). However, for post-structuralist thinkers, no matter how convincing such explanations are on their own terms, they do not allow for radical alternatives (i.e., other ways of conceiving and being in the world) and serve to solidify the shifting complexity of the world (into a system of thought). In Marxist thought, the primacy and permanence of capital is assumed; for post-structural thinkers, its permanence and importance in social process is constructed through language and practice – including the theories constructed by Marxist thinkers. Another example here is the theory of sexual development proposed (in different ways) by Freud and Lacan (to which we return in Chapter 4). This theory suggests that human beings are socialized into the subject positions at the heart of the so-called Oedipal family unit (i.e., the triad of Mother–Father–Son) and that they repress their natural sexual urges in accordance with social norms and expectations (so that, for example, sexual desire for the Mother on behalf of the Son is displaced because of the incest taboo). This is a convincing and widely cited theory of sexual development, but from a post-structural perspective it can be seen to be entwined in the processes that perpetuate the dominance of the heterosexual family unit (see Deleuze and Guattari, 1987, for a critique of psychoanalytical thought, and Žižec, 1999, for a post-Lacanian response). Explanatory theories, therefore, are bound into the making of the world, and in so doing serve to repress, divide and segregate.

Here, the reasons for geographers' interest in post-structuralism might become clearer; in a world composed of flows, movements and chaos, post-structuralists suggest that solidity is an illusion. One task for a post-structural geography, therefore, is to expose the practices that maintain this illusion. Crucially, it seems that geography itself is involved in imposing this sense of order

---

Box 3.7 Jacques Derrida (1930–   )

In its most basic form, Derrida's work can be described as a series of interventions designed to expose the impurity of language. Acknowledged as a key post-structuralist thinker, Derrida's writing takes issue with structural understandings of language (in particular the neat correspondence between signifier and signified) by seeking to subvert the meaning of text from within. This is manifest in writing that, by traditional academic standards, is often remarkably playful, obtuse and difficult. None the less, Derrida would insist that his writing cannot be judged in accordance with the rules of grammar, structure and communication that shackle conventional (and structural) accounts of social life. Instead, his work often seeks to open up texts to new readings and interpretations. In so doing, Derrida seeks to emphasize the potential of texts to create effects, stressing that academics can be truly creative (and critical) only when they adopt improper modes of thought and representation. In *Specters of Marx* (1994) the political implications of this deconstructive project were laid bare, suggesting that the language of politics had been eradicated, and there was a need for a 'new international' based on affinity and community (see Hussey, 2001). This attempt to create a dialogue with the language of classical Marxism (and, hence, the ghost of Marx) was read by many as an attempt

on the world, inventing concepts (e.g., place, space, nature) which reduce difference to sameness and potentially fail to do justice to the complexity of things. As
such, post-structural interest in the relations between knowledge and power has
percolated through geography's many subdisciplines, with many questioning
the 'truth claims' mapped out in a variety of geographical texts (e.g., Natter,
1995; Dixon and Jones, 1996; Sparke, 1998; Del Casino and Hanna, 2000). A
common assertion here is that geographical knowledge is traditionally *relational*,
so that the identity of a particular person or place is 'fixed' through the linguistic
construction of its Other. In simple terms, this means that the identity of one
place is built up as much through statements about what the place is not as
statements of what it is. Thus, binary oppositions of Self and Other are discursively mapped onto places that are 'here' and 'not here', 'close' and 'far',
'familiar' and 'alien'. For instance, it is apparent that familiar dualisms are used
to fix certain spaces in the popular imagination, so that they have become
imagined as either modern or primitive, cultured or wild, everyday or exotic
and so on. This implies that constructing the meaning of any place as belonging
to certain people or symbolizing a particular way of life relies on a set of (often
unstated) exclusions, whereby its representation distinguishes it from those
places which become, in effect, its Other. Yet at the same time, it appears that
any identity category seeks to deny this constitutive trace, so that the discourse
and language used to construct a place's identity becomes accepted as commonsensical, unproblematic and, under some circumstances, natural.

The idea that identities are discursively constructed, and accordingly need to
be *deconstructed*, is one that owes much to the ideas of **Jacques Derrida** (see
Box 3.7) on grammatology. Along with those other post-structuralist thinkers
who have problematized the relations of text, language and meaning (and here
we might also mention Blanchot, Lyotard and Foucault), Derrida's insistence

---

to reawaken the critical Left while demonstrating the limits of structuralist thinking.
His notion of textual deconstruction can therefore be seen as part of a wider ethical
concern that academia should not inflict violence on the world by placing it into
predetermined categories of Self and Other, reducing difference to sameness. Such
concerns with questioning the properness of academic language and thought are
also apparent in post-structuralist geographic writing (particularly that of Marcus
Doel), though writers like Gunner Olsson and Trevor Barnes have long explored the
potential of geographic writing to impose constancy on the world where there is none.
More widely, it is possible to discern Derrida's influence throughout the social sciences, with the adjective Derridean frequently used to describe those playful forms
of deconstruction that attempt to question the way we think about the world. As
such, while few geographers have sought to take Derrida's ideas forward in any
sustained manner, the implications of his work for the writing of geography are
profoundly important.

Further reading: Derrida (1991); Wolfreys (1998)

that everyday language is not neutral but bears the weight of cultural supposition and prejudice alerts geographers to the idea that difference is written into texts of all kinds (Derrida, 1991). In many ways, this questions the logic of de Saussure's claim (see Chapter 5) that language is based on a series of structured differences without positive terms (where a word or signifier is taken to signify something different from that which is signified by another word – so that 'x' is different from 'y'). For Derrida, when we describe something as having a certain characteristic ('x'), we inevitably recognize that it *lacks* another characteristic (i.e., is not 'y') and are able to speak the difference between these (so that one becomes deemed as lacking in relation to the other: 'x' > 'y'). In essence then, language is a play of signifiers that cannot articulate absolute difference, only lack or excess. The implication of Derrida's thinking is that the meaning of texts can never be pinned down; language is seen to defer, rather than yield, truth and meaning.

This can be illustrated by using a dictionary. For example, if we look up the term 'geography' in the *Oxford English Dictionary* (1990) we find it has three possible meanings: '1. The study of the earth's physical features, resources, and climate; 2. The main physical features of an area; 3. The layout or arrangement of rooms in a building.' If we then look up one of the words used to explain geography, for example, climate, then we find that it too has three meanings ('1. The prevailing weather conditions of an area; 2. A region with particular weather conditions; 3. The prevailing trend of opinion or public feeling'), all of which similarly defer to other words and so on. Tracking through the dictionary highlights how meaning is always intertextually deferred, always reliant on words that are themselves reliant on others and so on. Only when located in discourse and grounded by context do the words take on meaning, although they still mean different things in different contexts (as Derrida, 1990, p. 252, has stated, 'there is nothing outside the context'). This given, post-structuralists would argue that the idea that language can identify real and important distinctions between different types of people, places and objects appears dubious, given that the meaning of texts is always relational and embedded in an unstable context provided by other signifiers and texts. Accordingly, Derrida argues that a critical subversion of language is necessary in a society where texts serve to create distinctions between that which is Self and Other (and reduce difference to sameness).

Rejecting the binaryness of language, where the critical play of opposites determines the meaning of signifiers, Derrida's deconstructive method is one that seeks to undercut the truth claims inherent in any text. Accordingly, a Derridean-inspired strategy of deconstruction has been adopted by many geographers seeking to question the assumptions latent in representations of different spaces (e.g., Reichert, 1992). Described in its most simple form, this has entailed a critical engagement with text to expose the value-laden quality of the language it contains. The means by which this is achieved have varied widely, though common tactics designed to expose the dubious truth claims on which the creation of social and spatial hierarchies rest include identifying inconsistencies, contradictions and narrative silences within the text (Rose, 2000). Clearly, deconstruction cannot be applied in any formulaic or systematic sense; rather, it is seen to involve an interference with the text (Doel, 1999), one akin to an act of ploughing that cleaves the text open, forcing it out of itself. This is a form of critique, therefore, where the text is refracted back on the critical forces involved in its production. As Derrida argued, to deconstruct is not simply to dive beneath the surface of a text to understand its workings, but is to 'dredge' so that its composition may become evident before the 'sea text' recomposes, obscuring the conditions of its own existence.

This concern with the ways in which the world is brought into being through the realms of language is also mirrored in post-structural critiques of the unified subject. Here, understandings of human beings as autonomous and knowing subjects (i.e., entities that are profoundly aware of themselves and their place in the world) are challenged by ideas that imply that subjectivity is rooted in the body but is composed of and by a multiplicity of representations (Gregory, 1994a). Foucaultian analyses of subjectification have been particularly important in this regard (see Section 3.2.2). Stressing that there is no such thing as a 'pre-discursive' subject, Foucault suggested instead that subjectivity is brought into being through *discourses*. Here, discourses can be understood as groups of statements (whether spoken, written or visualized) which structure the way a thing is thought about, and the way we act on the basis of that thinking. These discourses are tied into complex power relations, often emanating from the social and cultural institutions that are important in giving a shape to the world. For instance, Rose (2000) outlines the importance of art galleries (and curators) in creating ideas about the distinctions between high and low culture, as well as between nature and culture. The gallery itself thus becomes a site where discourses are articulated through technologies of visual display, and where new subjectivities are created.

Beyond art galleries and museums, we might also think about a variety of institutional spaces in which discourses are articulated: hospitals, schools, courts, prisons, clinics, libraries and so on. Each of these spaces is a site of power/ knowledge where certain 'professionals' seek to construct ideas of social difference. In his ground-breaking works, Foucault explored how some of these discourses work to produce subjects. Most notably, he explored the working of psychiatry and 'mad-doctors' through the ages, exploring the distinctions between doctor/patient and sane/mad created through discourse (Foucault, 1967). Simply put, this stressed that madness and sanity are socially and discursively constructed concepts, with the boundary between madness and sanity seen to vary over both time and space in accordance with the localized nature of these discourses (in Chapter 4, we shall explore Foucault's contention that these discourses were mapped onto, and out of, the body). More widely, this Foucaultian take on identity suggests that all social categories are discursively constructed, with the sense of being a man or woman, young or old, straight or gay, able-bodied or disabled emanating from discourse. This implies that human identity is endlessly complex and fluid, and that the placing of people into particular pigeon-holes or categories is dependent on the discursive regimes (and power relations) that dominate at any one moment. In this way, discourse operates as the frame of reference through which particular types of knowledge make sense and through which we become bearers of its power/knowledge (M. Smith, 2000).

Foucault's take on social identity also implies that, if we are able to think in terms of the diffuse and multiple rather than classifying the fragmented and fractured in terms of ordered groups and wholes, the world would be more egalitarian (something outlined in his later work on the 'ethics of the self'). Similar post-structural concerns with difference and its social repression are present in the work of **Gilles Deleuze** (Box 3.8). While his wide-ranging work is often evasive and difficult, a key argument in his writing is the notion that pre-existing academic conceptualizations of self and other, culture and nature and human/non-human inhibit the development of radical thought. Positing the existence of a material world of flows, characterized by heterogeneity and difference, Deleuze suggests that the processes and energies which give consistency to this world (e.g., capitalist relations that create notions of value, or sexual relations that create notions of gender identity) block more productive relations. Crucial here is the notion of desiring-production, the name given by Deleuze to the process whereby desire brings flows together, producing new flows, new material and new effects. In the current epoch, Deleuze contended, desiring-production is harnessed in particular ways, to particular social ends, resulting in the production of human-subjects with certain desires (as well as anxieties and disgusts). Offering a way of thinking about this process without adopting the reactive language of pre-existing social science (particularly the languages of structural Marxism and Freudian psychoanalysis), Deleuze and Guattari (1987)

Box 3.8 Gilles Deleuze (1925–91)

Deleuze's early work consisted of critiques (Deleuze called them 'perversions') of the work of philosophers such as Spinoza, Bergson, Kant and Hume, working with (and against) their most radical and unconventional ideas. In the 1960s, this work coalesced into a more sustained (but constantly moving) elucidation of a non-totalizing mode of thinking that prefigured much post-structuralist thought. Here, the work of Nietzsche provided a key reference point, his heretical philosophy influencing Deleuze's espousal of radical ways of thinking and writing. Such experimental notions are certainly evident in Deleuze's most frequently cited works, *Anti-Oedipus* (1983) and *A Thousand Plateaus* (1987). These represented the output of a remarkable collaboration with Felix Guattari (often described as an 'anti-psychiatrist', working against established psychoanalytical theory and praxis). Replete with extraordinary metaphors and often impenetrable passages, these playful books none the less offer a remarkable attempt to rework the ideas of the two most important influences in twentieth-century thought – Marx and Freud – to develop a truly revolutionary and critical materialist philosophy. Summarizing the repressive effects of both Freudian and Marxist thought, these works instead offer an account where the energy of the world (its flows and movements) are socially organized and territorialized through symbolic and economic systems organized by state apparatuses. Outlining how capitalist processes of anti-production pacify and striate through an economy of desire centred on the Oedipal and a political economy centred on capital (which are in fact the same thing), Deleuze and

theorized the existence of *Bodies-without-Organs* to challenge established notions of human subjectivity. Rejecting the given boundaries and capabilities of the body as conceived of, and written about, in academic and popular discourse, this accordingly suggests that 'people' lack nothing if they are not repressed by the state apparatus of capitalism. Escaping this repression, the Bodies-without-Organs brings new bodies and identities into being, repressing an assemblage of objects, things, energies and bodies that raises new possibilities of existence. This concept suggests that the subject is an ongoing *process* and that the mechanical body of capitalism is a repressed body.

This is a complex and radical reconceptualization of subjectivity that suggests we are currently only partially Bodies-without-Organs, and that the boundaries of the body and subjectivity are more fluid than theorists often suggest. Moreover, the Body-without-Organs cannot be conceived of as being a visible body at all, in conventional frames of reference, existing in a smooth space/time whose shape is difficult to imagine (though an analogy here might be a successful football team: while the players on the pitch may vary from game to game, they form a unified whole whose combined effects can only be conceived of in terms of its unique totality). This is perhaps the appeal of post-structuralist thinking: rather than imposing consistency on the world it dares to imagine different ways of being. At the same time, it shifts the focus from re-representation of the world (a description of what seems to be going on) to a de-representation (the achievement of non-descriptive thought that is constitutive rather than representative) (Dillon, 2000). For Deleuze, for example, the intention is to dislodge forced sameness by exploring the differential relationality

Guattari suggest that people, objects and institutions are assembled into 'desiring machines'. This, they argue, involves syntheses between consumption, desire and production which serve to impose repetition in the world and, in the process, shape and repress the more creative potential of desire (see Holland, 1999). Opposing such repression, Deleuze and Guattari argue for differentiation and an acknowledgement that desiring machines can deterritorialize and decode the stability and force of the representations that create a mode of social reproduction suited to the needs of the capitalist economy. The way to escape the law of the signifier, and the tyranny of Oedipus, they suggest, is to become 'schizophrenic'; pushing the schizoid tendencies of capitalist-production to their limits through schizoanalysis rather than psychoanalysis. Rather than resolving the contradictions of capitalism, this is an analysis that runs an experimental line of flight *between* the contradictions, the force of which sweeps the opposing away. Thus, one of the main legacies of Deleuzism is a lexicon of terms which evoke this need for permanent revolution through new organizations of thought and energy – 'rhizomic' thought, 'nomadism' and the pursuit of 'lines of flight' being the most commonly cited. Anti-dialectical and fiercely critical of the canons of social science, Deleuze's work thus outlines a radical (and inherently political) social theory whose impacts have been profound in many disciplines.

Further reading: Buchanon (2000); Doel (2000)

immanent in a world of flows rather than creating holding formations that territorialize or solidify those flows. Seeking to escape the clutches of language, post-structuralism thus posits that totalizing theories and concepts are dominating and totalitarian (Peet, 1998). Its focus is on intervening in the relations between things in non-hierarchical, non-imposing ways that do not reduce difference to sameness.

Extending interests in text and language into all possible referents – bodies, flows, capital, money, nations, histories, objects – post-structuralism thus refuses to privilege any structure, process or agent in the making and unmaking of the social world. The question vexing many geographers is to how to translate this post-structural insistence on *relational materialism* into theory and practice. In Doel's estimation, such a translation/transformation is unnecessary, given that post-structuralism is inherently spatial. As he argues in his *Post-structuralist Geographies*:

> Rather than there being a post-structuralism that could get taken up by geography and geographers, I want to demonstrate that post-structuralism is always already spatial: that it attends from the off to the difference that space makes. It is the event of space, of spacing, that deconstructs. Speaking always as geographers, post-structuralists strain to become sensitive to what it is to space – to what happens when space takes place. (Doel, 1999, p. 10)

In Doel's text, the work of Derrida, Deleuze, Lyotard and Iragaray is heralded as 'difference-producing' thought that radicalizes geographic notions of situated knowledge. Doel accordingly contrasts 'pointilistic' geography (where spaces are predetermined, existing as ready-mades to be studied and represented) with a post-structuralist geography where nothing is predetermined and spaces only exist in so much as they are brought into being through folds of consistency. Developing this, Doel outlines concepts that are appropriate and 'becoming' for making sense of the 'infinitely adjusted chaos' of the world, alerting to the need for a geography that does not revolve around points. This is a geography that acknowledges that we live in a world of flow, movement and flux, which is lent consistency and seeming permanence through innumerable acts of folding. The task for the geographer (or 'origamist-cum-spatial scientist', as Doel puts it) is to 'open up' space and experiment with its rhythms and consistencies, affects and intensities. This conceptualization argues that nothing is given, and that master categories like capital and the phallus which are bequeathed explanatory power in some geographical accounts are in themselves assemblages which are attended to in different contexts. Some see Doel's efforts to elucidate a post-structural geography as a 'deeply disturbing' descent into relativism and amorality (Graham, 1995, p. 176; see also Pacione, 1999; Peet, 1998), but it is, together with the inventive writing of geographers such as Gunner Olsson, John Paul Jones and Trevor Barnes, beginning to inspire new ways of thinking geographically. Certainly, post-structural thought has impinged significantly on geographies of gender and sexuality (Probyn, 1996), while in areas as diverse as economic (Gibson-Graham, 2000) and historical geography (Wylie, 2000), its impacts are beginning to be felt, problematizing the distinction between words and things (and people and place) that have often hampered geographical thought (Holloway and Hubbard, 2001).

3.6 CONCLUSION

In this chapter we have endeavoured to provide an overview of some of the new theoretical impulses shaping contemporary human geography. Clearly this overview has been both partial and selective. Indeed, it has not been our intention to provide a comprehensive analysis of how geography is currently theorized, but rather to illustrate the varied and ever-changing nature of geographical thought. What should be clear is that human geography is very diverse in how it conceptualizes the world, drawing on a range of ideas both within and external to the discipline, but is unified in recognizing that such conceptualization necessitates an appreciation and use of theory. As stated in Chapter 1, in seeking to understand geography we cannot avoid theory.

In the second section of the book, *Practising Theoretical Geographies*, we try to ground the discussion in this and the previous chapter by demonstrating how the theoretical traditions discussed have been mobilized to think through and theorize five key concepts – the body, text, money, governance and globalization. Rather than provide a comprehensive analysis of each concept, each chapter is designed to illustrate how different geographical foci have been conceptualized and approached from a number of perspectives, each of which provides a different understanding of society. As such, each chapter makes evident that an understanding of key theories and ideas is essential if one wants to 'think geographically'. While the focus is primarily on geographical scholarship, the chapters endeavour to show how concepts derived from other disciplines have been invoked and developed by geographers, using appropriate case studies and examples to clarify the distinctive contribution of particular ideas. As we shall see, theory cannot be regarded as the pinnacle of geographical endeavour, telling those working in the valleys below, supposedly busy with mundane empirical work, how to proceed (Gregory, 1997). The relation between theory and practice is inevitably much more complex.

Practising Theoretical Geographies

Chapter 4   Geographies of the Body

4.1   INTRODUCING THE BODY

> If one thing is certain, it is that we all have a body. Everything we do we do with our bodies – when we think, speak, listen, eat, sleep, walk, relax, work and play – we 'use' our bodies. Every aspect of our lives is therefore embodied. (Nettleton and Watson, 1998, p. 1)

The above quotation seems relatively straightforward and commonsensical – we live our lives through our bodies. And, as Nast and Pile (1998a, p . 1) state, 'since we have bodies, we must be some place'. It seems logical then that any understanding of the spatiality of society must examine the geographies of the body (i.e., understanding how bodies occupy, use and create space). And yet, it is only in the last decade or so that geographers have started explicitly to consider the importance of the body in their analyses of society and space (for example, the edited collections by Nast and Pile, 1998b; Teather, 1999; Butler and Parr, 2000). In part, this interest in the body is connected to the discipline's 'cultural' turn (see Chapter 3). Indeed, given the growing attention devoted in the discipline to consumption and lifestyle issues (e.g., geographies of food, leisure and fashion), the idea that geographers could ignore either the experience or representation of the body appeared increasingly untenable. As research has subsequently suggested, the motivation of people to become involved in particular activities or practices in particular places is intimately connected to their own body image. At the same time, it has been suggested that those with certain (privileged and valued) types of body may seek to exclude 'other' bodies from their surroundings. Such assertions have emphasized the importance of the body as a locus for identities of all kinds (e.g., gendered, racialized, sexualized, disabled), as well as highlighting the potential for people to change the meaning of their bodies through the use of make-up, clothing, dieting, working out, prosthetics, implants or even plastic surgery.

But if geography was somewhat slow to embrace the body as an object of study, it is certainly not unique in this regard among the social sciences. Indeed, an important precept in Western thought since the time of Plato has been the separation of mind from body. In the Enlightenment period, this was elaborated by Descartes in his conception of the mind as an immaterial entity and the body as a material substance defined by its bulk, shape and mass. United to form 'human beings', this dualism between mind–body nevertheless proposed that it is the mind that is the basis of human thinking, feeling and acting, with the physical body being managed by the mind at the same time that it provides the mind with sensory input. This led to theorizing across the social sciences which privileged the mind as the seat of truth, knowledge and humanity, with the body rejected as an explicit theme in social, spatial and historical analysis. As a consequence, most social science has ignored the embodied nature of social life – the interactions between bodies – very often reducing human life to abstract relationships between human actors whose bodies are strangely effaced.

In many ways, this effacement of the body in social science left it to become a matter chiefly for biological, medical and sports science (see McCormack, 1999). These disciplines adopt a fairly straightforward approach to the body, suggesting that it is a natural product whose capabilities and uses are a product of its biology. This concurs with popular understandings of the body, with the *Oxford English Dictionary* defining a body as 'the physical structure, including flesh, bones and organs, of a person or animal, whether living or dead'. Adopting this view, the ability of people to do particular things is seen to be determined by their biology, with certain bodies understood to be better for performing particular tasks or skills. A medical interpretation of women's bodies, for example, suggests they are designed for carrying and nurturing children, whereas men's are bulkier and more muscular, making men better providers and protectors. This then is a conception of the body that, if used uncritically, can stereotype a person's social position and abilities; it effectively reduces and *essentializes* them in terms of their biological and genetic make-up. In such ways, biological differences between men and women, young and old, black and white, able-bodied and disabled may all be used to explain (and justify) inequalities between different groups. Over the course of human history, such essentialist arguments have been used to justify many invidious policies including eugenics (the forced sterilization of people), the incarceration of the disabled (e.g., in asylums or hospitals), apartheid, slavery and genocide (see Holloway and Hubbard, 2001).

Rejecting such biological essentialism, social scientists have mainly offered an account of social difference and inequality where it is the social meanings attached to the body that are crucial in shaping the dynamics of identity and difference (du Gay, 2000). From this *constructivist* perspective, identities are seen to be socially constructed rather than biologically determined. If we adopt this argument, no body can be seen as inherently better, stronger or more complete than any other; it is simply that society has come to value some bodies more than others. For example, feminist theorists have proposed that patriarchal structures generally privilege men's bodies over women's, while Marxist analyses suggest that (industrial) capitalism values strong, able-bodied workers over incomplete, sick or disabled individuals (Gleeson, 1998). Explicitly or otherwise, much social science theory has ignored the physical fleshiness of the body to examine the social structures and representations that generally privilege white, able-bodied, middle-aged, heterosexual male bodies over those of women, ethnic minorities, the elderly and sexual minorities. In other words, society is deemed the basis for identity, with the meanings associated with different bodies considered more important than the physicality of the body per se.

The basic constructivist argument is that identity is not biologically determined but is achieved through a process of socialization which encourages people to conform to established categories of belonging. Crucially, these categories are deemed 'natural', being mapped onto, and out of, particular physical bodies. This notion of social construction can be illustrated by contrasting the medical model of the disabled body with the social model of disability. The medical model of disability posits that problems disabled people face in society (e.g., underemployment, discrimination, negotiating the built environment) are the result of their impairment (e.g., their deviation from the biological 'norm'). From this perspective, overcoming such problems requires that the 'disabled' person overcome his/her bodily impairment through treatment and rehabilitation. The social model of disability, in contrast, posits that disabled people are disabled by society – it is not their bodies that impede them in everyday life, but rather the fact that the society creates an environment which is difficult to negotiate. In other words, it is not the body that disables, but the way that meaning is ascribed to the body by society. Similar arguments can be made in relation to the subordinate place of women in society, which, from a social constructivist perspective, is a result of women's bodies being represented as weaker than men's, supporting assertions that women are the 'weaker sex' (see McDowell, 1999).

As manifest in a glut of publications and journals (*Body and Society* being a notable example), discussions about the physical and social constitution of the body are now widespread in sociology, cultural studies, women's studies and even psychology, with the body acting as a key focus for debate across the social sciences (Smith, 2001). Drawing on theorists like Haraway (Box 1.3), who emphasizes the entwining of the social and the biological (as well as the cultural and the natural), few now hold to the idea that the body is solely social or biological. Instead, Longhurst (2000b) suggests that most regard the body as a material organization of flesh, bones and organs which is continually reconstituted by both self and society (see also Adams, 1995, on the shifting boundaries of the body). Engaging enthusiastically with this idea, many geographers are now exploring the constitution of the body in everyday life – or, as Rich (1986, p. 186) puts it, 'the geography closest in'. This involves often innovative studies of how bodies are formed, negotiated and understood in different spaces. But, as we describe below, examining embodied geographies does not simply involve 'adding' bodies to existing analyses of society and space. As the recent explosion of work concerned with bodies and identities illustrates, the body is a complex phenomenon which, if taken seriously, demands revision of many existing accounts of the relationship between people and place. It is the distinctive manner in which geographers have incorporated this 'social and biological' body into their understandings of spatial process that we explore in the remainder of this chapter.

4.2 MOVEMENT, REST, ENCOUNTER

As noted above, geography is a discipline that has traditionally ignored the body. For example, in the midst of geography's enthusiasm for quantification, human beings were aggregated out of existence, to the extent that people of different sizes, shapes, colours and ages were often reduced to points, flows and movements in space. Moreover, these movements and flows were often explained with reference to the rational decision-making processes made by conscious but disembodied actors. This then was a geography of the mind rather than the body. For example, in behavioural geography, which highlighted the role of the senses in acquiring information from the environment (see Chapter 2), the capabilities of human beings were largely understood in relation to their ability to process and interpret this information rather than the ability of their body to *feel* and *move* through space.

A notable exception was in the so-called *time geography* developed by geographers at Lund University, Sweden, in the 1960s. This contextual approach to understanding human spatial behaviour was based on the idea that space and time are resources on which individuals can draw in order to realize personal activities or projects. These projects are goal-oriented tasks which may be identified on a variety of scales (i.e., a project to get a degree may be broken up into separate projects involving attending lectures, writing essays, reading books; shopping may be broken up into grocery shopping, clothes shopping, picking up clothes from the dry cleaners, etc.). Based on the assumptions that people's ability to conduct different projects at the same time is limited, that movement between different locations in space takes time and that human beings are 'elementary' and indivisible 'particles' (i.e., a body cannot be in two places at once), this approach sought to examine the interweaving of people and projects in coherent 'blocks' of space and time. These ideas were most fully elucidated in the work of Hägerstrand (1975). He both provided a vocabulary to describe people's use of time-space and stressed the importance of space-time in shaping the daily movements necessary for bodily reproduction and 'development' (i.e., eating, sleeping, finding a partner, working, bringing up a child and so on). For Hägerstrand it was important to demonstrate that individuals routinely and repeatedly draw upon resources of time and space in the conduct of their everyday life. This concern with mapping the life-paths of different individuals and groups was manifest in one of the principal notational devices used by Hägerstrand – the *time-space map*. This diagrammatic representation mapped the scope of possible activity spaces based on the idea that a person moves between a variety of *stations* where they spend time on project-related activities. On any given day, the sum of these movements constitutes a daily path, while over longer periods daily experiences combine to produce a cumulative life-path, which simultaneously represents both the end result and context of people's actions (Pred, 1984). In the work of Gregory (1984) and Thrift (1983), this exploration of time-space routines provided a basis for understanding the recursive interaction of agency and structure, becoming an important concept in the development of *structuration* theory (see Chapter 2). This perspective stresses that individuals are knowledgeable about the social structures they produce and reproduce through their conduct, but are not always able to predict the consequences of their actions (see Bryant and Jary, 1997).

Yet even in the time-geography pioneered by the Lund School, where the human being was considered the central elementary particle of geographical enquiry, people were still conceived (and represented) as points in space, moving between different places (or 'stations') according to their position in wider social relations (see Pred, 1977). To a certain extent, it was geography's engagement with humanistic ideas (see Chapter 2) that reminded them that these points in space represented a real, breathing, feeling human being. The sociologist Anthony Giddens (1991) underlined this when he argued that the paths and movements mapped out by geographers offered a limited understanding of humanity because they failed to represent a 'living body-subject', endowed with memories, feelings, knowledge, information and goals – capabilities too rich to be captured by simple models or maps. Structuralist accounts were similarly disembodied, reducing humans to alienated units of labour – cold and lifeless (see Chapter 2). To the contrary, humanism seemed to offer a way of engaging with the sense of physically 'being' in the world, with the ideas of Edmund Husserl, Martin Heidegger and **Maurice Merleau-Ponty** (Box 4.1) being developed by those geographers intent on developing a more human-centred geography. In the main, such humanistic scholarship discussed the relationship between human identity and place identity in the abstract, but human geographers grounded this in specific times and places. In Chapter 5, for example, we will explore how Ley, Tuan, Relph, Buttimer, Lowenthal and others drew on texts and representations to describe the elusive 'sense of place' created through human practice. In a somewhat different vein, the Canadian geographer David Seamon (1979) developed a distinctive take on the phenomenology of being by exploring the way that bodies move through space. Though provoked by similar concerns to those voiced by Yi-Fu Tuan and Edward Relph (i.e., the seeming erosion of place identity by capitalist process), Seamon was prompted to examine the way places were constructed as a function of people's unique lifeworlds. To explore people's lifeworlds he contended that it was necessary to consider the relationships between people's behaviour (what people do in places) and their embodied experiences of place (see Rodaway, 1994).

Seamon (1979, p. 16) defined the methodology of phenomenology as 'a form of study which works to uncover and describe things and experiences – i.e., *phenomena* – as they are in their own terms'. Rejecting abstract theorization and categorization (e.g., making spatial laws), he developed an experiential framework for understanding the relationships between people and place. This had three related foci:

- Movement – a focus on how individual bodies move through space on a day-to-day or routine basis.
- Rest – a focus on how individual bodies find a place of dwelling or rest.
- Encounter – a focus on the ways in which bodies interact with other bodies and things in their everyday worlds.

This 'Triad of Environmental Experience' placed particular emphasis on the body as something which comes to 'know' its environment on its own terms. This may be an uncomfortable idea because we are so used to thinking about the ways in which our minds are our centres of experience, feeling and knowledge, but Seamon's interpretation suggested that our bodies too have intimate knowledge of the everyday spaces of our lives. The implication here is that we do not have to think about the way we move through space and interact physically with our surroundings as our body feels its way. This idea is obviously opposed to the tendency of Western thought to separate the mind from the body, where the body is seen as largely under the control of the mind, as the tool of the mind (R. Butler, 1999). Seamon is keen to break down this dualism. Instead of the human subject being theorized as a mind 'trapped' in, or working with, the body, he suggests that we consider individual people as 'body-subjects'. Following Merleau-Ponty (1940), the relation of a subject to the world is seen to be revealed in the purposive movements of the body – the body itself becomes the locus of intentionality (see also Cresswell, 1999).

In developing his ideas, Seamon employs an interesting descriptive metaphor for thinking about how individuals use space in their everyday routines – that of the 'body ballet'. This suggests that (to a certain extent) routine and repeated movements in familiar places can be thought of as choreographed (i.e., performed without thinking, as opposed to movements being constantly and consciously thought out in the mind, before being passed on as instructions to the body). Extending this metaphor to cover groups of people interacting with each other in particular places, Seamon uses the phrase 'place ballet' to describe the

---

Box 4.1 Maurice Merleau-Ponty (1908–1961)

Often described as a 'philosopher of consciousness', Maurice Merleau-Ponty is chiefly known as a philosopher who developed phenomenological ideas (see Chapter 2). Much of his early work involved collaboration with Jean-Paul Sartre, though later his dissatisfaction with the dualism between mind and matter (subject and object) implicit in Sartre's thinking led him to develop a different conception of existence. In works such as *The Phenomenology of Perception* (1940), Merleau-Ponty began to elucidate the importance of lived experience in grasping the nature of language, perception and the body. Rejecting the 'givenness' of the world, this is an account that privileges lived experience as the basis of perception (i.e., suggests that our understanding of the world is always embodied and time- and space-specific). This rejected the (widespread) idea that human consciousness is somehow abstract and autonomous (outside the body and the real world), proposing instead a phenomenology of the body which recognizes the importance of the encounter between body and world. This suggested that the primary access point

choreographed but complex movements of several bodies simultaneously. Unlike behavioural geography, where movement is reduced to something which can be measured and perhaps explained with reference to cognitive process, for humanistic geographers movement becomes something to be considered as a phenomenon in its own right – as an essential, dynamic and precognitive part of human experience. In Schutz's (1982) account, the constitution of the physical world occurs through the subject's own sense of its body in motion.

This 'choreography of existence' (Pred, 1977) had largely been ignored until Seamon's work (though Jane Jacobs's (1961) work on life in American cities referred to the 'pavement ballets' played out on its streets), and remained largely undeveloped by geographers until more recently, when converging interest in the body and *non-representational theory* has encouraged a re-exploration of movement and practice (see Nash, 2000). In Thrift's (1997, p. 146) summation, non-representational theory is concerned not so much with representations and texts (see Chapter 5) as with the 'mundane, everyday practices that shape the conduct of human beings towards others and themselves in particular sites'. This necessitates devoting attention to things that words and representations cannot express – the practical experiences of ordinary people that are rarely spoken of but constantly performed and felt. As he puts it, this focuses on the body, or more correctly, the body-subject, as it finds itself and remakes itself in a world that is constantly changing and becoming. Exploring the non-verbal and prediscursive ways people 'do' identities, there is now an extensive geographical literature on the ways people dance, walk, swim, ride or sit their identities (Nash, 2000), as well as the way they perform their identities through bodily gestures, modes of eating or styles of dressing (Valentine, 1999). For example, in Malbon's (1998) study of clubbing, he excavates the way that people create their own sense of place through dance, forming transitory communities of belonging through a shared experience of dancing. While this draws on humanistic ideas about the development of selfhood and identity through embodiment, it also develops ideas about the way the body is caught up in collective experiences

to the world is the body, and that knowledge of the world is always derived from embodied experience. In his later works (e.g., the unfinished *The Visible and the Invisible*), he elaborated this to stress that the body is not distinct from the mind, or the world, but is an element that, alongside these things, makes up the perceived and experienced world (as opposed to the world of hallucination and imagination). Read in parallel with the work of Martin Heidegger and Norbert-Schutz, Merleau-Ponty is a writer whose ideas are of especial interest to geographers as they offer a distinctive phenomenological perspective on concepts of place, space and being. While obviously influential to those working in a humanistic tradition (e.g., Seamon, 1979), Merleau-Ponty's ideas have been widely (albeit implicitly) adopted by those geographers who hold to the idea that it is the space of the body, rather than the conscious mind, that provides the basis of being in the world (see Thrift, 2000a).

Further reading: Langer (1989); Davidson (2000)

and power relations. The work of Michel Foucault has proved especially influential in this regard.

4.3 CIVILIZING AND DISCIPLINING THE BODY

In contrast to humanistic interpretations of the body acting as the basis of subjectivity via its being in the world, **Michel Foucault** (Box 4.2) suggested that the body-subject is an *effect* of power relations. This idea is perhaps difficult to grasp, being both anti-humanist but also post-structural. In many accounts, however, this is interpreted as meaning that individuals are created through discourse, their identities and sense of individualism being the product of the discourses that ripple through society (see also Chapter 3). This suggests that subject identities and categories that are used to describe body-subjects (e.g., male/female, black/white, sick/sane) are not given, but are created through representations, practices and performances. This is a critical theory of subject formation, where discourses enter into the constitution of the body and society, making distinctions and separations that become regarded as logical, acceptable and normal. Crucially, these include discourses and ideas about what particular types of body should look like and how it should be used. For example, his work on sexuality emphasized that specific sexual categories – the spinster, the masturbator, the prostitute, the good wife, the pornographer – were created through discourse, their identities consequently policed and regulated through

---

Box 4.2 Michel Foucault (1926–84)

Given the continual rereading and reintepretation of Foucault's work, it remains difficult to summarize his key ideas. Moreover, his often controversial life (and death) means that his work still excites considerable differences of opinion (and much overt criticism). None the less, there is little doubt that Foucault was among the leading thinkers of the twentieth century, his writing being widely cited in academia and beyond. Questioning many of the assumptions on which traditional academic enquiry rested, a key impulse in Foucault's earlier texts – *Madness and Civilisation* (1967) and *Discipline and Punish* (1977) in particular – was to explore the boundaries between normality and deviance, devoting attention to the historical treatment (and definition) of criminality, perversion and madness. Through such historical archaeologies of the Other, Foucault questioned the discursive claims on which concepts of normality and deviance rested, suggesting that the construction and ordering of society is created through discourses that work to discipline bodies (and minds). Arguing that these discourses emanate from innumerable points, Foucault also alerted people to the spatialized nature of this ordering, mapping the contours of the diverse webs of power in which bodies are caught up. This work has been of major interest to geographers (as well as historians), with those sections of Foucault's work that discussed the order present in particular spatial configurations inspiring many investigations of the power relations played out in specific settings (e.g., Ogborn, 1995; Hannah, 1997). Much of this has focused on the notion of surveillance, following Foucault's adoption of Bentham's panopticon as the quintessential model of modern social control. Finding echoes of panopticism in a

webs of disciplinary power. In relation to sexuality, such disciplinary techniques included punitive laws concerning the policing of particular sexual practices (e.g., the censorship and repression of same-sex desire) as well as the apparently enlightened and rational manner that we learn about sex through education. The net result, Foucault argues, was to discipline sexual bodies, making clear that certain sexual practices are pleasurable while others are in need of reform. Beyond discussion of sexuality, his work also highlighted the importance of public health, moral and legal discourse in the production and surveillance of disciplined bodies, with a particular focus on the eighteenth and nineteenth centuries.

In many ways, Foucault's writing on the regulation of bodies has over-shadowed other attempts to theorize the diverse techniques used to exercise control over bodies. For instance, in *The Civilising Process*, Norbert Elias (1978) outlined a related theory of the civilized body, exploring how the body has been transformed over the centuries into a polite and sophisticated object possessed and managed by its 'owner' in opposition to everything defined as animal. He suggested that today's notions of what is taken to be a proper and 'normal' body can only be understood by examining the ways in which the modern period enacted a civilizing process that changed notions of what human beings were supposed to be and how they were supposed to act. He suggested that a key trait of modernization was the idea that to be modern and advanced, people needed to distance themselves from primitive societies by changing the ways they used their bodies and adopting civilized ways of acting towards other

variety of spaces, both past and present, has alerted geographers to the way that discourse, power and knowledge come together in different spaces to shape human subjectivity and morality (Hannah, 1997). Beyond this obvious import into geographical scholarship, Foucault's later work on the 'technologies of the self' that maintain power relations has also been invoked by many geographers. As spelt out in the (incomplete) volumes of the *History of Sexuality*, this focused much more overtly on the way that individuals create *themselves* as subjects (and objects). For example, his work on the channelling of desire explored how people negotiate ethical relationship with one another, drawing on Nietzsche to critique the way sex was represented and understood in different epochs to identify the way human beings perform operations on their own bodies, conduct and way of being in order to attain a certain state of happiness, wisdom, perfection or immortality (Foucault, 1988, p. 221). This critical account has been inspirational for queer theorists (see Chapter 3) as well as more widely in the social sciences where it has raised important questions about the nature of governmentality, subjectivity and social order (see Chapter 7). Although some commentators have identified a schism between the earlier Foucault of disciplinarity, order and punishment, and the later Foucault of bodies, pleasures and ethics, both have had influence on those geographers seeking to excavate the way power is played out in (and through) space.

Further reading: Burchill *et al.* (1991); Philo (2000a); MacHill (1997)

people (as well as to animals and nature). In order to demonstrate his ideas and to chart the changing characteristics of acceptable behaviour and manners from the fifteenth century onwards, Elias explored changing ideas about the body in relation to good and bad manners. For example, he notes that in medieval times people would blow their nose with their fingers, adopting the 'civilized' handkerchief only in the seventeenth century. Similarly, he reports that it was common for people to talk to each other while defecating or urinating in public, communal areas (such as fields and streets) until late medieval times; and to eat with hands until the sixteenth century (see Jervis, 1999; Smith, 2001).

Through his 'figurational' analysis, Elias demonstrated that the raw material of the body is transformed into a civilized 'person' through codes of manners (Rojek, 1995). A key idea here is that these codes vary across both time and space, with 'modern' forms of body management (ways of dressing, walking, talking, eating and so on) being distinguished from those associated with previous, 'less civilized' periods (Giddens, 1991). This has led to current notions of a civilized body, where the boundaries between the inside and outside of the body are clearly defined, and the expulsion of substances from the body – liquids, solids and gases – is seen as impolite, something that should be done in private. This means, for instance, that we are expected to clean our bodies regularly to remove any traces of bodily substances (e.g., faeces, saliva, sweat). In the nineteenth century, when these ideas first became widespread, the spatial consequence of this was that cities changed to accommodate new flows of water and sewage; at the same time, these flows encouraged populations to conceive of themselves and their city in new terms (e.g., as more civilized). The body and the city can accordingly be seen as held in an intimate relationship (Sennett, 1994).

Elias's 'genealogy' of manners, whilst insightful on changing modes of body management, has not however proved as influential as Foucault's. Like Elias, Foucault's (1977) account of the changing nature of social control focused on the period when the medieval, feudal system was replaced by a quintessentially modern social order in the late eighteenth and nineteenth centuries. For Foucault, the body was less a reflection of this 'civilizing' process than a battleground on which social struggle was (and continues to be) played out. In other words, Foucault proposed that the idea that certain types of body are preferable to others was the result of power struggles between different groups, with the state seeking to impose its ideas about what was right and wrong by *disciplining* the body-subject. A focus on the specific institutions that tried to discipline the body-subject (including the judiciary, the medical profession and police) led Foucault to consider specific *spaces* of bodily management and reformation. In particular, Foucault's use of the *panopticon* as a general metaphor for the forms of spatial arrangement which were central to the disciplining of deviant individuals and behaviours suggested to geographers that specific principles of spatial segregation and surveillance are essential in the maintenance of social order. This panopticon model was spelt out by the social reformer Jeremy Bentham in a series of letters and correspondence from 1787 onwards, its name derived from the Greek for 'all-seeing eye'. Bentham advocated a new form of design for prisons in which principles of observation were crucial. A central feature of this design was that it would consist of numerous single cells positioned on the radii of a circle, each facing inwards towards an inspector's lodge from which it would be possible to see the actions of every inhabitant of every cell (through its iron grille) without being observed themselves. According to Bentham, the threat of continual observation would discourage misbehaviour, with the visibility of inmates maximized through their spatial separation. Bentham also believed the separation of inmates would inhibit the contagion of bad thoughts, bad behaviours and disease.

The geographer Chris Philo (1987) has explored the evolution and subsequent adoption of this panoptic design, describing how its blueprint was tailored and refined to specific local circumstances, as well as acting as a basis for the design of key institutions of reform, including workhouses, prisons and mental hospitals. In fact, few institutions slavishly followed Bentham's design, some allowing inmates to see and hear one another, others allowing them to see their keepers. None the less, new types of institutional setting began to emerge from the late eighteenth century, each seeking to impart order and discipline by bringing the building, its controllers and its inmates together in regulated space and time (Markus, 1993). Foucault's writing documented the way that the local and central state dispersed these sites the length and breadth of the country in a way that conveyed a general vision of social orderliness to the general population. In a wider sense then, the creation of such disciplinary sites demonstrated to Foucault that an expanded, unified and intensified form of surveillance was being used to discipline society in the modern era (see also Dandeker, 1990).

For Foucault, the incarceration and treatment of miscreants in these sites was only part of the story as to how state control came to be maintained through disciplinary power which focused on the body in such a way as to turn all citizens into 'good', docile citizens. More widely, he noted that the process of creating dedicated and productive citizens was institutionalized in state programmes of education, welfare and social policy designed to encourage people to recognize the desirability of having a normal, clean, healthy and productive bodies. This focuses attention on those 'places of formation' (Markus, 1993) where people were encouraged to participate in forms of self-surveillance, effecting an interiorization of power (Robinson, 2000). Such spaces include schools, libraries, community centres, swimming baths and other spaces of the state. For example, in schools one learns the importance of looking after one's body and presenting it to others. School rules and dress codes encourage conformity and participation in a way that is supposed to encourage each pupil to become a responsible individual by subsuming his/her individuality in the interests of the wider school community (see Fielding, 2000). Here, a focus on pupils' minds is matched by a focus on their bodies with cleanliness, healthiness and athleticism encouraged through periods set aside for physical education, team sports and even medical inspections. Investigating this, Armstrong quotes from 1908 school regulations:

Do not put fingers in the mouth. Do not pick nose or wipe the nose on the hand or sleeve. Do not wet the finger in the mouth when turning the leaves of books. Do not put pencils in the mouth, or money, or pins or anything except food and drink. Apple cores, candy, chewing gum, half eaten food, whistles or bean blowers are not to be swapped; pupils should never cough or sneeze in a person's face and should keep hands and face clean. (cited in Armstrong, 1993, p. 404)

Viewed from a Foucaultian perspective, a school becomes a place of constant surveillance where undesirable forms of behaviour, morality and appearance are discouraged through coercion and punishment, while good behaviour and learning are rewarded by the granting of privileges, good marks and praise from tutors.

Elaborating these ideas about the exercise of power, geographers have begun to think about the role of specific places in creating docile body-subjects, thinking about how the practices played out in different settings contribute to discourses that differentiate between good and bad bodies. In Linehan and Gruffudd's (2001) study of miners' bathhouses, for instance, the design of twentieth-century pithead baths is interpreted as designed to create ordered and clean bodies. Mirroring wider discourses concerning the boundaries of public and private bodies, their analysis suggests that washing systems sought to encourage particular ideas about bodily comportment. More widely, discourses of cleanliness and health have been diagnosed as a key mechanism by which people have been disciplined. For instance, the inclusion of bathing and swimming into school routines in the nineteenth century was viewed as a crucial step in the move toward cleanliness and hygiene, with the Bath and Washhouses Act 1846 making provision for public bathing and washing houses the length and breadth of Britain. These baths were strictly segregated between men and women, internally divided to separate dirty clothes and dirty bodies from things conceived as clean. They were spaces where bodies were appraised and sorted at the same time that they participated in an enjoyable leisure pursuit:

Great precautions are taken to safeguard clean children: separate washing boxes are provided and wiped out by an attendant after each occupant; children are numbered and graded unobtrusively; towels are kept quite separate; disinfectant soap is used; no loofahs or flesh brushes are used, but the hand only; underwear can be inspected if necessary while the children are under the water. (Campbell, 1918, p. 45)

So, whether one looks at bathhouses, school spaces, factories, asylums or prisons, it seems one can see disciplinary power being played out. Foucault's examination of spaces of incarceration has therefore inspired much geographical work on spaces of surveillance, and although much of this has been preoccupied with enclosed spaces, more widely it should be noted that Foucaultian ideas have been employed to explore the forms of regulation imposed in public space, particularly Closed Circuit Television (Fyfe, 1998; Fischer and Poland, 1998; Herbert, 1997).

4.4 CULTURAL CAPITAL AND BODY PROJECTION

While Foucaultian conceptions of the body question humanistic understandings that the body is the starting point for the constitution of the social world, some geographers have turned to other sources to explore the *cultural politics* of the body (see Section 3.1 on geography's 'cultural turn'). While such perspectives are not necessarily incompatible with Foucault's concern with power, particular emphasis is placed on the active and transformative role the body plays in relation to the capitalist processes that produce it (Longhurst, 2000b). Developing ideas about the connections between aesthetics, appearance and capital, a crucial notion here is that the body is tied into social processes which operate in favour of certain identities. More particularly, it has been suggested that the alteration and presentation of the body can be conceptualized as an *accumulation strategy*, being used by people to acquire money and prestige (Harvey, 2000a). Perhaps the best way to think about this is to compare the body to a work of art. Like a work of art, the body may be considered as something which has a value, with some bodies (and some works of art) considered more valuable than others. However, we realize that art has a value that is quite distinct from its usefulness in processes of production (its use value), needing to be understood as a form of *conspicuous consumption* whose worth derives from its symbolic value (Baudrillard, 1988). Accordingly, some people have a lavish taste in art, displaying their affluence through expensive paintings and sculptures which have no obvious use to them beyond this decorative and symbolic purpose. None the less, this 'wastefulness' distinguishes them from the less affluent; it is read as a sign of their status and refinement. In turn, this grants legitimacy to their cultural values and enhances the value of the art itself. As we shall see in Chapter 5, questions about the value of art therefore raise important questions about the role of signs in society; in postmodern society it is often asserted that the consumption of signs and symbols has become everything (Lash and Urry, 1994).

The implication here is that, in the same way that people buy art to assert their status, they use their bodies to accumulate and display wealth. An essential idea here is that the stylized appearance of the body can be used to communicate status and distinction. The notion of body language is well established, with certain postures and gestures being associated with 'good' upbringing. Moreover, it is obvious that the decoration of bodies (through clothing, make-up, jewellery and tattooing) has been an important means of signifying prestige and power since ancient times (Edensor, 2000). This is highlighted in the work of Erving Goffman (1959), who famously developed the notion that people are constantly concerned with *impression management*. Suggesting that people are like actors in a play, he argued that in public life we are forced to play roles which are not necessarily reflective of our 'true' selves; instead we conduct a performance designed to give a particular and favourable impression of ourselves. For example, dressing in a particular way is essentially a decision about how we present ourselves to others:

> When I rummage through my wardrobe in the morning I am not merely faced with a choice of what to wear. I am faced with a choice of images; the difference between a smart suit and pair of overalls, a leather skirt and a cotton dress, is not just one style but one of identity. You know you will be seen differently for the whole day, depending on what you put on; you will appear as a particular kind of woman with one particular identity that excludes others. (Williamson, 1986, p. 91)

Goffman's ideas thus spell out a sociology of co-presence, where the Self is a product of the social encounters played out in everyday life. Changing the way we present the body thus allows us to negotiate our identity, so that ultimately our character (or Self) becomes synonymous with the character we perform in social life.

Setting aside obvious criticisms of Goffman's ideas (e.g., his *symbolic interaction* perspective pays little attention to social structures), his work alerts us to the staging of identity through bodily presentation and manipulation. In relation to fashion, it suggests that clothing is symbolic as much as it is utilitarian, and when people choose clothes, they do so not only on the basis of price, durability or fit, but also on the basis of the messages they want to communicate about themselves (Lurie, 1992). For example, a soccer shirt may be functional (helping free up the body for movement in particular ways, and made of breathable fabrics) but is also symbolic as it indicates allegiance to a particular club (as well as suggesting that the wearer is the kind of person who thinks wearing a soccer shirt is fashionable). Of course, some may prioritize the symbolic over the functional, with Veblen's (1934) seminal account suggesting that

---

Box 4.3 Pierre Bourdieu (1930–2002)

Though he became a key thinker in post-war French sociology, and consequently a major influence in British cultural studies, Bourdieu's initial work was anthropological in focus. Inspired by his time on national service, his studies of Algerian social life were very much within the traditions of anthropological enquiry (i.e., rich description of a people's way of life, but little by way of analysis). Returning to study in Paris in 1960, his work began to engage with the canons of social science, particularly the work of Marx and Weber, at the same time reacting against the ideas being proposed by the other leading lights of the Parisian Left Bank – Sartre and his existentialism on the one hand, and Lévi-Strauss's structuralism on the other. Rejecting the determinism and voluntarism which he saw implicit in these accounts of social life, Bourdieu developed his own ideas about the distinctions (and choices) between objectivism and subjectivism (Jenkins, 1992). These evolved into a theory of social practice based around the neologisms of *habitus, field* and *symbolic capital*. As spelt out in *The Logic of Practice* (1990), these ideas seek to present an account of social life that suggests that behaviour is neither shaped by individual free will nor solely determined by overarching social

the haute couture adopted by the bourgeoisie was designed to symbolize their membership of the non-productive leisure class, exempt from the need to work.

Clothing therefore allows us to project a certain image, with the adoption of a particular mode of dressing communicating something about our social status (or the status we aspire to). Indeed, the idea that clothing and body presentation signify class identities has been important in cultural studies, where distinctions of high, low, mass, popular and elite culture are regarded as crucial in the making and unmaking of society (see Chapter 3). Here, **Pierre Bourdieu**'s (Box 4.3) ideas about *cultural capital* have been particularly influential for those theorizing the connections between body and capital accumulation. For Bourdieu, the desire to be fashionable is one of the means by which people indicate their distinctiveness:

> Like every form of taste, it unites and separates. Being the product of the conditioning associated with a particular class of conditions of existence, it unites all those who are the product of similar conditions while distinguishing them from all others. And it distinguishes them in an essential way, since taste is the basis of all one has . . . and all that one is. (Bourdieu, 1984, p. 56)

In the account offered by Bourdieu, fashion is closely connected to the *habitus* of particular groups, with the values of different classes manifest in the fashions they adopt. This implies that those belonging to particular class factions dress in ways that they believe is stylish, creating important distinctions between classes. Georg Simmel's (see Box 6.1) foundational analyses of modern society developed similar arguments, identifying an important contradiction in this process: people wear the latest fashions because they want to appear different but also because they want to seek affiliation with other fashionable people. In Bourdieu's work, clothing is described as a *materialization* of class taste; cultural

conditions. Pivotal here is the idea of habitus, a mode of being and understanding that is shared between members of social groups but varies across different social and cultural factions (Painter, 2000b). Habitus is therefore deemed the product and creator of social distinctions, being inculcated and reproduced through practices in a variety of fields (e.g., education, art, sports, religion). Offering an account of power, Bourdieu thus departed from deterministic materialist accounts by stressing the crucial role of the symbolic (or cultural) capital wielded by key social and cultural intermediaries. This suggested that society is shaped in a multitude of overlapping fields of power, with the creation of distinction through the privileging of particular modes of dressing, eating or speaking (for example) being deemed just one of the means by which society is reproduced. In geography, these ideas were widely cited in the midst of the discipline's 'cultural turn', though their theoretical implications have remained largely implicit in many investigations of social and cultural geography (but see Hubbard, 1996; Bridge, 2001).

Further reading: Jenkins (1992); Painter (2000b); Bridge (2001)

capital that can be converted into economic capital (and vice versa). This leads Bourdieu to posit the existence of 'constructed' class, with people able to be upwardly mobile by converting their cultural capital into economic capital (Turner, 1988).

What we need to remember here is that ideas about what is currently in vogue are largely determined by key 'cultural intermediaries' (i.e., designers and journalists) embedded in the fashion capitals of New York, Paris, London and Milan. Traditional interpretations of the fashion industry suggest that this leads to a vertical segregation of society where the latest fashions are created for the rich and famous, 'trickling down' to other (less affluent) groups over time. This results in a rapid turnover of fashions as the elite seek to maintain their distinct-iveness and one season's look is superseded by another's. For Simmel (1971), the net result of these cycles of fashion was deemed to be a relatively static social stratification, where people's class could fairly readily be gauged by their dress. However, this idea of a vertical differentiation of clothing has been thoroughly rejected by those who argue that style is not solely something associated with the upper classes, with designers often taking ideas from working-class and 'street' fashion (Wilson, 2001). Developing this interpretation of the cultural politics of fashion, Angela McRobbie (1994) has explored the market for second-hand dresses in London. In her study, it was frequently more affluent women who bought from second-hand stores while working-class women tended to buy more expensive clothing from high-street stores. But she stresses that this pattern is geographically differentiated, as buying (and wearing) second-hand clothes means different things in different places (see Gregson and Crewe, 1998, on 'car-boot' fairs and the spaces of second-hand clothing). Ironically, 'mix and match' styles that developed out of the second-hand clothes scene were later commodified by the fashion industry, appearing on the catwalk in designer shows. This suggests that the cultural valuation of different modes of bodily presentation is far from straightforward, being tied into complex chains of production and consumption (Jackson, 1999).

A further indication that the presentation of the body cannot be considered solely in class terms is found in the burgeoning literature on subcultures (see Chapter 3). Having its origins in the work of the Birmingham School (especially the work of Stuart Hall and Dick Hebdidge), such writing particularly high-lights the way that young people use material culture to indicate their member-ship of particular 'lifestyle' groups. Examples – mods, rockers, punks, goths, raggas, ravers and so on – suggest that, irrespective of wealth, the young can develop distinctive ways of dressing that mark them off as different from the mainstream. Often taking form in public space, these different groups typ-ically develop their own streetstyles which subvert or mock the mainstream. Hebdidge's original work on mods, for example, demonstrated how these essentially working-class youths signalled their dissatisfaction with their parents' generation and its values by wearing expensive Italian suits and having short, blow-dried hair. This rejection of traditional versions of working-class mascu-linity was to find its antithesis in the rugged leather and greased hair sported by the rockers (Hebdidge, 1979). More recently, the adoption of 'club' wear may help one gain admission to certain cultures (and spaces) of clubbing, as well as indicating one's rejection of other styles (and hence other lifestyles – see Malbon, 1998, on geographies of clubbing).

Taken together, this suggests that the relationship between social status and modes of dressing is complex, and some have even argued that there is now no connection at all between class and clothing, inferring that each individual develops his or her own style (Wilson, 2001). In some senses, this throws Bourdieu's interpretation of cultural capital into doubt, although it does not reject the idea that there is a cultural politics of the body. Accordingly, the way people dress to conform to or challenge existing social categories represents a continuing tradition in contemporary cultural studies. In geography, this has been manifest in some illuminating studies of how people still use clothing to project images of themselves that they think are appropriate in particular places. For example, Dwyer's (1999) work with young Muslim women in the UK demonstrates the difference between wearing (a Westernized) school uniform and a *shalwar kameez* (the loose tunic and trousers worn throughout South Asia). This demonstrates that choosing which to wear is an essentially political decision, making a different statement about the young women's identity according to the context in which it is worn. Even in schools with relaxed uniform rules, Dwyer showed that most young Muslim women wanted to wear 'Asian' clothes to school, but did not do so because of pressures to conform to 'Western' ideals. This work demonstrates an awareness of how class identities may intersect with racial, gender and sexual identities, something also explored in McDowell's (1995) work on 'power dressing' in the City of London (see Box 6.4). Such research suggests that the way we dress sends out profoundly important messages about our values and aspirations; beyond consideration of clothing, geographers are also examining the role of more permanent *body projects* (e.g., tattooing, piercing, prosthetics) in changing the meaning of the body (see Longhurst, 2000b).

4.5 SEXED BODIES AND SEXY BODIES

The ideas considered so far have highlighted the way that external forces and pressures encourage us to normalize our bodies. As a result, we generally dress in ways which are appropriate to particular settings, do not do certain things with our bodies when in public view, and make sure they are clean and free of dirt at all times. But we do not only do this because we are scared of appearing different (or 'out of place'); we are also driven by a desire to appear beautiful and attractive to others. As **Gill Valentine** (Box 4.4) writes, it is the desire to be seen as desirable that particularly encourages people to adopt *techniques of the self* designed to make the body appear sexy to others. This notion returns to the work of Foucault (1977, p. 155), and particularly his insistence that 'each individual exercises surveillance over and against himself'. This implies we constantly monitor and think about our own appearance because we are concerned about how others will see us. In short, we all wish to appear desirable to those who gaze upon us, and often seek to conform to some ideal of desirability to do so. Therefore, individuals (and especially, it seems, women) are supposed to be self-disciplined, to look after and sculpt their bodies – not only to bind, squeeze and enclose its bulk in fashionable underwear and clothes, but to *sculpt* it according to some ideal. In sum, whether we look at pornography or mainstream images, we find that certain types of body are deemed sexy or erotic, with the promise that by looking after our bodies (and buying 'beauty' products) we can become like (or have access to) these idealized bodies.

Here, we need to think about how this idealization of certain types of bodies has come about, and to think about how consumer culture, advertising and the media have created images of ideal bodies against which we are supposed to measure ourselves. If we start to examine the type of bodies that are defined as sexy, we find considerable variation over time and space; what was desirable in the past may seem odd today, and clearly Western and non-Western concepts may be very different. However, today it appears that a premium is placed on slenderness. For Susan Bordo (1993) the image of a slender body has been aspirational for women as it expresses an ideal of a well-managed, disciplined self. Here, there is an important link between the slender body and the *healthy* body, in that the slender body is depicted as available to anyone if they are vigilant of their food intake and pursue a healthy lifestyle:

> The perfect body is slender, fit and glowing. It does not smoke. If it drinks, it drinks in moderation. It also regulates its diet in terms of calories, carbohydrates, fats, salts and sugars. It exercises regularly and intensely. It showers frequently . . . It has proper muscle strength . . . It has appropriate aerobic capacity. (Edgley and Brissett, 1990, pp. 260–1)

Of course, anxieties about matching up to this body image are widespread, with compulsive disorders such as anorexia seen to result from pressures to diet in a

---

Box 4.4 Gill Valentine (1965–)

Gill Valentine, a Professor of Human Geography at Sheffield University, UK, has quickly established a reputation as a key thinker in social geography. Valentine established her reputation for timely, cutting-edge research primarily through her work on geographies of sexuality, writing of the time-space strategies and residential location decisions of lesbian women in the UK. This writing appeared at a time when British geographers were only beginning to acknowledge the existence of queer theory, and hence made many aware of the work of Butler, Weeks, Sedgwick and others. Her reputation as a leading writer on sexuality and space was consolidated with the collection *Mapping Desire* (co-edited with David Bell), which brought together an international field of authors exploring the spatial expressions and inflections of sexuality. None the less, this was not without personal consequences, with the validity of her work (and her own sexuality) being attacked – rarely in public, but privately through a 'hate' campaign (see Valentine, 1998, for a harrowing account of this). This has not prevented Valentine maintaining a prolific output of research that touches on the social and cultural consequences of contemporary trends in consumption – for example, the changing modes of food consumption, the

consumer society where food is sold as central to many social rituals. Anxieties about obesity as representing a failure of self-management are thus widely apparent, with sexist assumptions about women's rights to display their bodies serving to discourage women who consider themselves 'overweight' from sun-bathing in public parks and beaches (McDowell, 1999). Equally, returning to Valentine's (1999) discussion about food consumption, many obese women feel extremely uneasy about eating in public space for fear that their 'uncivilized eating' may be read as evidence of their gluttony. For men, concerns about body are couched more in terms of health than slenderness, a concern underpinned by gendered assumptions that men are more active than women. This is an idea promoted by those men's magazines that emphasize the importance of develop-ing an athletic, muscled body; the message seems to be that to be 'out of shape' is to be undesirable. As McCormack's (1999) perceptive reading of health and fitness discourse suggests, the fit body is also a flexible one, matched to the needs of the twenty-first century corporate workplace (see also Chapter 6 on the cultural geographies of money).

Sex, food and health, it seems, are fundamental in determining the type of relationships we have with our own bodies and those of others in contemporary society. It is often assumed that we will not be successful in finding a sexual partner unless we are concerned with how our bodies appear to the sexual gaze of others. But this concern with exercising constraint under the watchful gaze of other sexual bodies does not stop when people are in a sexual relationship. This has been demonstrated in the work of Robyn Longhurst (2000b), a geog-rapher whose work has become an important reference point for those inter-ested in gender, space and the body. Drawing on feminist theorists including Luce Iragaray and Elizabeth Grosz, her work on the pregnant body provides an interesting example of how pressures to fulfil idealized body images make some women feel uncomfortable in certain places. Interviewing pregnant women in Hamilton, New Zealand, she found that the Centre Park shopping centre – a

importance of cyberculture for children and the geographies of youth cultures (see Bell and Valentine, 1997; Skelton and Valentine, 1998). In relation to contemporary debates concerning the body, Valentine's work is exemplary in showing how space and place intersect with gender and sexuality to affect understandings of the body, with her work on food consumption (for example) indicative of how consumption practices are shaped by body images and take place in particular locations. From her perspective, bodies are 'the product of interactions . . . constituted by particular constellations of social relations' (Valentine, 1999: p. 330), and hence need to be understood in relation to the spaces within which they are oriented. Judith Butler's work is a key influence here, but Valentine continues to write primarily as a geog-rapher, emphasizing that bodies and their meanings change discursively and materially across space as much as they do across social groups (see Valentine, 2001).

Further reading: Bell and Valentine (1995); Valentine (2001)

shopping environment targeting middle- and high-income women – was experienced as an exclusionary space. This sense of exclusion was evident on a number of levels; for example, it was evident that window displays often incorporated idealized images of women that are normatively glamorous, sexy and attractive, but that pregnant women did not fit into this conception. Moreover, few shops provided clothing for pregnant mothers. More prosaically, those interviewed also reported that toilets, escalators and seating were not designed with the bodily form of pregnant women in mind. Concluding, Longhurst stresses that there are many social norms which pregnant women are expected to adhere to in terms of dress code, comportment and movement in public space. Because of cultural rules of pregnancy whereby women are not supposed to engage in sport, drink or smoke, or even have sex, it is therefore not surprising that some women find their usual public behaviours in public becoming unacceptable. In short, women whose bodies are sexed (and sexy) before they are pregnant take on different meanings during pregnancy, meaning that they may feel 'ugly and alien' in some places in which they previously felt welcome. This begins to imply a *moral geography* where a body considered desirable in one place is interpreted as a body of disgust elsewhere. The way that people shape their body space according to stereotypes of desire and disgust represents an emerging tradition in social and cultural geography (e.g., see Hubbard, 1999, on the exclusion of prostitutes' 'grotesque' bodies).

So far in this section we have discussed the gendering and sexing of bodies mainly from a constructivist perspective where the body is seen as a site of social inscription. This implies that the labelling of particular bodies as objects of desire or disgust is the result of social process. Yet such interpretations clash with those theories that view the body as a site of *performance*. This suggests the need to develop an approach which moves beyond dichotomies of structure/agency and nature/culture to explore how sexual identities are established and maintained through repeated and stylized performances in space. A key theorist here is Judith Butler (see Box 3.5), who has suggested that gender exists through bodily acts which are labelled as normal through visible repetition. Neither historically determined nor individually created, she conceptualizes gender as both a product of socialization and a dynamic project of the self, being made and remade through bodily performances. In effect, she suggests we are all obliged to perform our 'proper' gender, acting out a role which will be interpreted as male or female by others. However, unlike Goffman's interpretation, which separates the true Self from its public and embodied performance, Butler's work sees the psychic and bodily basis of identity as inseparable. This implies that no one can be considered to possess an identity which is either male or female *per se*, or even homosexual or heterosexual, but that these types of identity are always *becoming*. As Williams and Bendelow (1998, p. 126) argue, 'sex is no longer a bodily given upon which gender constructs are artificially imposed, but instead a "cultural norm" that governs the materialisation of bodies'. This implies that sexed bodies are not fixed but come into being through social norms of interpretation. Of course, the interpretation is not fixed over time and space, meaning that there are many opportunities for individuals to act out performances that raise questions about the links between different body types and different patterns of behaviour.

To date, this reconceptualization of the body as fluid and mutable has mainly been developed in relation to debates about the relation of sex and gender, where it has been employed to suggest that both gender and sex are performative rather than socially fixed (Hood-Williams and Harrison, 1998). Importantly, this interpretation leaves room for individuals to act out scripts of bodily identity in their own unique way. It is when performances deviate from the script that questions are raised about the 'givenness' of particular identities, and new sexual/gender identities may potentially emerge:

> The construction of coherence conceals the gender identities that run rampant within heterosexual, bisexual and gay and lesbian contexts in which gender does not necessarily follow from sex, and desire, or sexuality generally, does not seem to follow from gender; indeed, where none of these dimensions of significant corporeality express or reflect one another. When the disorganization and disaggregation of the field of bodies disrupts the regulatory fiction of heterosexual coherence, it seems that the expressive model loses its descriptive force, and that regulatory ideal is exposed as a norm and a fiction that disguises itself as a developmental law that regulates the sexual field that it purports to describe. (Butler, 1990b, p. 326)

The idea that some performances might shatter the coherence of taken-for-granted concepts of gender and sex has profound political consequences. In essence, social structures like heterosexism or patriarchy can be reimagined as regulatory 'fictions' maintained by millions of intersecting performances, capable of disruption. Butler shows this by describing how the parody of cultural conventions through *excessive* performances such as that of the ultra-masculine 'gay skinhead', the male drag artist or the feminine 'lipstick lesbian' offers a challenge to dominant heterosexual norms. The sight of two apparently 'macho' men kissing or holding hands thus disturbs assumptions about what is normal, exposing what Butler describes as the 'fiction' of compulsory heterosexuality (see also Grosz, 1992, 1994). Again, context is all important here, with these parodies having different effects dependent on the type of societies (and spaces) where they occur (McDowell, 1999). For example, Bell *et al.* (1994) have used Butler's work to explore how particular 'queer' performances in public spaces might challenge notions of citizenship based around heterosexual, family norms. This suggests that certain performances of the body disrupt not only masculine and feminine identities, but reclaim space for dissident groups like gays and lesbians. Likewise, Lisa Law's (1997) analysis of the performances of femininity embodied by female Philippine sex workers emphasizes that the adoption of 'Western' clothes, make-up and mannerisms may serve to resist the voyeuristic gaze of Western tourists and disrupt the idea that sex work is based on masculine power and feminine lack. Challenging Western fantasies of subservient and untainted Oriental sexuality, this allows the sex workers to negotiate spatially specific relationships with clients that are negotiated on the sex worker's own terms.

Here, it is evident that geographers are thinking about the body not simply as a site of knowledge/power, but also a site of resistance, a fleshy corporeality that may exert a stubborn recalcitrance and always provides the possibility of a counter-strategic inscription (Grosz, 1992). In effect, bodies are used to act out roles in various settings which conform or resist wider expectations (and perhaps do both at the same time). Such insights on performativity and embodiment should encourage us all to think about the way that we use our body, dieting, working out, picking, pruning, squeezing and decorating it to conform to or challenge some idealized view of an appropriate masculinity or femininity (Butler, 1990a). Returning to our earlier discussion of bodies, rest and move-ment, we might also think about the way we are encouraged to walk, stride, throw, move, sit, run and dance in accordance with gender norms (Young, 1990). This suggests that the gendered body is a complex site whose 'micro-geography' is the result of social, political and cultural inscription. Radcliffe (1999, p. 216) develops this argument in her examination of Ecuadorian concepts of the body, emphasizing that it is possible to extend feminist/queer theories of corporeality into a consideration of the way bodies are simul-taneously gendered, classed and racialized.

4.6   OTHERING THE BODY

As noted in Chapter 3, a growth area in human geography is the study of how power is articulated through *geographies of exclusion*. Seen as 'out of place' in particular spaces, the exclusion of certain people from some landscapes has been a widely observed phenomenon, evident at a variety of scales. One important aspect of research interrogating exclusionary processes has been to explore how bodies are implicated in this process, becoming, in effect, sites of Othering. In this manner, bodies are considered as marking off differences between Self and Other in ways that perpetuate distinctions between valued landscapes and 'places on the margin' (Shields, 1991). It is the way that feelings of revulsion attach to particular bodies, labelling them as Other, that we explore in this section, drawing especially on the work that has developed psycho-analytical theories about the relationship between self and society which is mediated through the psyche (e.g., Lukinbeal and Aitken, 1998; Nast, 1998; Pile, 1996; Sibley, 1995).

Most psychoanalytical accounts can in fact be traced back to the work of Sigmund Freud (1856–1939), who developed techniques designed to reveal fears and desires that reside in the unconscious mind. Later critized for his tendency to generalize on the basis of particular patients and case histories, his interpret-ations largely focused upon the formative years of socialization where (he argued) fundamental distinctions of self and other were developed by the infant. Identifying the tensions implicit in this process of child socialization, and the profound rupture that occurs when the infant realizes it is separate from its primary carer (in his account, the mother), Freud essentially developed a theory of socialization that suggested people suffer crises of identity if they do not conform with the positions at the heart of the 'Oedipus complex'. This Greek fable was invoked by Freud to suggest that 'natural' desire for the mother on behalf of the male child is seen to be repressed via an Oedipal castration complex, to be displaced onto a mother-substitute. At the same time, he suggested that the 'lack' of the female child is seen to be resolved only through the displacement of desire from mother to father, and hence to a father-substitute. Here, sexuality and infancy are the main ingredients of a theory of behaviour that took the unconscious mind to be the source of action (Ferrell, 1996).

For Freud, the normalization of identities like mother, father, son and daughter was deemed to be 'manufactured' by repressive socialization processes, with the desire for conjugal fidelity and the rearing of children deemed a predictable response to the forms of socialization that develop, and subsequently repress, infantile sexuality. Freudian psychoanalysis therefore offers a theory of how people form their own subjectivity, offering a reassuring and therapeutic account for those who are undergoing crises of identity. In essence, it tells us why we tend to conform with sexual and gender positions we do not always understand or identify with: the unconscious mind does not obey the laws of the rational mind, having an energy and drive of its own. Similarly, it describes why we do not always act upon our desires (particularly sexual ones) and why we repress certain feelings. However, Freudian psychoanalysis has been critiqued for its implicit sexism (the mother is regarded as responsible for childcare) and its insistence that sexual gratification is the basis of all desire. Moreover, his vague use of terms such as 'transference' and 'displacement' means that Freud's theory of the psyche remains elusive at times.

Conversely, Lacan famously extended and developed psychoanalytical ideas around a nuanced model of individuation which suggests the unconscious is structured like language. Focusing on the role of signifiers (see Chapter 5) in determining human desire, Lacan proposed that the notion of human subjectivity is illusory, and that the desire for completeness and self-identity drives people to seek identification with certain people and things in the world outside the self. This search for identity begins in what Lacan termed the Mirror stage, when an infant first conceives of itself as a self, and recognizes its separation from the world (as well as its mother). Seeking to resolve its lack, the infant reaches back into the Imaginary stage (that precedes the Mirror stage) and seeks identification with a mother-figure. Yet with the beginning of the Oedipal stage, and the entry of the 'Law of the Father', the subject becomes a body in pieces, separated from its fantasies and continually projecting itself into a world to find signifiers that resolve its sense of incompleteness. Here, the lack (of being) indicated in the Oedipal surrender of the first love object results in a constant oscillation between Real and Imaginary desire as the subject seeks to follow the symbolic imperative of the phallus. Given that no one possesses the phallus, every man is (symbolically) castrated; both the masculine and feminine are joined, oppressed by the Law of the Father (Ferrell, 1996). In this way, Lacanian psychoanalysis transfers the basis of sexual identity from the biological to the order of the Symbolic, the realm of Law and logic (Blum and Nast, 1996).

Given people's constant search for identity (i.e., their pursuit of selfhood and individuation), both Lacan's articulation of the fantasies of sexual difference (as symbolized in the phallus) and Freud's conception of libido have proved invaluable for explaining the basis of contemporary desires. However, as Rose (1993) argues, the negotiation of the self, and its complex amalgam of desire, anxiety, aggression, guilt and love, take place within and through the material and symbolic geographies of everyday life, with the psyche employing strategies to sustain its structure and relationship with the world (see also Lewis and Pile, 1996; Sommers, 1998; Davidson, 2000). Such ideas are more fully developed in packages of psychoanalytical thought that (arguably) pay more attention to social relations than the individualistic accounts offered by Freud and Lacan (du Gay, 2000). For example, the object-relations framework proposed by Melanie Klein, Julie Kristeva and Derek Winnicott suggests that the psyche is inherently social, being shaped by the political, cultural and environmental contexts in which people develop. Drives to repress particular sensations, or to seek identification with certain signifiers, are seen here as socially constructed, inculcated in infancy but subject to major variation across time and space. Drawing on such psychoanalytical theories about the importance of preserving self-identity (literally, the boundaries of the self) **David Sibley** (Box 4.5) has consequently argued that the urge to exclude 'threatening others' from one's proximity is connected to unconscious desires to maintain cleanliness and purity. These desires are depicted as the product of socialization, with the definition of what is *abject* and needs to be repressed being created through discourse, representations and practices that tell us what threatens our sense of identity. Drawing on Kristeva's (1982) influential *Powers of Horror*, and citing Douglas's (1966, p. 41) argument that 'dirt is matter out of place', Sibley has explored the ways in which this abject fear of the self being defiled or polluted is projected (or mapped) onto specific individuals or groups who are depicted as deviant or dangerous. These groups are largely defined by their bodily

---

Box 4.5 David Sibley (1940–   )

David Sibley, a Professor of Human Geography at the University of Hull, UK, has been researching the socio-spatial processes of exclusion for over two decades, with a particular interest in the marginalization of nomadic minorities, especially Gypsies. Having established a reputation for provocative and radical writing, for the past several years he has been a key proponent of the adoption of psychoanalytical ideas within geography. In particular, his book, *Geographies of Exclusion*, has been highly influential. In this text, Sibley develops the psychoanalytical work of Melanie Klein and Julia Kristeva to provide an account of the ways in which spaces are regulated against Others. Here, he uses Klein's conception of the border between Self and Other as a social and cultural process and Kristeva's concept of abjection (of defending the boundaries of the inner body against 'pollutants') to explore the idea of who 'belongs' in a space. In short, he argues that individuals seek to define and maintain a boundary between 'good' and 'bad' based on cultural appearance (e.g., disabled, black, female) or body codings (such as dress, style and so on).

David Sibley has thus developed one of the more convincing geographic interpretations of psychoanalytical ideas, arguing that *spatial* exclusion has been the dominant process used to create *social* boundaries in Western society. Exclusion becomes imagined as the key means by which hegemonic groups (normally white, middle-class and heterosexual) have been able to marginalize and control those who do not match their ideas of what is an acceptable way of living or behaving. Bad objects, and bad bodies, are distanced from these groups through processes designed to purify or sanitize; miscreants are cast out into the wilderness, nomads forced to occupy marginal sites, prostitutes obliged to work in liminal times and places, ethnic minorities described as illegal aliens and repatriated. This process of exclusion is also obviously manifest in the incarceration of bodies in institutional spaces (see Section 4.3). While these sites (madhouses, hospitals and asylums) have been designed to treat sick and ill bodies, it is also apparent that their location mirrors society's attitudes towards these groups. In most cases, those occupying these sites are both 'out of sight and out of mind', being physically and psychically distanced from mainstream society (Gleeson, 1998).

This exclusionary urge is also manifest in Nimbyism (the 'not-in-my-backyard' syndrome). This has traditionally been explained as a reaction to the perceived *negative externalities* (particularly environmental and aesthetic pollution) which might be caused by such developments, and the negative impact this might have on local property prices (Holloway and Hubbard, 2001). Such economic impacts are, to some extent, quantifiable; what is less measurable is the extent to which the Nimby syndrome can be taken as evidence for a more complex mixture of anxieties about populations regarded as Other. In this regard, geographers and others are doing much to question whether the opposition to groups such as foreign migrants or community homes for disabled people can be explained purely in economic terms. They suggest instead that opposition to these groups is founded on a unconscious fear of defilement. As

representations of people. Here, *spatial* exclusion and purification is a process which relies on the representation of certain groups as having bodies which are inferior to the imagined norm – they are dirty, diseased, smelly, impure and polluting. In moral panics about Other groups (e.g., travellers, the homeless, asylum seekers or prostitutes), he suggests that stereotyped and repetitive images are mobilized to depict them as a threat to the body of the nation. This prompts urges to create or repair boundaries, bequeathing social-spatial orders (and state policies) that marginalize particular groups. As such, he argues that understanding why people seek to exclude Others and purify what they see as 'their' space requires a careful examination of the 'placing' of anxieties.

Further reading: Sibley (1995, 2001)

such, to understand community opposition to these groups – those with different bodies – one must uncover the processes encouraging the maintenance of
both psychic and physical boundaries. An example of this is provided by Wilton
(1998), who draws on the work of both Freud and Kristeva to theorize the
community opposition in Los Angeles to community care facilities and welfare
services for the mentally ill, physically disabled people and people with AIDS.
He documents that, although many of the objectors to new facilities in their
area expressed themselves to be tolerant, sympathetic and accepting towards
disabled people in general, they nevertheless opposed these facilities, expressing
anxiety in public meetings, and characterizing the intended users as 'outsiders'.
Developing Freud's notion of the *uncanny* he suggests that those with a disability
are perceived to have incomplete or extraordinary bodies. This inscription of
certain bodies as 'out of the ordinary' is complemented, he suggests, by a desire
for abjection (as proposed by Kristeva); the desire to reject those things which
are part of the body politic, but which generate anxiety. Here, there is a recognition of the permeability of the human body and a fear of bodily boundaries
being transgressed by 'pollutants'. Since the integrity of the psyche is tied to the
body and linked to the world through body image, encountering the disabled
body proposes a threat and incites feelings of discomfort and rejection. Both
Freud and Kristeva argue that the uncanny can be experienced as a collective
phenomenon, with the proximity of difference generating anxiety at a scale
above that individually experienced. As such, the new disabled facilities are not
merely a threat to social order, but a threat to individual and collective identities.

Using this theoretical framework, Wilton explored community opposition to
disabled facilities (see also Dear *et al.*, 1997). While on one level the concern
focused on property values, declining neighbourhood character, a decrease in
safety to children and an increase in traffic and noise, analysis of secondary
sources such as newspaper articles and interviews with professionals revealed
that a discourse of individual and collective identity was also operating. For
example, in relation to an AIDS hospice for 25 people, the hospice director
reported:

> We got a couple of calls from this woman who said that she couldn't walk her
> dog down the street because she can't breathe the 'AIDS air' . . . We had an
> open patio by the hospice . . . we started getting complaints from people
> calling by; they didn't want to see these people with AIDS, these sick people.
> (cited in Wilton, 1998, p. 180)

Wilton argues that the spatial proximity of the hospice threatened (vulnerable)
people's sense of identity and that these people's feelings can be 'conceptualized
as emerging from confrontations with the uncanny or abject (in this case, the
hospice and its residents)'. In other words, the sense of purified self relies on
stereotypes of a diseased Other (i.e., people with AIDS) possessing bodies that
bring the threat of death close. Here, processes of exclusion are expressed
through an 'irrational' fear of contagion. In reacting to these fears the local
authority brought in new rules that morgue ambulances were not allowed to

stop outside homes (they had to go into an underground car park) and that all patients could not walk unaccompanied in local streets. In other words, they sought visually to remove the perceived threat so that residents no longer felt threatened by presence of AIDS in their community. The stigmatized body of people living with HIV, through collective representation and experience, thus becomes an object of disgust for many, resulting in the centrifugal forces that create geographies of exclusion (see also Watney, 1994).

4.7 CONCLUSION

In this chapter we have examined the varying ways in which the body has been theorized and empirically examined by geographers. Moving from conceptualizations of the body that see it as a collection of flesh, organs and bone controlled by an autonomous mind through to those that focus on its social inscription and (fractured) performance, we have illustrated the diverse ways in which the body has been incorporated into geographical scholarship. An implicit argument has been that there is a need to produce geographies that are embodied, and that a truly *human* geography needs to recognize the role of the body in shaping socio-spatial relations. But of course such an argument needs to be mindful of the tensions evident between different theories, which are by no means always compatible. Ultimately, perhaps, the notion of the body that a particular geographer works with will be informed by his/her own positionality, and indeed, own embodiment. The ability of the discipline to reflect on the way it constructs knowledge is therefore crucial for encouraging new perspectives and new takes on the body as geographers question their own 'being in the world'. After all, as we said at the beginning of this chapter, we all possess a body, and our understanding of our own body will impinge on the way that we theorize (and represent) other bodies.

Chapter 5   Geographies of Text

5.1 THE MEANING OF TEXT

As with many other terms enjoying widespread use among geographers, 'text' is one that has multiple and shifting meanings. In its 'everyday' sense, it refers simply to printed artefacts and sources that are written and read, though it is increasingly used to describe the much wider range of cultural products that communicate ideas across society (Rose, 2000). A disparate range of artefacts may then be referred to as texts, including books, comics and poems, but also music, television, painting, film and photography. From this, it should be immediately obvious that thinking about texts and textuality necessitates questioning traditional understandings of how ideas are circulated by the written word to think about the ability of a wide range of objects and practices to create meaning. None the less, a crucial idea underpinning all academic analyses of text is that communication relies on the existence of language in its written, spoken and metaphorical forms. To put this another way, it seems that the communication of ideas between different individuals and groups relies upon the existence of texts which convey meaning through specific combinations of words, sounds and images which may mean things in particular social and cultural contexts (but not others). To understand the meanings of texts, therefore, is to be able to decode their meaning in relation to conventions of language which can be spoken as stories, written, played, sung, filmed, painted and so on. Such concerns lie at the heart of cultural and literary studies, an expanding field of research that in itself has drawn on a diverse and sometimes bewildering range of theories to make sense of text (M. Smith, 2000).

Before we consider how geographers have engaged with these ideas about communication, it is necessary to understand why they have deemed it important to do so. Human geographers have always interpreted texts of different types to make sense of the relationships between people and place. For example, archival documents, diaries and reports may all be important for geographers seeking to document changing patterns of human activity, be they migratory movements, patterns of land use or shopping habits. But here, the extraction of quantitative or qualitative data from texts has generally proceeded in a relatively straightforward manner, whereby texts have been assumed to reveal the 'truth' of the world (i.e., they are *mimetic*). As such, the major concern for geographers using such sources has been that they are authentic (correctly attributed) and credible (that the writers believed what they were writing). If these can be confirmed, the researcher can be confident that the text is both a *valid* and *reliable* source of apparently accurate evidence (Kitchin and Tate, 2000). Accordingly, it is possible to identify certain written sources widely regarded as accurate and reliable, including surveys and censuses published by the state. In Britain, for example, there is a rich diversity of surveys and statistics published annually by the government on many facets of economic and social life. The fact that many of these are published on a number of spatial scales means they have lent themselves to geographical analysis and mapping.

While the use of official statistics, reports and documents as *secondary* sources of data (as opposed to the primary data constructed by the researcher) has been an important part of various geographical traditions (particularly those rooted in positivism), major questions have recently been raised about the veracity and usefulness of these texts as sources of factual information. For example, following the arguments of Foucault about the imbrication of knowledge and power (see Chapter 3), the creation of state archives and statistics has been identified as a primary means by which society is governed and disciplined (Robinson, 2000). Rather than simply collecting social 'facts', the state is thus implicated in a process of *producing* social knowledge that serves to normalize certain behaviours while making others seem anomalous (and undesirable). For some, this implies that 'official' sources manipulate the 'truth' to ideological ends, and cannot be relied on as an accurate mirror of social reality (May, 1997). Indeed, this means that official sources are largely discredited in some areas of research, to the extent that the reliability of crime figures has been brought into question by those studying geographies of crime (Lowman, 1992), and unemployment figures are treated with suspicion by economic geographers (see Green *et al.*, 1994).

But if texts are now rarely 'read' by geographers as sources of accurate information, this does not mean that they have been pushed to the margins of geographical enquiry. In fact, the opposite appears true, with geography's 'cultural turn' (see Chapter 3) encouraging increasing numbers of geographers to consider texts not merely as sources of information about the world but as objects of study in themselves. As we shall see, this has involved the analysis of both 'factual' and 'fictional' texts, with the line between them becoming increasingly blurred. For many, this distinction has become redundant, with both being seen as providing the 'maps of meaning' which people use for navigating the contemporary world (Jackson, 1989). When subject to critical interpretation, texts of all kinds begin to reveal partial, simplified and distorted representations of people and place, often shot through with notions that serve to reproduce social inequality. Given that many of these texts are produced in the powerful heartlands of the urban West, it is perhaps not surprising that texts often communicate dominant white, male visions of the world, marginalizing a whole range of 'other' groups. But at the same time, subaltern groups may create their own texts, subverting these dominant visions. For some geographers, texts therefore form the basis of a symbolic system of representation which lies at the apex of complex socio-spatial processes characterized by conflict and instability. As Gregory (1997, p. 73) puts it: 'Representation . . . is always a struggle – a conditional achievement – and those conditions (and consequences) mean that representation is always implicated in the play of power'.

In many senses, recent geographical interest in the textual can be interpreted as a belated response to the 'linguistic turn' in twentieth-century social theory. This is a term designating the trend for theorists to take language and linguistic representation as defining the ontological and epistemological basis (and limits) of their work. The implication here is that language does not simply reflect the real world, but constitutes it (i.e., there is no reality other than that which can be represented through, and by, language). Hence, many writers have rejected the assertion that language provides an obstacle to the development of theory, and instead have embraced the linguistic, seeing it as exemplary of the core aspects of social life. In many structural (Marxist) accounts, for example, society has been seen to be structured like a language, with language itself described as a structure which is reproduced as individuals draw on the rules of language in daily life (see Lévi-Strauss, 1969, on the 'deep grammar' of social myths and rituals). Accordingly, in the work of the Frankfurt School (see Chapter 2), notions of subjectivity were replaced with a notion of intersubjectivity in which 'world-constituting capacities are transferred from transcendental subjectivity to grammatical structures' (Habermas, 1988, p. 15). In other words, language (and the wider cultural industry) was deemed to be an instrument of oppression, necessitating a shift in the focus of critical theory from the economism of earlier Marxist traditions to an approach that considered the role of culture in relations of power – as superstructure to a materialist base (see especially Adorno and Horkheimer, 1972). In the work of other members of the Frankfurt School, this concern with language was to manifest itself in an experimental search for representations free from domination and ideological imprint (see especially Benjamin, 1955).

This chapter thus seeks to explore how geographers have engaged with some of these ideas about language, culture and power, considering how texts have been used by geographers to elucidate the recursive (two-way) relationship between society and space. More generally, it seeks to identify how geographers have drawn upon different intellectual traditions, methods and theories to think about the geographies of text. At the same time that it surveys these different ways of thinking about texts and textuality, it will seek to question the limits of text, particularly the distinction made between representational spaces and the spaces of the 'real' world. For this reason, the chapter begins with the traditional (though very limited conception) of what a text is – a written artefact. This is followed by a consideration of the moving image, discussing how geographers have explored the multiple geographies narrated in television, film and video. Finally, the chapter examines the arguments of those who have argued that the geographical landscape itself is a text, one that may be read to reveal its social production. Throughout, the chapter will consider how particular understandings of culture have informed the analysis of text, and how the slippery nature of language has ultimately challenged geographers' ability to identify single, fixed meanings of text.

5.2 GEOGRAPHIES OF LANGUAGE AND LITERATURE

Novels, poems and drama, often described as 'high' cultural forms (as distinct from the 'low' writing found in comics, magazines, fanzines or song lyrics), have long been examined in the social sciences and humanities. Written by those ostensibly skilled in the use and manipulation of language, these texts frequently offer deeply evocative accounts of life in particular times and places. Because of this, they offer rich pickings for geographers interested in examining the character of certain regions, particularly when the novel concerns people and places otherwise inaccessible to the researcher. Some authors have consequently been fêted by historical geographers because of their ability to weave beguiling and vivid 'word-pictures' of life in the past. Notable examples here might include Charles Dickens, whose novels serve to map out the geographies of Victorian London, and Thomas Hardy, whose works perform an equivalent task with respect to nineteenth-century rural Dorset (Barrell, 1982; Darby, 1948; Donald, 1999). Far from occurring in a blank landscape, the stories written by these authors are played out in 'real' landscapes whose physical forms, topography and appearance are made legible through a thoroughly spatialized language. In many of Dickens's books, for example, the plot unfolds in a landscape that is thickly described as one of danger and dread, with the fog of the capital enshrouding malodorous characters. Hardy's Wessex, meanwhile, is narrated as a green and pleasant landscape riven by seething class conflicts, its idyllic qualities the flip side of the human labour needed to work the land.

Brosseau (1994) suggests that such 'great' novels have often been taken by geographers as useful in mapping out the specific relationships that existed between people and place in a particular region. In many instances, these works claim credibility because the authors concerned were very familiar with the milieu of which they wrote. For historical geographers, therefore, novels such as *Tess of the d'Ubervilles* or *The Mayor of Casterbridge* give a better idea of what life in rural Dorset was like than do any number of census reports or documents (even allowing for the fact that Hardy replaced the place names of many Dorset towns with obscure pseudonyms!). Likewise, one can see that many contemporary novels offer topologically detailed accounts of life in specific towns or regions, and that these may capture many facets of everyday life that are effaced in academic accounts based on survey or ethnographic work. This is perhaps most obvious in those novels where the setting is emphasized as a significant component of the storyline (rather than an inconsequential backcloth against which the story unfolds). For instance, Tom Wolfe's *The Man in Full*, Bret Easton Ellis's *Less Than Zero* and Jay McInerary's *Brightness Falls* offer rich descriptions of the post-Fordist American metropolis, describing Atlanta, Los Angeles and New York respectively. Likewise, those seeking descriptions of life in contemporary London can dip into works by diverse writers including Martin Amis, Zadie

Smith, Hanif Kureishi, Nick Hornby, Geoff Nicholson, Michael Moorcock or Helen Fielding. Such novels are valuable not only because they offer detailed descriptions of individual buildings, neighbourhoods and locales, but because they also locate particular social groups and individuals in these spaces, mapping out the fractures of social class, race, gender, age and sexuality which characterize city life (for interesting accounts of literary London, and other cities, see Preston and Simpson-Housley, 1994).

Yet to regard simply novels as a source of factual geographical information clearly ignores the way authors imbue the places they describe with imaginative characteristics. As Pocock (1981b, p. 11) argues, the 'truth of fiction is a truth beyond mere facts' as 'fictive reality may contain more truth than everyday reality'. Underpinning this seemingly nonsensical statement is the idea that novels succeed in conveying and communicating the 'sense of place' that is immanent in given locations better than actually being in that location could. This idea relies on the fact that literature evokes the experience of being in place eloquently, with the intensely personal and deeply descriptive language used by the writer able to convey the elusive *genius loci* inherent in a place. Creative writing has certainly enabled many authors to express the reasons why places are special to them. The intention has often been to evoke in the reader a sense of place about somewhere they have not been or cannot ever physically go to (where, for example, the place is fictional, or set in a historical context). Accordingly, the analysis of literary texts to reveal the strong subjective meanings with which people imbue their surroundings forms a major tradition in humanistic geography.

As we saw in Chapter 2, humanistic theories about subjectivity, meaning and experience subtly shift the focus of geography from space to place. Such ideas reject a *mimetic* reading of text, where novels simply mirror the physical and social truths of a landscape, to posit a much more intricate notion of the written text, where the real and imagined collapse in a description that *refracts* the true human significance of particular places. Humanistic geography draws on ideas in the humanities about the study of literature, where scholars have developed ideas of *hermeneutics* in their attempt to understand how writers invest their text with their own personality and world-view (Atkinson, 1990). Understanding that authors write in a sometimes idiosyncratic manner, hermeneutics (literally, the 'art of interpretation') suggests that a text can be correctly and fully interpreted only if we understand what was in the author's mind as he or she wrote, questioning our own positionality in the process. The emphasis here is as much on excavating the world-view of the author (i.e., his/her background, development and state of mind) as it is on examining the language that is used. One formative influence here is Martin Heidegger's work, particularly the phenomenological ideas explored in *Being and Time* (1927). For Heidegger, words in texts are seen to show something beyond themselves – namely the lifeworld of the author – and need to be read in relation to the author's attitudes and practices. While hermeneutics stresses the essential connectedness of author and text, the impossibility of understanding either fully is also acknowledged. Hence, it is possible to talk of a hermeneutic circle, a continual reciprocity between text and reader, whereby we need to question continually our own presuppositions about the text as we seek to decode its meanings. These ideas are far from straightforward and, in Heidegger's account, are elaborated in a framework that emphasizes the difficulties that we have reflecting on our own being in the world (captured in his notion of *Dasein*). None the less, engagement with these ideas across the social sciences raised fundamental questions about how text should be interpreted, disturbing notions that texts contain truths that can be elicited through fixed methods.

Though Wright (1947) and Lowenthal (1961) were among the first geographers to suggest that novels could reveal human empathy with the environment, such ideas concerning the subjectivity inherent in the production and interpretation of text came to the forefront of the discipline with the rise of interest in humanistic packages of thought (particularly phenomenology and existentialism). Giving human agency primacy in the analysis of text, humanistic geographers such as Donald Meinig (1983), Anne Buttimer (1976), Douglas Pocock (1981a and b) and Yi-Fu Tuan (see Box 2.3) examined texts as resources that reveal the intricacies of human interaction with the environment. Generally, their studies focused on particular authors or texts, avoiding generalization in favour of specificity, though collectively they demonstrated that the world consists of a mosaic of special places whose uniqueness can only be understood from the perspective of the individuals who give them meaning. For example, Yi-Fu Tuan examined texts to explore the affective links between people and place (summed up in his concept of *topophilia*). In turn, he recognized that this was a highly personal and subjective endeavour, claiming that 'to know the environment is to know one's self' (Tuan, 1974). Likewise, Pocock's (1981a and b) attempts at developing a subject-centred human geography entailed interrogating fictional accounts of place. Recognizing literature's potential to transpose intangible human feelings about place into comprehensible forms, he emphasized the way specific novels and poems capture (and communicate) the ambience of particular spaces and regions. Others began to argue that there was much that geographers could learn from novelists in terms of writing style, with the adoption of a literary style seen as an appropriate way of communicating sense of place (Meinig, 1983).

Yet at the same time that geographers' nascent interest in text drew on humanistic philosophies, ideas of hermeneutics were also being taken up by those inspired by more 'critical' theories, particularly the Marxism of the Frankfurt School (see Chapter 2). In part, this uptake represented a critique of humanistic interpretations of text. Specifically, while humanistic geographers' enthusiasm to work with concepts from literary theory opened up new directions for geographical enquiry, the way in which they theorized text was seen as essentially reactionary by some (Sayer and Duncan, 1977). A widespread accusation was that humanistic analyses of literature were essentially nostalgic, using literature to identify a harmonious relationship between people and place which had seemingly been destroyed by progress and modernity. Coupled with this was the complaint that humanistic geography divorced the analysis of text from the way it was consumed and produced in specific social and political contexts, prioritizing agency over structure (Stoddart, 1986). Drawing on the insights of cultural Marxism, alternative modes of analysing text began to be explored. These acknowledged that texts were implicated in the reproduction of society, positing a recursive and complex dialectic between human agency and structure mediated through texts. Dismissing the idea that structures such as capitalism existed prior to the realization of social relations, this emphasized the *materiality* of text, particularly its role in altering people's consciousness (M. Smith, 2000).

This materialist conception of culture was one that was developed by the forerunners of cultural and media studies – Antonio Gramsci, Richard Hoggart and various members of the Birmingham School for Contemporary Cultural Studies being important influences. In different ways, each of these developed radical ideas about the 'work' that cultural texts perform in legitimating social relations, accentuating the need to examine texts in relation to ideological beliefs and structures. In the writing of Antonio Gramsci (see Box 3.3), for example, texts were seen as caught up in the process of hegemony, whereby the ideas of the ruling classes were imposed on other groups through the power of persuasion rather than the power of coercion. Reworking Marx's aphorism that the ruling ideas in any epoch are those of the ruling classes, Gramsci's neo-Marxist perspective alluded to the ideological role of the media in reproducing particular ideas about society (and the way society should be). Hegemony, in his account, represented a struggle for moral, political and intellectual leadership, played out in the mass media as much as in the workplace or market place (M. Smith, 2000). Writing in a very different context, the Welsh cultural analyst and literary critic **Raymond Williams** (Box 5.1) was to prove an important (if maverick) influence in cultural studies, his focus on the materiality of text becoming massively influential in cultural geography.

The ability of texts to impose (and, on occasion, contest) 'common-sense' meanings thus provoked geographers to consider the ideological beliefs sedimented in 'popular' expressions of culture, including advertisements, photo-

---

Box 5.1 Raymond Williams (1921–88)

Cultural critic Raymond Williams is perhaps best remembered for his insistence that culture is ordinary. By this he meant that culture needed to be reconceptualized as representing a whole way of life, rather than being understood solely as a term that described those artefacts and texts considered of economic (and cultural) value. In his own work, this was manifest in seminal examinations of the relation between industrialization and working-class culture, including studies of the formation of Welsh cultural identity. This focus on ordinary cultures (and working-class cultures in particular) was to map out a key trajectory for the subsequent development of media and cultural studies, though Williams's writing in fact encompassed a much wider range of topics, including literary criticism, drama, language and politics. For example, his *Keywords* (1976) provided a highly original overview of some of the most important words and expressions invoked in social and political struggles. For many geographers, however, Williams is best known for his book *The Country and the City* (1973), which explored the textual representation and

graphs, magazines, newspapers and even maps (see, for example, Harley, 1988; Short, 1991). Simultaneously, the adoption of terminology associated with *semiotics* (literally, the 'science of signs') became commonplace in geographical writing on text. Associated both with Charles Pierce and Ferdinand de Saussure, semiotics (or semiology) stresses that the meaning of language is, in effect, arbitrary, lacking constancy until it is given meaning through correspondence with other signs (Berger, 1988). Written language, as a sign, only signifies something when it is 'placed' in relation to other signs. Moreover, it is argued that signification remains specific to a given audience, so that texts are potentially *polysemous* (i.e., may be understood in conflicting ways by different social groups). This implies that the meaning of text is not intrinsic, but is structured through social codes and conventions which encourage certain 'readings' of text (Slater, 1998). In turn, these readings are seen to reproduce certain ideologies, values and philosophies as natural, universal and eternal.

The idea that texts contain signifiers that send particular ideologically charged messages to different social and cultural groups was accordingly influential to those geographers seeking a more rigorous methodological and theoretical framework for the interpretation of text – Burgess and Gold's (1985) collection brings together a representative sample. Burgess' (1985) own work, for example, illustrates how newspaper reports served to perpetuate racism through the selective and unrepresentative reporting of inner-city riots. In her account, the way that the text (and associated photography) encoded the story of the riots for its readers was indicative of the ability of a text to render an essentially biased and selective interpretation as 'common sense'. In the case of the rioting, this involved a consideration of the ability of the text to classify groups and individuals along racial lines, stereotyping non-white communities as inherently criminalized (see also Anderson, 1988; Wall, 1997). Here, the exclusions and narrative silences in the text are as important as what is included, with the selective and partial representation of people and place deemed a crucial means by which social inequality has been perpetuated (and justified); as

construction of urbanism and rurality. This represented a critical intervention in a long line of sociological writing about the distinction between town and country (including the work of Durkheim, Tonnies and Simmel) by stressing that this distinction was intimately connected to issues of power (and the class relations played out in town and country). Perhaps unsurprisingly, Williams' work was frequently cited by those seeking to sketch out the contours of a new cultural geography in the 1980s and 1990s (see especially Jackson, 1989, and Shields, 1991), and while his writing remained wedded to historical materialism, it remains influential for those geographers endeavouring to understand how culture acts as a signifying system through which social systems are communicated, reproduced, experienced and explored (see Mitchell, 1995).

Further reading: Williams (1973); Higgins (1999)

cultural theorist Stuart Hall (1990, p. 156) argued, 'whoever controls information about society is, to a greater or lesser extent, able to exert power in that reality'.

While a focus on newspaper and media reporting may imply something of a division between humanistic exploration of 'fictional' novels and materialist explorations of 'factual' media, the two became entwined within a reformulated cultural geography. Recognizing that both imaginative fiction and seemingly factual reportage have the ability to shape the cultural politics of everyday life, a trio of explorations into 'new' cultural geographies (i.e., Anderson and Gale, 1992; Barnes and Duncan, 1992; Duncan and Ley, 1993) began to spell out the importance of exploring the *discourses* immanent in a wide variety of written (and spoken) texts. Defining discourses as 'frameworks that embrace particular combinations of narratives, concepts, ideologies and signifying practices relevant to a particular realm of social action' (Barnes and Duncan, 1992, p. 12), the focus became the meanings that are transmitted and reported through different domains and texts. This implied that there may be varying representations of people or places circulating in different texts, but that, collectively, the embedding of discourses in social life serves to constitute these people and places (Holloway and Hubbard, 2001). Again, Michel Foucault's ideas on knowledge/power were an important influence (see Chapter 3). In his analysis, social meanings are not created by individuals (or structures) but by discourses. Disrupting any straightforward separation of text and a 'prediscursive' real world, Foucault's ideas of developing a critical genealogy of knowledge became widely (though not uncritically) adopted by geographers seeking to expose the importance of text in shaping the contours of everyday life (see Matless, 1992; Philo, 2000a).

In short, Foucault's ideas offered a fundamental challenge for those geographers who imagined that places (and people) have a real or essential existence outside the realms of language, encouraging a focus on the relations of discourse, knowledge and space (Barnes and Gregory, 1996). Here, it becomes important to distinguish between methods of *content analysis* (which considers the surface or manifest content of text) and *discourse analysis* (a way of analysing texts that thinks about content in relation to its effects). Focusing on the representation of place in a novel may well be interesting, but what has become more interesting for geographers is thinking about the role that that representation plays in creating social and cultural identities (Pile and Thrift, 1995). From this poststructuralist perspective, questions of what is true and false in a text are irrelevant; instead the focus is on the ability of the text to create reality through the 'invention' and documentation of difference. An example here is the invention of 'the disabled' as a distinct social category through discourses and representations which are historically and geographically contingent (so that, for example, understandings as to who is disabled, and why, have varied over time – see Chapter 4). Hence, through rhetorical strategies such as the construction of binary oppositions that ground meaning (e.g., disabled/abled, intelligent/stupid, black/white, culture/nature, urban/rural, male/female and so on), discourse creates socio-spatial identities which are conceived of in binary terms (so that, for example, ability can only be understood in relation to its inferior other, disability, or whiteness in relation to blackness).

Within a cultural geography that emphasizes theoretical diversity, fluidity and flux, this focus on discourse has seen geographers grappling with post-structuralist ideas about the construction of society, considering the active work that text and image performs in constituting the people and places that it apparently only describes (Sharp, 1996; Rose, 1997; Jones and Natter, 1999). Crucial here is Derrida's notion of *différance* (see Box 3.7), a term capturing the sense of difference inevitably written into any text (including, as Barnes, 1996, points out, geographical texts and representations):

> The sign represents the present in its absence. It takes the place of the present. We cannot grasp or show the thing, state the present, the being-present, when the present cannot be presented, we signify, we go through the detour of the sign. We take or give signs. We signal. The sign, in this sense, is a deferred presence . . . According to this classical semiology, the substitution of the sign for the thing itself is both secondary and provisional: secondary due to an original and lost presence from which the sign thus derives; provisional as concerns this final and missing presence. (Derrida, 1991, p. 60)

Elucidating the relations of difference internal to language and other cultural codes, Derrida has expanded upon these ideas at length, suggesting that things take their identity only from that which they are not. Such differential identities are also inherently unstable, so that, for example, the identity of the civilized, white European is haunted by the presence of the black and Oriental against which it defines itself (see Gregory, 1994a).

While such post-structural understandings of text have not entirely replaced materialist or humanistic readings (nor the use of semiotic frameworks of analysis), they have undeniably ushered in a new language of 'deconstruction' and 'destabilization' (Laurier, 1999). Simultaneously, they have encouraged geographers to extend the textual metaphor to encompass a wide range of cultural representations. For some, this is stretching the textual metaphor too far, neglecting issues of materiality in favour of a focus on a representation that is insubstantial and, perhaps, unreal:

> If all culture, and all the world, becomes a matter for representation, then we may lose purchase on the differences of material substance, whether that material is concrete, earth, paper, celluloid, and similarly, the power of the textual metaphor may be lost through over-extension. (Matless, 2000, p. 335)

None the less, recent work on music (Leyshon *et al.*, 1998), photography (Kinsman, 1995), public art (Hall, 1997) and websites and the Internet (Crang *et al.*, 1999) indicates that the textual metaphor currently enjoys wide currency among geographers, being employed to study all manner of 'new material'. In the next section, we therefore explore some of the potentials and pitfalls of extending the textual metaphor to different media, focusing on geographical interpretations of the moving image. As we shall see, geographical studies of film and television are engaging keenly with post-structural ideas about the instability of meaning, but, at times, this exposes the limits of the 'linguistic' and 'cultural turn'.

5.3 THE SPACES OF THE SCREEN

While geographers' engagement with 'writing worlds' has a lengthy precedent, the consideration of the representation of place via the moving image has a more recent pedigree. This is surprising given the contemporary ubiquity of cinema-going, video-renting and television-watching, not to mention the ease with which some can now access moving images via DVD, CD-ROM and Internet technologies. Collectively, such media appear massively important in shaping understandings of everyday life; television is watched more than five hours per day by 40 per cent of British adults, and cinema-going remains among one of the most popular leisure activities in the Western nations (Hubbard, 2002). Yet among geographers, academic snobbery appears to have discouraged examination of these popular media, with cultural geographers attracting accusations of elitism for their preoccupation with 'high' culture such as literature and fine art (see Thrift, 1999). Fighting this elitism, Aitken (1997) makes an effective case for 'couch-potato geography' by stressing that movies tell us something about the surfaces and mysteries of life. In his estimation, moving images are able to communicate senses of space, time and movement in a way that static, printed media are not. In this manner, he argues they are better able to capture the distinctive sense of place that adheres to specific settings (see also Higson, 1987). At the same time, he draws attention to the way filmic images narrate compelling stories about social space, potentially influencing the thought and action of the watching public.

Treating moving images as 'texts' which can be read and interpreted, a growing number of geographers have recently explored the ability of film and television to act as a repository of place meanings, examining the way certain cities or regions have been depicted. Examples here include Benton's (1995) analysis of the representation of Los Angeles in films like *Boyz 'n the Hood* and *Grand Canyon*, Aitken's (1991) consideration of the people-place transactions mapped out in the films of Scottish director Bill Forsyth, and Burgess's (1982) influential work on the representation of the Cambridgeshire fens through film and television documentary. The theoretical influences in this work are extremely varied (taking in humanism, behaviouralism and structuralism), though a common preoccupation is with the way that film-makers or television producers use particular settings to evoke particular feelings or moods. While it is self-evident that all films and television programmes have a geographical setting (even if this is simply a designer's set in a studio), these are fundamentally important in shaping audience responses. One obvious example of this is the way that soap operas gain credibility by being set in believable and 'realistic' settings (such as the British 'kitchen sink' soap opera *Eastenders*, which embeds its plots and characters in a familiar, if stereotyped, working-class district of London). In other cases, a contrast between setting and the behaviour of the actors can be used to comic effect, as noted in films like *Crocodile Dundee* or *Coming to America*, where an outsider's inability to cope with the rituals of city life becomes a source of humour.

Beyond this concern with describing the place images served up by film and television, a wider interest in geographic contexts of production and reception is also apparent. Interpreting moving images as having a source of emission, a channel of transmission and a space of reception (Kneale, 1999), this has highlighted the importance of film and television in circulating ideologically infused images of place to a mass audience. Certainly, improvements in communications technology have magnified the power of media companies, who have extended their global reach to broadcast to an international audience. While it was as recently as 1965 that the first commercial communications satellite (INTELSAT or Early Bird) was launched, today there are over 160 satellites in orbit enabling broadcasting companies to reach many nations still not served by a terrestrial television service (Robins, 1995b). The world's six largest media organizations – Rupert Murdoch's News International, Time Warner, Disney, Bertellsman, TCI and Viacom – all have a global presence, broadcasting to an international audience via their satellite subsidiaries (BSkyB Broadcasting, RTL, Fox Channel, CNN and so on). Accordingly, it is possible to discern a homogenization of global broadcasting, with audiences around the world being fed a remarkably similar diet of television and video (see Myers, 1999). This standardized diet of images has been implicated in the production of new forms of cultural identification, with Appadurai (1990) describing the emergence of a *global mediascape* produced by flows of images and information. In turn, these images serve to valorize (i.e., raise the value of) and promote particular lifestyles and ways of life, showing that cultural politics and political economy are entangled in increasingly dense global connections (see Chapter 8).

In Paul Virilio's (Box 8.1) estimation, the transformation of a modern world shaped by a mass movement of people into a postmodern one shaped by a mass movement of information has been brought about through such media technologies. The result of this, he argues, is that traditional notions of time and space have been destroyed as the world is bought to us via our computers, satellite televisions and video players, creating a 'placeless space' (see also Augé, 1995). Against this, Robins (1995b) is wary of claims that the media is *flattening* senses of space and time, noting that local media and film-makers can resist the deterritorializing tendencies of a Western-dominated media (see Bonnett, 2000a). But even if Virilio's description of the 'degree space zero' created through the global flows of information remains far-fetched, the moving image is certainly implicated in a process where distinctions of near and far are being destroyed, only to be reassembled in new topologies of Self and Other. As such, film, TV and video can be seen as integral to a global capitalist economy which thrives by constantly attaching values to particular people and places, and devaluing others. Shurmer-Smith and Hannam (1994) argue that the popular media are particularly important in the uneven production of space, bound into power relations at a variety of scales. At a international scale, for example, the media may be interpreted as an active agent of global hegemony. In this light, cinema and television may have even more importance than printed texts in creating global hierarchies of East/West, Developed/Developing and Self/ Other (Said, 1990). Certainly, Hollywood film can be regarded as a source of powerful images which legitimate and commodify white, middle-class, suburban ways of life while rendering those elsewhere exotic, alien and Other (something evident in films as diverse as *The Beach, Cast Away, The Last Emperor* or *Raiders of the Lost Ark*). The role of the media in securing intellectual and moral hegemony at a global scale was accordingly particularly pronounced in the twentieth century – the 'American century' – when the Hollywood dream factory offered a particularly seductive and reassuring vision of the virtues of mass consumption (Slater and Taylor, 1999).

Developing ideas about the imbrication of knowledge and power, the ability of moving images to construct identities has also been noted on other spatial scales. One notable example of this is provided in the now voluminous literature on cinematic representations of the city (see Clarke, 1997). Collectively, this suggests that cinematic images of the city are constructed within a complex and changing interplay of power relations, with representations of the city being culturally and historically contingent. None the less, Short (1996) suggests that the city is often filmed as a site of anonymity, crime and vice. In *film noir*, for example, the city becomes a brooding, threatening presence, a place of isolation and fear. Science fiction representations of the future city (e.g., *Metropolis, Things to Come, Alphaville* and *1984*) similarly paint a dystopian image of urban life (see Kitchin and Kneale, 2002), contrasted with the simple and idyllic nature of rural life (as exhibited in Merchant Ivory costume drama). This anti-urban/pro-rural representation is very common, far outweighing the small number of pro-urban films like *LA Story, Manhattan* and *Amélie from Montmartre* or rural horror films such as *The Blair Witch Project* or *The Texas Chain Saw Massacre*. Of course, from a post-structural perspective (see Chapter 3), the ability of any of these

---

Box 5.2 Roland Barthes (1915–80)
Barthes is best known as a literary critic and theorist who developed ideas of semiotics in new directions. Though influenced by Marx, his work cannot be viewed as quintessentially Marxist; rather, he could be described as a semiotician whose analyses of texts sought to expose the way they encoded myths. This idea was first articulated in *Mythologies* (1957), a pioneering but accessible study that identified how text and images communicate myths that structure social life. Therein, Barthes argued that text is bequeathed with the power to shape social attitudes and practices not just through its selectivity (i.e., excluding certain truths or meanings) but by courtesy of the way that it naturalizes various ideologies. The implication here is that the ideology of texts is both visible and invisible at the same time and, as such, Barthes's programme of denaturalizing ideology through the revelation of textual myths can be read as a forerunner of post-structural arguments that emphasize the textual deferment of meaning. In the majority of his early work, Barthes utilized the language of structural semiotics, albeit extending the notion of signifiers to

films to communicate particular ideas or senses of place is not fixed, but can only be understood in relation to other unstable systems of social signification, where signs are sutured to signifiers through the operation of social power (Jones and Natter, 1999). This is evident in (the many) geographic analyses of Ridley Scott's *Blade Runner* (e.g., Bruno, 1987; Harvey, 1989a; Dear, 2000), which suggest that the viewer's ability to read its nightmarish vision of the Los Angeles of 2019 as an extrapolation of current urban processes relies on recognizing its references to other films (e.g., the way it borrows motifs from *film noir*). These analyses suggest that a text cannot have an autonomous meaning, only a series of unstable meanings produced *intertextually* (Rose, 2000).

Working with post-structural notions of intertextuality has alerted geographers to the instability of moving images, and the fact that films may be interpreted differently depending on the (social, cultural, political and economic) positionality of the viewer: films may be viewed simultaneously in a variety of ways (Clarke, 1997; Dear, 2000). Here, a key argument is that it is only possible to interpret films and moving images by exploring the socio-spatial contexts in which they are consumed (see Aitken and Zonn, 1994). So, unlike work on printed media (e.g., Ryan, 1997), where the context of reception appears of less interest (presumably because it can be read anywhere), there has been much interest in theories of *spectatorship* among those exploring geographies of film (Kennedy and Lukinbeal, 1998). Here, ideas about practices of observation are often combined with an exploration of the objects being gazed at to create complex ideas about the pleasures of looking and knowing. Key influences here range from **Roland Barthes**' (Box 5.2) semiotic analyses of film, Crary's (1990) social history of viewing devices, and the psychoanalytical account offered by Mulvey (1989). In the latter, the ability of the camera to pull together a field of vision through its eye is implicated in the creation of gendered subjectivity, the camera's object of focus becoming the spectator's object of desire. Drawing heavily on Lacan (see Chapter 4), this suggests that film is important in helping people to identify or dis-identify with sexualized

include 'signs that did not look like signs' – clothing, entertainment, advertising and film. In *The Fashion System* (1967) this was developed into a notion of social distinction that no longer remained grounded in the realities of social life; the language of fashion was exposed (and attacked) as the basis of fashion itself. At this point, where Barthes began to perceive that nothing remained 'beyond' the text, he started to be less preoccupied with the connotation and meaning of texts and more with the pleasures created by the acts of writing and reading texts. The suggestion here is that texts mean nothing until they are read and given (intertextual) meaning by people. It is this latter theorization of texts as a field in which signifiers and signified can wander that has been particularly influential on post-structural theorists in geography and beyond.

Further reading: Duncan and Duncan (1988); Thody (1999)

figures, perpetuating the visual basis of sexual difference (Rose, 2000). The ability of film to suggest that particular bodies are desirable is one deemed important in structuring understandings of masculine and feminine bodies. In a slightly different manner, Barthes writes of his own narcissistic identification with the figures who are projected on to the cinema screen; part of cinema's power, he argues, is its ability to seduce the viewers, so that they become immersed in the spectacle of film. The lure of cinema and its flicker thus becomes Barthes's metaphor for the image-saturated nature of urban life, whereby we are seduced by the images before us, or else violently reject them.

Collectively, it is difficult to argue that these ideas add up to any coherent theory of spectatorship, though individually they offer some fascinating interpretations of the distinctive way in which people watch and experience film. To date, these have not been backed up by exhaustive empirical investigation; there have been few ethnographies of cinema-going. The reverse is true in relation to television viewing, whose importance in the practices of everyday life has been documented in many studies (e.g., Gauntlett and Hill, 1999; Silverstone, 1994). As opposed to the hypothesized film-spectator, who remains enthralled by the narrative unfolding (and *flicking*) on the cinema screen, the television viewer has been found to be a very different type of spectator. This is a mode of spectatorship which is perhaps described as distracted, centring on the *glance* rather than the gaze (Burgin, 1996). In an average evening's viewing, this means that a person is typically preparing food, reading a magazine or talking on the telephone at the same time that they are 'watching' television. Constantly switching between programmes is also a widespread practice, with individuals 'surfing' channels rather than immersing themselves in the narrative of any particular programme or feature. Furthermore, several studies of television watching have also indicated a complex negotiation of viewing between household members, so that different individuals may be allowed to watch only some (or some of) the programmes they wish (Kneale, 1999).

As yet, few geographic studies of domestic or leisure life have explicitly considered the way that 'watching the box' or 'going to the flicks' is implicated in the contemporary rituals of family and social life. Yet the fact that there appears to be a broad homology between urbanization and the moving image has acted as the impetus for some geographers to document the unfolding geographies of film and television. For instance, Donald (1999) argues that before the advent of mass broadcasting in the early twentieth century, the city was still emerging as a distinctive physical and mental space. For him, the nineteenth-century metropolis was characterized by a bewildering velocity and heterogeneity that needed to be negotiated by the urban dweller. Some coped better than others with this mass movement of people, communication and commerce, with Walter Benjamin (1955) famously suggesting that it was the streetwise *flâneur* (or 'man about town') who was most in tune with the rhythms of the city. The *flâneur* found his place in the city through his wanderings in the labyrinthine spaces of the city (see Rendell, 1998); for the masses, however, it was newspapers that provided the major guide to surviving, exploiting and enjoying the city. But it was cinema that allowed urban dwellers a more complete understanding of the city, as for the first time the moving city could be represented to seated spectators safely ensconced in the cinema auditorium. From this vantage point, they could gaze on the varied sites (and sights) of the city, its pleasures and dangers made legible to them in films that served to map out the city and its underworld. Cinema, in effect, gave everybody the opportunity of becoming a *flâneur*, experiencing the city in motion without leaving a space of leisure which offered amusement and distraction for all but the poorest city dwellers. Importantly, this was a space where women were as welcome as men, this incorporation in the public life of the city allowing them to escape the suburbs (Freidberg, 1993).

With cinema imagined as an essentially urban medium, it is unsurprising that television has often been hypothesized as a suburban form of entertainment and information. Underlining this, Silverstone (1994) suggests that it represents a unique technology, one that brought the public realm into the private, letting suburban dwellers become familiar with the ways of urban life from the comfort of their own home. Accordingly, he notes that television domesticates leisure to an unprecedented degree, simultaneously letting suburban dwellers know and *experience* the city without leaving their own homes. This ability of television to bring near and far into juxtaposition has been noted by several writers (e.g., Adams, 1992; Kneale, 1999), though few sustained geographical analyses of TV have been completed to date. In the context of postmodern theories where representation has fully entered the world of commodity production (Jameson, 1984), an analysis of televisual geographies should be a priority for geographers who wish to understand the postmodern (media) society. After all, as Kennedy and Lukinbeal (1998) stress, in a desensitized society where experiences are not immediately felt but instead are represented, film and television provide our guide to social interaction and to experiences of place. An analysis of how we live *through* television may therefore be an important avenue for future geographic research.

5.4 THEORIZING THE LANDSCAPE

Finally in this chapter, it is necessary to briefly consider the arguments of those who have sought to extend the notion of text to include the landscape itself. The definition of landscape is elusive, however. For some, it denotes a portion of the earth's surface, and is effectively synonymous with its shape and form. For others, it has more specific connotations, encapsulating a particular way of imagining and framing space:

> Landscape is in fact a way of seeing, a way of composing and harmonising the external world into a scene, a visual unity. The word landscape emerged in the Renaissance to denote a new relationship between humans and their environment. At the same time cartography, astronomy, architecture, survey-ing, land surveying, painting and many other arts and sciences were being revolutionised by application of formal mathematical and geometrical rules.

. . . Landscape is thus intimately linked with a new way of seeing the world as rationally-ordered, designed and harmonious. (Cosgrove, 1989, p. 121)

In **Denis Cosgrove**'s (Box 5.3) influential work, landscape implies a particular way of representing the (visible) world through cultural forms (e.g., landscape art, perspective drawings – even photographs from space) that serve to make the environment legible, coherent and pleasing to the viewer. In so doing, his work has drawn on the influence of Marxist cultural theorists and historians like Raymond Williams, John Berger and John Barrell to emphasize this way of seeing as inherently ideological. For instance, both Cosgrove (1984) and Cosgrove and Daniels (1988) explored eighteenth- and nineteenth-century traditions in landscape art, stressing that this mode of representation had close links with changes in land ownership and social relations in the countryside. In essence, such paintings were seen to incorporate an *iconography*, a set of symbols that create certain meanings of place in accordance with the interests of particular class groups. In turn, these symbols expressed a particular relationship between these groups and the landscape, so that the landscape was seen as the outcome of a particular mode of land ownership and husbandry. In short, the selective and stylized representation of landscape in art was interpreted as a statement of power, encouraging the preservation and maintenance of certain spaces and social relations (see Bender, 1992; Daniels, 1993; Nash, 1999).

This type of interpretation, which brings social and cultural theory to landscape interpretation, offers a distinctive approach to understanding landscape, one which can trace its lineaments back to the cultural geography pioneered by Carl Sauer and the Berkeley School in the 1920s and 1930s (see Jackson, 1989). In this tradition, the appearance of the natural landscape was seen to be transformed into a cultural landscape through the human practices and traditions indigenous to a particular area (providing 'a means of classifying areas according to the character of the human groups who occupy them' – Wagner and Mikesell, 1962, p. 2). Less overtly radical in orientation than the iconographic

---

Box 5.3 Denis Cosgrove (1948–   )

Professor of Cultural Geography at UCLA, Denis Cosgrove is acknowledged as a leading geographical figure whose work combines rigorous historical scholarship with critical theorizations of the role of representation. The notion of landscape has always been central to his work, which has been particularly concerned with the cultural meanings and significance of different landscapes – both physical and representational – in the contexts of historical projects of imperialism and modernization. For example, through examinations of the way art has represented landscape in Western Europe, he did much to show how John Berger's and Raymond Williams' cultural Marxism could be utilized to expose the idea of landscape as a power-laden 'way of seeing'. Similarly, through a series of studies of Palladian landscapes, the 'iconography' of sixteenth-century Venice, the spectacle of twentieth-century Rome, the writing of authors including John Ruskin, cosmography in early modern Europe and the envisioning of the globe, he has shown how a culturally sensitive investigation of representation generates specific insights

tradition pioneered by Cosgrove *et al.*, the Berkeley School's emphasis on mapping the distribution of material artefacts in the landscape continues to be an important influence, especially in North American geography. This is mirrored in the historical geographies of H. C. Darby (1948) and W. G. Hoskins (1955), which both offered authoritative surveys of the making of the English landscape. In the so-called 'new' cultural geography, however, the reading of landscape as caught up in political, social and economic process has encouraged more critical readings of landscape. The difference between these different traditions in cultural geography is subtle, and hotly debated (see Mitchell, 1995), but, in sum, it appears that the thrust of the new landscape studies is to consider landscape as part of a *process* of cultural politics, rather than as the outcome of that process.

The subject matter of the 'new' landscape studies is tremendously wide, and while iconographic analysis has been principally applied to historical texts and artefacts, it is also influential in geographic readings of contemporary landscapes. The journals *Landscape Research* and *Ecumene* publish many of these, the latter providing a particular focus on the importance of landscape aesthetics in the shaping of human-nature relations. Collectively, these stress that the idea of landscape remains a crucial means by which (Western) subjects make sense of their surroundings and negotiate their relations with the environment (Ryan, 1997). This stresses that, although the idea of landscape emerged as a particular facet of Enlightenment thinking, obviously related to human desires to conquer and civilize nature, its privileging as a way of imagining and picturing space remains tied to specific understandings of what is attractive and aesthetically pleasing. As Nash (1999) observes, the fact we take photographs and send postcards of specific urban and rural landscapes (and not others) underlines that landscape remains an important way of understanding and representing the distinctions between 'nature' and 'culture'. Moreover, as Seymour (2000) highlights, these questions of aesthetic value remain bound into power relations, so that certain landscapes and ways of life are privileged over others.

about the relations played out in different times and places. More broadly, his work has questioned the role of spatial images and representations in the making and communicating of knowledge. Much of this work reflects on the place of geography within the academy, elucidating the importance of specific 'geographical imaginations' in the making of identities. Furthermore, through his editorship of the journal *Ecumene*, Cosgrove has done much to encourage the development and trajectory of 'new' landscape studies which deconstruct established ways of seeing and representing the world. Though some commentators might deride the slew of landscape studies that have imitated Cosgrove's (suggesting the focus on representation often ignores social practice), there is little doubt that his work has offered a distinctive and important take on the politics of landscape that explores the *effects*, as well as the limits, of representation.

Further reading: Cosgrove (1984, 1994a, 1999)

This focus on landscape as a distinctive and visually coherent mode of representation has also witnessed stimulating attempts to bring textual theory into dialogue with feminist and post-colonial theory. For example, post-colonial critiques of Western modes of representing and imagining the developing world have pointed out the importance of landscape in imperialist and colonial traditions (Rogers, 1992; Kenney, 1995; Neumann, 1995; Phillips, 1997). Seymour (2000) vividly illustrates this, highlighting how the adoption of Georgian notions of landscape and estate management enabled colonizers to obscure the injustices and hardships that were apparent in the eighteenth-century plantations of the Caribbean. As she recounts, these islands were generally celebrated and represented as a luxuriant tropical paradise of great productive and financial value – a view that 'screened out controversies over slave labour and conduct, the dangers of tropical climates, sexual exploits on plantations and the fragility of West Indian society and economy' (Seymour, 2000, p. 209; see also Mitchell, 1994). Elsewhere, the idea that landscape is the product of a masculine gaze which aims to subdue and dominate a nature imagined as feminine has been vociferously debated (Duncan and Sharp, 1993; Rose, 1993). This clearly ties in with feminist critiques of traditional tropes of academic representation within geography, wherein male researchers and writers have often been accused of feigning a 'godlike' objectivity, positioning themselves outside the world which they represent through seemingly dispassionate texts and pictures (see Chapter 2). In deconstructing the colonial gaze, several commentators (including many drawing on psychoanalytical ideas of sexuality) have stressed the connections between masculinity and imperialism. Writing on the experiences of female travellers has accordingly highlighted the difference between their representations of the colonies and those produced within the white male traditions of exploration, conquest and surveillance (Blunt and Rose, 1994; Women and Geography Study Group, 1997).

This notion of landscape as a classed, gendered and racialized way of seeing is also highlighted in many analyses of landscapes of national identity. Herein, the mapping of ideas of (for example) Englishness onto certain rural and built landscapes has been seen as central in processes of exclusion which serve to render ethnic, sexual and disabled minorities invisible in dominant constructions of national identity and belonging (Kinsman, 1995). In Daniels's (1993, p. 5) view, 'landscapes, whether focusing on single monuments or framing stretches of scenery, provide visible shape to the nation'. In England, for instance, it is the rural landscape of the Home Counties that often provides the reference point in discussions of English national identity (Brace, 1999). This mythologization of the rural as the hearth of English values is evident in the many policies and strategies designed to prevent the incursion of modern urban influences into the countryside (or at least to ensure that they are incorporated sympathetically within a rural aesthetic). The connection between nationhood and identity as mediated through landscape has accordingly provided a key tradition in landscape studies, manifest in some lively and historically nuanced accounts of the role of visual culture in the legitimation of the nation-state (Lowenthal, 1991; Nash, 1993; Withers, 1996; Matless, 1998). As some commentators have been keen to point out (e.g., Taylor, 1991), the connection forged between English rurality and 'Britishness' has created tensions between projects of nationalism and the cultural heritage that may be significant in the Celtic diaspora of Wales, Scotland and Ireland (not to mention Cornwall or the Isle of Man). The fact that this analysis has been extended to consider the exclusions apparent in landscapes of 'national' sport further illustrates the pertinence of the landscape idea in geographical enquiry (Bale, 1993).

This wide-ranging definition of landscape indicates the way in which the text metaphor has been stretched to encompass many areas of geographical enquiry. This underlines that social space is constructed in the realms of both discourse and practice, and that it is impossible to conceive of any space outside the realms of language. Indeed, Jones and Natter (1999) argue that it is only through representation – words, images and data – that space exists, and that all spaces are 'written' and 'read'. In the work of Duncan and Duncan (1988), this logic is used to propose a method for interpreting the social production of space. In their writing, the instability of the meanings ascribed to the material landscape is played up, though the landscape is ultimately interpreted *intersubjectively* as a text which imposes limits on the way a space is conceived and used (see also Anderson, 1988; Duncan, 1990; Mills, 1993). In this way, society is seen to consist of discrete textual communities, each seeking to have its own preferred reading of text inscribed in the landscape. Such analyses are particularly apparent in readings of the production of the urban landscape, which has been considered by some as a remarkable synthesis of 'charisma and context' (Knox, 1991). Here, the townscape is interpreted as 'written' by architects, developers and planners who operate within specific socio-economic contexts, its architectural styles and forms invoking both ideology and power. The focus is on how this urban landscape 'works' within cultural practice, not just symbolizing power, but becoming an instrument of cultural power in itself. In the words of Lees (2001, p. 51), this involves a focus on the *performativity* of landscape, and its role in shaping social life. Returning to Matless's (2000) warning about neglecting the materiality of landscape, it is here we start to realize the limits of the textual metaphor; landscape is not simply perceived, it is used, occupied and transformed. Similarly, it is not just viewed, but smelt, heard, felt and *lived*.

Here, then, it is apparent that geographers have started to think about the ability of the urban landscape to *act* as a representation of itself, promoting particular practices through its appearance and design. Here, metaphors of text have been joined by those of theatre, spectacle and festival, with the city being reimagined as a setting embroiled in social, political, economic and cultural transactions between society and self. Consideration of the way specific buildings promote particular cultural values and social rituals has accordingly been emphasized in studies of memorialization and conservation (e.g., Kong, 1993; Johnson, 1996), while a more general consideration of the staged inauthenticity of the postmodern urban landscape is apparent in Harvey (1989a) and Soja (1996). Combining their own interests in radical political economy with post-structural ideas about the instability of meaning, each has developed stimulating and influential interpretations of the new urban forms emerging in the post-Fordist city (see Chapter 3). For Harvey, the depthlessness of the contemporary city, with its emphasis on surfaces and signs, is a means by which capitalism has sought both to attract and distract. For Soja, meanwhile, Lefebvre's (1991) ideas that space is simultaneously perceived, conceived and represented have been used to develop a 'post-Marxist' account that draws attention to the way that everyday settings can be decoded and recoded by embodied urban subjects (see Box 1.1).

Even if the conception of postmodernism as a particular epoch or phase of capital accumulation is somewhat limited, these accounts have been valuable for alerting geographers to the way that everyday landscapes now offer up an endless array of commodified signs, styles, metaphors and images. Moreover, with these signs and symbols decoupled from any authentic or fixed meaning they might have ever had, their voracious consumption via television, computer or cinema screen throws dialectic interpretations of sign and signifier into doubt. In some accounts of the postmodern consumer society – particularly that of **Jean Baudrillard** (Box 5.4) – the consumption of signs has become everything, their relation to real or authentic referents no longer an issue. Slipping into the seductive grasp of signs and simulacra, a widely noted tendency has been for consumers to buy into spaces that offer multiple opportunities to get lost in this mélange of signs and images. In Baudrillard's work, these are described as *hyperreal* because of the way they feign authenticity; examples include those contemporary shopping malls, theme parks and heritage centres that offer commodified fantasy versions of other places and times (see Shurmer-Smith and Hannam, 1994). An example here is the hyperreal Irish bar, a familiar sight in cities around the world. In most cases these offer a version of Irishness which is more 'authentically Irish' than that found in pubs in Ireland itself. Like the spaces of cinema, computer games and TV drama, these hyperreal pubs (and shopping centres, heritage parks and theme parks) are

---

Box 5.4 Jean Baudrillard (1929–)

For some, Baudrillard is *the* postmodern theorist. Though widely misunderstood, and evading easy comprehension, his portrayal of a society that is preoccupied with (and is) *hyperreal* has been widely cited, his neologism entering the lexicon of popular and academic debate. At its heart, Baudrillard's work takes issue with the basis of Marxist political economy, problematizing the idea that the capitalist system revolves around a series of unequal exchanges where the exchange value of an object exceeds its use value. Rejecting this division, his book *The Consumer Society* (1970) insisted that objects also have symbolic and sign values (i.e., they symbolize something to or about the owner that is unconnected to their potential utility). A simple example here would be a birthday card, which has an iconic and sign value beyond its usefulness as an object of decoration or its financial value (in effect, representing a token of affection). This rejection of the idea that objects can ever have an essential value based on the extent to which people need them led Baudrillard to undermine the distinction between real and imagined need (and true and false value). Replacing Marx's political economy with a generalized economy of desire, Baudrillard's subsequent work has sought to emphasize that consumption is a symbolic process, and that the process of consuming is more

representations, at once real and imagined. In the final analysis, by demolishing any easy distinction between image and reality, work on the postmodern city has therefore underlined the importance of reading space like a text, its consistencies only fixed through the stories it tells.

5.5 CONCLUSION

This chapter began by documenting geographers' motivations for examining text. To begin with, it was suggested that this was motivated by their concern to utilize a wide range of sources to make sense of the interactions they saw unfolding in spaces that were deemed as real. In the context of humanist thought, it appeared that these texts could evoke the sensuous meaning of real places, while for those inspired by Marxist theory, these texts were taken as ideologically infused representations prioritizing certain socio-spatial arrangements over others (i.e., shaping everyday reality). But in the light of post-structural ideas, which focus on the instability of text, the separation of language and reality seems to be less clear-cut. In fact, the latter sections of this chapter have emphasized that almost anything can be considered as a text that narrates and creates particular understandings of social space – even space itself! This type of understanding does not dismiss other conceptions of represented space out of hand, nor deny that a distinction between the textual and the substantial might be useful in some studies (see Matless, 2000). What it does indicate, however, is that geography is a discipline that balances its unique focus on the spatiality of text with an awareness of the debates unfolding in other areas of the humanities and social sciences. Far from being a casual ransacking, this has involved a careful engagement with ideas debates in social and cultural theory, one in which geographers' voices are increasingly acknowledged.

---

important than the object that is consumed. In work such as *America* (1988), this has spiralled into dizzying accounts of society's preoccupation with *simulacra* – representations or copies of other copies that are often more real than the real (i.e., hyperreal). An example cited by Baudrillard was Disneyworld, which he took to be emblematic of the corporate commodification of the sign (and as a metaphor for the depthlessness of American society). For Baudrillard, this problematization of image and reality throws everything into doubt, and suggests that a radical reworking of the basis on which we 'judge' the world is necessary to avoid the perpetuation of banal theory. In parallel with Debord's *The Society of the Spectacle* (1967), Bataille's work on excess and Deleuze's notion of desire, Baudrillard offers a crucial signpost to those geographers seeking to critique contemporary consumer society. At the same time, his work on the end of history, the depthlessness of modern society and the reversability of time offers a major challenge to established ontologies of knowledge.

Further reading: Gane (1994); R. G. Smith (1997)

Chapter 6   Geographies of Money

6.1 INTRODUCTION

Money is a multiple vision. Money is an economy. It is often described as the 'central nervous system' of capital, but like the central nervous system it is easier to see than to understand. Money is a sociology. In capitalism, according to some, it provides the 'real community' . . . a community in which rational calculation is mixed with a quasi-religious faith in the power of its bonds. Money is an anthropology. Its meanings are multiple. They deeply affect and are deeply affected by culture . . . Finally money is a geography and a curious geography too. (Leyshon and Thrift, 1997, p. 1)

In his voluminous *A History of Money*, Glyn Davies (1994) suggests we live in an age in which money means more to more people around the world than at any time in human history. Money's rhythms, manifestations and embodiments seemingly surround us, infiltrating our day-to-day existence in multiple ways. Despite this, or perhaps even because of this, the actual *qualities* of money are often subsumed by questions of quantity – money is often not thought about too hard, or for too long, beyond how much of it we possess (or perhaps more accurately, how much we lack) (Tickell, 1999). While money exhibits a curious geography, apparently being 'everywhere but nowhere in particular' (Harvey, 1989a, p. 167), it is only recently that geographers have paid systematic attention to it. Indeed, it has been somewhat common to make reference to the 'surprising' absence of geographic work on money prior to the 1980s, so that, compared with other social science disciplines, human geography has been seen as 'slow to recognize the importance of money and finance in the unfolding of social life' (Leyshon, 2000, p. 519).

The reasons for this neglect of monetary matters in geography are numerous. Speculating on these, Martin (1999, p. 3) suggests that since its earliest days as a subdiscipline of human geography, economic geography has been 'preoccupied with the industrial landscape', reflecting its origins in neoclassical writing on regional development and the space economy. For example, the triumvirate of location theorists – Von Thünen, Christaller and Lösch – whose work was to prove most influential in economic geography's quantitative revolution (see Barnes, 2001a), deemed money of little significance beyond its role as a unit of equivalence and calculation (i.e., as a measure of price, income, turnover and profit). Yet it is worth pointing out that one of those early works, Lösch's *The Economics of Location* (1949, translated in 1954) contained some material relating to financial aspects of the economic landscape, and a sequel was planned explicitly to consider the relationship between money and location. However, Lösch's death meant that such a work was never completed, leading Martin to hypothesize wistfully that maybe if that book had been written, 'the post-war development of economic geography and regional economics might not have neglected the study of money' (1999, p. 3).

It would of course be more than a little unfair to blame the lack of subsequent geographical work on money solely to any individual's premature demise, and Martin in fact outlines a range of works undertaken throughout the post-war period up until the late 1970s within both geography and regional economics. These include the works of Richardson (1972, 1973), who asserted that the overuse of neoclassical growth theory assumed away any regional role for money, alongside critiques by neoclassical thinkers such as Myrdal (1957) and Kerr (1965). Likewise, the political-economy critique offered by Massey (1973), Sayer (1976) and Harvey (1974, 1977; with Chatterjee, 1974) began to problematize neoclassical assumptions about quantification and economic exchange, pointing to the social relations that underpin capitalist financial transactions. None the less, despite their innovative nature, Martin (1999, p. 4) suggests that these works 'formed a partial and rather inchoate literature' that 'did little to stimulate other geographical work on finance'. In similar tones, Corbridge and Thrift (1994b) have suggested other reasons for the lack of focused attention on money during this period. These relate to a continuing focus on that which was assumed to be static and tangible (i.e., fixed points of production), and a concurrent preoccupation of economic geographers with productionism and labour relations (rather than finance and fiscal management).

However, in the wake of a range of works that have directly or indirectly placed money on the research agenda since the early 1980s, it has been suggested that geography's ignorance of financial and monetary issues may now 'appear curious' (Leyshon, 1995b, p. 531). Indeed, as we describe in this chapter, analysis of the geographies of money is increasingly moving into the mainstream of geographical enquiry. Numerous reasons for this growth of interest have been postulated. For example, Thrift (1994a) suggests that attention was stimulated in the 1980s by a rising awareness of the role of global finance in creating global economic, social and political turmoil (see also Corbridge and Thrift, 1994; Leyshon, 1995b). This was accompanied by innovative work by a number of key individuals, involving a growing engagement with ideas from outside geography. As we shall see, one important consequence of these stimuli has been a move beyond thinking about money in purely quantitative and economic terms, in that 'to concentrate attention narrowly on "the pound in your pocket" is to devalue the all-pervading significance of money' (Davies, 1994, p. 2).

In this chapter, we therefore highlight attempts to 'rescue' geography from such purely economic accounts of money, particularly those that have emphasized money's social, institutional and psychological effects in their attempt to bring money 'back to the social and cultural realm from which it should never have been allowed to escape' (Leyshon and Thrift, 1996, p. 1155). This is not to say that most work in economic geography suffers because of its inability to say anything meaningful about money, simply that we wish to focus upon that (largely post-positivist) work which takes money seriously as an object of study. We thus detail three interrelated sets of work, each of which approaches money from a different perspective and illustrates how geographers have drawn from literatures and theorists beyond the boundaries of traditional geographical enquiry. The first of these involves the tradition of political economy (and particularly Marxist political economy) and the insights that this has offered on global financial systems. The second relates to culturally nuanced geographies of money which explore its performance in different sites (including financial service centres). The third explores the social geographies of money, particularly the development of 'alternative' financial systems and institutions in marginal spaces. Throughout, we detail the development and consequences of the so-called 'new economic geography' and its important links to the 'cultural turn' (see Chapter 3). To begin with, however, we need to think about what we mean by 'money', exploring the different ways that it has been defined and conceptualized throughout history.

6.2 THINKING ABOUT MONEY

Throughout a large part of the history of humankind it was barter – the 'direct exchange of services and resources for mutual advantage' (Davies, 1994, p. 9) – that represented the only means by which goods and services could be exchanged. Historically, the main advantage of barter related to the *visibility* and *transparency* of the exchange process – what you saw was what you got, and if it was decided by either party that the exchange was not a fair one then either the exchange would not take place, or the quantities or qualities of the goods or services involved would be adapted until all parties were happy with their 'deal'. In many ways, however, this main advantage has been overshadowed, at least in many academic discussions, by a range of perceived disadvantages. Such disadvantages include: the absence of a common or generalized value standard by which participants could be assured that the exchange was fair and comparable (a problem that became increasingly important as trade developed and an increasing variety of goods and services became available for exchange); the need to find an exchange partner who both had the goods or services required and who was happy to accept the goods or services offered in exchange; and the costs of storing what were often necessarily 'real' objects or goods.

As such, and as the complexity of trade increased, such disadvantages have often been (implicitly and explicitly) drawn upon to support the view that money was 'invented' solely as a consequence of these disadvantages (see Crowther,

1940). In contrast, Davies describes how barter became increasingly sophisticated in response to this growing complexity, with, for example, certain commodities becoming preferred items of exchange because they were more easily
stored, easily carried or were more durable (that is, because of their qualities in
acting as media of exchange). Equally, established markets developed for barter-
ing in specific goods, easing the problems in finding suitable exchange partners.
So while (with hindsight) the use of money has subsequently and generally been
seen to offer major advantages over the process of barter, it is likely that the
process by which barter gave way to monetary exchange was more gradual than
many accounts suggest.

In particular, a range of so-called 'primitive' monies form an important linkage in this gradual development. Defining what constitutes a 'primitive money'
is problematic given the huge range of forms that have served as money, as well
as the variety of functions (some particularly narrow) that they have performed
throughout history. As such, very general depictions are often favoured, such as
Grierson's assertion that 'primitive money' denotes 'all money that is not a coin
or, like modern paper money, a derivative of coin' (Grierson, 1977, p. 14).
Despite these disagreements over definition, however, most writers on primitive
monies agree that barter was not the main factor in the origins and earliest
developments of money. For example, Davies notes that primitive money largely
originated in a variety of ornamental, ceremonial, religious rites, as well as
other 'non-economic' scenarios, such as bride and blood money (compensations
offered to the head of a family for the loss of a daughter's services, and for
killing or injuring somebody, respectively). Hence, primitive monies included
tributes, taxation, ransoms, bribery and other forms of payments, with the early
state increasingly utilizing money to enforce laws, thus enhancing the role of
primitive money within society. Forms of primitive money that have been identified therefore include amber, eggs, feathers, jade, leather, nails, pigs, rice, salt,
beads, ivory, yarns and so on (Davies, 1994).

The problem we face in talking about and defining such primitive monies
seemingly derives from our contemporary desire to compartmentalize aspects
of life into discrete categories such as 'the economic', 'the social' or 'the political', or, as Davies (1994, p. 24) argues, our inability 'to force ancient or recent
primitive fashions into modern moulds'. We perhaps find it difficult to comprehend how 'an object can be at the same time currency or money, a religious
symbol or a mere ornament' (Quiggin, 1949, p. 2). As Davies (1994, p. 26)
asserts, however, 'whatever barriers the state – or academics – may erect within
which to confine money, money has an innate ability . . . to jump over them'. As
we shall see, one of the key stimulants for recent geographical work on money
has been an increasing recognition that more modern forms of money perform
as wide a range of functions as their primitive antecedents. For now, though,
rather than seeing money as narrowly defined (i.e., as a replacement for the
inadequacies of barter invented by 'rational man'), we can instead note its
development as moving in a generalized sequence from barter, barter plus
primitive money, primitive money, primitive plus modern money, then (finally)
modern money (Davies, 1994). But even here we should be aware that modern

money has not completely usurped barter and primitive money, with both persisting in various forms.

It should be becoming apparent that the history (and development) of money is both surprising and colourful, contested and complex (see also Sinclair, 2000, on the development of sterling, 'the currency that ruled the world'). As noted above, debates concerning definitions of exactly what modern money is, as well as what it was in the past, have been most commonly conducted in relation to the wide range of functions it performs. In modern terms, these functions can be specific, general, concrete and/or abstract in nature, with the most commonly cited being that money represents a unit of account, a medium of exchange, a measure of value, a means of payment and a store of value (see Pollard, 2001). Disagreement here concerns which functions are most important in defining whether something is actually money or not; that is, which represents money's 'primary' and/or 'secondary' function. Such debates are difficult to resolve given that primary functions may change over time, and may also vary from place to place, with the secondary function in one place previously having been the primary function somewhere else. Further, given that a unit of account is an abstract feature, seemingly anything could potentially serve this function (e.g., a coin, a shell, a bead and so on).

In practice, however, even though an object may act as a unit of account and calculation, that does not necessarily mean that that object can perform any or all of money's many other functions. Importantly, and as alluded to above, a key advantage of money over barter is that the *convenience* of money is greatly enhanced if its abstract functions (its qualities of accounting and measuring) are linked to its more concrete functions (as a means of payment or medium of exchange) – that is, for example, it helps greatly if 'one's bank balance is kept in pounds, that one is paid in pounds, and that one pays others for purchases or services also in pounds' (Davies, 1994, p. 28). Of course, it could never be as

Box 6.1 Georg Simmel (1858–1918)
Along with Max Weber and Karl Marx, Georg Simmel was one of the leading German figures in the development of sociology in the late nineteenth and early twentieth centuries. Born in Berlin in 1858, Simmel taught sociology and philosophy at the University of Berlin before belatedly being appointed to a Chair at Strasbourg University in 1914, four years before his death. During his life, Simmel cemented his status as a leading theoretician of contemporary (modern) social phenomena, especially in relation to the themes of sexuality, sociability and money, while often evading easy categorization because of the breadth of his work. As a firm believer in the need to be philosophically informed, an underlying theme of much of Simmel's work concerned a focus on the relationship between the modern city and individual consciousness. In particular, he argued that, in the modern period, traditional 'affective ties' had become replaced by more formal ones, with abstract forms such as money increasing greatly in importance in people's lives. Through his notion of the 'blasé' attitude, Simmel explored the manner in which the complexities of, and hypersensitivity to, the modern experience is essentially 'managed' through a transformation in individual consciousness that leads to a filtering out of the detail and minutiae of modern existence into manageable levels of both

simple as that, with Davies going on to note how, for long periods, currency existed only as a unit of account, with multiple forms of 'money' being utilized outside this accounting system. This given, however, at a base level we can consider money as 'anything that is widely used for making payments and accounting for debts and credits' (Davies, 1994, p. 29).

In addition to debates around what money is, theorists have also grappled with how money and its impacts can be best interpreted. For example, money, and its effects on society, captured the attention of nineteenth- and early twentieth-century social theorists such as Karl Marx (see Box 2.4 and Section 2.4.1), Jürgen Habermas, John Maynard Keynes, Adam Smith and Georg Simmel (see Box 6.1) among many others. An analysis of these works reveal two predominate *discourses* (see Chapter 5) of money (Leyshon and Thrift, 1997). In the first, money is viewed as an 'enlightened force', offering innumerable possibilities to the possessor. In these accounts the benefits of wealth are highlighted and the justice of the free market is privileged. Here, the work of Baruch Spinoza and Adam Smith is important, suggesting, in different ways, that money is at the service of society, and works to its benefit. In a second, more prevalent discourse, however, money is represented as being out of control, a dehumanizing force that tears the fabric of society. This discourse is exemplified in Keynes's description of the monetary system as a 'species of illusion', 'an exercise in making uncertainty respectable' (Leyshon and Thrift, 1997, p. 33), or Marx's critique of money as the object against which all else is measured in the capitalist system (Roberts, 1994). From this perspective, the 'objectification' of money is seen as essentially antisocial, removing the subjective connections and qualitative relations between objects and individuals, reducing everything to its own form of abstraction (Marx, 1977).

Alongside Marx's powerful critique of capitalist society (see Chapter 2), the work of **Georg Simmel** (see Box 6.1) remains particularly influential for

intellectual and sensory stimulation. Whilst Simmel followed the likes of Marx and Durkheim in pointing to the emergence of a division of labour within the developing money economy, and its resultant economic and social effects, he also strove to examine its more cultural overtones. Through this focus, he explored the notion of the 'objectification' of modern life, especially through media such as money, the law and media communications. As such, the seminal, though somewhat neglected, *The Philosophy of Money* (1900, 1978) represented an attempt to analyse the effects of money on social and cultural life, while at the same time representing an attempt to generate a more general thesis on the philosophy of culture. Feminist critics such as Irigaray have voiced strong concerns over his elision of objectivity and maleness, the manner in which he naturalized the qualities of women, alongside more general criticism of his opposition of 'traditional' and modern life. However, Simmel's wide-ranging analysis of modern life continues to provoke engagement with his ideas across a range of disciplines, including geography.

Further reading: Frisby (1984); Kaern *et al.* (1990); Simmel (1978); Pryke and Allen (2000)

those who see money as exercising an invidious influence on society. In *The Philosophy of Money* (1978) Simmel explored money in relation to his notion of the objectification of modern (urban) life, outlining a number of its 'fundamental characteristics'. Like Marx, Simmel suggested that money is a medium of equivalence, reducing quality to quantity and destroying the essential 'form' and 'use' of any object. Through this principle of equivalence, money is seen as a pure form of exchange, having an exchange value that is abstracted from that used in barter (hence, Marx's distinction of use value and exchange value). Money thus represents a means of comparability, highlighting the commonality of things, and that anything can be bought and sold. Monetary value is mapped onto all aspects of society, so that even human life comes to have a financial value. Simmel's work, therefore, shows that money is much more than an economic entity, having profound effects on the nature of existence.

Taken together, we can see that both of these discourses of money suggest a definite relationship between money and society; in the first, money works for the good of society, in the second, money takes over society. The coexistence of the discourses has been vividly exemplified in recent years through the furore caused by the K Foundation's 'Burning of a Million Quid', whereby one million pounds (the rewards of their musical careers as the pop group, the KLF) in the form of 20 tight bundles of £50,000, was purposively burnt in an abandoned boathouse on the Isle of Jura in the Inner Hebrides (see Brook and Goodrick, 1997; Tickell, 1999). These events, and the subsequent tour of the United Kingdom in which the duo showed a 63-minute silent film *Watch the K Foundation Burn a Million Quid* and debated the group's actions, were reported in a BBC *Omnibus* documentary. Exemplifying the prevalence of both discourses in wider society, the tour also exposed a range of reactions to the film itself – 'it's horny'; 'it's symbolic'; 'spiritual'; 'it's a rave – they look exhausted, like zombies, so it's definitely a rave'; 'very indulgent'; 'very art' (*Omnibus*, 6 November 1995; and see Brook and Goodrick, 1997).

This furore was heightened by the fact that the burning marked the culmination of a series of events and stunts in which the K Foundation were 'primarily concerned with money: money as art, art as money. The possibility of meaning beyond money. To challenge the power of money' (Reid, 1994, p. 28). It had, for example, previously been the K Foundation's intention to host an exhibition entitled 'Money: a Major Body of Cash', which was to consist of seven pieces, all involving various amounts of cash nailed to, tied to, or simply standing on inanimate objects. The main work, 'Nailed to the Wall', featured one million pounds in mint £50 notes nailed to piece of skip pine, surrounded by a frame, which was to be auctioned at a reserve price of £500,000, thereby allowing the intriguing possibility of 'buying' one million pounds for half its monetary value (unless, of course, it became more valuable as a piece of art). After aborted attempts to site the exhibition, including an idea to take 'Nailed to the Wall' around the world – 'Money goes instantly around the world; we wanted to take it by hand and celebrate the end of cash' (cited in Brook and Goodrick, 1997, p. 9) – the idea of sending it all up in flames came to the fore.

In relation to the discourses of money, therefore, it is the idea of control (or the lack of it) which bears most relation to the K Foundation's exploits, most specifically through their 'nailing' of cash to inanimate objects, and secondly the idea of taking it around the world by hand. As one of the K Foundation's members argued during the *Omnibus* documentary, 'We nailed it to a bit of wood so it can't function as it wants to, but it's to do with controlling the money; because money tends to sort of control you if you've got it, it kind of dictates what you have to do with it, you either spend it, give it away, invest it, and we just wanted to be in control of it.' However, the main controversy to emerge, seemingly unexpected on the part of the K Foundation, exemplified the second main discourse, that of liberation (see Brook and Goodrick, 1997). De Abaitua (1995, p. 6) noted how the incident on Jura took place just as the UK's National Lottery was starting its weekly Saturday night run, when 'Cash was on everyone's lips: the moolah mania of £18 million prize money, the asinine debate over which charities deserve a cut of the proceeds, *The Sun's* "Have a go" column with its man-on-the-street indignation and another cash-for-scroungers moan. Sex and violence titillate us, but only money – serious amounts of money – raise the heckles of morality.' De Abaitua concluded, 'By burning everyone's dreams of being a millionaire the K Foundation touched the only nerve that could provide a truly horrified reaction in an age immured to the extreme' (1995, p. 7). Indeed, this difference in views, between where the K Foundation were 'coming from', and the reactions to their actions, clearly left both members more than a little troubled:

> You know, you want to make out that everything's fine, and that it's this fantastic art statement, and there's nothing wrong with it, but it's kind of riddled with flaws – the whole thing of burning the money I'm talking about . . . Every day you wake up, you go "oh God, yeah, OK, I've just burnt a million quid" . . . nobody thinks it's good, everybody thinks it was just a complete waste of time, everybody wants to know why you did it – you can't tell them why you did it, because you don't know why you did it. (Jimmy Cauty, K Foundation, *Omnibus*, 6 November 1995)

The coexistence of these discourses of money may then suggest that they are not as mutually exclusive as often portrayed. Leyshon and Thrift (1997), for example, argue that Simmel's work itself is somewhat 'schizophrenic' and contradictory in nature. On the one hand, Simmel suggests that money is devoid of innate qualities, instead acting as a stimulus for a range of possibilities and the opening up of the potential for greater freedom. In this way, Simmel argues that money leads to increased depersonalization as it induces inflated self-awareness and individualistic tendencies, threatening or even destroying affective ties to others (implicated in the emergence of a 'contractual' *Gesellschaft* society). On the other hand, Simmel also argues that this leads to a certain degree of dependence on others, as the earning and spending of money can only be sustained by social relations that are underlain by trust. In other words, whilst positing that money is pure, abstracted and objective, Simmel simultaneously notes that it is culturally and socially situated.

Irrespective of this, the views expressed within these two discourses of money have coalesced over time to create a dominant 'economic' understanding of money. Zelizer (1994) suggests this is based on five common assumptions. Firstly, money's functions and characteristics are seen to be situated outside society, so that it has a relationship with society but is definitely not social. The symbolic aspects of money are either considered as being largely inconsequential, or are paradoxically invoked to highlight the manner in which social life is becoming increasingly 'economic' in nature. Secondly, and following from this, a distinction is drawn between money and humanity, so that the latter is often described as warm, creative and even beautiful but the former is profane, vulgar and cold. Thirdly, all money is understood to be the same, with the only differences being differences of quantity, not quality (so that, for instance, a dollar always equals a dollar). Fourth, money, as the ultimate commodifier, is continually abstracting all areas of life into the realm of the economic, turning quality into quantity and transforming human love and labour into money. Finally, there is little room made for the ability of money to be transformed by social relations and values; this is a one-way street in which money transforms society, whilst being in itself pure and thus untransformable.

In recent years, a range of historical, sociological and anthropological critiques have emerged that have challenged this dominant understanding. These new accounts are epitomized in the work of the sociologist Viviana Zelizer (1989, 1994). In *The Social Meaning of Money*, Zelizer argues that 'money multiplies', documenting how money has been 'reshaped' throughout history, with new distinctions being created and new 'special' forms of money invented (e.g., credit money, which is based on profit yet to be realized). Consequently, Zelizer (1994, p. 18) proposes an 'alternative, differentiated model of money as shaped and reshaped by particular networks of social relations and varying systems of meanings' based around a (different) set of five assumptions. First, whilst accepting that money serves as a 'key rational tool' within the modern economic market, Zelizer argues that it also exists outside of this sphere, and is profoundly influenced by cultural and social structures. Second, Zelizer argues for more recognition of the importance of 'earmarked' and distinctive monies for different social contexts, exemplifying this idea by contrasting proper and inappropriate uses of monies in processes such as tipping (noting the reaction that such use and misuse can bring). Third, Zelizer contends that the idea of a single, general-purpose type of money is unsuitably narrow, suggesting that '[a] different, more inclusive coding is necessary, for certain monies can be indivisible (or divisible but not in mathematically predictable portions), non-fungible, non-portable, deeply subjective, and therefore qualitatively heterogeneous' (1994, p. 19). For example, a dollar does not always 'equal' a dollar – it does not always have the same value or mean the same thing, depending on whether it is a gift, a loan, a tip, a bribe, a fine, a credit or a debt. This idea is epitomized by such commonly understood notions as good money and bad money, blood money and dirty money, easy money and hard-earned money. Fourth, she posits that the assumption that money has no use value in itself is incorrect, since money, under certain circumstances, may become deeply personal and meaningful (see also Section 5.4 on Baudrillard's problematization of the relation of sign, exchange and use value). Finally, and as a result of the above assumptions, Zelizer (1994, p. 19) argues that the 'alleged freedom and unchecked power of money becomes improbable', since '[c]ultural and social structures set inevitable limits to the monetization process by introducing profound controls and restrictions on the flow and liquidity of monies'.

This critique of existing (economic) definitions of money is interesting in that it points to the fact that money is *socially produced*; that is, that it cannot exist outside society, and that it gains its functions and meanings through social practices. This argument is echoed in the work of Goux (1989), who similarly identifies money as having inseparable real, symbolic and imaginary aspects. The sociologist Nigel Dodd (1994) also suggests that the concept of money is highly differentiated and embedded in networks of human practices, custom and communication, so that money should in fact be conceived as *monies* brought together through social ritual and convention. As we shall see, geographers have not been immune to such arguments, and many have started to focus attention on the social and cultural aspects of money. Before we consider these approaches, however, let us first engage with political-economic accounts of money, accounts which have perhaps represented the dominant mode of thinking about money within geography until recent years, and which tended to draw from the second discourse of money outlined above.

6.3 THE POLITICAL ECONOMY OF MONEY

Nigel Thrift (1994b) contends that a key stimulant for interest in the geographies of money was the innovative and pioneering work of **David Harvey** (see Box 6.2). As noted in Chapter 2, Harvey has been a key figure in the development of human geography, particularly in terms of the discipline's engagement with Marxist critiques of the capitalist system and its inherent spatial contradictions and inequalities. If, as Leyshon (2000) suggests, areas of interest in the new geography of money and finance can be differentiated according to scale, Harvey's seminal text, *The Limits to Capital* (1982), focuses on the highest level of analysis, the economic system as a whole. With its chapters on money, credit and finance, Harvey's analysis highlights the importance of the financial system in sustaining and reproducing the capitalist economy through uneven development. In particular, he emphasizes how money and social power are inextricably interlinked, with money existing 'as the incarnation of general social power, independent of and external to particular production processes or specific commodities' (Harvey, 1982, p. 241).

Harvey has subsequently served to inspire many radical and critical thinkers within geography. With space as a central category of explanation, his work draws attention to the way in which 'the social power of money gives those individuals and institutions that possess it in abundance a privileged place within capitalism, so that over time the structure of the capitalist economy may be seen to be bending in line with the interests of money and finance' (Leyshon, 2000, p. 519). Harvey thus contends that money, in its multifarious forms, has played a key role in the reproduction of uneven development by creating and exploiting unequal interconnections and interdependencies on a global scale (see also Wallerstein (1974) on the emergence of the capitalist world system). This line of thought led Harvey to consider the ways in which the speed of economic life is accelerated in order to reduce the turnover time of capital (see Section 8.2), as well as to identify how new forms of money (e.g., credit money) have been created and mobilized to enable deals to be struck over vast distances. For instance, Harvey (1982) wrote of the importance of credit money ('fictitious capital') in attenuating the spatial and temporal crises of capitalism, showing how the speculative form of money can allow the switching of capital from one form of production to another. Simultaneously demonstrating the importance of finance markets in shaping the urban world (Harvey, 1985a), Harvey's work directly and indirectly spurred an increasing fascination amongst geographers in the ways in which new information technologies, communications services and bouts of financial deregulations in the 1980s and 1990s have served to make money increasingly mobile on a global basis (see Chapter 8). Harvey's work is also representative of a strong theme in much work on the dynamics of financial capital over the last two decades, that of political economy.

As Trevor Barnes (2000) outlines, political economy was a term first utilized in the early eighteenth century, being subsequently drawn upon by economists like Adam Smith and David Ricardo who emphasized two related theoretical aspects – the production and accumulation of wealth, and the highly politicized nature of the distribution and apportioning of any subsequent surplus. Marx (see Section 2.4.1) developed these ideas into his theory of revolutionary

Box 6.2 David Harvey (1935–)
Though David Harvey's early work was firmly within the idiom of spatial science (culminating in the publication (1969) of the wide-ranging exposition of positivist geographical method – *Explanation in Geography*), his engagement with the ideas of Marx has singled him out as perhaps the most influential proponent of Marxism in geography. Outlining his ideas about the relations between social inequality and spatial processes in the crusading text *Social Justice and the City* (1973), his work has subsequently proceeded through mainly theoretical readings of the relationship between the city and capitalism through the work of classical Marxist thinkers and the Frankfurt School. Following his remarkable attempt to interpret Marx's magnum opus, *Das Kapital*, for a human geography audience (*The Limits to Capital*, 1982), he adopted what he termed 'a dialectical and relational approach' to formulate a revised Marxism based on 'historical-geographical materialism'. The companion volumes *The Urbanization of Capital* (1985a) and *Consciousness and the Urban Experience* (1985b) demonstrated how such ideas could inform a geography that was at once radical, relevant and committed to change. Underpinning both was Harvey's keen understanding of capitalism's 'spatial fix', and a unique elucidation of the importance of urban form in capitalist societies. While this served to inspire a legion of geographers, it is notable that

change, whereby revolution would occur as a consequence of the inherent contradictions between production and distributional spheres. While the development of neoclassical economics in the late nineteenth century was critized by the likes of Marx for its ignorance of the political in political economy, it was widely drawn upon, relegating political-economy approaches to an essentially underground existence until the mid-twentieth century, when the work of Paul Baran (1957) in particular generated renewed interest. Since its emergence within human geography in the 'radical' late 1960s and early 1970s, its emphasis became increasingly widespread, entering debates concerning structure and agency, realism, locality, postmodernism and landscape (see Section 5.5). None the less, the way socio-spatial relations are affected by financial and monetary transactions remains a key focus, with Leyshon (1995b) identifying three related areas of interest: geopolitical economy, geoeconomics and geographies of financial exclusion (which we consider in Section 6.5).

Geopolitical economy, a term coined by Agnew and Corbridge (1989), relates to notions of shifting power relations (both geographical and structural) between states and markets, and those involved in regulating and operating those markets. One key idea in this literature is that money is a source of political power, invoking Gramsci's notion of hegemony (see Section 3.2) to explore how money is implicated in the construction of a world order dominated by an economic superpower (Ingham, 1994). Within this field, the way that powerful nation-states have been able effectively to impose their own order on the international financial system has been investigated through theoretically inclined works on the history and workings of capitalism (for example, Arrighi, 1994), alongside a range of empirical explorations of international financial regulation (such as Michie, 1992). These have stressed how British hegemony in the nineteenth century was tied into the acceptance of the gold-sterling standard, which

this endeavour did not create similar ripples among Marxist thinkers in other disciplines, who remained largely ignorant of the importance of space in social theory. An exception was Lefebvre (see Box 1.1), whose ideas on the abstraction and production of space were also to influence Harvey's (1989a) *The Condition of Postmodernity* (which focused on the increasingly diverse and fragmented cultural and architectural forms which served to legitimate the capitalist mode of production). Harvey's later work has indicated his willingness to engage with post-structural debates (particularly on the theorization of the body – see *Spaces of Hope*, 2000a), but his commitment to dialectical thinking as a radical source of transformative theory and practice remains unequivocal. As he wrote in *Justice, Nature and the Geography of Difference* (1996, p. 32) 'the task of critical analysis is not, surely, to prove the implausibility of foundational beliefs (or truths), but to find a more plausible and adequate basis for the foundational beliefs that make interpretation and political action meaningful, creative and possible'. For Harvey, Marxist theory continues to provide these foundational beliefs.

Further reading: Harvey (1999); Jones (1999)

governed international monetary relations between 1870 and 1914, and how the United States' hegemonic power relied upon the acceptance of the dollar-gold exchange system. Pegging international currencies to the dollar, this system allowed the construction of a relatively stable international monetary system between 1944 and 1971, underpinned by the Bretton Woods agreement. When the United States switched focus from international to internal financial matters, amid the economic turbulence created by the oil crisis of the early 1970s, this led to a substantially deregulated world of money with floating exchange rates (and hence, more opportunities to make profits on currency markets).

This deregulated international context, and the subsequent growth of *stateless monies*, has been explored by a number of geographers, who often portray this as representing the globalization of finance (e.g., Gill, 1992, 1993a; Swyngedouw, 1992). These deregulated global markets clearly benefit some nations more than others, with some nation-states having adapted more successfully to the imperatives of a global financial system by adopting neo-liberal fiscal policy. Here, the way that nation-states bequeath economic power to financial institutions can be seen to represent a form of bargaining whereby they are able to maintain their political power only by acceding their dominant influence in economic matters to the private sector (see also Chapter 7). For some, this suggests we have perhaps entered a 'post-hegemonic', deterritorialized era in which the power balance has shifted away from states and governments towards transnational corporate elites and global capital (see Gill 1993a, 1993b). On the other hand, explorations of the notion of 'hegemonic challenge' have focused on the potential for Japan to be a 'new economic hegemon' (Hellenier, 1993), though the rising importance of the Euro as the unified currency of the European Union suggests that the economic power of nation-states may have long ago been superseded by institutions whose influence is transnational rather than national (with the EU, G8 and NAFTA all emerging as potential economic hegemons for the twenty-first century).

Linked to work within geopolitical economy, research within *geoeconomics* has explored the continuing importance of the geographies of national monetary and financial systems in an age of increasing global flows of credit and finance (see Agnew, 1994). Here, interest has centred on the existence of a variety of 'economic worlds' that vary in terms of their abstractness, and their scale of existence and operation (see Storper, 1993). Explorations have been directed towards the national scale and 'national capitalisms' – the interrelationships between financial structures, state regulation and industrial organization – in striving to explain the different 'economic' rationalities of the leading national economies of the global capitalist system (see Lash and Urry, 1994). This has involved exploration of the forms of regulation and protectionism that specify a particular role for financiers and business in the life of the nation. Geographical work has outlined neo-liberal attempts by leading economies in North America, Europe and South-East Asia in the 1980s to reregulate their financial services industries in order to become more efficient and competitive, such as the new bargain struck between the UK government and finance in the 1980s (associated with the 1986 Financial Deregulation Act and the so-called 'Big Bang').

These events have led geographers to document the uneven growth of industries between and within regions, as new technologies and forms of organization follow financial restructuring. Martin (1999) thus outlines a growing body of work striving to analyse the spatial organization and operation of particular financial institutions, services and markets, alongside a less developed strand attempting to link regional financial flows and regional industrial development. Examples here include Daniels's (1986) work on the changing geography of banking resulting from financial deregulation, Gentle *et al.* (1991) on the decentralization of financial services in the UK and the geographies of those industries marketing new economic products and packages, such as e-commerce (Graham and Marvin, 2001).

On a regional and local level, attention has also revolved around the concept of 'institutional thickness' (Amin and Thrift, 1992), which refers to the importance of non-economic forces and embedded social relations in creating the 'success' of particular economic worlds such as Japan and the 'Third Italy' (see Section 7.3). Best (1990, p. 25) has illustrated how new principles of production and business organization, termed the 'new competition', are apparent in these 'wildly dissimilar institutional and cultural settings', being characterized, in turn, by 'an institutional complex of large firms, hierarchical and captive value-adding networks with large firms at the apex and vertical tiers of ever smaller firms, and industrial policy agencies of the central government' and 'networked groups of small firms, inter-firm collective service associations, and industrial policy agencies of local government'. This interest in flows of money and networks of financial trust re-emerges in work at different scales, including studies of the geographies of the world's pre-eminent financial centres – London, New York and Tokyo.

6.4 NETWORKS, BODIES, PERFORMANCE

While the political-economic perspective remains at the heart of geographical analyses of the geographies of money, it has increasingly been critiqued by approaches that fall under the rubric of what might be termed 'new' economic geography. Following the 'cultural turn' in human geography (see Chapter 3), there has been a sustained engagement with cultural and social theory by economic geographers, extending analyses to provide a more discursive understanding of money and economic life through recognition of the agency of individuals, institutions and financial organizations (e.g., Ford and Rowlingson, 1996; Leyshon and Thrift, 1996). This addresses the embeddedness and substantive role of social relations in shaping the space economy, simultaneously highlighting the hold which money has over different communities. 'New' economic geography is thus different from political-economy analyses in three main ways (Thrift and Olds, 1996). First, it is polycentric, composed of not one, but multiple, overlapping and non-universal narratives sensitive to differences across space and time. Second, it is much more open to voices from outside geography. Third, it reconceptualizes 'the economic', conceiving money beyond purely economic, abstracted terms by acknowledging its insubstantial nature (see Roberts, 1994). This demonstrates an engagement with post-structural ideas (see Section 3.4), and awareness that the power of money lies as much in its imagining as its reality:

> The word 'money' now refers to a configuration of oxides on a tape stored in a computer department of a bank. The connection between the oxides and the function of the exchange medium is arbitrary, revealing both its socially constituted character and the representation aspect of money sustained through language . . . 'money' indicates the great elasticity of language, and the way words refer to things that are a very great remove from them. (Poster, 1990, p. 13)

This thematic shift has thus led to a more inclusive debate around the wide variety of institutional and organizational practices that have eroded the concrete referentiality of money. In this section, we thus detail attempts to provide more discursive analyses of international financial centres, focusing especially on the way money is performed and articulated in financial centres – albeit that money itself is often hard to discern in these spaces.

Though many geographers have written of the changing spaces of financial centres (e.g., Pryke, 1991; Sassen, 1991), the work of **Nigel Thrift** (see Box 6.3) on the social and cultural life of financial centres stands out as a nuanced and

---

Box 6.3 Nigel Thrift (1949–)

A Professor within the Department of Geography at the University of Bristol, Nigel Thrift has been a prolific and influential contributor to a wide range of geographical debates and issues, not least the geographies of money. Renowned for bringing social theory into dialogue with more traditional geographic concepts of space and place, this is evident in a remarkable series of collaborative and individual projects that have introduced new ways of thinking about society and space. In his own words, Thrift suggests that understanding space and place is only possible if 'we stop looking at things in the usual way' (Thrift, 1999, p. 296). This has involved a constant search for new ways of conceiving of the world, rejecting grand theories in favour of more nuanced, complex and contingent ways of approaching human geography. Thrift's earlier work on geographies of time – particularly the space-time routines that structure everyday life – was more narrowly conceived in the traditions of positivist-behavioural enquiry (see, for example, Thrift, 1977). None the less, emerging from this was an emphasis on the duality of social structures, the idea that human practices and space-time routines were both mirror and mould of social structures. This led Thrift to become associated with the development of *structuration* approaches in human geography (as spelt out in his 1983 paper 'On the determination of social action in space and time') which offered a rapprochement between structure- and agency-dominated theories in human geography (see also Gregory, 1982). A focus on the worlds of money and finance allowed him to develop these ideas, resulting in increasingly sophisticated writing on the way that seemingly immutable structures (like capitalism) are sustained, and attended to, through practice. Much of this work is summarized in the collection *Spatial Formations* (1996), which shows the bene-

theoretically informed account of their role in managing flows of money. His interest in international financial centres is derived from two questions (Thrift, 1994c). The first relates to the persistence and necessity of international financial centres (such as the City of London) at a time of great advances of telecommunications, the apparent electronically induced hypermobility of money, and the notion that the world that we inhabit is effectively 'shrinking' as a consequence (see Allen, 1995). Here, Thrift wanted to consider whether their functions might melt away into a generalized 'space of flows' (Castells, 1996), giving rise to the 'end of geography' (O'Brien, 1991; see Chapter 8). The second related question focuses on the role played by the social and cultural structures of international financial centres, and the question of whether these have been intrinsically related to the economic successes of the centres or merely represent meaningless frills. In the case of London, for example, key foci for such analysis concern the rituals of dealing rooms and trading floors, the rules and regulations embedded in City institutions, right the way through to the conversations held in lodges and smoke-filled clubs throughout the Square Mile.

In attempting to answer these questions, Thrift (1994c) drew upon a range of literatures such as 'new international political economy', 'new economic sociology', cultural studies, 'reflexive modernization', organizational theory and 'new institutional economics'. In so doing, he moved away from the narrow, economic readings characteristic earlier works within this field to consider the social and cultural factors that play key roles in the maintenance of these

fits to be derived from an active engagement with social theory in making sense of spatial forms. Indeed, within *Spatial Formations*, the importance of social practice and performance were extended via Actor Network Theory and the work of Serres and Latour (see Chapter 7) as Thrift began to consider the importance of both human and non-human 'actants' in shaping the world: an example is his work on software as crucial in the reshaping of the global space economy. Abandoning any distinction between agency and structure, Thrift's work has thus offered a distinctive take on the way the world is bought into being, something particularly manifest in his recent espousal of 'non-representational theory'. He speaks of this as 'a radical attempt to wrench the social sciences and humanities out of their current emphasis on representation and interpretation by moving away from a view of the world based on contemplative models of thought and action towards theories of practice which amplify the potential of the flow of events' (Thrift, 2000c, p. 556). This offers a rebuke to those geographers who focus principally on representation and text (see Chapter 5) by arguing for a geography that takes practice seriously. Emphasizing the prediscursive, practical way that people engage with and create the world, Thrift calls for geographers to be 'observant participants' in the world rather than 'participant observers'. Mixing performance theory, phenomenology, organizational theory and Actor Network Theory, Thrift's recent work continues in a tradition of innovative geographical thinking and practice that exercises influence well beyond economic geography.

Further reading: Thrift (1983, 1996, 1999)

centres. 'New international political economy' is thus used to stress the importance of transnational financial elites; 'new economic sociology' to highlight the
socially constructed nature of institutions and money as a social and cultural
affair; and cultural studies to emphasize how, 'as money has progressively
dematerialized and become simply bits of information . . . so the potential for
discursive interpretation of money, and markets in money, has become greater
and greater' (Thrift 1994c, p. 332). To the uninitiated, drawing upon such a
range of literatures may seem more than a little daunting (if not potentially
bewildering), but it represents an example of the manner in which geographers
have been increasingly (and enthusiastically) exploring (and importing) theories
from outside the traditional realms of geographical enquiry.

After highlighting the relevance and importance of these literatures, Thrift
(1994c) moves to consider the locational determinants of international financial
centres. It is here that we see the first signs of his engagement with Actor
Network Theory (see Section 7.4) that more fully characterizes his later work
on international money, electronic networks and global cities. Like Dodd (see
Section 6.2), Thrift moves beyond traditional political-economy approaches to
theorizing money. However, his approach also represents a critique of Dodd's
more abstract and essentialist theorizing, by stressing the complexity of both
financial centres in themselves and monetary networks in general, a complexity
that is somewhat hidden by more abstract accounts. Thrift therefore argues
against what he terms the dominant account of the modern international financial system, an account which is focused on unimaginable sums of disembedded
and stateless monies being pushed around the world electronically, untainted
by human hands. This type of account, he argues, means that money 'becomes
a free-floating signifier circulating in an economic stratosphere'. Instead he
envisions an alternative account, based on a 'more human vision' in which
'hegemony is essentially contested, outcomes are always open to interpretation,
and geography matters' (Thrift, 1996, p. 214).

Thrift (1996) argues that the importance of particular forms of money in
international financial markets (e.g., internationalized credit money) poses a
challenge to conventional economic accounts of money, with older social obligations and agreements shrivelling and dying, to be replaced with new shared
understandings of risk, obligation, reciprocity and so on. In line with Dodd,
Thrift (1996) suggests international credit money needs to be seen as brought
into existence through a set of networks that are constituted by time, space and
information. This means that the global economy is now based on an understanding of money that is socially produced, maintained and worked at (see
also Allen and Pryke, 1994). Questioning orthodox 'economic' accounts of
geographies of money, the emphasis here is on 'the social relationships that
are involved in monetary transaction, rather than the objects which mediate
these relationships' (Thrift, 1996, p. 216). In addition, Thrift argues that international credit money 'constitutes and is constituted by *information*', whose
interpretation 'depends on ideas, expectations and symbolic associations' (1996,
p. 217). The importance of these concepts, argues Thrift, is best illustrated by
exploring the central preoccupation fuelling the production and transmission of

information – the assessment of risk. Noting its constantly changing morally and politically charged nature, he argues that within modern monetary systems risk has produced a paradox – while more is now known about risk (often in formalized systems of credit ratings), such knowledge is often used to produce new substitute forms of money, whose risk profile itself is unknown.

As Leyshon (1997a, p. 388) notes, up to this point Thrift's work can be clearly seen to parallel that of Dodd's, with 'reflexivity, spatiality, sociality, and regulation' figuring prominently in the ideas of both. However, despite the consensus over the existence of such properties, Thrift asserts that a monetary network, although often being thought of as abstracted, 'can never become an entirely abstract system, because it must remain a complex articulation of time, space, and information which, to some extent, defines how time, space and information are conceived' (1996, p. 219). More specifically, this complex articulation depends on agreed conventions, which in turn depend on credibility – upon trust that money assets will not decline in value:

> The existence of this trust clearly depends to a degree on the prior conditions in which a monetary network has been established (for example, the political means employed to validate money, or the institutional mechanisms for operating a payment system). But, such prior conditions need constant recharging through various confidence-building devices. The material and symbolic costs of building up the fiduciary dimension of international credit money . . . are great. Since the decline of Bretton Woods they have clearly become greater. (Thrift, 1996, p. 219)

Thrift notes that the decline of Bretton Woods demonstrated the contingent rather than necessary links between money and the state. From the Bretton Woods era where the international financial system was effectively run by nation-states, money capitalists being 'held in check' by state regulation of credit and state power in controlling what was defined as money, Thrift argues that we have moved into an era dominated by a return to power over the international financial system by money capitalists.

Within this system of weakened state control, he points to new structures of governance, understood as 'sources of rule', which can be seen to function outside of formal authority: what Rosenau and Czempiel (1992) have termed 'governance without government' (see Chapter 7). It is Thrift's analysis of these structures of governance, through the gaze of Actor Network Theory (see Section 7.4), that most clearly differentiates his analysis of money from that of Dodd's, as he sees monetary networks as embodied, rather than being made up of abstract properties. These networks, he suggests, are inherently unstable, needing constant effort and attention (see also Bingham, 1996):

> They are constantly redefined in interaction through resources which cannot themselves be considered as passive. The extent that these networks are maintained will depend upon the degree to which actor-networks are able to 'translate' situations, that is, bring together and define the bits and pieces

> needed to assemble a large and powerful network. . . . In turn, this process of translation demands the utilization of materials of association which are able to act at a distance, thus constructing time and space within these networks . . . Thus, in actor network theory, agency, power, and size are always uncertain capillary effects which have to be constantly worked on by an actor-network. They are achieved, they are not a right. (Thrift, 1996, p. 221)

Hence, money and monetary networks, instead of being theorized as abstract concepts and properties, are embodied – they are seen to be achievements produced and maintained by the conjoint action of actors, institutions and resources striving to 'improve their own representations of what money is, how it should be made, distributed and ordered' (Leyshon, 1997a, p. 389).

These networks of money in international centres are seen to have a number of characteristics that allow the financial system to operate; for example, co-operation between firms, employees who are constantly vigilant in the search for new businesses and social interactions between buyers and sellers. Above all else, it is the knowledge embedded in these networks that enables the 'world cities' to maintain their pre-eminence in an electronic space of flows (see Sassen, 1991; Allen and Pryke, 1994; Beaverstock *et al.*, 1999). Indeed, Thrift (1996) argues that the volume and speed of such flows may make it even more imperative to construct places that act as 'centres of comprehension'. With reference to the City of London, he argues that while the somewhat particular social and cul-tural structure of the City has always exerted a degree of influence over its economic success, in recent years these elements have become increasingly important, albeit in a changed form. Thrift considers the late 1950s to be a break between the 'old' and 'new' City, a break representing the point when it became a dynamic international financial centre after the gloom of the Second World War, while also representing the time around which there was a distinct change in many of the City's social and cultural characteristics. Elaborating this, he outlines how, in the pre-war period, the City (and its power to reproduce itself) was underlain by four 'foundation stones' – the City's 'essentially meso-corporatist' relationship with the British state, its social structure, its knowledge base and its spatial concentration (see also Kynaston's, 1994, 2001, definitive 'biographies' of the City).

Elaborating these ideas, Thrift (1994c, 1996) highlights the City's social struc-ture, arguing that its ability to reproduce itself was derived from a strong social structure based upon highly visible class, gender and ethnic divisions, which in turn generated strong senses of identity. This was clearly a world dominated by the bonds of mutual trust and knowledge disseminated among networks of white business*men*. In class terms, three distinct strata were present: the directors and partners (associated with aristocratic upbringings and practices), a profes-sional and managerial middle class (recruited from university and public school attendees) and, at the 'lowest' level, a clerical labour force. This strict social hierarchy led to the existence of a 'homosocial' environment in the City (see Mort, 1998, on homosociality). Thrift argues that this was based on intersections of class and masculinity that came together in the Square Mile to produce 'stifling forms of masculine identity based on quaint uniforms, exact dress codes, various boyish market rituals and japes' (Thrift, 1996, p. 238). This was compounded by a network of men-only social institutions, alongside a 'social schism' based around ethnicity. Here Thrift argues that a range of social groups were represented as 'foreign' to the City's collective body (a somewhat ambiguous construction in light of the overseas investors whose presence is a key to the success of a global financial centre).

In seeking to explain the social networks that underpinned the City in the early half of the twentieth century, Thrift (1994c, p. 342) thus alights on the narrative of 'gentlemanly' conduct, epitomized by the values of honour, courtesy and integrity and manifest in 'ideas of how to act, ways to talk, suitable clothing and so on'. Linked to both the City's aristocratic underpinnings and increasing professionalization, this narrative played a key role in the development of trust between contacts, with actors apparently being able to sense when something was not quite right, or when contacts 'did not fit'. This sober, conservative and gentlemanly ambience was mirrored in the City's buildings, which exuded an air of solidity and permanence (Black, 1996). Similar notions are explored in **Linda McDowell**'s (Box 6.4) research on the embodied and embedded nature of finance, and the multifarious ways in which masculinities and femininities are constructed in the City. Recognizing the City as a series of real places – 'places in which real people lived and went to work' – McDowell (1997, p. 3) focused on the social practices in the City, viewing it through the lens of the lives and careers of individual men and women working in the City's merchant banks. In highlighting the effects of the 'cultural turn' within geography, McDowell notes how she found 'the combination of an older materialist way of understanding the economy and new ways of thinking about economic behaviour as embedded and embodied, through symbolic meaning, representation and discourse, extremely liberating' (McDowell, 1997, p. 7). This allowed her the freedom to explore a wide range of sources from a wide range of disciplines, ultimately resulting in her ability to interlace profitably a range of literatures to uncover the complexities of waged work in the City.

In her work on *Capital Culture*, McDowell (1997) focuses on the changing social worlds of the City of London. Like Thrift, she notes that the City has changed since the beginning of the 1960s, largely as a consequence of a range of mutations in the extent and nature of international financial systems. The manner in which the City has responded to the threats and opportunities presented by this new world of money required the making of new networks in the City, so that the ability of this 'community of money' to reproduce itself over time was not brought into question (see Thrift, 1994c, pp. 345–6). In considering why and how the City has remained successful in the face of these changes and threats, Thrift suggests that a change in the City's social structure to a more heterogeneous make-up was a crucial factor. Addressing this, McDowell focuses on the way that women have been enrolled in these networks of money in various ways, and how this inclusion has been encouraged and discouraged by various institutions, individuals and rituals.

McDowell notes at the outset of *Capital Culture* (1997) that much popular and academic literature surrounding the analysis of the 'feminization' of work in the urban West has waxed lyrical about the feminized attributes of observed management structures, styles and practices, seemingly justifying a degree of optimism regarding the success and empowerment of women in the work sphere more generally (see also Christopherson, 1995). However, she notes that recent years have also witnessed an increasing breadth of theoretically grounded studies of service-based economies. A key trend within these works has been the increased importance placed on the role of work and workplaces in socially constructing workers as embodied beings. Through notions of the gendering of organizations, work being constructed as emotional labour and how 'feeling' is managed in relation to different bodies in workplace situations and interactions, therefore, McDowell seeks to add a 'specifically geographical imagination' in analysing how the 'location and the physical construction of the workplace – its site and layout, the external appearance and the internal layout of its buildings and surrounding environment – also affects, as well as reflects, the social construction of work and workers and the relations of power, control and dominance that structure relations between them' (McDowell, 1997, p. 12). Of course, such issues are of importance in 'back room' office spaces, telephone call centres and data processing facilities just as much as they are in corporate office spaces (see Crang, 1999).

In considering these issues, McDowell emphasizes the importance of the performances that are played out in the spaces of the City – its boardrooms, dealing rooms and offices (as well as its clubs, pubs and gyms – see McCormack, 1999, on the importance of the latter in contemporary workplaces). Here, McDowell invokes the notion that workplaces are *stages* on which everyday interactions and behaviours are played out (Goffman, 1959). Focusing on the body as a culturally inscribed and performed entity (see Chapter 4), this allows

---

Box 6.4 Linda McDowell (1949–)

Along with Doreen Massey (see Box 1.2), Linda McDowell has been perhaps the most important influence on the trajectory of feminist theory in geography since its inception in the 1970s. Working from a broadly socialist-feminist perspective, her work on the intersections of patriarchy and capitalism was to generate a number of insightful analyses of the way that the feminization of the workforce in the late twentieth century was implicated in the construction of both spatial and gender divides. These ideas were spelt out in a series of journal articles on urban segregation (1983), industrial relations in the post-Fordist era (1991) and, latterly, the performance of gender identity, the embodied and embedded nature of work and the multifarious ways in which masculinities and femininities are constructed in workplaces in the City of London (1995, 1997). Throughout, attention to the way that women have been marginalized in various spaces and sectors of work has allowed McDowell to develop important ideas about the invidious effects of socio-spatial processes on women's quality of life. The evolution of McDowell's thinking to some extent mirrors that in feminist geography more generally: from earlier considerations of gendered divisions of labour, her emphasis has shifted to exploration

her to explore how the economic, social and cultural facets of the City entwine in networks of money. She highlights that, at the same time that there has been a growth in the number of women entering the City in professional positions, 'occupational sex stereotyping and the institutional and everyday structures of workplace interactions have maintained and reproduced gendered patterns of inequality at work' (McDowell, 1997, p. 204). Here, she stresses that despite their growing numbers, City women continue to be constructed as 'different' both through embedded patterns of domination and subordination within City firms, institutions and organizations, as well as in workplace rules about dress and appearance (see Halford and Savage, 1993). McDowell concludes that, despite the fact that many occupations are increasingly characterized by their performatively or interactively nuanced nature (epitomized by traits most often characterized as feminine), finance remains dominated by male values.

Like Thrift, McDowell points to the social and cultural rituals that have enabled London to maintain its pre-eminent position in international financial markets. The City of London – like New York, Tokyo and other rising financial centres such as Singapore and Frankfurt – has clearly changed, and some of the character and arcane ritual has been jettisoned in favour of a more relaxed and cosmopolitan atmosphere (see Kynaston, 2001). Yet much remains the same, with networks of money and the embedded knowledge they contain necessitating strong continuities. Above all else, this points to the continuing importance of geographic proximity in the life of the City, so that face-to-face contacts between knowledge-rich individuals remain crucial, even in a global space of flows (see Chapter 8). In times of financial boom (such as post-'Big Bang', in the late 1980s), this triggers excessive demand for property in the City, meaning that office rents in London remain some of the highest in the world (see Pryke, 1991). Thrift (1994c) accordingly concludes that international centres will remain of importance in the foreseeable future because they meet interpretative

of the way gender is performed and embodied in different spaces. Her text *Gender, Identity and Place* (1999) therefore represents a state-of-the-art summary of what feminism has bought to the theory and practice of geography, devoting attention to the multiple forms of femininity and sexuality which challenge the patriarchal values implicit in different spaces and landscapes. This also shows her interest in theories of the body (a theme explicit in her work on her studies of performance in banking and finance), while more recent work (2000b) also shows a developing engagement with masculinity, emphasizing the often assumed-away manner in which gender issues concern men as well as women. Meanwhile, her co-editorship with J. Sharp of *A Feminist Glossary of Human Geography* (1999) and its companion volume, *Space, Gender, Knowledge* (1997), indicates her continuing desire to gain widespread acceptance for feminist enquiry within a discipline still redolent of sexism and homophobia.

Further reading: McDowell (1997, 1999)

needs that cannot be satisfied electronically, and that the social and cultural determinants of their success may become more, rather than less, important.

6.5 EXCLUSION, INCLUSION, RESISTANCE

While work on financial centres shows the influence of geography's 'cultural turn', this influence is equally evident in work on the implications of financial restructuring and the creation of geographies of financial exclusion. The early body of this work arose from attention being devoted to how banks and financial institutions were responding to the emergence of an international financial system which offered new threats and opportunities (see Leyshon and Thrift, 1995; Moran, 1991). Here, interest focused on the manner in which much of the developing world was being excluded from the international financial system due to its indebtedness to international banks (see Corbridge, 1992, 1993b) and how the global financial system was instead focusing on the three regional blocs of the industrialized world, North America, Europe and South-East Asia, each co-ordinated by an international financial centre (New York, London and Tokyo respectively) (O'Brien, 1991; Hirst and Thompson, 1992; Sassen, 1991). As banks abandoned the developing world, they turned increasingly to the developed countries for their new customer base. Castells (1989, p. 37) thus depicted large parts of the developing world as moving from a 'structural position of exploitation to a structural position of irrelevance' in relation to global capitalism.

Through these new markets in the developed world, the 1980s became characterized as a period of rapid growth within the financial services industry, and witnessed the initiation of a credit boom within core capitalist countries (Leyshon and Thrift, 1993). Large amounts of credit were provided for construction industries, for the purchase of property (Warf, 1994), for increasingly

---

Box 6.5 Andrew Leyshon (1962–   )

Now Professor within the School of Geography at the University of Nottingham, the economic geographer Andrew Leyshon has been a key contributor (alongside long-term collaborator Nigel Thrift) to the development of the 'new' economic geographies of money, emphasizing that the economy is also cultural. Starting from a somewhat 'traditional' economic-geography stance, underpinned by a political-economy conception of money, Leyshon and Thrift initially investigated ideas of financial 'regions', international financial systems and the process of financial infrastructure withdrawal. By the early 1990s, unhappy with the narrowness of this approach, they sought to retheorize the geographies of money, utilizing social theory more broadly, investigating the ways in which financial institutions worked to create geographies of financial exclusion and how alternative financial systems were created on the ground to cope with such exclusions (Leyshon and Thrift, 1997). Leyshon's work (along with Thrift) has therefore been influential in developing a more discursive approach to money that extends beyond purely economic considerations to pay more attention to social and cultural processes, practices

aggressive rounds of corporate restructuring (Clark, 1989) and for personal loans and other credit facilities in order to support the consumption of goods and services (Ford, 1988, 1991; Berthoud and Kempson, 1992). By the late 1980s, however, household indebtedness levels were more than 90 per cent of disposable income in both the United States of America and Japan, and more than 100 per cent of disposable income in the UK (Bank for International Settlements, 1992, p. 107). The good times were at an end, and in the wake of a glut of financial crises, the 1990s witnessed 'debt coming home' in the form of the 'developed countries debt crisis', founded in personal, corporate and property-related liabilities (Berthoud and Kempson, 1992; Ford, 1988, 1991; Warf, 1994). As a consequence, financial service firms were forced to rediscover the merits of caution, with a general redirection of credit away from poorer social groups towards richer groups as part of a strategy of risk avoidance.

Given the restructuring of the financial system and the exclusions this has created within developed countries, geographers have begun to trace how the financial services industry has retreated to a largely middle-class heartland in the search for fee-income and investment accounts (Mitchell, 1990; Christopherson, 1993) while simultaneously withdrawing its services from certain poorer communities. Here, the work of Nigel Thrift – working with **Andrew Leyshon** (see Box 6.5) – has again been important. In Leyshon and Thrift's wide-ranging research, they have traced the linkages between the extensive restructuring in the financial services sector, the withdrawal of financial services from poorer areas and the effects of targeted investment in a volatile market. For example, they have examined how as much as 15 per cent of some bank branch networks in the UK were closed down in the early 1990s, most of which were in low-income, inner-city areas. Moreover, they chart how the unsuccessful, and ultimately recession-inducing, foray by the British Conservative Government into the European Exchange Rate Mechanism (ERM) in the early 1990s had severe effects on the British housing market, turning it into 'a vehicle for

and outcomes – emphasizing the constructedness and 'power' of money in shaping life across a range of spatial scales (as documented in a trilogy of articles in *Progress in Human Geography*, 1995b, 1997a, 1998). However, while advocating the development of 'new' economic geographies, Leyshon (1995c) also notes the dangers of overly concentrating on the cultural at the expense of the material, pointing to the relative lack of work on poverty in contemporary geography and the need to tackle widespread social and financial exclusion. Leyshon's recent work includes analysis of monetary networks in financial centres and the geography of local currency systems, alongside a developing interest in the geographies of music, with a particular focus on how software formats, electronic distribution systems and e-commerce more generally are transforming the global consumption and production of music.

Further reading: Leyshon (1995b); Leyshon and Thrift (1997); Lee *et al.* (2002)

financial ruin and spatial entrapment' for many, as inflation, and subsequently interest rates, rose (Leyshon, 1995b, p. 536).

In exploring the theoretical underpinnings of these processes of financial infrastructure withdrawal, Leyshon and Thrift have drawn upon the works of the economists Gary Dymski and John Veitch (1992, 1995, 1996). In drawing on this work, Leyshon and Thrift (1995, p. 314) have argued that a strong relationship exists between the ease of access to capital and the economic power of the borrower, a 'structural bias' that may be explained by understanding that the cost of money is effectively determined 'by the level of risk which a financial institution believes it incurs in lending money to a borrower'. This risk is determined firstly by reference to the length of time that the money will be out on loan, hence favouring those firms who can pay back such loans quickly (that is, those firms with greater financial resources). Secondly, risk is determined by the purpose of the loan, with money effectively being cheaper when it is borrowed to purchase specified, tangible assets (such as property), rather than non-specific purposes. Thirdly, risk is also determined by the perceived 'creditworthiness' of the borrower, itself determined in part by an indication of the current wealth of the borrower (and this may take many forms), and by estimates of the borrower's future financial status. Importantly, such information may be more or less readily available. Dymski and Veitch have also been drawn upon to highlight the contrasting accessibility of sources of capital between 'spot' credit markets (where large amounts of capital are available at very short notice as a result of the fact that the creditworthiness of the borrowers is known beforehand, thereby favouring the top-rated borrowers) and 'contract' credit markets (where information on the borrower's creditworthiness is not so readily on display, and where subsequently the balance of power shifts in favour of the lender).

Consequently, Leyshon and Thrift (1995, p. 315) argue that 'if gaining access to credit from the financial system is determined in large measure by income and wealth, then the geography of income and wealth to a large extent determines the geography of access to the financial system'. Moreover, through Dymski and Veitch's notion of 'financial dynamics', this relationship is seen to be circular, in that geographical variations in access to the financial system deepen and accentuate prevailing levels of uneven development; in other words, 'rich areas tend to get richer and poor areas poorer because of the way in which the financial system discriminates between people and communities on the basis of risk' (Leyshon and Thrift, 1995, p. 315). As Philo (1995) notes, this results in the creation of areas cut off from the worlds of institutional finance, where few have bank accounts, it is difficult to obtain a mortgage, and insurance is sky-high. This leads to a situation where those most in need of good financial services and advice (i.e., those living in poverty) are unable to access even basic services. Even cash point machines (ATMs) may be notoriously absent in some 'no-go' areas.

Though this work on the role of financial institutions has its antecedents in earlier neo-Weberian 'managerial' theories on the key gatekeepers who control access to resources (see Hamnett and Randolph, 1988; Knox, 1994),

Leyshon and Thrift's work has arguably led to a broader appreciation of exclusion and inclusion in relation to the financial system by highlighting the interdependent nature of the social, the cultural and the economic. This is not to say that their approach to financial infrastructure withdrawal has been beyond criticism. For example, Ford and Rowlingson (1996) argue that it characterizes the financial system in 'narrow' terms. They note that, in general, research tends to focus on 'regulated', 'formal' or 'high-street based' sources of credit, such as banks, mortgage lenders and occasionally credit from major retailers, failing to acknowledge the far greater range of financial institutions within the regulated market such as hire purchase companies, local shop credit, cheque traders and mail order firms, and the existence of other sources of credit such as pawnbrokers, money lenders and alternative financial systems such as credit unions and LETS (local exchange trading systems). So, in the same way that retail geographers have paid attention to informal sites of shopping (e.g., car-boot fairs, junk shops, garage sales – see Williams and Windebank, 2000), economic geographers have begun to explore the importance of these alternative sources of money, particularly for indebted and poor households.

Subsequent research has therefore begun to address other systems of financial services and credit which provide a range of facilities to those marginalized from the 'mainstream' financial services as well as alternative sources of credit to those who can access mainstream services. These include community development banks (Taub, 1988); rotating savings and credit associations (ROSCAs) (Ardener, 1995); local exchange trading systems (LETS) (Lee, 1996); and credit unions (Fuller, 1998; Fuller and Jonas, 2002a, 2002b). As a consequence of these financial services often developing 'bottom up' from largely practical initiatives or through institutional templates moving from the developing world to the developed, they had, Leyshon and Thrift (1996) argued, previously been ignored by the academic gaze, a neglect that Fuller (1998) suggests can be understood through analogy to the status of social and ethnic minorities within society and in academic work. Drawing on Sibley's (1990) argument that the location and economic status of minorities is not only determined by the dominant forces in society but also through their own agency, Fuller argues that accounts that privilege banks as all-powerful institutions fail to recognize the agency of borrowers and savers. In essence, these accounts had elaborated a geography of finance and credit essentially limited to concern over the provision of such facilities and finance from these sources. The affluent and powerful – the banks and building societies – were seen as holding all the power.

By holding this power, they were perceived to be able to relegate groups whom they considered to be a bad risk (for whatever reason) to areas outside the financial 'mainstream'. While expressing concern for their predicaments, the mainstream sources of credit would argue that they are 'businesses, not charities', and that they do not provide social services (Hunter, 1993). Moreover, it had been implicitly presumed that minority groups, as defined by a lack of creditworthiness, suffered through lack of access to 'mainstream' credit and financial infrastructure, and lack of power and control over the source and determinants of that creditworthiness. For example, much of the information surrounding moneylending is characterized by anecdotal evidence and media images which have subsequently tended to 'sensationalise moneylending, portraying moneylenders as the exploiters of the vulnerable, as usurers who make large profits on the backs of the poor and the weak' (Ford and Rowlingson, 1996; see Daly and Walsh, 1988). Whilst such 'mainstream' financial institutions were viewed as being proactive, excluding for sound economic reasons, borrowers' lack of involvement with banks and building societies would be cast in terms of helpless *reactions* to the mainstream players' agendas, turning to sources they would not normally use. In contrast, Ford and Rowlingson (1996) argue that people possess, in principle at least, a degree of choice and scope, with an ability to express (proactively) a preference between mainstream sources and those which are regarded (or represented) as less 'mainstream'/formal/ regulated (see Fuller and Jonas, 2002a). As a consequence, it is argued that institutionally led processes of financial exclusion are not the whole story.

Recent empirical research has sought, therefore, to investigate notions of financial citizenship and 'local monies', which 'represent highly diverse, and possibly temporary, alternative ways of organizing local economies and communities' (Lee, 1999, p. 223). In investigating one example of these, Fuller and Jonas (2002a) have explored the potential for British credit union development to play a key role in countering the effects of poverty and financial exclusion. With a focus on 'community' credit unions (financial co-operatives that are owned and operated by their members, who are usually drawn from a common bond area defined by place of residence and/or work) they have been examining local capacities for credit union development in selected localities, the absorption of local credit unions into community economic development (CED) initiatives and trends within the wider credit union movement as these increasingly impact upon local development trajectories. In so doing they have focused on the growing interrelationships between the local and national contexts of credit union development, highlighting the manner in which the role, identity and philosophy of British credit union development are currently being appropriated by the state (albeit with the help of certain key players from within the credit union movement) and given legitimacy through the state's emphasis on social exclusion policy. They argue that this appropriation has a number of important implications for the future development trends and trajectories of British credit unions and their role in carving out 'spaces of hope' (see Harvey, 2000a) amid the landscapes of poverty and despair that otherwise have been created through the spatially uneven workings of global finance (Philo, 1995).

In particular, Fuller and Jonas (2002a) stress how, along with other 'local monies' such as local exchange trading systems (LETS), credit unions are recognized to be increasingly practical and vital to the economic stability of localities and communities otherwise adversely affected by economic restructuring and financial withdrawal, with this role being given added significance by the British Labour Government, which now views support for credit union development as central to its policies on social and financial exclusion (Social Exclusion Unit, 1998; HM Treasury, 1999; HM Government, 1999). Elsewhere, they have analysed how these institutional forms become embedded in the landscape, and how their supporting social networks and institutions are (or are not) reproduced over time and, as such, question their supposed 'alternative' nature (Fuller and Jonas, 2002b; see also Lee *et al.*, 2002). Similar work on local exchange trading systems (LETS) has explored notions of value, barter, work, social movements, and empowerment, alongside its use as a vehicle in examining broader conceptualizations of money in and of itself (see Lee, 1999; North, 1999; Williams, 1996).

Interestingly, this focus on alternative financial systems has led some to explore the division between academic and activist, and the role of the academy in the increasingly vociferous campaign which has been waged in policy and public spheres to hold the 'mainstream' players to account for their actions. As such, there is a developing trend within academic (and geographical) circles for the inclusionary and emancipatory potential of these 'alternative' forms of financial systems to be both explored and engaged with, professionally and privately, beyond the academy (see Fuller, 1999; North, 1999). This shows that there are real and important links between theory and practice, with many geographers concerned not just to make sense of, but also to intervene in, the world (a theme captured in the rubric of 'critical geography' – see Chapter 3).

6.6 CONCLUSION

We began this chapter by noting how the study of money within geography is a relatively recent phenomenon, developing rapidly since the early 1980s to the extent that it now represents a burgeoning field of interest and inquiry within economic geography. Despite this recent development, geographers have drawn upon an increasingly wide range of theoretical perspectives and viewpoints in striving to understand the geographies of money. While the political-economy tradition still strongly influences much work, the effects of the 'cultural turn' and the creation of a 'new' economic geography have witnessed increasing emphasis being placed on the social and cultural facets of money and its geographies, with 'new' literatures being plundered beyond the traditional geographical realm in order to develop understandings of what money is, how it works and its effects on society at large. However, in a sense, there is nothing new at all about this 'new' emphasis on the social and cultural within the study of money. The reading of this chapter might seem to imply that, in recent years, the social and cultural aspects of money have been added to previously 'economic' analyses, with an implication that all previous 'economic' analyses have excluded the 'social' and 'cultural'. For many Marxists (amongst others), however, money is, and always has been, theorized fundamentally as a social relation, with the exchange of commodities and labour for money theorized as having social consequences. As such, money in all its forms is always-already a social relation, and as such it is not a question of adding on the social and cultural aspects, or analysing the transformation of money by societal relations and values, but exploring their relation, dialectically or otherwise. While there is undoubtedly much to be gained from the 'new' ideas and 'new' theories being developed as the geographical study of money progresses, there is also therefore much to be learnt from old(er) theories and ideas, as often they (or their underlying themes) return in new guises and forms, with different nuances, from different sources, at different times. The task for the geographer is to think geographically about money, and use these ideas, whether new or old, to further understanding of money's curious geography.

Chapter 7   Geographies of Governance

7.1 THE MEANING OF GOVERNANCE

This chapter examines ways that geographers have sought to make sense of relationships between the sovereign state (embodied in local, regional and national governments), the market (private enterprise) and civil society (broadly defined as 'the public'). Traditionally, this has been of interest mainly to political geographers, who have tended to examine the role of the state in the regulation of the market and civil society, but more recently this has extended to a wider concern among geographers with the way that public and business interests are involved in maintaining social order. As this chapter will explain, this has entailed a move away from traditional analyses of *government* and its control of society and space to a conceptualization of *governance* based on flexible and facilitative forms of partnership between government representatives, businesses and other non-government agents. According to Stoker (1998) this conceptualization of governance became increasingly popular in the social sciences during the 1990s, so that its dictionary definition (i.e., as a synonym for government) has been superseded. Here, traditional governmental structures, policies and institutions are deemed to be just one component of governance which embraces a wide range of institutions and actors working together on a formal and informal basis to produce policy outcomes. The concept of governance thus extends beyond the formal institutional structures of authority and decision-making associated with government – for example, general elections, political parties, policy-making and referenda – to embrace the wider networks which shape society.

In part, contemporary geographic interest in governance has resulted from the awareness that politics is currently undergoing something of a transformation. Central here is the idea that the sovereign state is no longer the primary anchor of political regulation (Jessop, 1995). Instead, the boundaries between the three spheres of the state, the market and civil society, so clearly distinguishable and demarcated in early analyses, have collapsed as policy-making is enacted both through and beyond the mechanisms of the state (Amin and Hausner, 1997). Increasingly, governance involves a shift from centralized and bureaucratic forms of decision-making to a plurality of coexisting networks and partnerships that interact as overlapping webs of relationships at diverse spatial scales, from the neighbourhood to the globe (Healey *et al.*, 1995; Painter, 2000a).

One example of this is the way that non-governmental organizations are becoming involved in the governance of everyday life both in the West and non-West. Charities, agencies, consultants and other non-elected bodies may become significant in shaping the social character of different places, with some areas (e.g., British inner cities) being subject to the influence of multiple, and often overlapping, organizations, from Task Forces and Development Corporations through to Enterprise Councils and National Health Service Trusts. Typical features exhibited by these non-state or quasi-state bodies are relative autonomy from the state, organizational interdependence, ongoing negotiated interaction and self-organization, and mutual or transactional trust among members (Rhodes, 1997). The resulting fragmentation of responsibilities between different organizations means that the sovereign state becomes only one of many agencies competing for resources and control of agendas (Davoudi, 1995). In this sense, the concept of governance directs attention to the proliferation and fragmentation of the service delivery mechanisms that exist to devise and implement policies.

As we shall see in this chapter, thinking about governance rather than government, and facilitation rather than diktat, has forced geographers to develop new perspectives on political power and social order. The chapter reviews some of these ideas, paying particular attention to the emergence of theories which extend analysis of *power* in politics beyond issues of party politics and class control to its wider (and often more subtle) manifestations in the politics of everyday life. This has seen political geographers engage with emerging concepts in cultural, social and economic geography, as well as theoretical frameworks derived from other disciplines. As we shall see, the theoretical roots of thinking about governance are extremely varied, ranging from classical Marxist theories of class conflict through to Foucaultian social theory (Stoker, 1998). Unsurprisingly, geographic literature on the subject is also extremely eclectic.

To try to understand how geographers have thought about governance, this chapter is divided into five main sections. The first describes the way that geographers and other theorists have attempted to identify key transitions in the nature of governance via the recognition of distinct modes of governance. Outlining the way such modes have been used to characterize transformations in global, national and local politics, this section focuses particularly on the move towards entrepreneurial forms of governance. Here, we explore the link between these changes and the associated shift in orientation of state policies from welfare protection to the promotion of economic development and competitiveness. In the second section, we examine how geographers have utilized (and developed) the conceptual tools of political science – especially coalition and regime theories – to make sense of the new modes of governance emerging at the local (and especially urban) scale. Extending this, we then turn in our next section to describe the way that neo-Marxist ideas theorize these shifts in governance as part and parcel of a wide shift in the nature of (global) regulation. In the fourth section, we explore some of the alternative ways geographers have begun to work with fluid notions of structure and agency through the adoption of Actor Network Theory, which offers a different take on political power. Finally, we explore the important changes occurring in civil society by examining geographers' interpretations of 'citizenship'. Throughout, we focus primarily on the forms of governance emerging in the urban West, though in passing we should note that the debates we highlight are also being worked through in other contexts (see Leftwich, 1993; Radcliffe and Westwood, 1996).

7.2 CHANGING MODES OF GOVERNANCE

It has been widely argued that geographers' increasing emphasis on questions of governance has been provoked by recent transitions in the nature of politics (Painter, 1995; Hubbard and Hall, 1998; Low, 2001). What is particularly evident, certainly in the West, is that trends of privatization and political conservatism have been evident, with a concurrent rise in the popularity of 'neo-liberal' thinking (Pierson, 1998). Though this term covers a range of disparate ideas, the key thread running through neo-liberalism is that free markets are the most efficient mechanisms for regulating the production and distribution of goods and services in society. Proponents argue, accordingly, that state intervention in the market should be minimized on the grounds that it undermines the efficiency of markets, and that only minimal state intervention is necessary to ensure the fairness of business practice. This is by no means a new idea, having antecedents in the economic liberalism of Adam Smith that was to prove so influential in the Victorian era, yet its contemporary inflection by the New Right arguably loses much of the subtlety of Smith's writing in favour of an unabashed celebration of the excesses of the free market (Hutton, 1995). In the 1980s, this was to reach its apogee in the Thatcherite and Reaganite politics that dominated the UK and USA respectively, though the logic of liberalism spread beyond the Western core through a development doctrine couched in terms of 'structural adjustment, privatisation, deregulation, free trade and market based development' (Slater, 1995, p. 68). The implication here was that non-Western countries had to be opened up as never before, and were expected to roll back the frontiers of the state to facilitate Western-style development and financial discipline. Notably, this neo-liberalism was encouraged by the structural adjustment programmes imposed by the International Monetary Fund and World Trade Organization in the wake of the 1980s debt crisis, while more recent international agreements such as the General Agreement on Tariffs and Trade and the creation of extended free-trade zones such as the North American Free Trade Agreement Area have also promulgated this laissez-faire logic (see Chapter 8 on economic globalization).

In many ways, the (re)turn to neo-liberalism represents an interesting reversal of policy thinking and management priorities from the political ideas that dominated the post-war period, when strong state intervention was seen as a necessary precursor to effective social reproduction. At this time, the negative impacts of the Industrial Revolution on landscape and society gave rise to the view that the operation of the private market was irrational and inefficient – thereby giving rise to a range of consequential problems that required state intervention to safeguard the public interest. In Britain, this resulted in the construction of a bureaucratized and centralized 'Keynesian' welfare state, with a state-controlled system of welfare, education and public health. At the same time, fiscal policy was subject to strong state control. The maintenance of this Keynesian welfare state was crucial to the success of Fordist (mass) production, ensuring a growing body of affluent consumers to buy the goods realized through the refinement of the factory assembly line, rising productivity and the expansion of productive capacities (Swyngedouw, 1989).

Now, conversely, it is these very principles and practices that are considered by many politicians to be the source of social problems. Following the rise of the New Right in the 1980s, the welfare state has been gradually disassembled as privatization has become the dominant trend in many sectors of social life. The consequences of this are certainly evident in the transformations that have occurred in the nature of urban life, where privatization and the 'hollowing out' of the state are dominant leitmotifs. Studies of the transformations in the nature of urban governance have consequently highlighted the fiscal pressures facing city governors (Pinch, 1995), simultaneously stressing that city regions are expected to become engines of local economic growth through the formation of partnerships between public and private sectors (Brotchie *et al.*, 1995; Newman and Thornley, 1996). A key concept here is that of *entrepreneurialism*: cities are no longer regarded as passive places in the international arena, but adopt entre-preneurial practices which are designed to promote competitive advantage on the national and global stage:

> The new entrepreneurialism has as its centrepiece the notion of public-private partnership in which a traditional local boosterism is integrated with the use of local governmental powers to try and attract external sources of funding, new direct investments or new employment sources. (Harvey, 1989b, p. 7)

Perhaps most important here is the way cities have been (re)positioning them-selves through marketing and promotional strategies designed to enhance their image and prospects of attracting additional inward investment (Ashworth and Voogd, 1990; Kearns and Philo, 1993; Hubbard and Hall, 1998).

Significantly, these strategies include the use of flagship projects as ways to 'reimage' the city and promote its potential for international development and investment (Olds, 1995). Examples include the redevelopment of London's Docklands, New York's Battery Park, Barcelona's Olympic Marina, Birming-ham's Brindley Place, Berlin's remodelled Potsdamer Platz, Lisbon's Expo Centre and so on. Spectacular in form, these developments are intensely pro-moted and heavily mediated (see Chapter 5 on the representation of landscape).

Of course, there is no guarantee that such schemes, or the publicity they generate, will create additional revenue for the city, and some are financial disasters (Anderson, 2002). Yet most are underwritten by the state and financed by private-sector capital. In most cases this means that the public sector bears the losses whilst private sector investors (including large corporate developers and financial institutions such as investment banks and insurance fund managers) reap the benefits. Private capital is thus attracted by the reduced risk implicit in such public-private partnership initiatives, creating a growing 'demand' for entrepreneurial development (Gaffikin and Warf, 1993; Swyngedouw, 2000). At the same time, it is notable that most schemes are targeted at a new global elite, so that these urban development schemes supply working, living and leisure spaces for those who actually have little commitment to a particular city and live in the essentially self-contained 'islands of the cosmopolitan archipelago' (Bauman, 2000, p. 57). In many cases these areas involve the transformation or gentrification of redundant or 'low-grade' sites with redevelopment potential in or around the older quarters of city centres (see Section 3.1 on theories of gentrification). This underlines the fact that entrepreneurialism represents a speculative approach to the management of cities, privileging certain groups and values, which contrasts with the ostensibly professionalized, bureaucratized and democratic managerial governance dominant in the post-war period (Harvey, 1989b).

A significant dimension in the adoption of entrepreneurial strategies is the creation of a suitable local political environment which is supportive of neo-liberal economic development (Newman and Thornley, 1996). This often involves the introduction of new political/administrative arrangements, such as public-private partnerships, as well as the creation of quasi-autonomous organizations ('quangos') like Urban Development Corporations (UDCs) or Training Enterprise Councils (TECs). Such partnerships exhibit varied geographies, being spatially diffuse in some cases, locally embedded and focused in others. They can also cross sectoral divides to unite groups or agencies with different functional remits or interests. Most notably, from the point of view of urban governance, they draw together public and private sector actors around a shared strategic focus and sense of civic vision. Moreover, some partnerships may reinforce the prevailing governance structures whilst others may challenge them. According to Ling, partnership is generally portrayed as returning politics to the people, but there is a glaring absence of evidence to justify such claims. There is, he says, a considerable body of anecdotal rhetoric and assertion about the public benefits of partnership from a variety of academic and non-academic sources. However, without appropriate empirical evidence, we cannot determine whether policies and initiatives failed in the past because of lack of partnership or confirm that new partnership arrangements have demonstrably improved outcomes (Ling, 2000). Local partnerships can become a new technical form of area management, in the organization and operation of which local people participate rarely and even then only at a formal, tokenistic level. Despite these problems, Parkinson (1998) suggests that the innovations and flexibility of partnerships as compared with traditional local government structures is bound to have an energizing effect upon local authorities.

Geographers have been quick to outline the essential attributes of such partnerships, theorizing their formation in relation to the changing interests of both the state and private business (Peck, 1995; Peck and Tickell, 1995; Newman and Thornley, 1996; Painter, 1998). This work makes the important point that partnerships do not exist in a vacuum, but emerge from an existing institutional culture. Even where they are established for ostensibly economic ends they are more than economic or political entities; partnerships are social and cultural constructs and their variable nature reflects the diversity of the social, economic, political, cultural and spatial environments in which they emerge. Significantly, the entrepreneurial phase of British local government in the 1980s coincided with severe reductions in the funding available to local authorities from central government block grants and the curtailment of their tax-generating powers. Arguably, this situation compelled local authorities to embrace a much more entrepreneurial approach to raising revenue. This included entering new alliances with the private sector and becoming more actively involved in economic development initiatives (Stoker, 1998). A further change in central government policy during the 1990s intensified this entrepreneurial approach by emphasizing notions of competitiveness. Central government consequently became more selective in allocating exchequer funding for urban development and localities were obliged to create partnerships to compete with other area-based partnerships for urban regeneration funds through City Challenge and the Single Regeneration Budget (Oatley, 1998). Local authorities were also often impelled to become members of broader partnership alliances to satisfy the bid criteria specified by central government. Hall (2001) suggests that this fostered three-way partnership models which could include the community and voluntary spheres of civil society in addition to the state and private sectors. While it is perhaps too early to judge their impacts, the aim of the later policies has ostensibly been to broaden access to power, transform the operations of local government and provide more sustainable forms of urban regeneration (Oatley, 1998; Hall, 2001).

In sum, the new urban governance involves city governors self-consciously adapting to new pressures by privatizing or contracting out some of their traditional functions, divesting others to community groups and reconstituting their role as competitive and proactive (entrepreneurial) managers of the remaining activities (Hambleton, 1998). All of these developments combined to create a dynamic and volatile environment in which the ability to create and sustain successful partnerships is of paramount importance and the politics of partnership formation and maintenance have taken centre stage. Yet, explaining exactly why these new forms of governance have emerged is problematic, and both old and new theoretical materials have been invoked in attempts to make sense of governance. We review some of these theories in the following three sections.

7.3 COALITIONS AND REGIMES

Despite Lovering's (1995) criticisms of the fashion for myopic 'local' research, an emphasis on exploring governance at the local level has continued to thrive in academic work on governance (Leyshon, 1997b). Key questions here include how cities and regions are able to create sufficient 'institutional capacity' to promote and govern themselves given that many previously centralized urban functions are being devolved and privatized. *Growth coalition theory* has been used extensively in the fields of political science, sociology and urban geography to explore this issue (Stoker, 1998). Such growth coalition theories are closely allied to 'elite' theories in political science (which can be traced back to Marx) and draw mainly upon research reports of the experiences of North American cities (Peterson, 1981; Logan and Molotch, 1987; Cox and Mair, 1988). This research suggests that it is urban elites (i.e., coalitions of dynamic businessmen, real estate developers, banks, newspaper proprietors and proactive city hall politicians, led usually by a charismatic mayor or politician) who transform 'their' city. From the perspective of Marxist political science, growth coalitions are read as place-bound phenomena, having a vested interest in embedding capital in their locale (Cox, 1998).

The work of Logan and Molotch (1987) is especially influential here, describing the characteristics of 'growth elites' – people who share a common pro-growth mentality. These elite 'growth coalitions' are defined by Logan and Molotch as significant groupings of influential actors who seek growth at almost any cost. Members of the growth coalition usually stand to benefit from the population expansion and increased land values associated with 'growth strategy'. They also tend to be highly active in local government politics because they have much to gain from their involvement in the system. The political machinery tends, accordingly, to be weighted in their favour and work in their interests. However, growth coalitions usually extend their influence by actively working to persuade others that growth will benefit everyone. Typically, a consensus is sought through persuading the wider public of the benefits of the idea of the city as a 'growth machine', the potential of which is captured in a combination of visionary development projects and boosterist imagery. The importance of the local media in such growth coalitions is therefore obvious, playing an important supportive role in highlighting the wider merits of the projects and creating a positive environment for investment (as well as persuasively pre-empting local criticism by 'selling' the growth vision to the local population). In effect, the 'story' narrated by the elite becomes the dominant narrative of city development and receives widespread approval from the general populace. In this view, a 'unified' city interest is achieved that purports to benefit all residents of the city including the members of the elite coalition. Where opposition to the growth coalition is expressed, the media typically represents its multiple voices as a unified group with the single interest of opposing the growth machine so that the overall picture is one of either universal support for the growth machine or a very polarized situation comprised of two camps who are either pro- or anti-economic development (Hall, 2001). There are then important links between the perspectives of growth coalition theory and the ideas of hegemony proposed by Gramsci (see Box 3.3): the symbolic framing of the city becomes all-important in the legitimation of urban policy (Boyle, 1997).

Critics of growth coalition theory have argued that its narrow conceptualization of power obscures the multitude of conflicts, compromises and other political manoeuvrings that constitute the policy-making and implementation agenda of cities (Stone and Sanders, 1987). They argue that the naïve view of power in growth coalition theory, which assumes the ability of a growth coalition to exercise control over resources and people, fails to account for the processes which create and shape this power. In many ways, it draws on Marxist theories of social relations which have been accused of eviscerating urban politics by ignoring the cultural creativity and bargaining explicit in city politics (Collinge and Hall, 1997). Arguably, the variety of forms of coalition and the motivations of their members are far more diverse than allowed for in growth coalition theory (Stone, 1989; Stoker, 1995). Consequently, growth coalition theory often fails to account for the diversity of coalitions found in different cities (Ward, 1996; Hubbard and Hall, 1998). In Britain, for example, not all town halls are entrepreneurial and there are many examples of local authorities and partnerships committed to no-growth, low-growth or anti-growth development strategies whilst others have subscribed to strategies with a political bias towards the provision of welfare services at the expense of economic development (Hall, 2001). As such, Logan has admitted that 'after two decades of research, we are still unsure whether growth machines make a difference to urban development' (Logan *et al.* 1997, p. 624).

Since its inception in the United States in the late 1980s, through the pioneering works of Richard Elkin (1987) and **Clarence Stone** (see Box 7.1), *regime theory* has flourished as an alternative approach to analysing city politics in North

---

Box 7.1 Clarence Stone (1935–   )

The US political scientist Clarence Stone was one of the pioneers in the 1980s of urban regime theory, which has since become one of the dominant approaches to the study of urban political power. Regime theory emphasizes the variety of regimes over time and space and is usually employed as a research tool to carry out empirical investigations through the method of case studies. Stone's groundbreaking theoretical account of regime theory is embedded in his detailed case study of Atlanta, Georgia, in the USA (1989). Stone was frustrated by the economistic explanations of city politics advanced by both right- and left-wing commentators in the 1980s. He developed regime theory as a direct response to the economic determinism propounded by Peterson's *City Limits* (1981). He challenged Peterson's claim that there was a unitary or common city-wide interest in promoting economic development which, Peterson argued, would benefit everyone within the city limits. There was no allowance made for political conflict in Peterson's model of economic imperatives. By demonstrating the relative autonomy of the state and politics from capitalism, Stone also sought to dispel simplistic Marxist explanations which portrayed the state as an appendage of the economic mode of production. In short, he wished to put politics, which was being sidelined by the economistic approaches, back on the agenda of urban

America and beyond. In contrast to elite theories which see power as consolidated, regime theory views power as a diffuse resource and draws upon Weberian pluralist traditions in political science which conceive of political power as negotiated and dispersed (being derived from the work of the sociologist Max Weber). Here, different 'power clusters' (Dahl, 1961) control different spheres of urban life, and are granted the power to act through popular consent (as expressed at the ballot box). Grounded empirically in a host of detailed single-city case studies, regime theory claims to offer a more sophisticated account of urban politics than growth coalition theory. Regime theory acknowledges that urban decision-making is diffuse, fragmented and non-hierarchical and recognizes the 'meshing of interests' that brings both governmental and non-governmental actors within the ambit of governance (Ward, 1996). It also acknowledges the importance of local business interests in local governance but without succumbing to the economic determinism or structuralism of growth coalition theory:

> Specifically [regime analysis] recognises the enormous political importance of privately controlled investment, but does so without going so far as to embrace economic determinism. In assuming that political economy is about the relationship between politics and economics, regime analysts explore the middle ground between, on the one side pluralists . . . and on the other side structuralists. (Stone, 1993, p. 2)

Regime theory differs importantly from pluralist (positivist) conceptions by focusing on the ways that diverse groups compensate for their individual lack of power by combining to form a more powerful collective regime. These regimes are rarely formed from scratch, but are ongoing and constantly shifting

---

inquiry. He did this by operationalizing the concept of a regime as a public-private coalition. This enabled him to emphasize the 'political' in political economy and allowed him to bridge the research gap between the exhausted Weberian tradition of static community-power studies and the Marxist economic determinism of political economists. Stone deployed regime theory to identify institutions and actors in the state, market and civil sectors through whom urban policy and politics were negotiated and brokered in relation to a particular urban issue. In his view, to understand urban policy-making, it is necessary to consider how the limited resources commanded by public officials are melded together with those of private actors to produce a capacity to govern. The arrangements by which such coalitions are created can be called regimes – in the case of localities, urban regimes (see Stone *et al.*, 1994, pp. 223–4). This formulation of regime theory permitted detailed empirical investigation of crucial substantive issues in the context of changing relations between a variety of agents in the field of urban governance while extending theoretical debates on the nature of urban power.

Further reading: Stone (1996); Stoker (1995)

phenomena, taking different forms as structures of capitalism shift. Here, a decisive shift has been that from Fordist production to post-Fordism: a political economy based on economies of scale to one based on economies of scope (Swyngedouw, 1989).

The critical argument of regime theory is that political power is not inherently available to any specific individual or agency but has to be created by the members of a regime coming together to blend their resources, skills and purposes into a long-term coalition, or regime, to produce the capacity required to achieve agreed aims. This is a way of thinking about power as 'creative production' and constitutes a move away from the view of power as 'control' which fuelled the debates between the elite and pluralist schools:

> What is at issue is not so much domination and subordination as a capacity to act and accomplish goals. The power struggle concerns not control and resistance, but gaining and fusing a capacity to act – power *to*, not power *over*. (Stone, 1989, p. 229)

In regime theory, politics is not restricted to acts of domination by an elite and consent or resistance from the ruled. In a complex and fragmented society no single group can exercise complete control over its environment, and all groups, including governmental institutions, are driven to co-operate with others who may have resources essential to the achievement of policy aims. As the task of government becomes more complex in the contemporary 'network society' (see Chapter 8), effective government institutions must co-operate, and blend their capacities, with more non-governmental actors. Thus, the establishment of a viable regime is the ultimate act of power in the context of an emerging system of governance (Stoker, 1998). There are then clear parallels between the issue-focused 'capacity-building' dimension of regime theory and the current trend of 'enabling' partnership formation in cities (see Section 7.2).

Collinge and Hall (1997) provide a succinct summary of fundamental differences between growth coalition theory and regime theory. They conclude their comparison with the following summary:

> There is . . . an underlying difference between neo-Marxist theories of hegemony [growth coalition theory], with their formal analysis of the state and its relationships to the structures of capital and class in which empirical investigation is neglected, and regime theory with its more open-ended investigation of political process in which there is greater empirical emphasis, but in which the form of the state apparatus and its structural relationship to economic interests are neglected. (Collinge and Hall, 1997, p. 135)

They suggest that useful lessons can be drawn from regime theory, with a stronger emphasis upon political dynamics being of benefit to growth coalition theory by illustrating the ways in which politics mediates between strategies and structures, or between the direction and form of urban governance. Stoker (1995) similarly argues that the framework for analysis provided by regime theory, with its layered conceptions of power and politics, yields a more subtle understanding of politics than that provided by rival theories including growth coalition theory and 'hyperpluralist' approaches – even where the latter prioritize empirical description over theoretical development in recognition of postmodern times (see Chapter 3). Regime theory also lends itself to sophisticated classifications of a variety of different types of regime which can be employed heuristically for research and analysis purposes (Stone has himself provided a working classification matrix). Nevertheless, even Stone concedes that it is a theory in need of development. In particular, he suggests that regime theory needs to avoid the 'localist' trap and place its micro-political analysis in the context of the broader political environment.

This criticism is one that strikes at the heart of debates in urban politics. In many ways, regime theory has a strong functional emphasis, being rooted in the traditions of positivist social science (see Chapter 2). For many, this is an uncritical approach that fails to situate governance adequately within the broader framework of Marxist political economy (Le Galés, 1998). Commentators from within the structuralist political-economy perspective have also critized the absence of a convincing theoretical framework, arguing that without a wider explanatory context regime theory amounts to little more than the construction of typologies of regimes based on 'ideal types' (Cox, 1991; Ward, 1996). Arguing this, Collinge and Hall invert the criticisms about the need to upgrade regime theory by linking it with a wider 'neo-Marxist' explanatory framework:

> [Growth coalition] theory provides a powerful overall framework for understanding urban governance. But this approach can usefully be extended and developed by addressing the issues raised by regime theory, in demonstrating that politics matters, its concern with capacity building and with the investigation of case studies. Our understanding of the locally networked state, and of the patterns that are summarized under the broad headings of 'Fordist' and 'post-Fordist', can be advanced by opening a dialogue between neo-Marxism and neo-pluralism. (Collinge and Hall, 1997, p. 140)

Some regime theorists thus claim that regime theory bridges the gap between the pluralist power studies in the Weberian tradition (which focus on the measurement of perceived 'status' in the community) and the excesses of Marxist analyses which ignore the nuances of local culture (Le Galés, 1998). However, most of the case studies carried out in regime theory remain city-specific and tend to concentrate on the internal dynamics of the dominant regime or partnership to the detriment of contextual forces. In response, some have eschewed regime theory in favour of a 'neo-Marxist' regulation framework that updates earlier attempts to develop a holistic account of state formation (see Jonas and Wilson, 1999; Lauria, 1997; Mayer, 1995). We explore such theories in our next section.

7.4 REGULATION THEORIES

Adopting a local focus offers one particular geographical take on urban politics, but, according to Mayer (1995), the shape and form of local politics need to be understood in relation to the changes wrought by globalization (see Chapter 8). Specifically, she suggests that it is the increasingly porous nature of national boundaries that provides the basis for other changes in governance, namely, the reassertion of the urban; the growth of competitive entrepreneurialism; and the emergence of new forms of complex collaborative action. The first of these concerns the rescaling of politics in an era of 'perforated' national sovereignty. A key symptom of this is the lack of control which nations have over the international money supply (see Chapter 6). This means that the traditional role of central government is superseded by a need to 'think global, act local'. In other words, it is perceived that the city can respond more readily than the nation-state to the fast times ushered in by globalization, and is therefore better situated to harness hypermobile global capital (Krugman, 1991; Kresl, 1995). The orchestrated promotion of competitive subnational areas, particularly cities, is seen to be decisive as traditional (national) urban hierarchies give way to new networks of investment and flow centring on key 'world cities' in the new economic and political mega-regions (such as the European Union and the North American Free Trade Agreement Area).

In relation to the second of these changes, Mayer contends that globalization has encouraged more 'entrepreneurial' governance because traditional policy fields are seen as staid and conservative in an global era that ostensibly demands flexibility. In this new 'flexible' policy arena, social policies are typically subordinated to economic polices and labour policies to the pursuit of competitive local economic development. Thirdly, Mayer writes of the importance of integrating increasingly complex and diffuse fields of policy without compromising competitiveness. As described in Section 7.1 (above), the sphere of local political action has therefore expanded beyond the realm of traditional local authority bureaucracy to encompass a range of private and semi-public interests. This trend has been accompanied by new bargaining systems and new forms of public-private collaboration in which the role of local bureaucracy is redefined in relation to the interests of businesses and real estate interests – which may be simultaneously local and global.

From this perspective, the emergence of complex modes of governance at the local scale represents an adaptive response to the challenges instigated by globalization. Thus, an important avenue of investigation for researchers is exploring the way that local politics are implicated in the search for social systems that can effectively regulate the global capitalist economy (Amin and Hausner, 1997; Jessop, 1997b; Stoker, 1998). Rejecting crude notions that global changes drive local transformations (implicit in growth coalition and regime theories), this involves engagement with the ideas of the 'Parisian' Regulation School, a neo-Marxist group of writers who have sought to theorize the transition from an overarching Fordist to a flexible post-Fordist Mode of Regulation. Put crudely, these theories suggest that the state has responded to the breakdown of the

Fordist mode of mass production and mass consumption by developing new forms of societal regulation or governance.

According to regulation theory, the state is recomposing itself, organizing in line with the transition to a new post-Fordist logic of wealth accumulation and distribution (Le Galés, 1998). As we have seen, included in the list of the state's new regulatory adaptations are closer and more collaborative relationships with business, the sharing of responsibilities for welfare with the private and civil sectors, and the development of new 'entrepreneurial' management styles in public administration purposes (Stoker, 1998). This reorganization of the state opens up opportunities for new territorial networks, or localism, as part of the new governance package. While many commentators are cautious about the strength of the connection between the post-Fordist Modes of Regulation and the rise of entrepreneurialism as part of the new localism, there is a strand of literature which explores this very connection (Mayer, 1995; Painter, 1995; Newman and Thornley, 1996).

Though regulation theory works with Marxist ideas (see Chapter 2), it departs from many structural interpretations by not presupposing the existence of fixed economic, social and political structures. Instead, as Goodwin and Painter (1996) argue, regulation theory explores how the state is itself caught up in the crises of capitalism; far from simply reacting to wider shifts in the nature of capital accumulation, the transformation or crisis of the state is deemed to be implicated in crises of capital accumulation. Consequently, reorganizations of governance (including the local state) may result in the emergence of new, stable modes of capital accumulation (and the achievement of a 'successful' Mode of Regulation). Goodwin and Painter (1996, p. 638) outline the precepts of regulation theory as follows:

- Social systems are complex and contradictory, with inbuilt tendencies towards rupture and crisis (mirroring Marxist accounts of the inherent crisis-prone nature of capitalism).
- The regulation of a social system refers to the processes which mitigate contradictions, displacing these crises in time or space.
- Regulation is not inevitable or 'natural', but involves intentional actions (however, such actions may have unintended outcomes).
- Regulation is an emergent feature of social systems, so that effective regulation (the emergence of a stable Mode of Regulation) only occurs through the interaction of a number of separate elements of the system.
- Regulation is a social process, and remains prone to contradiction and crisis, undermining established Modes of Regulation.
- When Modes of Regulation fail, there is a need for re-regulation (i.e., an attempt to restore the Mode of Regulation) or the need to construct new social systems to produce a new Mode of Regulation.

Painter (1995), drawing upon the work of Alain Lipietz, argues that for regulation theorists the fate of the post-war 'Keynesian' welfare state is linked to the abandonment of the Fordist mode of capital accumulation. This echoes

Harvey's (1989b) neo-Marxist political-economy approach that links the transformation from managerial to entrepreneurial governance to the paradigmatic shift from the rigid mass production of Fordism to the flexible accumulation of post-Fordism (see also Section 8.2). Similarly, it resonates with **Bob Jessop**'s (Box 7.2) assertion that Fordism can be theorized as a system of economic production (based on mass production), a regime of accumulation and a Mode of Regulation. In the Fordist Mode of Regulation depicted by Jessop, the national economic space was the fundamental geographical unit of organization, with the state having sovereign control over wealth accumulation and wage relations within its boundaries. The Fordist state was, accordingly, characterized by a high degree of centralized political regulation and spatial integration as regions and localities were subordinated to the stabilizing macroeconomic and redistribution priorities of the central state. At the same time, the state was responsible for ensuring certain standards of living, fuelling the demand for the manufactured goods that sustained processes of capital accumulation.

According to Jessop (1994), regulation theory is not limited to analysis of the crisis of Fordism but also focuses on questions of social cohesion and capital/labour relations. This argument is echoed elsewhere:

> Perhaps the principle contribution of the regulation approach lies in the integration of the role of political and social relations (state action and legislature, social institutions, behavioural norms and habits, political practices) – the so-called 'mode of social regulation' (MSR) – into the conception of capitalist reproduction and crises. (Tickell and Peck, 1992, p. 192)

For Jessop and others, the transformation to a post-Fordist Mode of Regulation needs to be understood as a response to the contradictions of government as much as to the breakdown of Fordist production processes, the collapse of the

---

Box 7.2 Bob Jessop (1946–)

Bob Jessop is a Professor of Sociology at Lancaster University. His work develops broad interests in political economy (particularly the transition between Fordism and post-Fordism) alongside empirical investigations of the political economies of post-war Britain. His most recent research deals with three main areas: current changes in the capitalist economy linked to globalization and the knowledge-driven economy; welfare-state restructuring; and issues of governance, 'meta-governance' and the failure of regulation. Jessop's arguments about the role of the state in securing the conditions for stable post-Fordist accumulation overlap with his writings on the emergence of the 'workfare' state. In such accounts, the national state is seen to be 'hollowed out' through the transfer of intervention powers and responsibilities upwards, downwards and sideways to reflect the rescaling of economic activities and forms of competition. He regards this as part and parcel of the transition from Fordism to post-Fordism, with the structural crises in capitalism having strained social and political institutions and undermined the mixed economy and welfare liberalism associated with the Fordist model. He argues that social welfare regimes oriented to redistribution are accordingly supplanted by policies more concerned to increase the flexibility of the workforce and to reduce the social

Bretton Woods agreement that underpinned international financial stability (see Chapter 6), or the 'globalization' of economic activities and spaces (see Chapter 8). While the state was successful in displacing certain crises in the Fordist era, it arguably created others. This included the state's inability to resolve a range of national economic management issues and social legitimation crises – particularly stagflation (combined price inflation and economic stagnation), lagging industries, taxation for public sector expansion and industrial relations revolts.

The crisis of British Fordism, for example, may be seen to be state-induced, in that the state was part of the problems besetting the floundering British economy in the 1970s. Similarly, the social systems existing in other nations seemed equally unable to regulate Fordism in a sustainable manner, triggering the transition to post-Fordism. This was embodied in the reorientation of the state and the adoption of the free-market-oriented 'neo-liberal' models of governance which became popular in the closing decades of the Millennium. Thus, under neo-liberal regimes the traditional welfare state is 'rolled back' to create new synergies between devolved forms of management, private consumption, deregulated service provision and flexible working practices. The high-cost redistributionalist policies of the old welfare state are supplanted by selective intervention measures which require less taxation and fewer public sector resources. Public sector funding is accordingly diverted away from the welfare sector towards economic restructuring and promotion in line with flexible pro-competitiveness policies.

Responding to such accounts of the 'decline' of the interventionist post-war 'Keynesian' welfare state, **Ash Amin** (Box 7.3) and Nigel Thrift (1994c) take issue with views that present the state's influence on the space economy as being undermined by globalization or other market driven forces – pointing to the creation of unifying supranational bodies as well as localized subnational institutions. They suggest that these may constitute new forms of state

wage considered as a cost of production. Associated changes include a reorientation of state policies from general welfare protection to the promotion of competitiveness on different scales, including the local or urban as well as the triad (e.g., EU). This is reflected in an increased emphasis on entrepreneurialism. While there is continuing disagreement about the exact nature and mutability of these trends, Jessop (1994, 1997a) suggests that they are generated by the institutional logic of the emerging post-Fordist accumulation regime. None the less, there are different forms of workfare regime that reflect national variations despite the current hegemony of neo-liberalism. More recently, Jessop (1997b) has addressed the limits of economic guidance in relation to the governance of complexity and the complexity of governance. Collectively, Jessop's work illustrates a geographic sensitivity to the structures of governance implicated in the transition from one Mode of Regulation to another, with his distinctive take on regulation theory meaning his work is frequently cited (and used) by geographers (see Hall and Hubbard, 1996).

Further reading: Jessop (1994, 1997a, 1997b, 1999)

intervention rather than representing a withering away or replacement of state regulation. Likewise, Martin and Sunley (1997) are critical of much of the governance literature on regulation theory, which, they argue, is vague in concept, exaggerated in theory and lacking in empirical content. While state regulation may be changing, they suggest that what is emerging is far more complex, experimental and confused than the picture presented by the proponents of the simplified models of the post-Fordist state. The state may lose some powers of intervention in particular spheres of socioeconomic life, but it compensates by expanding or reinforcing them in others. States are developing new capacities and structures to exert new forms of political and economic power across space. They suggest that it may be more accurate to characterize governance changes as a change in the *mode* of state intervention rather than a withdrawal or weakening of government.

Drawing on case examples, Martin and Sunley (1997) identify two complementary types of state–economy relations which they consider will become the model for future debate. The first of these is the influential *micro-social relations model* that draws upon 'bottom-up' social systems as found in the north of Italy, where cities and regions exist with vibrant micro-network connections between workers, institutions and firms. These flexible production nodes in the 'Third Italy' are renowned for their production of textiles (Como), ceramics (Sassuolo) and shoes (Ancona), with their dense agglomeration of firms allowing them to outperform rival regions (Amin and Thrift, 1992). The second model takes the view that the most successful economies are those that have deliberately deployed co-ordinated policies at both micro- and macro-levels. This *co-ordinated networked state model* of development applies to Germany, Sweden, Switzerland and Japan as well as the late industrializing and highly competitive tiger economies of East Asia and Europe (Holtham and Kay, 1994; Sheridan, 1993). The typical conception of this model is one which views the state less as a bureaucracy and more as a capacity-builder underpinning a dense structure of policy

---

Box 7.3 Ash Amin (1955–   )

Ash Amin is a Professor of Geography at the University of Durham. His research work has resulted in numerous publications on comparative urban and regional change in the context of structural change, European integration and internationalization. Collectively, this has developed geographical understanding of post-Fordism, globalization and new forms of political expression: his work on post-Fordism (in particular) is regarded as a near definitive description of the 'spatial switching' and restructuring associated with the decline of manufacturing and the rise of the 'informational economy'. Most recently, his work has addressed the social economy and participatory politics in the context of a multicultural and multi-ethnic European Union. Throughout these diverse research strands, Amin's emphasis has been on changing forms of governance; a key motif has been recognition of the complex modes of governance that represent an adaptive response to the challenges presented by the transition to post-Fordism. Thus, a key avenue of Amin's investigation has been to elucidate the *institutional thickness* necessary to embed the economic life of firms and markets in post-Fordist spaces of agglomeration. Amin notes that this 'thickness' is constructed and institutional-

networks that connect public, private and voluntary sector actors through sustainable formal and informal channels (Weiss and Hobson, 1995).

Thus, while some commentators describe changes in governance in terms of diminishing intervention or the death of the nation-state and the hollowed-out state, others view them as a change in quality rather the quantity of intervention or as a *redirection* of intervention (see O'Neill, 1997). Certainly, the apparent dismantling and fragmenting of state systems of central intervention in deference to the restructuring forces of global competition should not mask other forms of state support for regions and localities within the state. Employing the language of regulation theory, we thus need to remember that the central state remains an adaptive or enabling agency which encourages the construction of stable social systems through its intervention in numerous sites of regulation (e.g., labour markets, financial systems, service provision, consumption practices and so on). Indigenous growth and local governance may be the new buzzwords of economics and politics but the role of the central state in moulding these developments and shaping Modes of Regulation remains crucial (see Amin and Tomaney, 1995). Indeed, for many commentators it is the differences in qualitative state input at the national level that account for the variations in competitive performance between and within national capitalisms (Hutton, 1995; Newlands, 1995; Berger and Dore, 1996). This underlines the fact that Modes of Regulation take on markedly different forms in different nations. Whatever the case, a major concern for many critical commentators is that the selective promotion of some areas, combined with a retrenchment or reconstitution of welfare spending, will widen social and spatial inequalities and thereby undermine the geographic integration and social cohesion secured by the welfare state (Moulaert, 2000; Swyngedouw, 2000).

ized differently in different spaces (from the historic legacies of the City of London through to the recent formation of *neo-Marshallian* nodes in the Third Italy), and is accordingly critical of approaches which oversimplify the complexity of contemporary governance by seeking to explain them in a single theory. Instead, he has adopted a network perspective to explore the multiple geographies of the city, holding to the idea that governance involves webs articulated across different spatial scales (Amin and Graham, 1997). Amin also disagrees with those commentators who insist that current trends in the post-Fordist state are following a clear and irresistible path and argues that these trends are not inevitable but are a consequence of a deliberate and reversible policy (Amin and Tomaney, 1995). He is also optimistic about the potential of emerging forms of associative urban governance that unite state, market and civil society (see Amin and Graham, 1997).

Further reading: Amin and Thrift (1992); Amin and Hausner (1997)

7.5 ACTOR AND POLICY NETWORKS

While there appears to be some continuity in the coherence of governance itself as a practice, Ling (2000) suggests that the literature theorizing governance amounts to little more than methodological anarchy and definitional chaos. Certainly, growth coalition, regime and regulation theories, though under-pinned by certain key ideas about the state, differ widely in their conception of power, as well as their scale of analysis. Another common feature is that the tripartite distinction between the state, market and civil society is assumed in all approaches, even though the distinctions between them are increasingly blurred as all sectors are fused in the melting pot of mutated governance. The three categories become enmeshed and overlapping as governance generates more of those institutions and relationships that facilitate the enhancement of capacity power – namely, partnership alliances. The proliferation of such partnerships is a fruitful area for geographical investigation using growth coalition, regime and regulation theories, although the instability of such partnerships makes that task increasingly difficult. Certainly, unpacking such complexities as multiple membership of a multitude of partnerships that may coexist at various scales in overlapping and nested webs of networks, presents geographers with increas-ingly mutable and difficult-to-pin-down research targets.

One important theoretical impetus for making sense of how policy and decision-making are *produced* on a variety of interrelated scales is Actor Network Theory (hereafter referred to as ANT). Bingham and Thrift (2000) argue that

---

Box 7.4 Bruno Latour (1947–   )

Inspired by the work of Michel Foucault, the French theorist Bruno Latour is best known for his work on the form and content of scientific knowledge. This has explored the practices of science and the ways in which scientists represent their activities and findings. From this, Latour produced an alternative understanding of the process of scientific discovery, articulated most famously in *Science in Action* (1987). This portrayed scientists as entrepreneurs, actively engaged in the pursuit of political and economic influence, as well as academic acclaim. One of the ways that they do this is by creating simplified areas of knowledge which are presented as self-evident. He calls these uncontested areas 'black boxes'. For Latour, this approach accorded science an undue authority and status, thereby allowing it to engage in the uncontested production of 'truth'. The principle of the black box can perhaps be illustrated by the example of a motor car, with the engine of the car serving (for most) as the unexamined black box of the socio-technical system that allows drivers to get where they want to go. The contents and workings of the black box are relied upon but remain unexamined. Black-boxing is thus a way of simplify-ing the world so that users and innovators can get on with their work; as long as the actors behave as if the black box is sealed, the construction of 'knowledge' and 'truth' can continue. Latour argued that the biggest and most successful scientific constructions are thus assembled through the accretion of black boxes – the big-gest and most ambitious scientific projects are built upon large numbers of black boxes. However, for Latour the construction of knowledge through the epistemo-logical use of black boxes was not enough to guarantee the success of a scientific

ANT originates within studies of science, French intellectual culture and, above all, the writing of Michael Serres and **Bruno Latour** (Box 7.4). Latour (1993) developed an account of networks on the basis that these intermediary arrangements are much more interesting than the two 'extremes' of micro- and macro-level analysis. He also argued that it was essential to develop an account of networks which incorporates non-human elements as actants, on the grounds that that they can be just as important as human actants in any particular study. In Latour's work, power is viewed as the 'performative' ability to get others to perform action rather than as a stock of influence residing in any particular person or institution. It not the inevitable outcome of irresistible forces but the fluid effect of a mobilizing capacity to achieve aims through enacted inter-actions between the agents of a network. Power is creatively composed and reproduced not through unchangeable structures or institutions but through the recurring performance of networks of interaction. While these enacted patterns are inherently unstable and mutable, they can nevertheless congeal into discernible channels through which the continually reproduced power configurations flow. The durability of certain arrangements is sustained by the enrolment of actants who subscribe to, and produce, apparently stable and orderly patterns of action.

From the perspective of ANT, the key to the stability and transformation of such 'coherent' power configurations is to understand how actors are enrolled to perform within them. The relevance and potential attraction of Latour's work for the analysis of governance should be obvious. His emphasis

---

endeavour; it was also necessary for the scientist to enrol allies by convincing them to share the same visions or goals. To do this, a whole panoply of strategic manoeuvering and tactical actions are required (see Latour, 1987, for an extensive and detailed list of these options). Latour used these insights about scientific activity to make a more general point about research methodologies in other fields of social investigation. In summary, Latour adopted an 'open' approach to the study of social phenomena which viewed the world as a 'relational network' of objects, people and representations (including knowledge about the world). This extends notions of agency to non-humans, with the performative production of power through network interactions seen as involving the enrolment of actants in the networks. In a somewhat similar way to political theorists, who define power as being 'capacity to act' (e.g., Stone, 1993), this suggests that power is networked and that actants can only mobilize their capacity to change the world by enrolling others in 'their' network. Accordingly, Latour's work is frequently cited by those working with Actor Network Theory; although his work has never used this term explicitly (and now dismisses its core concepts), many of those working with ANT claim to be influenced by his writing. Alongside this theoretical contribution, his attack on essentialist notions of science should make geographers mindful of the fact that their knowledge production also relies on the formation of supportive networks that obscure the taken-for-granted 'black boxes' of geographic truism.

Further reading: Latour (1987, 1993); Kendall and Wickham (1999)

on networked interaction coincides conveniently with the increasingly explicit promotion of the partnership approach to governance with its associated emphasis on new relations and patterns of engagement – that is, the incorporation of non-governmental actors into the formulation of policy-making and regulatory frameworks through networking, negotiation, performance standards, bargaining systems and coalitions (Stone, 1993).

In essence, ANT offers an analytical framework for making sense of social relations and struggles of all kinds, avoiding overgeneralization or the search for 'deep' structures in favour of descriptions of the associations that bring society into being (see, for example, Latour, 1987, 1993; Law, 1992). This suggests that power does not 'belong' to particular groups, politicians or individuals, but is a composition produced by a network comprised of a combination of heterogeneous entities (even though it might be 'attributed' to one of them). As Murdoch and Marsden (1995) argue, the powerful are not those who hold political power, but those who enrol, enlist and coerce people and things into networks and associations that allow them to enact their policies. These networks are not spatially constrained, so that a network that allows particular policies to be pursued in a specific city may extend globally, involving representatives of local community groups, global corporations, national media companies, visitors and so on. This means that non-local actors can often exercise power at a distance, and that those located in the centre of a network may be physically distant from those with whom they are associated. Networks can be 'fat' or 'thin', 'deep' or 'shallow'; their effectiveness does not depend on their size or shape but the extent to which they create 'ability to act'.

This ability to act relies upon the type and strength of association between different actors in the network, something that may rely on the existence of *discourses* (see Chapter 5) and representations that give those in the network a sense of identity or purpose. This emphasizes that materials, technologies and texts are a crucial part of networks, and that 'actants' in networks may be non-human as well as human. For example, 'town plans' are just as enmeshed in planning networks as urban planners. ANT recognizes that the capacity to catalyse change or maintain stability is not limited to human beings and that a wide variety of things can bring the world into existence and sustain it. Accordingly, examination of the circulation of things and people around networks is an essential feature of ANT. When enrolled in networks, these actants hold each other in positions that define the identities of subject/objects and their ability to do things (Murdoch, 1997). In the context of political life, this means considering the management of networks and flows of information, discourse, documents, ideas and representations as much as it involves thinking about the social relations between people. In other areas of geography, ANT is provoking radical reconceptualization of the distinctions between object/subject, such as in those innovative analyses of 'animal geographies' that acknowledge that animals have agency too (Whatmore, 1999).

ANT has ushered in a new language of 'actants' enrolled in the networks of 'immutable mobiles' which bring the world into being. Open to notions of complexity, and mindful of the fact that the world is always in flux or in the process of becoming, ANT thus avoids making totalizing claims (meaning that it is very much in keeping with postmodern, and, arguably, post-structural thought – see Section 3.4). As Whatmore (1999, p. 27) argues, for those working with ANT, 'agency, and by implication, power, is decentred, spun out between social actors rather than seen as a manifestation of unitary intent'. Moreover, given that Michael Serres and Bruno Latour have used geographical metaphors frequently in their work, ANT seems to offer a distinctly spatial way of describing or mapping, rather than understanding, the world.

In relation to urban politics, such insights have been taken up primarily in policy network studies, which combine detailed, and sometimes quantitative, analysis of relations between agents, politicians and institutions with an attempt to specify what is actually important in shaping urban policy (Rhodes, 1997). As well as thinking about the associations between local and non-local actors, this has involved examination of the power of marketing brochures, planning documents, videos, websites and e-mail communications to bring networks into being. Thinking about how actors like city councils enrol key organizations (Chambers of Commerce, Tourist Boards, Training and Enterprise Councils, Regional Development Agencies), individuals (local celebrities, dignitaries, visitors, residents) and collectivities (community groups, residents' associations, traders' associations) into a network that speaks and acts for the city thus represents an important avenue for research in urban governance. At the same time, recognizing that such networks need to be attended to (i.e., require constant attention and maintenance), ANT alerts us to the way that apparent transitions from one Mode of Regulation to another are brought into being – not from 'above' or 'below', but through networked acts of weaving and pleating (Bingham and Thrift, 2000).

Actor Network Theory has been particularly important for problematizing taken-for-granted questions of scale and boundedness in geography. Amin and Graham (1997) illustrate this when they refer to the 'within' and 'withoutness' of cities, suggesting that cities are manifold formations created in the midst of tangled networks which exist at different scales simultaneously. ANT can also be used to demonstrate how the new networked practices of governance can 'enfeeble' particular actors whilst simultaneously empowering others (Hubbard and Hall, 1998; Lauria, 1997). A recent example of the enfeeblement of local government is provided by McGuirk (2000). She illustrates how the influence of local authority planners in Dublin was diminished through their being locked outside the newly emerging policy networks. This positioning left the planners unable to grasp the opportunities for local empowerment that emerged from the new context of governance. McGuirk suggests that new governing networks of special purpose agencies, central government incentives and public-private partnerships were established to mediate a new urban regeneration oriented approach to city development. Employing a Latourian conception of power allows McGuirk to diagnose the reasons why Dublin's planners were left outside the new networks, identified as the narrowly defined role of planning as a bureaucratic regulatory activity and its perceived history of inefficiency and failure. The Latourian approach also enables her to explain why the local authority planners failed to exploit opportunities provided by the changes in governance. Their commitment to traditional planning 'scripts' and anti-entrepreneurial discourses prevented them from mobilizing the performative capacities that could have enabled them to insert themselves into the new order. McGuirk's findings allow her to suggest how local planning authorities might insert themselves more effectively within the 'powered-up' networks of interaction that typify new forms of governance.

7.6 CITIZENSHIP, GOVERNANCE AND SOCIAL JUSTICE

Shifting focus from the institutions and networks of formal governance, many geographers have decried the state-centred notions of politics with which regime, growth coalition and regulation theories work. Specifically, they are critical of the tendency to ignore the way that political relations within and across society are deemed to be shaped primarily by decisions enacted by the state (whether working in partnership with the market or not). They are particularly anxious to look beyond the arenas of the state and market to understand the conduct of urban politics in what is often termed civil society. Often conceptualized as equivalent to the public sphere (see Habermas, 1989), this term is perhaps best understood as representing all those elements of society outside government (including business interests). However, the definition of this term is not unproblematic. Indeed, while Habermas (1989) regarded the public sphere as a political counterpoint to the state and market, it is sometimes portrayed as a non-political sphere where social and individual identities are reproduced through a range of social practices (see Johnston, 2000). Civil society is therefore a relatively loose term which can be taken to encompass either a wide range of activities and groups outside the formal mechanism of politics or a range of spaces that exists between the private spaces of home (on the one hand) and the private spaces of the state (on the other). But either way, civil society is often posited as the arena where social reproduction is actually negotiated and where relations between different race, gender, class and age groups are played out. As such, civil society is a space of negotiation where new relationships between the state, market and citizens are constructed (Yeates, 2001).

For Habermas, membership of civil society is not granted on an equal basis, but involves individuals leaving the realms of their private lives to enter a public sphere of rights, obligations and responsibilities. These include, for example, political rights to freedom of speech, right to assembly, equality before the law, freedom from violence, protection of private property and the right to vote. Such rights clearly come at a cost and, in recognizing themselves as members of civil society, individuals have to pay taxes, respect the law, maintain certain standards of behaviour and so on. The way these rights and responsibilities are played out in everyday life is every bit as political as the decisions and policies made in the 'corridors of power'; Low (2001) suggests that lively informal politics always accompany the institutional machinations of party politics.

Conceptualizing power as diffuse and relational (as in Foucault – see Chapter

3), the emphasis here is on the way the politics of 'everyday life' grants political legitimacy to particular groups, with access to the public sphere deemed a key means to staking claims to economic and social power. A key notion is that of *citizenship*. Although the term citizenship can be understood in different ways (and at a variety of scales), it is principally used to refer to the (social, economic and political) rights and responsibilities which underpin both the construction of the nation-state and civil society. Here, a crucial notion is that nations are constructed around values, attitudes and practices which encourage some behaviours and discourage others. It is widely understood that if individuals fail to subscribe to these national standards and norms then they are not considered worthy of full citizenship in terms of entitlements and benefits. While Susan Smith (1989b) suggests that forms of citizenship may be institutionalized and imagined very differently across national boundaries, a widely noted trend has been for national citizenships in the urban West to be based around socially constructed visions of liberty and equality which, none the less, serve to marginalize women, ethnic minorities, the disabled and so on (Bennet, 1993; Whelan *et al.*, 1994; Clarke and Staeheli, 1995; Ferman, 1996; Ramsay, 1996).

Extending analysis of politics to embrace the *cultural politics* of everyday life, work on citizenship has demonstrated geographers' enthusiasm to link formerly unconnected concepts. An example here is the work on sexual citizenship, which has seen geographers critically evaluate how political norms and expectations reinforce heterosexual identities. Smith (1989b, p. 151) refers specifically to the example of Australia, where notions of citizenship have been constructed based on notions of 'mateship' and 'fraternity' which are simultaneously racialized, gendered and sexualized. This, she argues, results in rights of citizenship for Australians that are not liberatory but instead represent an institutionalization of sexual, gender and racial inequality. Here Smith draws on the theories of sexual and social contract developed by Carole Patemen which suggest that civil society is, in effect, a patriarchal construction that serves to limit women's participation and rights in the public sphere. For Pateman (1988, p. 20), the idea that the 'social state of nature' is inhabited not by isolated individuals but by 'families' appears to be particularly important in determining the importance of the family as the 'natural' basis of civil life. Consequently, she asserts that the historic development of civic society has revolved around specific associations between private space, sexuality and desire. Invoking contractual and democratic theories of the state, she suggests that individuals are only able to leave this space and enter a public space of rights, property ownership and citizenship if their interests are subordinate to the wider interests of the state. As such, it appears that civil society can be conceptualized as a *heterosexual* (as well as patriarchal) construction in that it serves to make entry into the public realm very difficult for those whose sexual lives are judged immoral. For example, Bell (1995) notes that both men and women who do not conform to dominant sexual standards and expectations are effectively invisible to the state in respect of entitlements (but not in terms of obligations), while, conversely, good sexual citizens are rewarded in terms of medical, welfare and housing provision (see also Section 3.3 on 'queer theory').

Many communities and individuals are politically marginalized by virtue of their lifestyle (whether defined by their sexuality, religion or ethnicity). Moreover, with the wealthy increasingly providing their own private pension and insurance cover and opting out of public welfare, and the welfare state being continuously eroded, it is the less affluent who are often stigmatized as 'bad' citizens. Those who have well-paid employment increasingly complain about the 'welfare' drain on the exchequer (and their tax contributions) arising from the need to offer financial assistance to the unemployed. Where the debate involves calls for the replacement of welfare by *workfare* – with its emphasis on the civic responsibility that individuals have to seek work – unemployment and poverty are redefined as individual, personal problems (relating to the lack of *will* to work) rather than structural ones (to do with the lack of jobs) (Painter, 1995; Peck, 1996).

Some writers make an explicit connection here between the *social exclusion* of particular groups and transitions in the role of the state (Byrne, 1999; Ferguson and Hughes, 2000). With paternalistic state corporatism (and its emphasis on 'client-citizen' relationships) giving way to a more market-oriented relationship, good citizens are deemed to be those knowledgeable 'self-governing' consumers who take responsibility for their own choices. In this new corporatist model the state takes on a new managerial role, with the rhetoric of social exclusion used to justify state intervention in these fragmented communities of 'non-consumers'. Many of the newer area-based approaches to local development fall into the category of approaches designed to tackle the 'social exclusion' of those who do not conform with the dominant model of citizenship (Delanty, 2000). Conceptually, these strategies claim to avoid the weaknesses of traditional approaches to tackling poverty by creating critical social infrastructure (Room, 1995). Parkinson (1998) sees a positive correlation between community-based partnerships and social inclusion, suggesting that the flexibility of partnerships, and their innovative capacity to overcome the bureaucratic inertia of the state, can provide energizing effects for 'local' citizens. The literature on state privatization, deregulation and urban regeneration is replete with concrete and complex examples of the ways in which both affinity-based communities and area-based communities are mobilized to reorder relationships between the state and civil society (see Amin and Hausner, 1997; Byrne, 1999). However, concern has also been expressed that the mobilization of community through local partnerships could become a new vehicle of bureaucratic control in poor neighbourhoods as success or failure to discharge duties and obligations is used to 'manage' the political inclusion or exclusion of groups from 'mainstream' society (see Mohan, 2000). This suggests that such 'communities' are reconstituted as new territories for the administration of individual and collective existence – a surface upon which moral relations among people may be administered (Rose, 1996).

Currently, political geographers are extending this interest in civil society and citizenship to explore how different groups are attempting to assert their civil rights through acts of resistance and civil disobedience. Specific attention here has been devoted to the rise of 'New Social Movements', single-issue pressure groups designed to bring attention to issues such as gay rights, environmentalism, road-building, animal exploitation, disabled access, racism and so on. This often involves highly symbolic appropriations of public space – such as the formation of 'Temporary Autonomous Zones' where dominant ideologies and practices may be resisted (Routledge, 1997). By adopting tactics well beyond those conventionally associated with community groups (i.e., drawing up petitions, writing to politicians and organizing public meetings), these activists employ forms of action that may bind individuals together in 'neo-tribes' whose values oppose dominant modes of thought and action (Maffesoli, 1996). In some instances, this results in unlikely alliances as different class, ethnic and lifestyle interests come together – however fleetingly – to oppose a seeming threat to a particular community. Recent protests against motorway construction in Britain, for example, have witnessed green activists, New Age travellers and retired army colonels standing alongside one another against the bulldozers, attempting to prevent the 'desecration' of the idyllic (and idealized) English countryside (Cresswell, 1996). More widely, it is notable that anti-globalization protests (e.g., opposition to the World Trade Organization) have involved the creation of international networks of communication and dissent (Routledge, 1997).

Quite why there should have been an explosion of popular activism and grass-roots politics has been the subject of much popular conjecture as well as academic debate. On one level, this do-it-yourself (DIY) activism has been portrayed as a manifestation of people's dissatisfaction with conventional party politics and state-sponsored planning systems as means of resolving socio-spatial conflicts (McKay, 1996). In a broader sense, however, it has been postulated that this dissatisfaction is merely a facet of a globalizing world which lacks security, certainty and order (see Chapter 8). With the order formerly guaranteed by the (modern) state breaking down in the face of economic and political turbulence, many commentators have therefore suggested that contemporary society is characterized by contingency, ambivalence and ambient risk. Perhaps the most forceful and widely cited version of this argument is contained in Ulrich Beck's description of a *Risk Society* (1986), which (although labelled as 'late' rather than postmodern) has generated unprecedented levels of anxiety.

Beck suggests that with the global media making the public aware of an ever-increasing number of risks, each individual is constantly faced by choices which force him or her to face the likelihood of being affected by a threat. In such circumstances, he argues, risk has become the dominant leitmotif that structures forms of sociality, running palpably through all areas of social life. In caricature, he suggests this has resulted from the breakdown of the stable modes of social regulation associated with the industrial capitalist process and their replacement by the more diffuse and amorphous flexible production systems associated with post-industrial accumulation processes. Forms of (national) state regulation, financial management and welfarism appear increasingly unable to provide certainty and order in the face of global fluctuation and instability, while transnational organizations such as the United Nations, World Bank and International Labour Organization seem distant, obscure and out of touch (see also Doel and Clarke, 1997). This perceived 'breakdown' and rupture of the organizations, laws and procedures which managed risks for people in industrial society, Beck argues, have prompted individuals to confront *reflexively* local problems and manufacture new certainties in an era characterized by global flux, fluidity and uncertainty (see Chapter 8). Citizen mobilization thus represents an attempt at dealing with risk and social fragmentation at a time when informal politics seems a more likely route to recognition and rights than a formal politics obsessed with growth and restructuring.

While many groups are currently seeking to expand citizenship rights, Low (2001) contends that there has been a major reaction to new social movements and growing opposition to the idea of ever-expanding citizenship rights. While much of this is associated with the New Right and the neo-liberal backlash against social difference (see Chapter 3 on revanchist New York), it is evident that the New Left also imposes limits on who is entitled to citizenship as sexual minorities, 'bogus' asylum seekers, single mothers, travellers and the homeless find their civil and public rights challenged (see Cooper, 1998, on the limits of New Labour's multiculturalism in the UK). Tangible differences in citizens' rights – and resulting differences in quality of life – thus continue to raise important questions about the limits (and effects) of democracy. After all, the omission of particular people and places from the decision-making mechanisms that shape their social and economic destinies is one of the fundamental forms of social exclusion (Winchester and White, 1988). Therefore, questions of *social justice* remain at the heart of debates concerning the fairness and inclusiveness of political policies and structures of governance.

As Merrifield and Swyngedouw (1996) argue, ideals of social justice concern what a just society should be like. Difficulties arise, however, when it is realized that there are as many views as to what constitutes social justice as there are people, ranging from utilitarian liberalism (the good of society outweighing the needs of individuals) to social egalitarianism (where each individual is viewed as equally deserving) (D. M. Smith, 1994). In an era where postmodern ideas are requiring geographers to think about the different senses of morality and justice

---

Box 7.5 David M. Smith (1936–   )

A Professor of Geography at Queen Mary, University of London, for thirty years David Smith has examined issues of inequality, social justice, moral philosophy and normative ethics from a geographical perspective. His early work focused on the geographies of welfare – 'who gets what, *where*, and how' (Smith, 1977, p. 7), the inequalities in these arrangements, and how they might be made more equal through resource distribution and planning. As with David Harvey's (1973) work, this opened up questions of what *should* be, along with what is. Smith then pursued a systematic exploration of, and engagement with, models of social justice. More recently, Smith's work on the role of ethics and moral philosophy in geography more broadly has culminated in the book *Moral Geographies* (2000). In this wide-ranging work, he examines the moral significance of concepts of landscape, location and place, proximity, distance and community, space and territory, justice and nature. He then explores how these concepts are employed in politics, planning,

subscribed to by particular groups and individuals (see Chapter 3), this raises intriguing questions. Merrifield's (2000c) exploration of the politics being played out on the streets of New York provides a good illustration of the issues. Discussing the zero tolerance techniques enacted by a partnership of multi-national corporations, the New York police, business improvement associations and city governors, he describes the common reaction of the Left to the 'cleaning up' of the streets as one of regret and disapproval. Yet he tempers this with an awareness that it is dangerous to romanticize 'sleaze', and the assertion that a sanitized urban landscape (characterized by bland office corporations, MTV, fast-food outlets and Virgin megastores) is not necessarily 'better' or 'worse' than the shabby urbanism it replaced (which was similarly typified by social exploitation, conflict and aggression).

Engaging with critical theory geographers including David Harvey (1996, 2000a) and **David Smith** (Box 7.5) have argued that postmodern relativism should not invalidate explorations of social justice, but should revitalize them by alerting us to the way that discourses of fairness and justice are constructed through governance. They suggest that there is no one notion of social justice that must be invoked in different situations (see also Harvey, 1992a), but insist that geographers need to confront the fairness of the political and social processes which produced those situations. Justice, then, is not given but is seen to be constructed and negotiated by members of society via processes of governance. This is why laws change as we negotiate how society is operated, and why rights vary across space:

> Like space, time, and nature, 'justice' is a socially constructed set of beliefs, discourses and institutions expressive of social relations and contested configurations of power that have everything to do with regulating and ordering material social practices within place. (Harvey, 1996, p. 330)

This notion of social justice as institutionalized and regulated obliges geographers to think about the (un)fairness and (in)equality implicit in new forms of

development and so on. At the core of his analysis are several key questions, such as: does distance diminish responsibility? should we interfere with the lives of those we do not know? is there a distinction between private and public space? which values and morals, if any, are absolute, and which are cultural, communal or personal? and are universal rights consistent with respect for difference? These questions are explored through case studies relating to genocide and rescue during the Holocaust, conflicts over space between Israel and Palestine, and social tensions in post-apartheid South Africa. While it might be argued that his work is more concerned with the distributive effects of policy rather than governance per se, his work continues to demonstrate how geographers can attempt to assess the 'fairness' of different situations.

Further reading: Smith (1994, 2000); Proctor and Smith (1999)

politics. This is especially pressing in situations where a welfare-based politics of redistribution has been undermined and replaced by a politics of growth. For example, in many Western cities entrepreneurial modes of governance have enabled radical forms of geographical reorganization, being implicated in processes of polarization as the walls between rich and poor become marked out in the fortified barriers between carceral city spaces and new dreamscapes of postmodern consumption (see Dear, 2000). Similarly, the net results of many entrepreneurial policies have been a net transfer of wealth from the less well-off to urban elites (Harvey, 1989a). Work on urban politics has continually highlighted such invidious outcomes of urban policy, and suggested policies that might better address local economic development while retaining minimal standards of living in the city. This includes the suggestion of mechanisms to minimize exploitation, liberate marginalized groups and empower the oppressed. Alert to both the processes and outcomes of contemporary politics, geographical work on governance is thus well placed to inform policy debates and contribute to the continuing project of critical geography (see Chapter 3).

7.7 CONCLUSION

In this chapter we highlighted contemporary changes in modes of governance and saw that a number of theories have been developed to make sense of these. Foremost among these changes was a transformation from centralized, bureaucratized government to a plurality of self-organizing, coexisting networks and partnerships that interact at diverse spatial scales. To explain these emerging developments, geographers have drawn on ideas derived from political science, sociology and economics, invoking theoretical frameworks originating in the work of figures as diverse as Marx, Weber, Dahl, Foucault, Latour and so on. Here, we considered these ideas under three main headings. The first of these involved an examination of the utility of growth coalition and urban regime theories drawn from the work of political scientists. This, we argued, is producing a growing body of research designed to examine the extent and manner in which partnership co-ordination has become a core feature of modern governance. The second attempt at explicating governance invoked regulation theory, which places more emphasis on the connectivity of local and global. This approach is influenced by theories about the emergence of a flexible post-Fordist society. It stresses the contradictions and complexities of change by analysing institutional reform and complex governance as part of the transformation of modern capitalism. This suggests that the mass production and hierarchical political institutions that regulated capitalism under Fordism have yielded in a variety of ways as the relation between capital and labour is reworked. A third (expanding) field of inquiry for geographers in relation to governance is the use of Actor Network Theory as a basis for understanding the interactions and roles of partnerships and networks as they constitute and represent themselves in response to the changing policy environment.

In reviewing these three very different theories about the creation of new modes and structures of governance, we also underlined geographers' continual interest in questions of scale. For instance, we noted in passing that geographers are interested in exploring the extent to which governance is implicated in the construction of a 'new localism' which appears to be linked to the risks and uncertainties associated with the intensifying market challenges of globalization. We showed this through our examination of work on the governance of cities – although similar debates are being played out in the context of rural politics too (see Murdoch and Marsden, 1995). At the same time, we saw how geographers are problematizing distinctions of local, national and global governance through perspectives that suggest that local governance involves global actors, including some of the transnational companies that are deemed 'footloose' (of course, the converse is also apparent, with 'local' actors implicated in global politics – one of the foci of our next chapter). We also learned that the most recent models of governance have major implications for citizenship and do not always sit easily with rhetoric of empowerment, partnership and subsidarity that is the heart of contemporary (Western) governance. With the growing acceptance of postmodern thinking, the 'social' and 'political' notions of citizenship associated with modernity have, in many respects, been superseded by the 'cultural' question. In some instances, this 'cultural turn' can lead to an exclusion of the social or the political. It other cases, it can reflect attempts to reintegrate the social and political dimensions into a wider 'cultural' understanding of society. With their unique geopolitical focus on the spatiality of governance, geographers are playing a pivotal role in debates about these changes. In sum, we have seen that, like economic and social theory, political theory has also undergone a fundamental (but largely unheralded) 'spatial turn'.

Chapter 8   Geographies of Globalization

8.1 INTRODUCTION

> A bizarre adventure happened to space on the road to globalisation: it lost its importance while gaining in significance. (Bauman, 2000, p. 110)

Globalization is currently something of a buzzword, being used as shorthand for a bewildering range of social, economic, political and cultural changes in the contemporary world. For example, since the demise of the Cold War, symbolized by the fall of the Berlin Wall, the notion of globalization is invoked on an increasingly widespread basis to depict a growing political consensus across the world, as the ideological battle of Communism and Western capitalism has given way to a new neo-liberal, global agenda. Equally, by creating an increasingly connected world in which frontiers and borders have become permeable, globalization, it is argued, has facilitated instant communication and information exchange, bequeathing a 'global village'. Further, globalization is seen as strengthening the dominance of a capitalist world system, with transnational corporations supplanting the role of the nation-state in a truly interdependent global economy. In each case, the fact that all parts of the world are becoming subject to the same sorts of influences is deemed to be a good explanation as to why certain things are occurring, seemingly requiring us to 'think global' even when we are considering the local and the everyday (Holloway and Hubbard, 2001).

In this sense, globalization has become a new meta-narrative – a fashionable 'grand theory' that seems to account for many changes in the contemporary world. Yet at the same time it is something that demands to be explained and theorized in itself; there is no agreed definition of what the term actually means and rival accounts of the concept proliferate in the literature. Hence, globalization is a schizophrenic concept, deployed to describe both the cosmopolitanism characteristic of the (late) modern world or, conversely, the erasure of cultural difference in the face of a standardized global culture (Bauman, 2000). It can also be used just as readily to imply the homogenization of space or its differentiation through increased hybridization (Friedmann, 1999). In short, globalization is a highly contested, fuzzy and ill-defined concept (see Markusen, 1999).

Indeed, the debates and issues covered by the globalization discourse are so wide-ranging that we cannot attempt to deal with all of them here. Instead, we will concentrate on some geographical interpretations of globalization, high-lighting competing accounts of the importance of globalization in the recon-figuration of economic and social life (some issues relating to globalization in the political sphere are discussed in Chapter 7).

In this chapter, we highlight some of the key contributions made by geog-raphers and those in cognate disciplines as they have attempted to make sense of globalization (both as a set of processes and as the disputed outcome of those processes). We take as our starting point the idea that the relations of space and time, if not profoundly transformed, have at least changed in ways that demand that geographers think carefully about the scale and speed of the processes that shape the world. In our first section, we accordingly describe the speeding up, spreading out and linking up of activities that are seen by many to be the basis of globalization. In the second part of the chapter we examine the idea that such globalization processes are underpinned by key transitions in the evolution of the world system (namely, the emergence of a truly global economy). While this focuses on the economic power of an 'exterritorial' global elite, in the following section, we examine the arguments of those who have written about globaliza-tion as a cultural rather than economic phenomenon. Noting a tension between those who foresee the end of cultural diversity and those who argue for a more 'progressive sense of place', we highlight how researchers are seeking to make sense of the local–global nexus. This leads on to a consideration of globaliza-tion as creating a new space of flows; a single power network made up of a multiplicity of smaller networks, each of which demands careful analysis and examination. Throughout, we examine how geographic theories – which, after all, originate in specific times and places – have been turned to global ends, used to help make sense of new times and new places.

8.2 SPACE, TIME AND MOBILITY

Though there is much disagreement about globalization, it seems that most commentators do at least agree that the last thirty or so years have seen a major 'speeding up' of the world. This has meant that distance has become less of an obstacle to movement and communication, with the distances between different places declining in significance. Consequently, *friction of distance* has been effect-ively reduced through a combination of technological innovations and trans-port improvements which, according to Harvey (1989a), occurred in two main phases. The first was at the end of the nineteenth century, as new 'enabling' technologies such as the telegraph, wireless, telephone, train and steamship permitted speedier flows of goods and faster communications (see Schivelbusch, 1986). While this led to an immediate rise in international trade, it was the technological advances of the 1980s and 1990s that effected a truly *global* com-munications revolution. At the heart of this revolution was the development of the Internet and the World Wide Web, an 'Infobahn' that allows virtually instantaneous transmission of text, pictures and sounds across the world (see Kitchin, 1998; Dodge and Kitchin, 2000). At the same time, many people now possess mobile telephones which allow them to contact people around the world at a fraction of the cost that their parent's generation would have expected to have paid. The proliferation of space satellites and high-speed telephone links via fibre-optic cables has meant that 'weightless' goods and products (such as information) can be transported almost instantaneously across the globe as electronic flows. Likewise, the advent of affordable air travel, high-speed international trains and the explosion of motorway networks in the second half of the twentieth century has reduced the long-haul movement times of people and goods.

As such, the connections between different localities and nations have intensified dramatically over recent years, creating a situation where we are seeing unquestionably faster flows of goods, information and people around the world than ever before. Portentously, the cultural theorist Marshall McLuhan (see Box 8.3) spoke of the coming of a 'global village' in the 1960s; by the 1990s it seemed that this global village had arrived. Today, we live in a world where momentous world events can be beamed 'live' into our homes via satellite technology; where products and ideas from abroad are routinely incorporated into our lives; where the political decisions that shape our destinies are as likely to be debated overseas as in our own government; and where many people expect to work outside their country of birth for long periods. In short, it seems that we are living in a world where interactions of all types have been 'stretched' over space to the extent that formerly autonomous nations and locales have been drawn into contact with one another.

Donald Janelle (1969) was among the first to write of this apparent 'shrinking' of the world, coining the notion of *space-time convergence*. In his estimation, the reducing importance of distance as an obstacle to movement meant that measurement of space was being supplanted by an emphasis on the measurement of time (see also Leyshon, 1995a). This altered perception of time and space has subsequently encouraged geographers to study relative distance rather than absolute location, deeming that the former is vitally important in a world where 'time is money' (Castells, 1996). Some geographers would no doubt point out that this has always been the case, and that the world is not constantly speeding up, being instead characterized by different senses of speed and slowness (see Thrift, 1999). None the less, the apparently new-found elasticity of space and time ushered in by recent technical innovation is being mirrored in the way that geographers are conceiving of the relationship between space and time. Here, three further concepts have been pivotal: *time-space distantiation*, *time-space compression* and *global infrastructure provision* (Held and McGrew, 2000).

The first of these refers to the idea that formerly independent people, organizations and places now connect or interact with each other over vast distances on a routine and real-time (i.e., synchronous) basis thanks to new communications technologies (Giddens, 1991). This new shared social space is distinct from the face-to-face interaction that occurs in territorial space in that economic and social actors who may have existed in areas formerly isolated from one another can interact and become interdependent. Face-to-face interactions are being augmented and displaced by distantiated interaction as people engage in regular and recurring contact with people and organizations that are 'physically distant' but highly accessible through telecommunications technologies such as electronic mail and the Internet. On this basis, a growing number of people have more frequent contact with friends, colleagues and 'associates' on the far side of the world through new technology than with family, friends and acquaintances living in their immediate neighbourhood. As we shall see, this linking up creates the possibility that more uniformities will emerge as common standards, languages and practices are diffused and adopted across the globe.

Writing of this stretching of social relations, Giddens (1991, p. 29) suggests that the integration of places in synchronous time produces a 'global present' where events, people and issues intrude into our everyday lives. Urry (2000) suggests that this produces a montage or collage effect, so that our experience and consciousness is a mix of near and far, close and distant. This is well illustrated in the news programmes we watch on television, which bring a mixture of stories from around the world to our homes, often in a *hyperreal* manner. Baudrillard's (1995) analysis of the Gulf War as a globally mediated spectacle that 'did not take place' – at least only in the defined and memorable visual sequences that substituted for real death and suffering in the Middle East – offers a provocative example of the collapse of space in the midst of such a symbolic exchange (see Chapter 5). This blurred experience of space has its corollary, Urry argues, in the emergence of *instantaneous time*. This includes a number of characteristics that distinguish it from the routinized (and *national*) clock time associated with industrialization and modernization (see Urry, 2000b, p. 129):

- The increasing importance of global time.
- The increasing disposability of products, places and images.
- The growing volatility of fashion, style, products, ideas and images.
- The breakdown of distinctions of day and night (and week and weekend, home and work and so on) as new technologies change the way we live and work.
- The idea of a 24-hour society (hence the emphasis on evening economies or the importance of round-the-clock financial trading).
- The diminishing importance of family rituals (such as mealtimes).
- The growth of 'just-in-time' production, so that workers are expected to be more flexible in their working hours (and companies lay claim to their whole life, not just the period that they are paid to work).
- The sense that the pace of life is speeding up and has perhaps got too fast (producing notions of risk).

While this list is far from exhaustive, Urry's argument is that an ordered and disciplining national time has been undermined by a global time that reschedules people's activities and results in more flexible and varied ways of living. In many ways, this is a restatement of the idea that the world is 'speeding up', but what is crucial here is that the speeding up is seen to result in people using (and experiencing) space and time in new ways. The subtext here is that people are increasingly shaping their lives in accordance with their perception of a global world. The inverse of this, of course, is that these people are creating a faster world through the way that they work, rest and play (particularly through the connections they forge with those who are in different nations).

An influential account of the potential impacts of instantaneous time is presented in the work of **Paul Virilio** (see Box 8.1). Virilio's unrestrained and sometimes apocalyptic writings suggest that speed is rendering human vision, rational reflection and normal consciousness obsolete (Luke and O'Tuathail, 2000). An exponent of the 'geography is history' thesis, Virilio (1991, p. 15) equates the demise of 'classical' Euclidean space with the postmodern critique of grand narrative (see Chapter 3). In his view, the contemporary tendency to use technology to simulate reality privileges mediated information to the detriment of meaning. It is this very technology, with its emphasis on the priorities of time and its urgency for speed, that contributes to the obliteration of material space and its replacement by an 'accidental heterogeneous space' where instantaneous translation is the norm. As he outlines it, the priorities of the new 'technological time' thus bear no relation to any calendar of events or any sense of collective memory. These new time-stresses construct a permanent present of mediated flux, 'an unbounded, timeless intensity that is destroying the tempo of a progressively degraded society' (Virilio, 1991, p. 12). Like Urry's instantaneous time, this represents a changed sense of time, and an 'over-exposed' sense of global belongingness (see Shurmer-Smith and Hannam, 1994). Jameson (1984) equates this with postmodernism, arguing that we need to develop new cognitive and mental maps (see Chapter 2) to make sense of these 'fast' times.

Box 8.1 Paul Virilio (1932–)

The French urbanist Paul Virilio is best known for his 'war model' of the growth of the modern city and the evolution of human society. He is also well known as a theorist of speed, credited with inventing the term *dromology* to refer to the 'logic' of speed. Virilio argues that technical developments in the fields of telecommunications and transportation have led to an erosion of the physical to the point where space is no longer a resource, but a burden – the so-called 'geography is history' thesis. The argument here is essentially that traditional space is going through a crisis as the dominance of the physical presence is eroded by transient electronic space. In the age of the Internet, cyberspace and the global mass media, *speed distance* obliterates the physical dimension of distance, physical boundaries are superseded by systems of electronic communication and surveillance, and notions of 'here' and 'there' lose their traditional relevance. The significance of property boundaries, walls and fences diminishes as permanent physical obstacles give way to an infinity of telematic openings; the placeless *televisual screen* has replaced the window in the private room and the meeting place of the public city square as the new zone of access, interaction and control. In the era of the screen interface of computers, television and teleconference, people occupy

For Leyshon (1995a), the concept of *time-space compression* advanced by David Harvey (Box 6.2) provides the explanatory dimension (or propulsive force) required to account for this obliteration of physical distance and its replacement by speed distance. Harvey argues that it is the underlying rules relating to the flows of capital that account for the acceleration of modern life. As we saw in Chapter 2, the essence of capitalism is the pursuit of profit; Harvey suggests that space is organized so as to maximize such profits by facilitating the growth of production whilst reproducing labour power. In the latest phase of capitalism, which Harvey terms post-Fordism, this involves radical transformation of both space and time. One manifestation of this is the stretching of social life identified by Giddens (1991), whereby capital is circulated ever more widely around the world into new (and profitable) markets; another is the collapsing of time identified by Urry (2000b), where the accelerated pace of life is seen to reduce the turnover time of capital (the time taken for investment to return a profit).

The clearest statement of Harvey's views on global transformation is in *The Condition of Postmodernity* (1989a). Starting by detailing the new communication technologies that are resulting in the compression of time and space, Harvey (1989a, p. 240) brilliantly evokes how this changes 'how we represent the world to ourselves'. This leads him to describe how we learn to cope with this sense of compression, acting according to our changed perception of the way the world works. One symptom of this, as we saw in Chapter 6, is the accelerated speed of financial transactions, with the idea that 'time is money' encouraging traders and dealers to extend and speed up processes of economic exchange lest they miss out on key business opportunities (Leyshon and Thrift, 1996). Equally, the idea that economic exchange needs to be quick entails a parallel acceleration in consumption habits (hence, fast food, home delivery, service 'while you wait', etc.). Both sets of change have a disorienting and disruptive impact upon

transportation and transmission time instead of physically inhabiting space. Thanks to space satellite technology, their living space is transformed into a form of global broadcast studio where 'everywhere' is instantaneously available. Through the screen interface all localization and all position are telescoped and the old cadastral certainties disappear. The obliteration of space by speed has involved a loss of anticipatory control and foresight. It is a world of flux, adaptation and risk: we constantly destroy the world we have known and re-create the world as we have not known it. It is a world of constant crisis where the crisis of (space) dimension as geometric narrative becomes the crisis of the whole. Widely read across the social sciences, Virilio has nevertheless been critized for failing to give sufficient attention to the corporeality of the body in his thinking (see Chapter 4). It is also argued that his accounts of the homogenization of global communications may overemphasize the creation of placelessness; the new technology may have the counter-effect of provoking a backlash and a renewed celebration of the specificity of physical place.

Further reading: Virilio (1991); Armitage (2000); Luke and O'Tuathail (2000)

political-economic practices (as well as cultural and social life). Harvey thus makes a distinction between modern 'rational' production processes and the 'irrational' consumerist outcomes of globalization, showing how myths of increased consumer choice and reflexivity are implicated in the making of a more flexible and 'soft' capitalism (see also Chapter 3 on the postmodern city).

Significantly, Harvey asserts that although the spatial switching of capital occurs on a more and more rapid basis, this does not mean that the significance of space is decreasing. Ironically, as spatial barriers diminish in importance, it has been argued that we become more aware of the value of place (see also Swyngedouw, 1989). For example, the heightened competition associated with the disappearance of spatial barriers forces capitalists to pay much closer attention to relative locational advantages precisely because they now have the power to exploit minor differences between places. But if capitalist elites are becoming more sensitized to the spatially differentiated qualities of world geography, then so too are the 'local' elites who advertise the 'special' qualities of their place to make it more attractive to capitalist investors. As we described in Chapter 7, entrepreneurial forms of place packaging, reimaging and branding may be seen as a response to globalization. Harvey goes further by suggesting that such political actions differentiate space in ways that encourage space-time compression. New economic and social policies are continually adopted and new styles of governance flourish in the intensifying efforts to enhance the competitive status of places in the battle to lure peripatetic (constantly moving) capital that values the option of mobility so highly:

> We thus approach the central paradox: the less important the spatial barriers, the greater the sensitivity of capital to the variations of place within space, and the greater the incentive for places to be differentiated in ways attractive to capital. The result has been the production of fragmentation, insecurity and ephemeral uneven development within a highly unified global space economy of capital flows. (Harvey, 1989a, p. 197)

Bringing Marx's ideas about the need for capital to seek ever more profitable sites for its reproduction into dialogue with theories about the cultural and social production of space (especially Jameson, 1984; Bourdieu, 1990; and Lefebvre, 1991), Harvey thus portrays globalization as the outcome of capitalist processes that create and exploit spatial – and social – difference at the same time that they bring all places within capital's grasp. In his work on entrepreneurial policy (e.g., the redevelopment of Baltimore inner harbour – see Harvey, 1989b), this dialectic between the differentiating and universalizing tendencies of capital is clearly etched, with Harvey describing the serialization of spectacular architectural projects designed to mark out a particular territory as a good business environment (see also Olds, 1995; Short and Kim, 1999).

Harvey therefore sees globalization as the latest of capitalism's 'spatial fixes' – a compression of time and space that surmounts the crises of global Fordism and allows a new round of *flexible* capital production (i.e., post-Fordism) to be realized. Targeting the rhetoric that has accompanied this (e.g., the 'think global, act local' discourse that demands increased flexibility in a 'risky' and 'fast-moving' world), he argues that globalization is a powerful idea which is employed to repackage and justify some of the oldest and most insidious ideas of Darwinism, including the idea that it is 'natural' for there to be winners and losers in an evolving society (and hence the idea that capitalism is natural). He is accordingly anxious to outline the potentially deleterious impacts of flexible, global capital for human life (cf. Lefebvre, 1991, on the experience of abstract capitalist space, and Lyotard, 1993, on the way that 'dead' capital feeds off the living). As he puts it, the purported freedom provided by the globalization process is simply propelling us, faster and faster, towards death. In the post-modern world of global capitalism, the stress of maintaining the pace of being constantly opportunistic and competitive in a world without moorings is taking its toll on health and quality of life. We are not moving towards any of the emancipatory freedoms promised by the modernist vision, he argues, but are instead embracing the ephemeral, the fashionable and the new. Virtually all aspects of human life have thus become more superficial and volatile. Harvey concludes that change is the only thing that is consistent in a world of rapid disposability and transience, where style is privileged over substance.

Showing how the cultural and economic intertwine to create the myth of a natural yet volatile global economy (see also Gibson-Graham, 1996), Harvey's work has been influential for theorists of globalization because of the critical attention devoted to the *reflexive* nature of globalization (which is, after all, sustained through the conjoint action of individuals the world over). What his work also begins to do is show that the global economy is a complex achievement, and that adequate *global infrastructure provision* – a central nervous system – is required to articulate global capitalism. Held and McGrew (2000) draw on Harvey to suggest that the reorganization of space around 'hubs' that control global movements of people, goods and movement is an important consequence of time-space compression. These are those spaces that exhibit a critical density of institutional and other infrastructure. Examples of this infrastructure include the ISDN networks and servers that allow global elites to communicate at a distance; the global financial markets (see Chapter 6) which trade on a 24-hour basis via stock exchanges across the world; international airports; and so on (see Graham and Marvin, 2001).

More importantly, perhaps, these hubs of global control represent concentrations of the knowledge-rich individuals whose job it is to 'attend' to the global financial architecture on a daily basis (repairing it in moments of global crisis or slump). Reflexivity and networking are consequently at the heart of Thrift's (1994b, 1996) understanding of the global economy, with knowledge-rich workers, firms and institutions needed to establish and maintain global flows (see Chapter 6). While new technologies have a centrifugal potential to de-materialize and decentralize these 'epistemic communities', making it possible for them to be located anywhere provided workers are electronically connected, a countervailing centripetal propensity is evident as new forms of global control have emerged and clustered together in particular localities (something we return to in our subsequent discussion of the world cities that are crucial in the articulation of global flows – see Section 8.5). This underlines the major contra-diction with which theorists of globalization grapple: why is place still important in an era of space-time compression? Ultimately, it is this conundrum – and the tension between local and global – that lies at the heart of many debates about globalization. We start to show how this relation between local and global has been theorized in our next section, which explores the economic geographies of global production and consumption.

8.3 THE GEOGRAPHY OF THE GLOBAL ECONOMY

As work on communication and mobilities makes clear, globalization is neither an abstract system nor the final outcome of economic, social and political processes. Rather, globalization is an ongoing *process*, involving the mass mobil-ity of capital, people, goods and ideas. While some (like Harvey) suggest that this process has resulted in a truly global economy, a unified global society and a shared global politics, others suggest that these flows are far from global, and touch down only in particular places. Urry (2000b, p. 13), for instance, speaks of the 'partial development of an emergent level of the global', and contends that while shock waves may spill out chaotically from one part of the world to another, there may still be parts of the world that are not subject to globaliza-tion. This argument is certainly evident in debates about economic globaliza-tion, where it is acknowledged that global capital has largely bypassed the less developed nations and remains embedded in the core nations (particularly the urban West). For example, Hirst and Thompson (1999) are particularly dismis-sive of the idea of a global economy, pointing to the geographical unevenness associated with the omission of large parts of the world, including most of the continents of Africa and Asia, from many of the integrating activities purported

---

Box 8.2 Immanuel Wallerstein (1930–)

Immanuel Wallerstein produced one of the most influential arguments for viewing the world as a single economic system. Wallerstein's primary unit of analysis is the world-system, a unit that is presumed to have an autonomous development cap-acity over and above the social processes and relationships of its constituent soci-eties or states. For Wallerstein, there have been three types of world-system: *world-empires*, the international trading empires that featured prominently in early and middle history; *world-economies*, where nation-states are integrated in a single capitalist economy; and *world-socialism*, the yet to be achieved political-economic system that will replace both the nation-state and capitalism. The modern world-system (i.e., the global economy) corresponds to the second of these systems. Wallerstein's interpretation of the global economy as a single world market com-posed of competing nation-states is clearly a political-economy approach and shares many similarities with Marxist analyses of capitalist development. These similarities include a critical view of market (capitalist) forces and the importance of external relations between rich and poor countries in perpetuating economic inequality. He views the relationship between the rich (core) and poor (periphery) countries as essentially exploitative with the poor nations being accorded a

to be associated with globalization. Their analysis of capital flows and trade information underlines that capital is concentrating in the advanced countries rather than spreading employment or other opportunities across the globe. The current world order, they argue, is an internationalized economy that is controlled by hegemonic nation-states and organized into dominant super-blocs (dominated by the triad of the United States, Japan and selected European countries).

This creates what **Immanuel Wallerstein** (1984; see Box 8.2) identifies as a three-tier stratification of the world into a Western core, a poverty-stricken periphery and an emergent semi-periphery (the stabilizing political force between these economic extremes). Wallerstein's 'world-systems theory' therefore adopts a political-economy perspective on the importance of space in international relations. Hence, while traditional perspectives on geopolitics focused on the struggle for strategic control over vital heartland areas, or a nation's position in the global hierarchy of power relations, Wallerstein (1984) interprets international relations in terms of the dynamics of the capitalist world economy. This approach suggests that geopolitical analysis cannot proceed on a country-by-country basis, but needs to consider the division of labour which exists on a world scale (cf. Massey, 1994). In Wallerstein's account, it is the structural logic and rhythms of the capitalist system that creates a particular role for nations in the world economy (though Agnew, 1998, has amended this political-economy model to allow for the formative influence of sociocultural and political processes in the creation of a more complex and layered world territorial hierarchy, which he calls the 'geopolitical economy').

Of course, this type of analysis does not throw into doubt the idea that economic globalization is occurring, or that there has been an increased volume of economic exchange across the globe in the last twenty to thirty years. But even here we must tread warily, with Paul Knox (1996) suggesting that

---

dependent role in the relationship. However, according to Wallerstein, the long-term historical record reveals that the relative strengths and weaknesses of countries over time can result in adaptations to the world-system with countries moving in and out of core and periphery status. He identified an intermediate category of semi-periphery that served as a relegation zone for failing core countries and a promotion division for successful Third World countries. The main variables explaining the movement of countries between these three zones and creating the New International Division of Labour (NIDL) were suggested by Wallerstein to be the practices of large business corporations and regulatory activities of individual nation-states. Wallerstein's 'world-systems theory' has been hailed by some commentators, including Anthony Giddens (1990, pp. 68–70), as an early version of globalization theory. However, others have argued that the existence of a world-system which is integrated exclusively on an economic basis does not imply global unification and that political and cultural integration exists only as a remote possibility for Wallerstein in his utopian formulation of world socialism (see Waters, 2001).

Further reading: Wallerstein (1974, 1984); Taylor and Flint (1999); Taylor (1999b)

globalization is not necessarily a new phenomenon. He argues that a globalized infrastructure of unitary nation-states, together with international agencies and institutions, global forms of communication, a standardized system of global time, international competitions and prizes, and shared notions of citizenship and human rights, had all been established by the mid-nineteenth century, having antecedents in the mercantilism of the fifteenth and sixteenth centuries (see also Wallerstein, 1974, on the growth of a modern world-system based on the logic of the market).

What is distinctive about more recent globalization, according to Knox, is that there has been a decisive increase in the proportion of the world's economic activity that is transnational in scope. This refers to the fact that the flows of goods, capital and information that take place within and between companies are becoming more important than imports and exports between nations. Viewed from a behavioural perspective (see Chapter 2), this can be explained with reference to the decision-making processes of business elites, which are shaped by perceptions of a global world and the idea that spreading production facilities across the world's surface is a way of enhancing profits. Moreover, the fact that these elites are often in charge of flexible and vast conglomerations means that they are able to act on their instincts, creating global companies.

Therefore, while commodities and products have been traded *between* nations for hundreds, and perhaps thousands, of years, today a significant proportion of these international transactions occur *within* one company. For some, the decisive factor underpinning globalization is that a major increase has occurred in the proportion of world trade that is conducted by transnational corporations (or TNCs). Broadly defined, a TNC is any company that has investments and activities that span international boundaries and that has production facilities (factories, assembly plants), offices or research establishments in several nations. Many of the largest TNCs are household names throughout the world because they produce so-called *global products* – a phrase used to refer to those consumer and household goods which are produced, marketed and sold under the same branding worldwide. Notable examples here include Coca-Cola, Benetton clothing, Marlboro cigarettes, Nike sportswear, the Sony Walkman, the Windows operating system and Ford motor cars. Indeed, a widely noted trend is for these products to be marketed using images and discourses of globalization, with consumers sold the idea that buying a particular product connects them into a global culture (G. Myers, 1998). This is often defined by advertisers around Western ideals of environmental concern, respect for difference and (perhaps paradoxically) the celebration of conspicuous consumption (see Section 8.4).

Beyond these manufacturers of mass-produced consumer goods, some of the most powerful TNCs are involved in oil and petrochemical production, pharmaceuticals and aerospace. Yet it is also important to note that many TNCs are service sector-based, playing a crucial role in maintaining a globally integrated financial system which sees billions of dollars of stocks, shares, bonds and futures traded every day. Processes of financial homogenization in the late twentieth century are conspiring to make national financial systems increasingly similar, as witnessed in the equalization of short-term interest rates and the introduction of standardized forms of market regulation (Leyshon and Thrift, 1997) and, perhaps, in the globalization of certain currencies (especially the US dollar) and the creation of a new European currency in the European Union. A further illustration of this is the advent of virtual money, which cannot be considered to belong to any particular nation. The credit cards issued by Visa, Mastercard and American Express potentially allow many of us to benefit from this speeding up and stretching of monetary transactions. This means that it is entirely possible for us to tap into the networks of global finance every time we use an ATM, obtaining money in local currency wherever we are in the world (assuming there is an ATM there). Thus, the need to translate paper money from one currency to another has virtually been obliterated, with the large financial corporations and institutions who manage these flows of virtual money – NatWest, Citicorp, J. P. Morgan, Soloman Incorporation, Hong Kong Shanghai Bank (HSBC) – now among the largest employers in the world (see also Chapter 6).

Yet whatever business they are in, the majority of TNCs aim to have a strategic presence in the global market for a number of reasons – both supply- and market-oriented. Here, it is necessary to distinguish between a company's urge to seek the most profitable location to make its product (i.e., to seek locations where the supply of raw materials, labour and infrastructure is most conducive to producing a commodity at lowest cost) and its desire to open up new profitable markets for that good. An example that might help to illustrate the factors at work here is that of Nike. As the leading athletic sportswear company in the world, Nike needs little introduction. In 1996, its annual revenue was reported as $6.5 billion, a figure comparable with the gross domestic product of some small nations. Considering that the company was only founded in 1965 (in Beaverstown, Oregon), this represents a phenomenal expansion. In part, the company's success can be explained with reference to its offshore production operations which have allowed it to shift the labour-intensive processes of shoe assembly from nation to nation as local costs of production change. This has meant that virtually all of the company's shoe manufacturing is currently in the Far East, where low-cost wages are an obvious attraction (Schoenberger, 1996). Nike's principal offshore operations are thus in five Asian countries – China, South Korea, Taiwan, Vietnam and Indonesia – where the employment of women and young people on ultra-low wages allows the company to accelerate the rate at which it accumulates and reinvests profit. In the future, of course, it is entirely possible that this accelerated growth might be more easily achieved in another locale, meaning that the current operations might be abandoned in favour of less expensive places. In this sense, TNCs like Nike are depicted as increasingly *footloose* in their search for profit, able to deploy their activities across international boundaries with seeming impunity.

Widely regarded as 'the primary shaper of the global economy' (Dicken, 1998, p. 177), TNCs are the focus of many fears and hopes about globalization in the new millennium (Waters, 2001). The reasons for this are connected both to the sheer magnitude of many TNCs (many have turnovers in excess of the gross national product of individual nations) as well as their seemingly footloose nature. Barff (1995) suggests that TNCs switch investment from country to country through the constant realignment of their corporate networks, resulting in rapid shifts in the geography of production chains on an international and global scale. Displaying little loyalty to place, a TNC's decision suddenly to shift production from one nation to another as markets fluctuate may have deleterious impacts on relations with 'indigenous' supplier firms and producer services reliant on the TNC. The exceptions to this footloose logic are the research and development, technology, finance and marketing wings of TNCs, which tend to stay embedded in the core nations (especially North America, Japan and the European Union). This implicates TNCs in the making of a New International Division of Labour (NIDL) whereby the periphery develops low-skilled standardized operations such as manufacturing assembly or routine data entry and the global core retains high-skill knowledge- or technology-rich industries (Sayer and Walker, 1992; Barff, 1995). In this context, it is worth noting that 97 of the 100 largest TNCs' headquarters are in the core nations (Short and Kim, 1999).

For these reasons, the debate about the impacts of TNCs tends to polarize commentators between those who regard them as parasitic and those who view them more positively. The Japanese writer Kenichi Ohmae (1990, 1995) falls into the latter camp, being a leading advocate of the 'borderless world'. He sees globalization as the inevitable spread of Western free-market ideals across the globe, creating new opportunities for job creation, high mass consumption and wealth worldwide. In the new 'consumer democracy', Ohmae argues, the increasing dominance of consumers over the state is 'melting away' national economic borders to create a global market. Stateless corporations, or transnational companies (TNCs), are accordingly replacing nationally embedded multinational companies (MNCs) as the prime movers of an increasingly interlinked economy. This economy, Ohmae argues, is now so powerful it has absorbed most consumers and corporations, made traditional national borders almost disappear and pushed old-style politics, bureaucracy and the military towards the status of declining industries. In this 'new' world the nation-state is deemed to lack the flexibility necessary to compete globally (being too small for many modern purposes and too large for others) and is being supplanted by new spatial configurations in the drive towards globalization. In Ohmae's view we are witnessing the emergence of a 'borderless world' in which the boundaries of traditional nation-states become obsolete and city-states become the main sites of political and economic power. Again, we might note that 41 of the largest 100 TNCs have their headquarters in Paris, New York or Tokyo (Short and Kim, 1999).

Ohmae's work has been very influential in the fields of business management and amongst 'boosterist' politicians and public sector managers concerned about the challenges faced in an era of intensified competition between business firms and places seeking to attract investment (see Chapter 7). However, many geographers (e.g., Leyshon, 1997b; Roberts, 1995) are dismissive of Ohmae's interpretation of the economics of globalization. For them, it is significant that

Ohmae's ideas are deployed prescriptively by business strategists and political leaders and they are not surprised that many of those speaking up for the growth-generating potential of TNCs are business gurus and advocates of neo-liberalism. These are the very people, they argue, with most to gain from deploying caricature versions of globalization in politically loaded ways. Kevin Cox (1997) makes a similar point when he 'unpacks' uncritical globalization discourses like those of Ohmae which, he argues, mask the function of 'naturalizing' neo-liberal capitalism as a necessary and inevitable order. In Cox's view, uncritical globalization discourses are part of the international class struggle, designed to serve the interests of those aligned to transnational capital by overcoming earlier territorial resistance. Moreover, he implies that these discourses are dangerous because they deflect attention from real trends and disguise the relentless neo-liberal agendas of the dominant super-bloc powers.

For Cox, to adopt the assumptions and language of economic globalization is essentially to surrender to the sense of inevitability produced by the concept. He thus warns of the need to distinguish between reality (the world as it is) and discourses aimed at becoming reality. Roberts (1995) dismisses suggestions that globalization is a myth but, like Cox, assaults the hegemony of globalization discourses, reiterating that globalization has a discursive as well as a materialist dimension. For Roberts, globalization involves a material reshaping of scalar relations through an iterative set of discourses and socio-spatial practices. These globalization discourses are deemed to be self-affirming and self-propagating, containing both an explanation of the world as it is and a prescriptive plan of action. As such, Roberts argues for a more detailed examination of their production and dissemination, launching a blistering attack on geographers for their tendency to dismiss the discursive basis of globalization as immaterial in relation to its seeming rootedness in political economy.

For Cox and Roberts (among others), accepting the ideas of globalization proposed by neo-liberal business gurus is regarded as highly dangerous. Rather than constituting a good explanatory framework, such discourses are seen to be implicated in the perpetuation of globalization. Consequently, some theorists are unwilling to dismiss such discourses out of hand, carefully acknowledging the role of discourse in the contested construction of a new world order (e.g., Mitchell, 1995; Barnes, 1996; Gibson-Graham, 1996; Agnew, 1999). Influenced by the post-structural ideas of Foucault, Derrida, Latour, Law and others (see Chapter 3), these theorists believe that major changes are under way but they do not accept that the outcomes predicted by globalist discourses are clear-cut or predetermined. Some believe, like Cox, that the hegemony of capital may be the dominant force shaping most aspects of social life but they allow for inflections and resistance through the mediation of discourse (as well as action and protest in concrete situations – see Routledge, 1995). This means that discourses that contradict Ohmae's upbeat assessment of global process (like Schoenberger's (1996), account of the inequalities and exploitation wrought by Nike) might also affect the trajectory of globalization.

It is worth noting here that there is no shortage of geographers who challenge Ohmae's thesis of a 'borderless world'. For instance, Dicken (1997) has stated that it is a gross error to assume that TNCs have usurped nation-states as the controllers of the global economy. Dicken argues there is a discernible trend towards the internationalization of economic activity, which he characterizes as a 'global shift', but that the power of TNCs to bypass the regulatory controls of nation-states is still open to debate. The evidence he considers indicates that there is no major shift towards the creation of truly global companies in recent decades, with most large companies continuing to be multinational (i.e., MNCs) rather than truly transnational (TNCs). He insists that the notion of a truly footloose global firm is a myth, with even the most 'globalized' of firms being historically *produced* and embedded in particular nations. Of course, the locational behaviour of TNCs (using the term in a loose generic sense) makes them significant actors in the process of globalization but Dicken argues that government actions are also highly significant in establishing and sustaining national comparative advantages – as illustrated in the formation of supra-national integrated markets based on multilateral political agreements (e.g., the North American Free Trade Agreement or European Union).

Dicken (1997) also notes the bewildering variety of organizational forms involved in modern production and concludes that diversity will continue for the foreseeable future. However, he acknowledges some clearly observable trends in the operation of 'global' companies, the most notable being a growing emphasis on global networks. He argues that TNCs appear to be rationalizing their geographically dispersed operations into more tightly integrated networks organized around world cities (see also Taylor, 2001). This development of more complex organizational networks *within* TNCs has been accompanied by an upsurge in the number of external collaborations with other firms. Thus, the major car manufacturing corporations in America, Europe and Japan are becoming aligned as strategic global conglomerates – with Ford, Volvo and Mazda combining to compete with General Motors and Toyota. Similar trends towards the creation of conglomerates and alliances are evident in the service sector spheres of banking and finance (see Daniels and Lever, 1996; Wood, 1991) and the media (Robins and Cornford, 1994; Robins, 1995b). These restructurings and strategic alliances both represent and stimulate the changes occurring in the global economy – such as intensified competition, technological change, production and marketing of new products.

Ultimately, Dicken (1997) suggests that conceiving of TNCs as a homo-geneous population of giant firms, all pursuing somewhat similar objectives in similar ways, is wholly inadequate. Emphasizing diversity rather than uniform-ity, Dicken concludes that much of the diversity arises from the relationship between a TNC and its home country (as well as the nations that host its many branch plants). In his book *Global Shift* (1998), Dicken provides detailed empir-ical evidence to show that the impacts of TNCs on different nations (and nations on TNCs) are highly variable, casting doubt over claims that the nation-state is no longer important in the global economy (see also Allen, 1995; Dunning, 1993). Prominent in Dicken's work is consideration of the way state policy and legal frameworks impinge on the practices of TNCs. This alerts us to the interdependency that is created between a TNC and a host (with some 'footloose' firms becoming firmly embedded in localities). Though much of the writing on TNCs accordingly focuses on the labour-capital/supply-demand relations that are at the heart of global capitalism, researchers are beginning to produce accounts that are more attuned to the social and cultural practices of TNCs, exploring the way that global discourses and business practices encourage particular firms to 'go global' in particular ways (e.g., Gertler, 1997; Schoenberger, 1996). This enculturated perspective on the global economy is yet another symptom of geography's 'cultural turn' (see Chapter 3).

8.4 A GLOBAL SENSE OF PLACE

While much has been made of the economic impacts of globalization, the 'annihilation of space by time' has also prompted geographers to think about the way that a *global culture* is being spread around the world. The key actors in this process are the Western news, film and broadcasting corporations that dominate the world's media. The world's six largest media organizations – as we detailed in Chapter 5 – all have a global presence, broadcasting to an international audience via their satellite subsidiaries. Accordingly, it is possible to discern a homogenization of global broadcasting:

> Irrespective of where they live, audiences around the world are fed a broadly similar diet of television. The same kind of programmes are scheduled at the same times of the day . . . Soap operas and quiz shows account for most of the daytime slots while children's programmes predominate in the early evening. These are followed by family viewing, the mid-evening news, drama, sport and adult television. The significance of this standard format is that it generates demands for particular types of programming, much of which is international in origin. (Clark, 1997, p. 126)

Some commentators argue this standardized diet of images is producing new forms of cultural identification as people become exposed to lifestyles, activities and values which transcend the frontiers of national communities. Appadurai (1990) describes the emergence of a *global mediascape* produced by flows of images and information via printed media, television, music and film. As we saw in Chapter 5, these images serve to valorize (i.e., raise the value of) particular lifestyles and places, showing that it is necessary to consider the entwining of the political economy and cultural economy when theorizing global flows of money, information and goods.

While Appadurai's notion of a global mediascape seems an apposite description of the homogenization of global media, it is **Marshall McLuhan** (see Box. 8.3) who is often credited with alerting us to the spatial consequences of the communication revolution. It was McLuhan who first coined the term 'global village' in the 1960s to describe the new geographical and communications order that was taking shape at that time:

After three thousand years of explosion by means of fragmentary and mechanical technologies, the Western world is imploding. During the mechanical ages we had extended our bodies in space. Today, after more than a century of electronic technology we have extended our central nervous system itself in a global embrace, abolishing both space and time as far as our planet is concerned. (McLuhan, 1964, p. 16)

McLuhan's arguments related principally to the detraditionalizing tendencies effected by distantiation and the stretching of social relations. One of his key ideas was that language would be standardized by the imperatives of instantaneous communication, with written and printed communication being supplanted by synchronous modes of talking with people on the other side of the world (hence, his prediction of a global village based on 'neo-tribal' communication). McLuhan's predictions of the cultural changes associated with globalization have been widely acclaimed as offering surprisingly accurate insights into the possible effects of the communication revolution. However, his work has been subject to some misinterpretation, with some commentators seizing on his prediction of the detraditionalization of local modes of communication as presaging the 'end of geography'. This type of interpretation suggests that global flows of people, goods and information are dissolving geographical boundaries and diversity so that there may be no differences worthy of geographical analysis in the resulting global village (O'Brien, 1991). But the demise of geography has been vehemently rejected by many others, who argue that new differences are being produced by the very processes that threaten global uniformity (Allen and Hamnett, 1995).

Another take on McLuhan is taken by political economists who explore the spread of Western capitalism and the part it plays in the formation of contemporary global systems. The sociologist Leslie Sklair (1991), for example, examines the idea that globalization is obliterating difference and suggests that that the world is being reorganized into a global economic system with the

---

Box 8.3 Herbert Marshall McLuhan (1911–80)

The Canadian writer Marshall McLuhan has been hugely influential since the 1960s through his idea that modern media re-create the world in the image of a global village. His books *Understanding Media* (1964) and *The Medium is the Message* (1967) addressed two key questions about the modern world: what are communications and how do they affect humanity? His answers to these questions traced the entire process of communication from the invention of the printing press to the electronic age. The kernel of his argument was that societies have always been shaped more by the nature of the medium by which people communicate than by the content of the communication. It is the medium *itself* that is most influential, not the ideas and information that the medium disseminates. In short, the *medium is the message*. McLuhan suggested that the invention of the printing press, with its emphasis on using the eye rather than the ear, had encouraged people to be introspective, individualistic and self-centred. As such, it was an 'isolating' technology

global media firmly implicated in the exploitation and inequality wrought by capitalism:

> All those who argue that it is the medium not the message that characterises this revolution are entirely wrong . . . The central messages are still and more powerfully those of the capitalist global system. McLuhan's famous 'the medium is the message' is true to the extent that corporations, increasingly transnational corporations, control the media to propagate *their* message, as McLuhan himself occasionally acknowledges. (Sklair, 1991, p. 74)

Sklair turns McLuhan's ideas around completely by concluding that the medium *is* the message because the message has engulfed the medium (Sklair, 1991). The mass media are described as a tool of cultural manipulation and imperialism for the dominant agents of contemporary capitalism (i.e., TNCs based in the West) because they create a market hungry for Western commodities and lifestyles and limit the possibilities of effective resistance to this version of 'the good life'. The geographer Kevin Robins (1995b) also links the changing global reach of the media to transitions in capitalism. Robins argues that culture and the media are enslaved by growth imperatives, with the electronic communication networks of the conglomerates 'managing and massaging' audiences even as they serve them. In passing, we might note important connections here between these ideas and the cultural materialism that seeks to expose the ideological underpinning of texts and textuality (see Chapter 5); for Hodge and Kress (1988, p. 3), it is clear that 'dominant groups attempt to represent the world in forms that reflect their own interests, the interests of their power'.

From this perspective, cultural globalization can be viewed as an expansion which has involved the incorporation of all parts of the world into capitalist production and consumption practices that took shape in the West. Accordingly, it is perhaps better to refer to globalization as representing the 'Westernization' or even 'Americanization' of world culture, a process whereby all nations have

---

that was inimical to the creation and maintenance of a cohesive, interdependent society. The electronic media, in contrast, are a 'connecting' technology that is reshaping and restructuring patterns of social interaction and interdependence by exposing and linking us instantly to the concerns of others from a multitude of places and sources. They have reconstituted discourse on a global scale by undermining the cult of individualism associated with print discourse by compelling us to live and participate in a global village of simultaneous happenings. The result is a redefinition of the world through imagining it as a single, related and interdependent place – that is, the emergence of a new consciousness of the world community as a 'global village'.

Further reading: McLuhan (1964); McLuhan and Fiore (1967)

seemingly been persuaded of the benefits of Western-style capitalism. In considering this argument, we might perhaps start thinking of the landscapes which actively promote modern consumer practices designed to encourage and reproduce global capitalism. For example, anyone who has travelled internationally cannot help but have noticed that there are many places that look similar no matter what country one is in. The French anthropologist Marc Augé (1995) offers the examples of airport departure lounges, railway terminals and shopping malls, settings which are decorated in a similar manner, have identical shops and food outlets and are enveloped by the same piped muzak irrespective of international context. Inevitably, they will be populated by people dressed in similar ways (jeans, designer T-shirts, sportswear for the young, business suits and casual wear for older people), reading internationally syndicated magazines and comics or pausing to play video games which are the same the world over. For Augé, these settings – together with the landscapes of hotels, sports centres, restaurants (and even motorways) – extend capitalist consumer values into the far corners of the globe, simultaneously symbolizing the sense of speed, efficiency and *supermodernity* that lies at the heart of global capitalism.

Yet perhaps the most frequently cited example of a global landscape is that of the fast-food restaurant, particularly McDonald's (which has over 18,000 branches in 90 countries). With McDonald's recently expanding into the former Communist bloc, some commentators have even redubbed globalization as the *McDonaldization* of society, suggesting that the fast-food restaurant has become the organizational force representing and extending the process of consumer capitalism further into the realm of everyday interaction and local identity:

> McDonaldization . . . is the process by which the principles of the fast-food restaurant are coming to dominate more and more sectors of American society as well as of the rest of the world. (Ritzer, 1993, p. 1)

Ritzer contends that everything from pizza to ice cream, from alcohol to fried chicken is dominated by the McDonald's mentality. Seemingly, we no longer have to go to the chains; rather, they come to us, in city centres, malls, motorway service stations, schools and military bases, hospitals and airports, even aeroplanes and football stadia. Moreover, Ritzer claims that McDonaldization has apparently extended its reach into areas that are increasingly remote from the heart of the fast-food business – book retailing, fashion, childcare, sports, news production and so on. His basis for this claim rests on the idea that McDonald's encapsulates five themes at the heart of global capitalism – efficiency, calculability, predictability, technological advancement and control. Connected to this is the proliferation of 'McJobs' – Douglas Coupland's (1991) term for the low-status, low-skill, low-pay jobs taken by the characters in his satire of consumer society, *Generation X*.

Several commentators have suggested that McDonaldization is one clear symptom of the replacement of 'indigenous' local cultures by a seemingly rational and *supermodern* global culture defined by American consumer values (Featherstone, 1990; Rojek, 1995). But, if we consider such accounts in the light of structural theories concerning the making of spatial difference through capitalist process, their limitations become sharply etched. In fact, few geographers suggest that the distinctiveness of local places has been lost as a result of globalization. Instead, they have been keen to stress that there is not one single global culture – nor hermetically sealed local ones – but that everywhere there is a complex interaction of local and global. In this sense, they have drawn on post-colonial ideas (see Chapter 3) to highlight the cultural *hybridity* created through the intersection of international, national and local ways of life. In the past, hybridity was something that was noted principally in border areas where languages, rituals and fashions mixed to create new cultural forms (exemplified by the Tex-Mex music, fashion and food that have become associated with the US–Mexican border area). Today we can see hybrid cultures being created everywhere as global and local intertwine in sometimes unexpected ways.

This notion of hybridity is one that begins to emphasize why grand theories of global change are in danger of oversimplifying the effects that globalization has on different people's lives. After all, even if McDonald's restaurants are similar everywhere, this does not mean that they are identical (e.g., McDonald's in Tokyo sells a Teriyaki McBurger); nor does it mean that McDonald's restaurants are used by the same kind of people in the same kinds of way irrespective of location. Bhabha (1994) thus utilizes this critical notion of hybridity when he speaks of the way that cultural globalization can challenge Western processes of Othering. Here, the authenticity of dominant culture is shown to be negotiable, stoking an 'identity politics' based on group affiliation (Barber, 1995; Friedmann, 1999). The significance of globalization here is not simply that it has undermined state citizenship but that it has complicated the geography of community. The diminution of the role of nationhood as a force of community allows and facilitates the development of alternative frameworks of solidarity which may be more multidimensional, fluid and uncertain (Scholte, 2000). Ironically, such diasporic and transnational communities, whether defined in relation to race, gender or sexuality, pose major challenges to globalization (as well as to the notions of citizenship inherent in the notion of the nation-state – see Chapter 7).

A similarly optimistic interpretation of hybridization has been advanced by Doreen Massey (see Box 1.2) in her work on a 'progressive sense of place'. Like Harvey (Section 8.2), Massey (1991, 1993) explores the interplay of local and global by elucidating the tension between space and place. She begins by critiquing humanistic assertions that places are strongly bounded locales whose stability and fixity provides a firm locus for Being (see Chapter 2). She does this by juxtaposing Heidegger's summation that places offer uniqueness with the idea that places have multiple identities. Writing of the everyday experiences of people (such as the experience of walking along a shopping street in any British city), she contends that places are always manifold, fluid and unbounded, highlighting the connections between such places and the rest of the world (from the diverse products and people that can be found there to the constant flow of traffic that takes people elsewhere). This leads her to propose that places are unique articulations of many facets of globalization that weave together and meet at a particular locus. Lacking seamless, coherent identities, such places can have multiple identities, and these coexisting multiple identities can be a source of either richness or conflict (or both). For Massey (1991), specific places are not static or passive receptors of the global; they are part of a 'relational' process that integrates local and global, creating a consciousness of links with the wider world.

Acknowledging the inequalities associated with the power geometries of space-time compression, Massey argues that there is a lot more shaping our 'sense of place' than the bounded experiences contained in place. Consequently, Massey suggests we should not idealize the local but embrace it as a relational and relative concept, open to movement and flow. This approach argues against those accounts that suggest that globalization creates homogenization or that it threatens local ways of life. Yet, at the same time, it recognizes that globalization recontextualizes locality in ways that are ambiguous, equivocal and potentially progressive. Similar notions are developed by Amin and Thrift (1994a), who reject polarized accounts of the global and local as oppositional forces. They point out that, while official attempts to differentiate places are problematic (e.g., through place promotion – see Chapter 7), the success of localities in a global economy will depend upon their ability to embrace the global. They contend that it is 'only through the construction of adaptable institutional mixes that places can hold down the local' (Amin and Thrift, 1994a, p. 260). This implies that adaptable localities with a suitable local infrastructure (or 'thickness') can make effective and progressive links with the global (something of major concern to policy-makers struggling to reconcile local and global). This articulation of a 'global sense of place' is crucially important for geographers seeking to transcend the dichotomy between accounts that portend the end of geography, or, conversely, its enhanced importance in a global era (see McDowell, 1997). Such ideas begin to theorize place as 'articulated moments' in globalized networks, encouraging geographers to think about places as caught up in a global 'space of flows' (Castells, 1996).

8.5 TOWARDS A GEOGRAPHY OF FLOWS

The realization that the commonplace activities of daily life are not residual products of globalization but are themselves formative of the global is important in encouraging geographers to conceive of space and place in more imaginative ways (Flusty, 2001). While positivist, humanistic, behavioural and Marxist theorists have tended to treat places atomistically (i.e., as discrete spatial entities), globalization is encouraging many to analyse the real connections that join different parts of the world. This emphasis on connectivity, flow and the 'traffic in things' (Jackson, 1999) is informed by debates about displacement, movement and speed (drawing on the ideas of Virilio in particular – see Box 8.1) as well as work on Actor Networks (see Chapter 7). Unfortunately, given the tendency for geographers to focus on what exists within places, rather than what moves through them, there is a serious deficit of data concerning the nature of these global flows (Taylor, 2000). None the less, information about the volume and direction of flows of workers (via international migration), capital (via international banking), products (via import/export), ideas (via the movement of academics and cultural commentators) and even pollution (via dumping policies) begins to indicate the existence of a global 'space of flows' (see Smith and Timberlake, 1995).

For many commentators, it is these very movements and flows that constitute globalization. Doing away with distinctions of 'inside' and 'outside' (e.g., the idea that places are contained within a global world that shapes their destiny), this is effectively a post-structural account in which flow becomes everything. For instance, rather than being a global economy made up of flows, these flows are the global economy. To that extent, what is interesting about places is not their fixed position within an imploding global network (Virilio, 1999), but the way that flows drift in and drift out, speed up and slow down, contract and expand, within them (cf. Jameson, 1984). In short, global network formation is always subject to a double movement of speed and slowness, of contraction and expansion (Doel, 1999). This 'relational materialism' (Law and Mol, 1995, p. 277) demands consideration of the way that human and non-human actants are implicated in the articulation of this global network, and the way that this network is maintained through conjoint action (see Beaverstock et al., 2002).

Against this, others hold to a more structural interpretation of linkage, especially those who investigate world city formation, where world cities are called upon to fulfil particular tasks by the structures of global capitalism. A key theorist of these global structures is **Manuel Castells** (Box 8.4), whose multi-volume *The Information Age* (1996, 1997, 1998) identifies global networks as part and parcel of a global *informational capitalism*. He argues that these networks are becoming the new organizing and managing principles (or 'social morphology') of capitalism, with recent advances in information technology providing the material infrastructure for the diffusion of the networking principle throughout society. Insofar as the logic of networks is diffusing into all spheres of human activity, Castells contends, it is also radically modifying the production, consumption and experience of space. Until the 1970s, according to Castells, modern society was constituted as 'spaces of places', such as nations, cities and regions. Contemporary network society, on the other hand, is constituted as spaces of flows, an entangled knot of linkages, connections and relations across space (Taylor et al., 2001). Castells describes this 'space of flows' as having three levels: the infrastructural, the organizational and the social. The first refers to the hard and soft technology that enables global communication, the second to the hubs and nodes that allow the network to operate, and the third to the networks of global elites that are of paramount importance in the information age. All three have distinctive geographies, with presence or absence in these networks being 'critical sources of domination and change in our society' (Castells, 1996, p. 469).

The political geographer Peter Taylor has sought to reconcile and clarify Castells's work in relation to his own interests in world cities, modernities and world-systems (which draws on heavily on Wallerstein's, 1974, world-systems theory). Taylor observes that Castells's treatment of 'command and control centres' is quite conventional in terms of the global cities literature, following, for example, Sassen's (1991) identification of London, New York and Tokyo at the top of a global urban hierarchy. According to Taylor (1999a), the principal contribution of Castells to the world/global cities literature is instead to position the world city network into a richer and more comprehensive theoretical context, making it one important network within a particular layer of the space of flows, the new spatial logic of the informational age. Identifying world cities as the most direct illustration of hubs and nodes in the new spatial logic of the informational age allows Castells to emphasize the uneven articulation of global flows, which he reads as 'critical for the distribution of wealth and power in the world' (Taylor, 1999a).

Though Taylor agrees with this summation, he remains concerned by Castells' (1996) conflation of the concepts of world city and mega-city. For Taylor, these two conceptions of contemporary large cities have a very different provenance: economic-functional (in the case of world cities) and demographic-statistical (in the case of mega-cities). However, Castells does not use size as the defining quality of mega-cities and compounds the confusion by describing mega-cities as one of the new urban forms of the informational age, with the growth of mega-cities described 'the most important transformation of urban forms world-wide' (Castells, 1996, p. 403). He also characterizes mega-cities as 'the nodal points, and the power centres of the new spatial form/process of the information age: the space of flows' (Castells, 1996, p. 410). This usage of the

---

Box 8.4 Manuel Castells (1942–   )

An influential writer in many fields of research, the polymath Manuel Castells is Professor of Sociology and of Urban Planning at the University of California, Berkeley. Born in Spain in 1942, Castells has taught and researched in more than twenty universities outside the United States and has published over twenty books. Castells's early work in the field of urban sociology and neo-Marxism emphasized the importance of space and helped to reorient urban geography. His books *The Urban Question* (1972 [1977, English translation]) and *City, Class and Power* (1978) drew on Marxist theory to assert that urban life and urban space were a product of the industrial system under capitalism and were ultimately shaped by class antagonism. In the 1980s Castells moved away from his earlier rigid structuralist approach and his book on urban protest movements, *The City and the Grassroots* (1983), acknowledged that the imperatives of economic development and class control were not straightforwardly stamped across space. Instead, Castells allowed for human agency within his Marxist framework and argued through a series of case studies that spatial relations reflected the types and patterns of opposition and resistance encountered by the dominant economic forces and elite classes. Castells's work in the 1990s sought to establish the importance of the emerging information society. He argued that the transition to the era of informationalism represented a profound break from industrialism, which itself had constituted a profound break from the previous era of agrarianism. Therefore, informationalism amounted to far more than the latest (Kondratiev) cycle of technological innovation driving the successive waves of capitalist development. Castells's

term mega-cities by Castells overlaps considerably with his deployment of the term global cities. Taylor argues that this conflation detracts from the clarity of Castells' work and he goes on to clarify the two terms theoretically and empirically (see Taylor, 1999c, 2000, 2001).

However, Taylor also makes the point that Castells' conception of global cities as 'embedded flow processes' rather than places usefully directs attention away from what cities contain (the case study approach) to their connections with other cities (the relational approach). Similarly, he stresses that Castells raises crucial points about space and place. This boils down to the idea that 'spaces of places' have not disappeared with the coming of a 'space of flows', with world cities (for instance) acting as nodes in networks as well as distinctive places (Taylor *et al.*, 2001). In this way, world cities have become privileged places in the contemporary world economy. According to Knox (1995), it is world cities that house the 'knowledge elite' which exacts the economic reflexivity that has become crucial for economic success. Knox (1995, p. 236) therefore refers to world cities as 'nodal points that function as control centres for the interdependent skein of material, financial and cultural flows which, together, support and sustain globalization'. In a similar manner, Storper (1997, p. 222) refers to world cities as 'privileged sites', suggesting they are critical places in the perpetuation of global capitalism. World cities are deemed to contain the economic, cultural and institutional infrastructure that channels national and provincial resources into the global economy and that transmits the impulses of globalization back to national and provincial centres.

---

later work has as its main aim the formulation of a systematic theory of the information society that takes account of the fundamental effects of the information technology on the contemporary world. His best-selling book *The Rise of the Network Society* (1996), the first of his three-volume study on the economy, society and culture of the 'Information Age', is an account of the economic and social dynamics of the new information era. It argues that the global economy is now characterized by accelerating, and in some cases instantaneous, flows and exchanges of information, capital and communication. The new spatial logic of the informational age is termed the 'space of flows'. This new space is, according to Castells, 'the material organization of time-sharing practices that work through flows' (p. 412). It has three layers: the electronic impulses in networks, the places which constitute the nodes and hubs of networks and the spatial organization of cosmopolitan elites in terms of work, play and movement. These flows shape both production and consumption, and their networks reflect and create distinctive cultures. The growing dependence upon, and difficulty in regulating, the new modes of informational flow confer enormous, and potentially unaccountable, power on those who control them. Castells links informationalism to processes of globalization which, he argues, marginalize those places and people excluded from the global networks, creating new and highly segmented social and spatial structures.

Further reading: Castells (1996, 2000)

Castells's structural take on globalization has then been especially influential in the literature on world cities. The initial identification of 'world city formation' (Friedmann and Wolff, 1982) followed upon the recognition of the major restructuring of the world economy in the 1970s. Frobel *et al.* (1980) delineated a New International Division of Labour which reflected the worldwide production strategies adopted by major corporations who had developed new 'global reach' (see Section 8.3). This 'new' global economy required command and control points in order to function effectively; world cities were deemed to be such points. Consequently, world cities were viewed as the places where TNCs had their headquarters, and from where the New International Division of Labour was organized. Updating these ideas, Castells (1996) suggested that the world city network was one important layer in this space of flows but argued that it no longer played the same role in the articulation of these flows as it did in the 1970s and 1980s. Then, the majority of corporate headquarters were located in major Western cities; now, new communications technologies do not require headquarter functions to be carried out only in the largest cities. In addition, the 1990s witnessed the rising importance of capital flows within so-called 'emerging markets', bypassing the corporate headquarters of the urban West. In response, TNC headquarters have often decentralized, seeking new and cheaper locations away from world city centres (which are characterized by high rents). In relation to this, it is interesting that London is home to only three of the world's largest 100 TNCs (Short and Kim, 1999), but is still commonly referred to as a world city.

Yet, if the presence of corporate headquarters is not the key distinguishing characteristic of world cities, what is? Saskia Sassen (1994) provides a possible answer, simultaneously explaining why some economic functions continue to concentrate in cities despite the decentralizing potential of electronic communications. For Sassen, it is crucial to consider the role of *advanced producer services*, defined as those corporate activities that enable the world economy to operate through the expert assistance they give to both public and private corporations. Covering such activities as banking, accountancy, insurance, advertising, public relations, law and management consultancy, these services went 'global' at the same time as their main clients, the TNCs. However, the globalization of advanced producer services involved more than the 'global servicing' of TNCs, with many advanced producer services becoming TNCs in their own right. The most obvious example here is the banking sector, which includes some of the biggest TNCs – which are themselves served by other advanced producer services such as law partnerships. These advanced producer service TNCs may have begun their global strategy by following clients to world cities, but their continued success has required more proactive strategies. Global service corporations have thus been adept at producing their own commodities, including new financial products; new advertising packages; new forms of multi-jurisdictional law; and so on (see Beaverstock *et al.*, 2000).

The one thing that all of these share is dependence on specialized knowledge. Their state-of-the-art commodities are produced by bringing together different forms of expertise to meet the specific needs of clients. In order to be able to put together such packages, firms need to be embedded in knowledge-rich environments. Sassen (1996) suggests that world cities provide such environments and that face-to-face contacts between experts are facilitated by the clustering together of knowledge-rich personnel in cities. Ironically, these world cities are becoming more, rather than less, important in a global era, and although the rise of the Pacific Rim means that cities such as Singapore, Vancouver or Los Angeles have taken on a new strategic importance, London, New York and Tokyo have unquestionably maintained their pre-eminence as global hubs (Taylor, 2001). Ultimately, this again highlights the tension that exists between the deterritorializing centrifugal impulses of capitalism (which threaten to undermine place identities in the interests of mobility) and the re-territorializing centripetal tendencies that create a highly differentiated world of places (so that some places are more profitable and powerful than others).

8.6 CONCLUSION

In this chapter, we have explored the way that geographers have tried to make sense of globalization. As we have seen, this endeavour has been rendered problematic by the fact that globalization remains a highly contested term. For some, it signals the end of geography and the death of place; for others it has heightened the salience of place in social, economic and political life. Likewise, some regard it as a destructive force that wreaks havoc across the world, but others see it as benevolent and potentially emancipatory. What appears to be generally agreed is that globalization necessitates new theories of space and time, and that many existing theories seem inadequate for making sense of the processes and outcomes of global change. In a world where time-space compression is changing popular understandings of speed and distance, it seems that academic theories must change too. Effectively summarizing many of the debates about understanding a 'hyperactive' world, Thrift concludes that the world has become more complex and difficult to comprehend, but that this does not preclude geographers making critical interventions:

> Certainly there is an electronic space of flows. Of course the world has speeded up. But because the world is more difficult to understand does not mean that nothing is understandable. The space of flows doesn't reach everyone. Speed isn't everything. The story is as much in what is missing from these accounts as in what is there. (Thrift, 1995, p. 24)

This has led to some innovative attempts to adapt theoretical tools suitable for making sense of global times, challenging the understandings of globalization proposed by business gurus and neo-liberal politicians. Taylor *et al.* (2001) stress that this is not simply a question of geographers adapting existing theoretical tools evolved in the context of the local or national to explore issues at a different scale. Rather, it involves interrogation of the meaning of scale within geographical study, resulting in new understandings of the complex articulation of local and global. Hence, geographic debates about globalization are replete with neologisms like hybridity, supermodernity, glocalization and the 'space of flows', which may, in time, come to be as important in understandings of the way the world works as established geographical concepts of space and place.

As in a previous chapters, what this shows is that the philosophical perspective which geographers adopt, and the conceptual tools that they use, are crucially important in changing the way they relate to their objects of study. More crucially, perhaps, it actually changes what they take to be their object of study – Pieterse (2000, p. xvi) maintains that globalization is inevitably 'framed by language and epistemology'. For instance, depending on their allegience to particular packages of philosophical thought, geographers can approach globalization as a discourse that needs to be deconstructed, a global consciousness that needs to be empathized with, an attitude that needs to be explained, a set of processes that need to be critiqued or a space of flows that needs to be mapped. Perhaps, in the final analysis, it is all of these things, in which case humanistic, behavioural, positivist, post-structural, Actor Network and Marxist perspectives (not to mention feminist, queer and post-colonial theories) may all explain something of globalization. On the other hand, one may prefer to discount some (or all!) of these theorizations, dismissing those theories which promise to reveal preordained global orders because there is no single point for inquiry nor a single spatial or other logic waiting to be revealed (Barnes, 1996). This postmodern position offers yet another perspective, where there can be no single definition of globalization. The concept of globalization is elusive and yet remains pivotal to any exploration of the geography of the contemporary world. Perhaps all we can be sure of is that geography is not dead, it is merely moving with the times; we live today in global times.

Conclusion

Chapter 9 Final Words

9.1 THINKING GEOGRAPHICALLY

> We shall not cease from exploration. And the end of all our exploring will be to arrive where we started and know the place for the first time. (T. S. Eliot, *Little Gidding*)

Our principal aim in this book has been to stress the importance of engaging with theory, illustrating that thinking in different ways inevitably (and profoundly) affects the way that geographical knowledge is produced. We have done this by, firstly, outlining some of the distinctive theoretical approaches in geography and, secondly, by showing how five key geographical concepts have been theorized in relation to these approaches. Consequently, we have not sought to provide a comprehensive history of geographic thought or an expansive overview of contemporary human geography's '-ologies' and '-isms', but rather have sought to explain why engaging with theory is an important, necessary and stimulating part of being a geographer. Central to our thesis is the notion that 'thinking geographically' is a basic point of departure for understanding ourselves and the world in which we live. The more we learn about the world, and our place within it, the more questions are raised about the basis of our understanding. After all, the world is constantly changing. Hence, our theoretical efforts are also always changing.

This constant struggle to understand a changing world leads, as you have probably realized by now, to one of the most obvious features of theory – that is, the lack of agreement about it. Whether one looks at literature on geographical theory or at wider philosophical debates about the status of knowledge, disagreement about fundamental concepts and ideas is evident. Some theories appear to be mutually incompatible in some respects while complementing one another in other ways. This is quite common in relation to social theories – there is often a degree of overlap between them despite the apparent antipathy that may exist between those working in different theoretical traditions (witness, for example, the often vituperative confrontations between humanistic and behavioural geographers, Marxist and humanist geographers, Marxist and post-structural geographers and so on). Often, it seems the main task of theorists has been to fortify their own position against criticism whilst lobbing plenty of 'critical bombs' into the territory of the opposition. Hence, the weaknesses highlighted in any particular theory do not materialize out of nowhere – they either are exposed by those working in other theoretical traditions or arise internally as a result of defensive refinement which seeks to pre-empt critical attack from outside. You might recall, for example, that many of the proponents of the Marxist tradition have not abandoned it in the face of numerous criticisms from postmodernist and post-structuralist theories. Instead, they have gone on to refine and supplement their theoretical frameworks so that Marxism remains – for them at least – a useful approach to analysis (see Section 3.2.1).

This raises another point that you may have noticed as you progressed through the book; namely, that different theories have not only 'thrived' at particular times, they have come to dominate geographic debate. This does not mean that they became the *only* theoretical position accepted by geographers at a particular time; it simply means that one approach was the driving force in theoretical debate, so that geographers in other traditions felt obliged to justify their own approaches in relation to this 'dominant' approach. Yet it is important to note that the popularity of particular approaches at particular moments is reflective of a range of factors, not just their ability to offer new or different possibilities for advancing understanding. For example, a theory's popularity is also dependent on its apparent usefulness in relation to contemporary social issues, its ability to capture the imagination of researchers, the role of key individuals within the discipline promoting its use and development, the formation of a 'critical mass' of proponents and so on – all of which have to be understood in relation to the shifting institutional cultures of higher education. In respect of the latter, John Gold (1992) argues that behaviouralism, for example, started to fade from prominence from the discipline at the end of the 1970s not only because its ideas were challenged by humanists and structuralists, but also because it failed to achieve critical mass as postgraduate students adopting behavioural approaches did not achieve academic posts at this time as a result of the political-economic climate. Consequently, a generation of behavioural geographers was denied the opportunity to promote, advance and educate others in behavioural ideas, and the next generation of postgraduates and those remaining in the academy tended to pursue other theoretical ideas. As we noted in Chapter 2, disciplinary geography has thus moved through successive phases of intellectual and theoretical development, with its current plurality leading to the suggestion that geography is best characterized as a *singular diversity* in which different theories and ideas coexist in a creative tension, intermingling and cross-fertilizing to produce new theoretical outlooks.

Given geography's singular diversity, throughout our account we have been careful not to privilege overly any one approach, seeking instead to compare and contrast positions in order to reveal how the construction and adoption of different theoretical approaches shapes geographers' understanding of particular phenomena. This has been a careful tactic on our behalf. While most academic books seek to create a coherent theoretical argument, seeking to persuade readers of the merits of a particular approach for understanding and explaining the world around us, we have merely tried to provide the conceptual tools needed to engage critically with such texts and begin to evaluate their arguments. While it has been tempting for us to forward our own opinions as to the most appropriate and valid means through which to think geographically, we feel it has been more pedagogically constructive to allow you to make your own decisions about which approach seems most plausible in explaining the world.

This tactic may present the confident reader with an exciting menu of approaches from which to choose but to the uninitiated it may seem like a bewildering collection of contrasting frameworks (at best) or a chaotic recapitulation of unrelated ideas (at worst). To make sense of the choices available it is necessary to spend time relating them to one another: by comparing and contrasting the various options one can obtain a good understanding of their relative strengths and weaknesses. The more skill and acumen one exercises in this, the more control one is likely to have over the subject matter. The analogy of a remote-controlled television may usefully illustrate what we mean here. The remote control initially gives you the choice of flicking continually between perhaps 20 or more channels. You may stay at this superficial channel-hopping level without ever really getting your bearings. Alternatively, you can make the effort to compare the style, form and content of each channel until you are in a position to make your own judgements about what the different channels have to offer. Ultimately you should be in a position to make your own informed and judicious choices as to which is your favourite channel(s) and the extent to which you wish to engage with the other channels. Perhaps at a later stage you might switch channels again, or turn off! In any event, it is extremely helpful to develop a comparative overview of theoretical approaches in human geography.

Here, it is important to remember that each theoretical framework is differently formulated in relation to the four axes set out in Section 1.1 – ontology, epistemology, ideology and methodology. Each of these axes needs to be considered in evaluating the salience and value of a theoretical approach. One way to explore these axes and to start to think about how you conceptualize each is to ask yourself the following questions (adapted from Kitchin and Tate, 2000):

- *Am I naturalist or anti-naturalist?* This is a question about epistemology and how we can come to know the world. A naturalist approach suggests that geographers can research the social, economic and political world in much the same way that (most) scientists research the natural world. For example, we can adopt the scientific methods used in biology, chemistry or physics and apply them to human geography. Anti-naturalism, as its name implies, suggests that such an adaptation is invalid. In general, naturalists would tend to subscribe to approaches such as empiricism, positivism, realism and behaviouralism, which seek to explain the wider world, while anti-naturalists subscribe to more interpretative approaches, which search for meaning via humanism, feminism, post-colonialism and so on.
- *Do I think research should be value-free or action-orientated?* This is a question about ideology and the extent to which you think research should actively seek to change the world or whether it should merely seek to understand it. Generally, approaches such as positivism, behaviouralism and humanism would

claim to be value-free, whereas frameworks such as Marxism and feminism are often understood as critical and action-orientated.

- *Do I think research is objective or situated in nature?* This is an epistemological question concerning whether knowledge can be gained in an objective and neutral fashion. Both naturalist and anti-naturalist approaches can adopt an epistemological positions where the researcher is considered an objective recorder and observer of the world. This position has been challenged by those subscribing to feminist, postmodern and post-structural approaches who alternatively contend that knowledge is situated, affected by personal values of the researcher and the context in which the research takes place (see Section 1.2).

- *Do I think there is a geography or many geographies?* This is an ontological (and epistemological) question about what can be known. Some, including many proponents of postmodernism and post-structuralism (as well as forms of feminism) argue that no one theory can fully account for the complexity of society, as so many geographies are required to capture the multidimensional nature of the world (see Section 3.3). Against this, some hold to grand theory, believing that the task of the academic is to construct a theory that can reveal *the* truth about the world.

- *Am I a realist or idealist?* This is an ontological question concerning the question of existence; the issue of validity in claiming that something exists. Realists argue that a 'real' world exists regardless of conceptions of it: that the world and the people living on it have a concrete existence beyond what we think about the world. Anti-realists (or metaphysical idealists) contend that the world only exists in the mind – reality is constituted in thought and language – and there is no logical reason to suggest that it has material existence beyond our thoughts. In essence, the question is can we only study how people come to construct their world or is there a real world that we can know (and measure)? In human geography, humanistic and post-structuralist approaches are generally more concerned with the former, positivism, realism and Marxism with the latter.

- *Do I think that human geography is best understood through agency or structural explanation?* Changing tack slightly, another way to evaluate which approach most suits your views is to consider your understanding of how society works. The structure–agency debate essentially concerns the extent to which social actions are constrained by social structures. Some approaches consider that social actions are highly structured and largely outside the control of individuals (e.g., Marxism). Other approaches consider individuals as completely self-autonomous, free to act as they like (e.g., behaviouralism). Other approaches accept that there is a play-off between structure and agency, recognizing that individuals make their own decisions but that these decisions are framed within broader structures (e.g., structuration and realism).

While these questions rather simplistically address a complex set of issues, by working through them it should be possible to start to see whether different approaches match your world-view. Another approach is to try applying each approach to the world around you and to see which one seems to work for you as an analytical tool. For instance, this might consist of applying learning and understanding to everyday life – whether this concerns current affairs, local politics, race relations, unemployment and poverty, sex and shopping, love or hate. As you think about such issues, and simply 'get on' with your life, you will find that theory provides you with an understanding of the world, and allows you to understand your place in it (hence Thrift's (1999, p. 334) description of theory as 'a practical means for getting on'). More particularly, it might involve student project or dissertation work, when the aim should be not just to collect data solely for the sake of collecting data, but to engage with theories about how the world works (through the testing of hypotheses, the rejection of established ideas or the refinement of existing concepts, for example).

Here, it is important to remember that any personal theoretical outlook will also inform the topic chosen for investigation and how that topic is approached. That is, theory can change what is studied and how it is investigated. For instance, approaching a subject such as consumer behaviour through the lens of structuralist, post-structuralist, positivist or humanistic theories will lead the investigator to prioritize certain factors, and to study and elaborate the notion of consumption in very different ways (e.g., as an inauthentic process of creating profit through the triumph of exchange over use value, a means of acquiring identity through the purchase of signs and symbols, a rational process of meeting needs or a way of projecting oneself in the world). Each of these interpretations is interesting, and no one can be deemed 'wrong'; however, depending on which theory we subscribe to, we will 'do' very different geographies. This is very much what we have attempted in our last five chapters, each of which shows that theory inevitably informs the way geographers look at particular subjects/objects. Equally, one's topic can influence the theoretical approach adopted, with, for example, an interest in multiculturalism perhaps leading to engagements with post-colonial theory. As such, it is necessary to be *reflexive*; to reflect on the interrelationship between theory and praxis and how this shapes one's understanding, seeking always to internally critique one's approach; to appreciate the *situatedness* of one's knowledge production (see Section 1.2).

Regardless of how the personal salience of each approach is explored, it should be appreciated that there is no right or wrong way of thinking geographically. Each approach has its critics and each has moral and political effects, by informing teaching, research, actions and policy. To put it bluntly, there is no pure thought, no pure theory. As we stated at the outset of the book, the relationship between theory and praxis does not allow for pure thought: the relation of theory and praxis is much too complex. Our exploration of the way that five key concepts in human geography have been viewed through the lens of different theories has brought this into sharper focus. Simply put, those studying these concepts have not been able to avoid theory. Even those seeking to document the geographies of bodies, texts, money, governance and globalization in narrowly empirical terms inevitably work with particular understandings of the way the world works. Equally, those writing in a more abstract sense about these concepts develop ideas informed by praxis. Geographical praxis then is always infused with theory, to the extent that disentangling theory and praxis for the purpose of writing a book like this is no easy task.

But even though it is hard to distinguish exactly what theory is, we ultimately wish to convince you merely of the need to 'think geographically'. Engaging critically with geographic ideas – whether in an abstract or a concrete way – is essential if one is to become a geographer. We appreciate that such engagement can be difficult, especially where authors use an unfamiliar and difficult vocabulary to communicate what are often straightforward ideas. However, we suggest that the struggle is worth it, because it provides an enriched view and understanding of past and present thought. Here, wider reading is important in increasing familiarity with the subtle inflections of particular schools of geographic thought and how they propose to understand the world: 'if theory is the food of geography, read on . . . '. With reading, one's ideas and thoughts evolve as new ideas and evidence come to light, and sometimes an initial position is dropped as a new understanding is constructed. All geographers are in this constant state of transition, continually refining and reworking their theories in the light of fresh evidence and critique. Hence, the concepts a geographer invokes in one particular moment (e.g., place, space, location, power, flow, resistance, landscape, consumption, text, desire, capital, the body, production and so on) may not be the ones they find useful or meaningful in the next. By thinking about old concepts in new ways and new concepts in old ways, theoretical materials are assembled and cajoled into frameworks that might help to make sense of the world – or at least prompt new ways of thinking. Theory is, therefore, never fixed; it is there to be rethought, reworked and recast as the discipline (and the world) changes.

9.2 FUTURE GEOGRAPHIC THOUGHT?

As we have detailed throughout this book, geography is a theoretically plural, synthetic and constantly evolving discipline. If one thing seems certain, then, it is that geographic thought is going to continue to evolve as new theories are created and woven into the lexicon of the discipline. How this evolution will unfold, however, is very difficult to predict. In Chapter 3, we suggested that critical, postmodern and post-structural theories look set to drive theoretical advancement over the next few years, accompanied by other long-standing approaches such as feminism and Marxism. We have little doubt that these approaches will be endlessly refined in attempts to make them more robust in the face of criticism and in time that will be accompanied by new theoretical frameworks. As the popularity of some approaches grows, others will lose appeal and become less fashionable, gradually fading from prominence. This is not to say that they are necessarily less valid, especially for those who still subscribe to their central tenets, merely that they are no longer in vogue. This is not to advocate a simple, paradigmatic understanding of knowledge production, where theoretical schools compete with the victor replacing the loser (see Chapter 2), but rather to acknowledge the messiness and plurality of geography's theoretical landscape.

While some of the impetus for change will emerge from within the discipline, much will be derived from the importation of ideas from across the humanities and social sciences. Indeed, the broad engagement with social theory looks set to continue, with theoretical and empirical links to other disciplines continuing to be forged. However, we feel it unlikely, in the foreseeable future at least, that this will produce a post-disciplinary landscape. At best, this landscape will be partial, as disciplinary identities will continue to be maintained for both administrative and political reasons. We will accordingly continue to have separate and demarcated schools of knowledge. Here, it is recognized that disciplines, in broad terms, approach the same foci from varying perspectives, so that while there are similarities in explanation, there are also varying insights. Human geography's unique contribution in this respect is its insistence on recognizing the salience of space, place and human–nature relations: factors often 'forgotten' or neglected by other disciplines (although, as we note in Chapter 3, this is changing). Geographic thought remains unique in its insistence on grounding theory, developing a distinctly spatial take on the workings of society, economy and polity by developing theories which take seriously the difference that space makes. After all, things do not happen outside of space and time, and always take *place*. There will always be a place for 'thinking geographically'.

References

Abler, R., Adams, J. and Gould, P. (1971) *Spatial Organisation: The Geographer's View of the World.* New Jersey, Prentice Hall.

Adams, P. (1992) 'Television as gathering place', *Annals, Association of American Geographers*, **82**, 117–35.

Adams, P. (1995) 'A reconsideration of personal boundaries in space-time', *Annals, Association of American Geographers*, **85**, 267–85.

Adorno, T. and Horkheimer, M. (1972) [1947] *Dialectic of Enlightenment.* New York, Continuum.

Agnew, J. (1987) *Place and Politics.* Boston, Allen and Unwin.

Agnew, J. (1994) 'The territorial trap: the geographical assumptions of international relations theory', *Review of International Political Economy*, **1**, 53–80.

Agnew, J. (1998) *Geopolitics: Revisioning World Politics.* London, Routledge.

Agnew, J. (1999) 'The new geopolitics of power', in D. Massey, J. Allen, and P. Sarre (eds), *Human Geography Today.* Cambridge, Polity Press.

Agnew, J. and Corbridge, S. (1989) 'The new geopolitics: the dynamics of geopolitical disorder', in R. J. Johnston and P. J. Taylor (eds), *A World in Crisis?* Oxford, Blackwell.

Aitken, S. (1991) 'A transactional geography of the image-event: the films of Scottish director, Bill Forsyth', *Transactions, Institute of British Geographers*, **16**, 105–18.

Aitken, S. (1992) 'Person-environment theories in contemporary perceptual and behavioural geography II: the influence of ecological, environmental learning, society/structural trans-actional and transformational theories', *Progress in Human Geography*, **16**, 553–62.

Aitken, S. (1997) 'Analysis of texts: armchair theory and couch-potato geography', in R. Flowerdew and D. Martin, (eds), *Methods in Human Geography: A Guide for Students Doing a Research Project.* London, Longman.

Aitken, S. and Zonn, L. (eds) (1994) *Place, Power, Situation, Spectacle.* Lanham, MA, Rowman and Littlefield.

Allen, J. (1995) 'Crossing borders: footloose multinationals?', in J. Allen and C. Hamnett (eds), *A Shrinking World: Global Unevenness and Inequality.* Oxford, Oxford University Press.

Allen, J. and Hamnett, C. (eds) (1995) *A Shrinking World: Global Unevenness and Inequality.* Oxford, Oxford University Press.

Allen, J. and Pryke, M. (1994) 'The production of service space', *Environment and Planning D – Society and Space*, **12**, 453–76.

Amin, A. and Graham, S. (1997) 'The ordinary city', paper presented to the Institute of British Geographers/Royal Geographical Society Annual Conference, University of Exeter, January.

Amin, A. and Hausner, J. (1997) 'Interactive governance and social complexity', in A. Amin and J. Hausner, (eds), *Beyond Market and Hierarchy: Interactive Government and Social Complexity.* Cheltenham, Edward Elgar.

Amin, A. and Thrift, N. (1992) 'Neo-Marshallian nodes in global networks', *International Journal of Urban and Regional Research*, **16**, 571–87.

Amin, A. and Thrift, N. (1994a) 'Holding down the global', in A. Amin and N. Thrift (eds), *Globalisation, Institutions and Regional Development in Europe.* Oxford, Oxford University Press.

Amin, A. and Thrift, N. (1994b) 'Living in the global', in A. Amin and N. Thrift, (eds), *Globalisation, Institutions and Regional Development in Europe.* Oxford, Oxford University Press.

Amin, A. and Thrift, N. (1997) 'Globalisation, socio-economics, territoriality', in R. Lee and J. Wills (eds), *Geographies of Economies.* London, Arnold.

Amin, A. and Tomaney, J. (1995) 'The challenge of cohesion', in A. Amin and J. Tomaney (eds), *Behind the Myth of European Union: Prospects for Cohesion.* London, Routledge.

Anderson, J. (2002) 'Gambling politics or successful entrepreneurialism in a social-democratic city: Copenhagen', in F. Moulaert, E. Sywgedouw and A. Rodriguez (eds), *Urbanising Globalisation: Urban Redevelopment and Social Polarisation in the European City*. Oxford, Oxford University Press.

Anderson, K. (1988) 'Cultural hegemony and the race definition process in Chinatown, Vancouver', *Environment and Planning D – Society and Space*, **6**, 127–49.

Anderson, K. and Gale, F. (eds) (1992) *Inventing Places: Studies in Cultural Geography*. Melbourne, Longman.

Appadurai, A. (1990) 'Disjuncture and difference in the global cultural economy', *Theory, Culture and Society* **7**(2/3), 295–310.

Ardener, S. (1995) 'Women making money go round: ROSCAs revisited', in S. Ardener and S. Burman (eds.), *Money-go-rounds: The Importance of Rotating Savings and Credit Associations for Women*. Oxford, Berg.

Armitage, J. (2000) *Paul Virilio – from Modernism to Hypermodernism and Beyond*. London, Sage.

Armstrong, D. (1993) 'Public health spaces and the fabrication of identity', *Sociology*, **27**, 393–410.

Arrighi, G. (1994) *The Long Twentieth Century*. London, Verso.

Asworth, G. J. and Voogd, H. (1990) *Selling the City: Marketing Approaches in Public Sector Urban Planning*. London, Belhaven.

Atkinson, P. (1990) *The Ethnographic Imagination: Textual Construction of Reality*. London, Routledge.

Augé, M. (1995) *Non-Places: An Introduction to the Anthropology of Supermodernity*. London, Verso.

Bale, J. (1993) *Landscapes of Modern Sport*. Leicester, Leicester University Press.

Bank for International Settlements (1992) *Recent Developments in International Interbank Relations*. Basle, Bank for International Settlements.

Baran, P. A. (1957) *The Political Economy of Growth*. New York, Monthly Review Press.

Barber, B. (1995) *Jihad v. McWorld*. New York, Ballantine.

Barff, R. (1995) 'Multinational corporations and the new international division of labour', in R. J. Johnston, P. J. Taylor, and M. Watts (eds), *Geographies of Global Change: Remapping the World in the Late Twentieth Century*. Oxford, Blackwell.

Barnes, T. (1995) 'Political economy I: "the culture, stupid"', *Progress in Human Geography*, **19**, 423–31.

Barnes, T. (1996) *Logics of Dislocation: Models, Metaphors, and Meanings of Economic Space*. New York, Guilford.

Barnes, T. (2000) 'Political economy', in R. J. Johnston, D. Gregory, G. Pratt and M. Watts (eds), *The Dictionary of Human Geography*. Oxford, Blackwell.

Barnes, T. (2001a) 'Retheorizing economic geography: from the Quantitative Revolution to the Cultural Turn', *Annals, Association of American Geographers*, **91**, 546–65.

Barnes, T. (2001b) 'Lives lived and tales told: biographies of geography's quantitative revolution', *Environment and Planning D – Society and Space*, **19**, 409–29.

Barnes, T. and Duncan, J. (eds) (1992) *Writing Worlds: Discourse, Text and Metaphor in the Representation of Landscapes*. London, Routledge.

Barnes, T. and Gregory, D. (eds) (1996) *Reading Human Geography: The Poetics and Politics of Inquiry*. London, Arnold.

Barnett, C. (1998) 'The cultural turn: fashion or progress in human geography', *Antipode*, **30**, 379–94.

Barrell, J. (1982) 'Geographies of Hardy's Wessex', *Journal of Historical Geography*, **81**, 347–61.

Barthes, R. (1957) [1972] *Mythologies*. London, Jonathan Cape.

Barthes, R. (1967) *The Fashion System*. London, Jonathan Cape.

Baudrillard, J. (1970) *The Consumer Society: Myths and Structures*. Paris, Doneul.

Baudrillard, J. (1988) *America*. London, Verso.

Baudrillard, J. (1995) *The Gulf War Did Not Take Place*. Sydney, Power.

Bauman, Z. (1998) *Globalization: The Human Consequences*. Cambridge, Polity.

Bauman, Z. (2000) *Community: Seeking Security in an Insecure World*. Cambridge, Polity.

Beaverstock, J. V., Doel, M., Hubbard, P. and Taylor, P. (2002) 'Attending to the world: competition, cooperation and connectivity in the world city network', *Global Networks*, **2** (2), 95–116.

Beaverstock, J., Smith, R. G., Taylor, P. J. (1999) 'The long arm of the law: London's law firms in a globalizing economy', *Environment and Planning A*, **31**, 1857–76.

Beaverstock, J., Smith, R., Taylor, P., Walker, D. and Lorimer, H. (2000) 'Globalisation and world cities: some measurement methodologies', *Applied Geography*, **20**, 43–63.

Beck, U. (1986) *Risk Society: Towards a New Modernity*. London, Sage.

Beemyn, B. (ed.) (1997) *Creating a Place for Ourselves: Lesbian, Gay and Bisexual Community Histories*. London, Routledge.

Bell, D. (1995) 'Pleasure and danger: the paradoxical spaces of sexual citizenship', *Political Geography*, **14**, 139–53.

Bell, D., Binnie, J., Cream, J. and Valentine, G. (1994) 'All hyped up and no place to go', *Gender, Place and Culture*, **1**, 31–47.

Bell, D. and Valentine, G. (1995) 'Introduction: orientations', in D. Bell and G. Valentine (eds), *Mapping Desire: Geographies of Sexuality*. London, Routledge.

Bell, D. and Valentine, G. (1997) *Consuming Geographies: We Are Where We Eat*. London, Routledge.

Bell, M. (1994) 'Images, myths and alternative geographies of the Third World', in D. Gregory, R. Martin and G. Smith (eds), *Human Geography: Society, Space and Social Science*. London, Macmillan.

Bell, M., Butlin, R. and Heffernan, M. (eds) (1995) *Geography and Imperialism 1820–1940*. Manchester, Manchester University Press.

Bender, B. (1992) *Landscape Politics and Perspectives*. Oxford, Berg.

Benjamin, W. (1955) *Paris – Capital of the Nineteenth Century*. Berlin, Suhrkamp Verlag.

Benko, G. and Strohmayer, U. (1997) *Space and Social Theory*. Oxford, Blackwell.

Bennet, L. (1993) 'Harold Washington and the black urban regime', *Urban Affairs Quarterly*, **28**, 423–40.

Benton, L. (1995) 'Would the real/reel Los Angeles please stand up?', *Urban Geography*, **16**, 144–64.

Berger, J. (1988) *Media Analysis Techniques*. London, Sage.

Berger, S. and Dore, R. (eds) (1996) *National Diversity and Global Capitalism*. Ithaca, NY, Cornell University Press.

Berman, M. (1982) *All That Is Solid Melts Into Air*. New York, Verso.

Berry, B. J. L. (1967) *Geographies of Market Centers and Retail Distribution*. Englewood Cliffs, Prentice Hall.

Berthoud, R. and Kempson, E. (1992) *Credit and Debt: The PSI Report*. London, Policy Studies Institute.

Best, M. H. (1990) *The New Competition: Institutions of Industrial Restructuring*. Cambridge, Polity.

Best, S. and Kellner, D. (1991) *Postmodern Theory*. Basingstoke, Macmillan.

Best, S. and Kellner, D. (1997) *The Postmodern Turn*. New York, Guilford.

Bhabha, H. (1994) *The Location of Culture*. London, Routledge.

Bhaskar, R. (1978) *A Realist Theory of Science*. Brighton, Harvester.

Bingham, N. (1996) 'Objections from technological determinism towards geographies of relations', *Environment and Planning D – Society and Space*, **14**, 635–58.

Bingham, N. and Thrift, N. (2000) 'Michael Serres and Bruno Latour', in M. Crang and N. Thrift (eds), *Thinking Space*. London, Routledge.

Binnie, J. and Valentine, G. (1999) 'Geographies of sexuality – a review of progress', *Progress in Human Geography*, **23**, 175–87.

Bird, J. H. (1989) *The Changing World of Geography: A Critical Guide to Concepts and Methods*. Oxford, Clarendon Press.

Black, I. (1996) 'Symbolic capital: the London and Westminster Bank headquarters, 1836–38', *Landscape Research*, **21**, 55–72.

Blaikie, P. (1985) *The Political Economy of Soil Erosion*. Harlow, Longman.

Blaut, J. (1993) *The Colonizer's Model of the World: Geographical Diffusionism and Eurocentric History*. New York, Guilford.

Blum, V. and Nast, H. (1996) 'Where's the difference? The heterosexualisation of alterity in Henri Lefebvre and Jacques Lacan', *Environment and Planning D – Society and Space*, **14**, 559–80.

Blunt, A. and Rose, G. (eds) (1994) *Writing Women and Space: Colonial and Post-colonial Geographies.* New York, Guilford.

Blunt, A. and Wills, J. (2000) *Dissident Geographies: An Introduction to Radical Ideas and Practice.* London, Prentice Hall.

Bondi, L. (1992) 'Symbolism in urban landscapes', *Progress in Human Geography,* **16**, 157–70.

Bondi, L. (1997) 'Sexing the city', in R. Fincher and J. Jacobs (eds), *Cities of Difference.* New York, Guilford.

Bonnett, A. (2000a) 'Trinh', in M. Crang and N. Thrift (eds), *Thinking Space.* London, Routledge.

Bonnett, A. (2000b) *White Identities.* Harlow, Prentice Hall.

Bordo, S. (1993) *Unbearable Weight: Feminism, Western Culture and the Body.* Berkeley, University of California Press.

Bourdieu, P. (1984) *Distinction.* London, Routledge.

Bourdieu, P. (1988) *Homo Academicus.* Cambridge, Polity.

Bourdieu, P. (1990) *The Logic of Practice.* Cambridge, Polity.

Boyle, M. (1997) 'Civic boosterism in the politics of local economic development: institutional positions and strategic orientations in the consumption of hallmark events', *Environment and Planning A,* **29**, 1975–97.

Brace, C. (1999) 'Finding England everywhere: regional identity and the construction of national identity, 1890–1940', *Ecumene,* **6**, 90–109.

Bridge, G. (2001) 'Bourdieu, rational action and the time-space strategy of gentrification', *Transactions, Institute of British Geographers,* **26**, 205–16.

Brook, C. and Goodrick, A. (1997) *K Foundation Burn a Million Quid.* London, Ellipsis.

Brosseau, M. (1994) 'Geography's literature', *Progress in Human Geography,* **18**, 333–53.

Brotchie, J., Batty, M., Blakely, E., Hall, P. and Newton, P. (1995) *Cities in Competition: Productive and Sustainable Cities in the Twenty-first Century.* Melbourne, Longman.

Bruno, G. (1987) 'Ramble city: postmodernism and Blade Runner', **41** (October), 61–74.

Bryant, C. G. A. and Jary, D. (1997) *Anthony Giddens: Critical Assessments.* London, Routledge.

Bryant, R. L. (1992) 'Political ecology: an emerging research agenda in Third-World studies', *Political Geography,* **11**, 12–36.

Buchanon, I. (2000) *Deleuzism: A Metacommentary.* Durham, Duke University Press.

Burchill, G., Gordon, C. and Miller, P. (eds) (1991) *The Foucault Effect.* London, Harvester Wheatsheaf.

Burgess, J. (1982) 'Filming the fens', in J. R. Gold and J. Burgess (eds), *Valued Environments.* London, Allen and Unwin.

Burgess, J. (1985) 'News from nowhere: the press, riots and the myth of the inner city', in J. Burgess and J. R. Gold (eds), *Geography, the Media and Popular Culture.* London, Croom Helm.

Burgess, J. and Gold, J. R. (eds) (1985) *Geography, the Media and Popular Culture.* London, Croom Helm.

Burgin, V. (1996) *In/different Spaces.* Albany, State University of New York Press.

Butler, J. (1990a) *Gender Trouble: Feminism and the Subversion of Identity.* New York, Routledge.

Butler, J. (1990b) 'Gender trouble, feminist theory and psychoanalytic discourse', in D. Nicholson (ed.), *Feminism/Post-modernism.* London, Routledge.

Butler, J. (1993) *Bodies That Matter: On the Discursive Limits of Sex.* London, Routledge.

Butler, J. (1999) *Subjects of Desire.* New York, Columbia University Press.

Butler, R. (1999) 'The body', in P. Cloke, P. Crang, and M. Goodwin (eds), *Introducing Human Geographies.* London, Arnold.

Butler, R. and Parr, H. (2000) (eds) *Mind and Body Spaces: Geographies of Illness, Impairment and Disability.* London, Routledge.

Buttimer, A. (1976) 'Grasping the dynamism of the lifeworld', *Annals, Association of American Geographers,* **66**, 277–92.

Byrne, D. (1999) *Social Exclusion.* Buckingham, Open University Press.

Callinicos, A. (1990) *Against Post-modernism: A Marxist Critique.* New York, St Amrin's Press.

Callinicos, A. (1991) *The Revenge of History: Marxism and the East European Revolutions.* London, Routledge.

Campbell, A. (1918) *Report on Public Baths and Wash-houses in the United Kingdom*. London, Carnegie United Kingdom Trust.

Castells, M. (1977) *The Urban Question*. London, Arnold.

Castells, M. (1978) *City, Class and Power*. London, Macmillan.

Castells, M. (1983) *The City and the Grassroots*. Berkeley, University of California Press.

Castells, M. (1989) *The Informational City*. Oxford, Blackwell.

Castells, M. (1996) *The Rise of the Network Society: The Information Age: Economy, Society, and Culture Volume I*. Oxford, Blackwell.

Castells, M. (1997) *The Power of Identity: The Information Age: Economy, Society, and Culture Volume II*. Oxford, Blackwell.

Castells, M. (1998) *The End of Millennium: The Information Age: Economy, Society, and Culture Volume III*. Oxford, Blackwell.

Castells, M. (2000) 'Materials for an exploratory theory of the network society', *British Journal of Sociology*, **51**, 5–24.

Castree, N. (1999) 'Envisioning capitalism: geography and the renewal of Marxian political economy', *Transactions, Institute of British Geographers*, **24**, 137–59.

Castree, N. (2000) 'Nature', in R. Johnston, D. Gregory, G. Pratt and M. Watts (eds), *The Dictionary of Human Geography*. Oxford, Blackwell.

Castree, N. and Sparke, M. (2000) 'Professional geography and the corporatization of the academy', *Antipode*, **32**, 222–9.

Chorley, R. and Haggett, P. (1967) *Models in Geography*. London, Methuen.

Chorley, R. and Haggett, P. (1969) *Network Analysis in Geography*. London, Methuen.

Chouinard, V. and Grant, A. (1996) 'On being not even anywhere near "the project"', in N. Duncan (ed.) *Bodyspace*. London, Routledge.

Christopherson, S. (1993) 'Market rules and territorial outcomes: the case of the United States', *International Journal of Urban and Regional Research*, **17**, 274–88.

Christopherson, S. (1995) 'Women's place in the world', in R. Johnston, P. Taylor and M. Watts (eds), *Geographies of Global Change*. Oxford, Blackwell.

Cixous, H. (1981) 'Castration or decapitation?', *Signs*, **7**, 41–55.

Clark, D. (1997) *Urban World, Global Cities*. London, Routledge.

Clark, G. L. (1989) 'Remaking the map of corporate capitalism: the arbitrage economy of the 1980s', *Environment and Planning A*, **21**, 997–1000.

Clarke, D. (ed.) (1997) *The Cinematic City*. London, Routledge.

Clarke, S. and Staeheli, L. (1995) 'Gender, place and citizenship', in J. Garber (ed.), *Gender in Urban Research*. London, Sage.

Cloke, P. (1993) 'Enculturating political economy: a day in the life of a rural geographer', in C. Philo, P. Cloke, N. Thrift, M. Doel and M. Phillips (eds), *Writing the Rural*. London, PCP Press.

Cloke, P. and Little, J. (1997) (eds) *Contested Countryside Cultures*. London, Routledge.

Cloke, P., Philo, C. and Sadler, D. (1991) *Approaching Human Geography*. London, PCP Press.

Collinge, C. and Hall, S. (1997) 'Hegemony and regime theory in urban governance: towards a theory of the locally networked state', in N. Jewson and S. MacGregor (eds), *Transforming Cities: Contested Governance and New Spatial Divisions*, London, Routledge.

Cook, I., Crouch, D., Naylor, S. and Ryan, J. (2000) 'Foreword', in I. Cook, D. Crouch, S. Naylor and J. Ryan (eds), *Cultural Turns/Geographical Turns*. Harlow, Prentice Hall.

Cooke, P. (1989) *Localities: The Changing Face of Urban Britain*. London, Unwin Hyman.

Cooper, D. (1998) 'Regard between strangers: diversity, equality and the reconstruction of public space', *Critical Social Policy*, **18**, 465–92.

Corbridge, S. (1986) *Capitalist World Development: A Critique of Radical Development Geography*. Basingstoke, Macmillan.

Corbridge, S. (1992) 'Discipline and punish: the new right and the policing of the international debt crisis', *Geoforum*, **23**, 285–301.

Corbridge, S. (1993a) 'Colonialism, post-colonialism and the political geography of the Third World', in P. J. Taylor (ed.), *Political Geography of the Twentieth Century: A Global Analysis*. New York, Guilford.

Corbridge, S. (1993b) *Debt and Development*. Oxford, Blackwell.

Corbridge, S. and Thrift, N. (1994) 'Money, power and space: introduction and overview', in S. Corbridge, R. Martin and N. Thrift (eds.), *Money, Power and Space*. Oxford, Blackwell.

Cosgrove, D. (1984) *Social Formation and Symbolic Landscape*. Madison, University of Wisconsin Press.

Cosgrove, D. (1989) 'Geography is everywhere: culture and symbolism in human landscapes', in D. Gregory and R. Walford (eds), *Horizons in Human Geography*. London, Macmillan.

Cosgrove, D. (1994a) 'Contested global visions: one-world, whole-earth, and the Apollo space photographs', *Annals, Association of American Geographers*, **84**, 270–94.

Cosgrove, D. (1994b) 'Postmodern tremblings: a reply to Michael Dear', *Annals, Asssociation of Amercian Geographers*, **84**, 305–7.

Cosgrove, D. (1999) *Mappings*. London, Reaktion.

Cosgrove, D. and Daniels, S. (1988) *The Iconography of Landscape: Essays on the Symbolic Representation, Design and Use of Past Environments*. Cambridge, Cambridge University Press.

Cosgrove, D. and Jackson, P. (1987) 'New directions in cultural geography', *Area*, **19**, 95–101.

Coupland, D. (1991) *Generation X*. London, Abacus.

Cox, K. (1981) 'Bourgeois thought and the behavioural geography debate', in K. Cox and R. G. Golledge (eds), *Behavioural Problems in Geography Revisited*. London, Methuen.

Cox, K. (1991) 'Questions of abstraction in studies in the new urban politics', *Journal of Urban Affairs*, **13**, 267–80.

Cox, K. (1997) 'Globalisation and geographies of workers' struggles in the late twentieth century', in R. Lee and J. Wills (eds), *Geographies of Economies*. London, Arnold.

Cox, K. (1998) 'Spaces of dependence, spaces of engagement and the politics of scale, or: looking for local politics', *Political Geography*, **17**, 1–23.

Cox, K. and Mair, A. (1988) 'Locality and community in the politics of local economic development', *Annals, Association of American Geographers*, **78**, 307–25.

Cox, K. and Mair, A. (1989) 'Book review essay: urban growth machine and the politics of local economic development', *International Journal of Urban and Regional Research*, **13**, 137–46.

Crang, M. (1998) *Cultural Geography*. London, Routledge.

Crang, M. and Thrift, N. (2000a) 'Introduction', in M. Crang and N. Thrift (eds), *Thinking Space*. London, Routledge.

Crang, M. and Thrift, N. (eds) (2000b) *Thinking Space*. London, Routledge.

Crang, M., Crang, P. and May, J. (eds) (1999) *Virtual Geographies*. London, Routledge.

Crang, P. (2000) 'Organisational geographies: surveillance display and the spaces of power in business organisations', in J. Sharp, P. Routledge, C. Philo and R. Paddison (eds), *Entanglements of Power*. London, Routledge.

Crary, J. (1990) *Techniques of the Observer*. Cambridge, MA, MIT Press.

Cream, J. (1995) 'Resolving riddles: the sexed body', in D. Bell and G. Valentine (eds), *Mapping Desire*. London, Routledge.

Cresswell, T. (1996) *In Place/Out of Place: Geography, Ideology and Transgression*. Minneapolis, University of Minnesota Press.

Cresswell, T. (1999) 'Embodiment, power and the politics of mobility: the case of female tramps and hobos', *Transactions, Institute of British Geographers*, **24**, 175–92.

Cresswell, T. (2000) 'Falling down: resistance as diagnostic' in J. Sharp, P. Routledge, C. Philo and R. Paddison (eds), *Entanglements of Power*. London, Routledge.

Crowther, G. B. (1940) *An Outline of Money*. London, Thomas Nelson and Sons.

Crush, J. (ed.) (1995) *The Power of Development*. London, Routledge.

Culler, D. (1997) *Literary Theory: A Very Short Introduction*. Oxford, Oxford University Press.

Curry, M. (1991) 'Postmodernism, language and the strains of modernism', *Annals, Association of American Geographers*, **81**, 210–28.

Curry, M. (1995) 'On space and spatial practice in contemporary geography' in C. Earle, K. Mathewson and M. Kenzer (eds), *Concepts in Human Geography*. Lanham, MA, Rowman and Littlefield.

Dahl, R. (1961) *Who Governs?* New Haven, Yale University Press.

Daly, M. and Walsh, J. (1988) *Moneylending and Low Income Families*. London, Combat Poverty Agency.

Dandeker, C. (1990) *Surveillance, Power, Modernity: Bureaucracy and Discipline from 1700 to Present*. Cambridge, Polity.

Daniels, P. W. (1986) 'Foreign banks and metropolitan development: a comparison of London and New York', *Tijdschrift voor Economische en Sociale Geografie*, **77**, 269–87.

Daniels, P. W. and Lever, W. F. (eds) (1996) *The Global Economy in Transition*. Harlow, Addison-Wesley Longman.

Daniels, S. (1993) *Fields of Vision: Landscape Imagery and National Landscapes in England and the United States*. Cambridge, Polity.

Darby, H. C. (1948) 'The regional geography of Thomas Hardy's Wessex', *Geographical Review*, **38**, 426–43.

Davidson, J. (2000) 'A phenomenology of fear: Merleau-Ponty and agoraphobic life-worlds', *Sociology of Health and Illness*, **22**, 640–60.

Davies, G. (1994) *A History of Money: From Ancient Times to the Present Day*. Cardiff, University of Wales Press.

Davis, T. (1995) 'The diversity of queer politics and the redefinition of sexual identity and community in urban spaces', in D. Bell and G. Valentine (eds), *Mapping Desire: Geographies of Sexuality*. London, Routledge.

Davoudi, S. (1995) 'Dilemmas of urban governance', in P. Healey, S. Cameron, S. Davoudi, S. Graham and A. Madani-Pour (eds), *Managing Cities: The New Urban Context*. Chichester, John Wiley and Sons.

De Abaitua, M. (1995) 'K Sera', *The Observer*, 5 November 1995, Preview Magazine.

Dear, M. (1988) 'The postmodern challenge: reconstructing human geography', *Transactions, Institute of British Geographers*, **13**, 262–74.

Dear, M. (2000) *The Postmodern Urban Condition*. Oxford, Blackwell.

Dear, M. and Flusty, S. (1998) 'Post-modern urbanism', *Annals, Association of American Geographers*, **88**, 50–72.

Dear, M., Wilton, R., Gaber, S. and Takahashi, L. (1997) 'Seeing people differently: the socio-spatial construction of disability', *Environment and Planning D – Society and Space*, **15**, 455–80.

Debord, G. (1967) *The Society of the Spectacle*. London, Rebel Press.

de Certeau, M. (1981) *The Practice of Everyday Life*. Berkeley, University of California Press.

Del Casino, V. J. and Hanna, S. P. (2000) 'Representations and identities in tourist map spaces', *Progress in Human Geography*, **24**, 23–46.

Delanty, G. (2000) *Modernity and Postmodernity: Knowledge, Power and Self*. London, Sage.

Deleuze, G. and Guattari, F. (1983) *Anti-Oedipus: Capitalism and Schizophrenia*. London, Athlone.

Deleuze, G. and Guattari, F. (1987) *A Thousand Plateaus*. London, Athlone.

Demeritt, D. (1998) 'Science, social constructivism, and nature', in B. Braun and N. Castree (eds), *Remaking Nature: Nature at the Millennium*. New York, Routledge.

Department of Education and Science and the Welsh Office (1990) *Geography Working Group's Interim Report*. London, HMSO.

Derrida, J. (1976) *On Grammatology*. Baltimore, John Hopkins University Press.

Derrida, J. (1990) *Limited Inc*. Paris, Galilee.

Derrida, J. (1991) *A Derrida Reader: Between the Blinds*. Brighton, Harvester Wheatsheaf.

Derrida, J. (1994) *Specters of Marx*. London, Routledge.

Desforges, L. and Jones, R. (2001) 'Bilingualism and geographical knowledge: a case study of students at the University of Wales, Aberystwyth', *Social and Cultural Geography*, **2**(3), 333–46.

Dicken, P. (1997) 'Transnational corporations and nation states', *International Science Journal*, **151**, 77–89.

Dicken, P. (1998) *Global Shift: Transforming the World Economy*, 3rd edn. London, Paul Chapman.

Dillon, M. (2000) 'Post-structuralism, complexity and poetics', *Theory, Culture and Society*, **17**, 1–26.

Dixon, D. P. and Jones III, J. P. (1996) 'For a supercalifragilisticexpialidocious scientific geography', *Annals, Association of American Geographers*, **86**, 767–79.

Dodd, N. (1994) *The Sociology of Money: Economics, Reason and Contemporary Society*. Cambridge, Polity.

Dodds, K. (2000) *Geopolitics in a Changing World*. Harlow, Prentice Hall.

Dodge, M. and Kitchin, R. (2000) *Mapping Cyberspace*. London, Routledge.

Doel, M. (1999) *Post-structuralist Geographies: The Diabolical Art of Spatial Science*. Edinburgh, Edinburgh University Press.

Doel, M. (2000) 'Un-glunking geography: spatial science after Dr Seuss and Giles Deleuze', in M. Crang and N. Thrift (eds), *Thinking Space*. London, Routledge.

Doel, M. and Clark, D. B. (1997) 'Transpolitical urbanism: suburban anomaly and ambient fear', *Space and Culture*, **2**, 13–37.

Domosh, M. (1991) 'Towards a feminist historiography of geography', *Transactions, Institute of British Geographers*, **16**, 95–115.

Donald, J. (1999) *Imagining the Modern City*. London, Athlone.

Douglas, M. (1966) *Purity and Danger*. Harmondsworth, Penguin.

Driver, F. (1992) 'Geography's empire: histories of geographical knowledge', *Environment and Planning D – Society and Space*, **10**, 23–40.

Driver, F. (1995) 'Geographical traditions: thinking the history of geography', *Transactions, Institute of British Geographers*, **20**, 403–4.

du Gay, P. (2000) 'Identity, sociology, history', in P. du Gay, J. Evans and P. Redman (eds), *Identity: A Reader*. London, Sage.

du Gay, P., Evans, J. and Redman, P. (2000) *Identity: A Reader*. London, Sage.

Duncan, J. (1990) *The City as Text: The Politics of Landscape Interpretation in the Kandyan Kingdom*. Cambridge, Cambridge University Press.

Duncan, J. (2000) 'Place', in R. Johnston, D. Gregory, G. Pratt and M. Watts (eds), *The Dictionary of Human Geography*. Oxford, Blackwell.

Duncan, J. and Duncan, N. (1988) '(Re)reading the landscape', *Environment and Planning D – Society and Space*, **6**, 117–26.

Duncan, J. and Ley, D. (1993) *Place/Culture/Representation*. London, Routledge.

Duncan, N. and Sharp, J. (1993) 'Confronting representation(s)', *Environment and Planning D – Society and Space*, **11**, 473–86.

Dunford, M. (1981) *Historical Materialism and Geography*. Research Paper in Geography, No. 4. Falmer, University of Sussex.

Dunning, J. (1993) *Globalisation, Economic Restructuring and Development*. Mimeograph, Department of Economics, University of Reading.

Dwyer, C. (1999) 'Veiled meanings: young British Muslims and the negotiation of differences', *Gender, Place, Culture*, **6**, 5–26.

Dyck, I. (1997) 'Dialogue with difference: a tale of two studies', in J. P. Jones, H. Nast and S. Roberts, (eds), *Thresholds in Feminist Geography: Difference, Methodology, Representation*. Lanham, MA, Rowman and Littlefield.

Dymski, G. A. and Veitch, J. M. (1992) 'Race and the financial dynamics of urban growth: L.A. as Fay Wray', in G. Riposa and G. Dersch (eds), *City of Angels*. Los Angeles, Kendal/Hunt Press.

Dymski, G. A. and Veitch, J. M. (1995) 'Taking it to the bank: race, credit, and income in Los Angeles', in R. D. Bullard, J. E. Grigsby and C. Lee (eds), *Residential Apartheid: The American Legacy*. Los Angeles, Centre for Afro-American Studies, UCLA.

Dymski, G. A. and Veitch, J. M. (1996) 'Financial transformation and the metropolis: booms, busts, and banking in Los Angeles', *Environment and Planning A*, **28**, 1233–60.

Eagleton, T. (1996) *The Illusions of Post-modernism*. Oxford, Blackwell.

Edensor, T. (2000) 'Moving through the city', in D. Bell and A. Haddour (eds), *City Visions*. Harlow, Prentice Hall.

Edgely, C. and Brissett, D. (1990) 'Health nazis and the cult of the perfect body', *Symbolic Interaction*, **13**, 257–79.

Elias, N. (1978) *The Civilising Process: The History of Manners*. New York, Pantheon Books.

Elkin, S. (1987) *City and Regime in the American Republic*. Chicago, University of Chicago Press.

Ellis, J. M. (1989) *Against Deconstruction*. Princeton, NJ, Princeton University Press.

Entrikin, N. (1991) *The Betweenness of Place*. Baltimore, John Hopkins University Press.

Eyles, J. and Smith, D. M. (1988) *Qualitative Methods in Human Geography*. London, Polity.

Featherstone, M. (ed.) (1990) *Global Culture: Nationalism, Globalisation and Modernity*. London, Sage.

Ferguson, R. and Hughes, G. (2000) 'Welfare: from security to responsibility', in G. Hughes and R. Ferguson (eds), *Ordering Lives: Family, Work and Welfare*. London, Routledge.

Ferman, B. (1996) *Challenging the Growth Machine: Neighbourhood Politics in Chicago and Pittsburg*. Lawrence, KS, University of Kansas Press.

Ferrell, R. (1996) *Passion in Theory: Conceptions of Freud and Lacan*. London, Routledge

Fielding, S. (2000) 'Walk on the left! Children's geographies and the primary school', in S. L. Holloway and G. Valentine (eds), *Children's Geographies*. London, Routledge.

Fischer, B. and Poland, B. (1998) 'Exclusion, risk and social control: reflections on community policing and public health', *Geoforum*, **29**, 187–97.

Flowerdew, R. and Martin, D. (1997) *Methods in Human Geography*, Harlow, Longman.

Flusty, S. (2001) 'Adventures of a barong; a worm's eye view of global formation', in C. Minca (ed.), *Postmodern Geography: Theory and Praxis*. Oxford, Blackwell.

Foord, J. and Gregson, N. (1986) 'Patriarchy: towards a reconceptualisation', *Antipode*, **18**, 186–211.

Ford, J. (1988) *The Indebted Society: Credit and Default in the 1980s*. London, Routledge.

Ford, J. (1991) *Consuming Credit: Debt and Poverty in the UK*. London, Child Poverty Action Group.

Ford J. and Rowlingson, K. (1996) 'Low-income households and credit: exclusion, preference, and inclusion', *Environment and Planning A*, **28**, 1345–60.

Forest, B. (1995) 'West Hollywood as symbol: the significance of place in the construction of a gay identity', *Environment and Planning D: Society and Space*, **13**, 133–57.

Forgacs, D. (1984) *Formations: Of Nations and Peoples*. London, Routledge.

Forgacs, D. (2000) *The Gramsci Reader: Selected Writings, 1916–1935*. New York, New York University Press.

Foucault, M. (1967) *Madness and Civilization*. London, Tavistock.

Foucault, M. (1977) *Discipline and Punish*. Harmondsworth, Penguin.

Foucault, M. (1981) *The History of Sexuality, Volume One*. Harmondsworth, Penguin.

Foucault, M. (1988) *The Care of the Self: The History of Sexuality, Volume Three*. Harmondsworth, Penguin.

Freidberg, A. (1993) *Window Shopping: Cinema and the Postmodern*. Berkeley, University of California Press.

Freire, P. (1970) *Pedagogy of the Oppressed*. Harmondsworth, Penguin.

Friedmann, J. (1999) 'The hybridisation of the bush and the abhorrence of the roots', in M. Featherstone and S. Lash (eds), *Spaces of Culture*. London, Sage.

Friedmann, J. and Wolff, G. (1982) 'World city formation: an agenda for research and action', *International Journal of Urban and Regional Research*, **6**, 309–44.

Frisby, D. (1984) *Georg Simmel*. London, Tavistock.

Frobel, F., Heinrichs, J. and Kreye, O. (1980) *The New International Division of Labour*. Cambridge, Cambridge University Press.

Fuller, D. (1998) 'Credit Union development: financial inclusion and exclusion', *Geoforum*, **29**, 145–58.

Fuller, D. (1999) 'Part of the action, or "going native"? Learning to cope with the politics of integration', *Area*, **31**, 221–7.

Fuller, D. and Jonas, A. E. G. (2002a) 'Institutionalising future geographies of financial inclusion: national legitimacy versus local autonomy in the British Credit Union Movement', *Antipode*, **34**(1), 91–117.

Fuller, D. and Jonas, A. E. G. (2002b) 'Constructing and contesting "alternative economic spaces": community credit unions and the British Credit Union Movement', in R. Lee, A. Leyshon and C. Williams (eds), *Alternative Economic Spaces: Rethinking the 'Economic' in Economic Geography*. London, Sage.

Fyfe, N. (1998) *Images of the Street*. London, Routledge.

Gaffikin, F. and Warf, B. (1993) 'Urban policy and the post-Keynesian state in the United Kingdom and the United States', *International Journal of Urban and Regional Research*, **17**, 67–84.

Gale, F. (1992) 'A view of the world through the eyes of a cultural geographer', in A. Rogers, H. Viles and A. Goudie (eds), *The Student's Companion to Geography*. Oxford, Blackwell.

Gane, M. (1994) *Baudrillard: Critical and Fatal Theory*. London, Sage.

Garrison, W. (1956) 'Applicability of statistical inference to geographical research', *Geographical Review*, **46**, 427–9.

Gauntlett, D. and Hill, A. (1999) *TV Living: Television, Culture and Everyday Life*. London, Routledge.

Gentle, C. J. S., Marshall, J. N. and Coombes, M. G. (1991) 'Business reorganization and regional development: the case of the British building societies movement' *Environment and Planning A*, **23**, 1759–77.

Gertler, M. (1997) 'Between the global and the local: the spatial limits to productive capital', in K. Cox (ed.), *Spaces of Globalisation: Reasserting the Power of the Local*. New York, Guilford.

Gibson-Graham, J. K. (1996) *The End of Capitalism*. Oxford, Blackwell.

Gibson-Graham, J. K. (2000) 'Poststructural interventions', in T. Barnes and E. Sheppard (eds), *A Companion to Economic Geography*. Oxford, Blackwell.

Giddens, A. (1984) *The Constitution of Society: An Outline of the Theory of Structuration*. Cambridge, Polity.

Giddens, A. (1990) *The Consequences of Modernity*. Cambridge, Polity.

Giddens, A. (1991) *Modernity and Self-identity*. Cambridge, Polity.

Gill, S. (1992) 'Economic globalization and the internationalization of authority: limits and contradictions', *Geoforum*, **23**, 269–83.

Gill, S. (1993a) 'Global finance, monetary policy and cooperation among the group of seven, 1944–92' in P. Cerny (ed.), *Finance and World Politics: Markets, Regimes and States in the Post-Hegemonic Era*. Aldershot, Edward Elgar.

Gill, S. (1993b) 'Gramsci and global politics: towards a post-hegemonic research agenda', in S. Gill (ed.), *Gramsci, Historical Materialism and International Relations*. Cambridge, Cambridge University Press.

Gleeson, B. (1996) 'A geography for disabled people?', *Transactions of the Institute of British Geographers*, **21**, 387–96.

Gleeson, B. (1998) 'The social space of disability in colonial Melbourne', in N. Fyfe (ed.), *Images of the Streets*. London, Routledge.

Gleeson, B. (1999) *Geographies of Disability*. London, Routledge.

Goffman, E. (1959) *The Presentation of Self in Everyday Life*. Harmondsworth, Penguin.

Gold, J. R. (1980) *An Introduction to Behavioural Geography*. Oxford, Oxford University Press.

Gold, J. R. (1992) 'Image and environment: the decline of cognitive-behaviouralism in human geography and grounds for regeneration', *Geoforum*, **23**, 239–47.

Golledge, R. G. (1981) 'Misconceptions, misinterpretations and misrepresentations of behavioral approaches in human geography', *Environment and Planning A*, **13**, 1325–44.

Golledge, R. G. (1991) 'Cognition of physical and built environment', in T. Garling and D. Evans (eds), *Environment, Cognition, Action*. Oxford, Oxford University Press.

Golledge, R. G. (1993) 'Geography and the disabled: a survey with special reference to vision impaired and blind peoples', *Transactions, Institute of British Geographers*, **18**, 63–85.

Golledge, R. G. (1996) 'A response to Imrie and Gleeson', *Transactions, Institute of British Geographers*, **21**(2), 404–11.

Golledge R. G. and Stimson, R. J. (1997) *Spatial Behavior: A Geographic Perspective*. New York, Guilford.

Goodey, B. and Gold, J. R. (1985) 'Behavioural and perceptual geography – from retrospect to prospect', *Progress in Human Geography*, **9**, 585–95.

Goodwin, M. and Painter, J. (1996) 'Local governance, the crisis of Fordism and the changing geographies of regulation', *Transactions, Institute of British Geographers*, **21**, 635–48.

Goux, J. (1989) *Symbolic Economies after Marx and Freud*. New York, Cornell University Press.

Graham, E. (1995) 'Postmodernism and the possibility of a new human geography', *Scottish Geographical Magazine*, **11**, 175–8.

Graham, S. and Marvin, S. (2001) *Splintering Urbanism: Networked Infrastructures, Technological Mobilities and the Urban Condition*. London, Routledge.

Gramsci, A. (1971) *Selections from the Prison Notebooks of Antonio Gramsci*, ed. and trans. by Q. Hoare and G. Nowell-Smith. London, Lawrence and Wishart.

Greed, C. (1993) *Creating Gendered Realities*. London, Routledge.

Green, A., Owen, D. W. and Winnett, C. M. (1994) 'The changing geography of recession: analyses of local unemployment', *Transactions, Institute of British Geographers*, **19**, 142–62.

Gregory, D. (1978) *Ideology, Science and Human Geography*. London, Hutchinson.

Gregory, D. (1982) 'A realist conception of the social', *Transactions, Institute of British Geographers*, **7**, 254–6.

Gregory, D. (1984) 'Space, time and politics in social theory: an interview with Anthony Giddens', *Environment and Planning D – Society and Space*, **2**, 123–32.

Gregory, D. (1994a) *Geographical Imaginations*. Oxford, Blackwell.

Gregory, D. (1994b) 'Social theory and human geography', in D. Gregory, R. Martin and G. Smith (eds), *Human Geography: Society, Space and Social Science*. London, Macmillan.

Gregory, D. (1997) *Explorations in Critical Human Geography* (Hettner Lecture 1997). University of Heidelberg, Department of Geography.

Gregory, D. (2000a) 'Said', in M. Crang and N. Thrift (eds), *Thinking Space*. London, Routledge.

Gregory, D. (2000b) 'Post-colonialism', in R. J. Johnston, D. Gregory, G. Pratt and M. Watts (eds), *The Dictionary of Human Geography*. Oxford, Blackwell.

Gregory, S. (1963) *Statistical Methods and the Geographer*. London, Longman.

Gregson, N. and Crewe, L. (1998) 'Dusting down second-hand Rose: gendered identities and the world of second-hand goods', *Gender, Place, Culture*, **5**, 77–100.

Grierson, P. (1977) *The Origins of Money*. London, Athlone.

Grosz, E. (1992) 'Bodies-cities', in B. Colomina (ed.), *Sexuality and Space*. London, Routledge.

Grosz, E. (1994) *Volatile Bodies: Towards a Corporal Feminism*. Indiana, Indiana University Press.

Guelke, L. (1974) 'An idealist alternative to human geography', *Annals, Association of American Geographers*, **63**, 19–202.

Habermas, J. (1988) *On the Logic of the Social Sciences*. Cambridge, Polity.

Habermas, J. (1989) *The Structural Transformation of the Public Sphere*. Cambridge, MA, MIT Press.

Hägerstrand, T. (1975) 'Diorama, path and project', *Tijdschrift voor Economische en Sociale Geografie*, **73**, 323–39.

Haggett, P. (1965) *Locational Analysis in Human Geography*. London, Arnold.

Haggett, P. (1975) *Geography: A Modern Synthesis*. London, Heinemann.

Haggett, P. (1981) 'Geography', in R. J. Johnston (ed.), *The Dictionary of Human Geography*. Oxford, Blackwell.

Haggett, P. (1990) *The Geographer's Art*. Oxford, Blackwell.

Haggett, P. (2001) *Geography: A Global Synthesis*. Harlow, Prentice Hall.

Halfacree, K. (1993) 'Locality and social representations: space discourse and alternative definitions of the rural', *Journal of Rural Studies*, **9**, 23–8.

Halford, S. and Savage, M. (1993) 'Changing the culture of the organization: gender and cultural restructuring in banking and local government', paper presented to the Urban Change and Conflict Conference, University of Sheffield, 14–16 September.

Hall, S. (1990) 'Encoding/decoding', in S. During (ed.), *The Cultural Studies Reader*. London, Routledge.

Hall, S. (1996) 'Introduction', in S. Hall (ed.), *Representation: Cultural Representations and Signifying Practices*. London, Sage.

Hall, T. (1997) 'Images of industry in the post-industrial city: Raymond Mason and Birmingham', *Ecumene*, **4**, 46–68.

Hall, T. (2001) *Urban Geography*, 2nd edn. London, Routledge.

Hall, T. and Hubbard, P. (1996) 'The entrepreneurial city: new urban politics, new urban geographies?', *Progress in Human Geography*, **20**, 153–74.

Hambleton, R. (1998) 'Competition and contracting in UK local government', in N. Oatley (ed.), *Cities, Economic Competition and Urban Policy*. London, Paul Chapman.

Hamnett, C. and Randolph, W. (1988) *Cities, Housing and Profit*. London, Hutchinson.

Hannah, M. (1997) 'Imperfect panopticism' in G. Benko and U. Strohmayer (eds), *Space and Social Theory*. Oxford, Blackwell.

Hanson, S. (1992) 'Geography and feminism: worlds in collision?' *Annals, Association of American Geographers*, **82**, 569–86.

Haraway, D. (1985) 'A manifesto for cyborgs: science, technology, and social feminism in the 1980s', *Socialist Review*, **80**, 65–107.

Haraway, D. (1991) *Simians, Cyborgs and Women*. London, Free Association Press.

Harley, B. (1988) 'Maps, knowledge and power', in D. Cosgrove and S. Daniels (eds), *The Iconography of Landscape: Essays on the Symbolic Representation, Design and Use of Past Environments*. Cambridge, Cambridge University Press.

Harley, B. (1992) 'Deconstructing the map', in T. Barnes and J. Duncan (eds), *Writing Worlds*. London, Routledge.

Hartshorne, R. (1939) *The Nature of Geography: A Critical Survey of Current Thought in the Light of the Past*. Chicago, Rand McNally.

Hartshorne, R. (1959) *Perspective on the Nature of Geography*. Chicago, Rand McNally.

Harvey, D. (1969) *Explanation in Geography*. Oxford, Blackwell.

Harvey, D. (1970) 'Behavioural postulates and the construction of theory in human geography', *Geographica Polonica*, **18**, 217–45.

Harvey, D. (1972) 'What is theory?', in N. Graves (ed.), *New Movements in the Study and Teaching of Geography*. London, Maurice Temple Smith.

Harvey, D. (1973) *Social Justice and the City*. London, Edward Arnold.

Harvey, D. (1974) 'Class, monopoly rent, finance capitals and the urban revolution', *Regional Studies*, **8**, 239–55.

Harvey, D. (1977) 'Government policies, financial institutions and neighbourhood change in United States cities', in M. Harloe (ed.), *Captive Cities: Studies in the Political Economy of Cities and Regions*. London, John Wiley and Sons.

Harvey, D. (1982) *The Limits to Capital*. Oxford, Blackwell.

Harvey, D. (1985a) *The Urbanization of Capital: Studies in the History and Theory of Capitalist Urbanization*. Oxford, Blackwell.

Harvey, D. (1985b) *Consciousness and the Urban Experience*. Oxford, Blackwell.

Harvey, D. (1989a) *The Condition of Postmodernity: An Enquiry into the Origins of Cultural Changes*. Oxford, Blackwell.

Harvey, D. (1989b) 'From managerialism to entrepreneurialism: the transformation of governance in late capitalism', *Geografiska Annaler*, **71B**, 3–17.

Harvey, D. (1989c) *The Urban Experience*. Oxford, Blackwell.

Harvey, D. (1992a) 'Social justice, postmodernism and the city', *International Journal of Urban and Regional Research*, **16**, 588–601.

Harvey, D. (1992b) 'Postmodern morality plays', *Antipode*, **24**, 300–26.

Harvey, D. (1996) *Justice, Nature and the Geography of Difference*. Oxford, Blackwell.

Harvey, D. (1999) 'On fatal flaws and fatal distractions', *Progress in Human Geography*, **23**, 556–78.

Harvey, D. (2000a) *Spaces of Hope*. Edinburgh, Edinburgh University Press.

Harvey, D. (2000b) 'Reinventing geography (interview)', *New Left Review*, **4**, 75–97.

Harvey, D. and Chatterjee, L. (1974) 'Absolute rent and the restructuring of space by government and financial institutions', *Antipode*, **6**, 22–36.

Healey, P., Cameron, S., Davoudi, S., Graham, S. and Madani-Pour, A. (eds) (1995) *Managing Cities: The New Urban Context*. Chichester, John Wiley and Sons.

Hebdidge, D. (1979) *Subcultures: The Meaning of Style*. London, Routledge.

Heidegger, M. (1927) [1987] *Being and Time*. Oxford, Blackwell.

Held, D. and McGrew, A. (2000) 'The great globalisation debate: an introduction', in D. Held and A. McGrew (eds), *The Global Transformations Reader: An Introduction to the Globalisation Debate*. Cambridge, Polity.

Hellenier, E. (1993) 'The challenge from the East: Japan's financial rise and the changing global order', in P. Cerny (ed.), *Finance and World Politics: Markets, Regimes and States in the Post-Hegemonic Era*. Aldershot, Edward Elgar.

Herbert, S. (1997) *Policing Space*. Minneapolis, University of Minnesota Press.

Herbert, S. (2000) 'For ethnography', *Progress in Human Geography*, **24**, 550–68.

Herman, E. and McChesney, R. (1997) *The Global Media: The New Missionaries of Corporate Capitalism*. London, Cassell.

Higgins, J. (1999) *Raymond Williams: Literature, Marxism and Cultural Materialism*. London, Routledge.

Higson, A. (1987) 'The landscapes of television', *Landscape Research*, **12**, 8–13.

Hill, M. R. (1981) 'Positivism: a "hidden" philosophy in geography', in M. E. Harvey and B. P. Holly (eds), *Themes in Geographic Thought*. London, Croom Helm.

Hirst, P. and Thompson, G. (1992) 'The problem of "globalization": international economic relations, national economic management and the formation of trading blocs', *Economy and Society*, **21**, 357–96.

Hirst, P. and Thompson, G. (1999) *Globalisation in Question*, 2nd edn. Cambridge, Polity.

HM Government (1999) *A Better Quality of Life: A Strategy for Sustainable Development for the United Kingdom*. London, HMSO.

HM Treasury (1999) *Credit Unions of the Future*. Report of the Credit Union Taskforce, November 1999.

Hodge, R. and Kress, G. (1988) *Social Semiotics*. Cambridge, Polity.

Holland, E. W. (1999) *Deleuze and Guattari's Anti-Oedipus: An Introduction to Schizoanalysis*. London, Routledge.

Holloway, L. and Hubbard, P. (2001) *People and Place: The Extraordinary Geographies of Everyday Life*. Harlow, Prentice Hall.

Holtham, G. and Kay, J. (1994) 'The assessment: institutions of economic policy', *Oxford Review of Economic Policy*, **10**, 1–16.

Hood-Williams, J. and Harrison, W. (1998) 'Trouble with gender', *Sociological Review*, **49**, 73–92.

hooks, b. (1991) *Yearning: Race, Gender and Cultural Politics*. Chicago, South End Press.

hooks, b. (1992) *Teaching to Transgress: Education As the Practice of Freedom*. London, Routledge.

Hoskins, W. G. (1955) *The Making of the English Landscape*. London, Penguin.

Hubbard, P. (1996) 'Urban design and city regeneration: social representations of entrepreneurial landscapes', *Urban Studies*, **33**, 1441–61.

Hubbard, P. (1999) *Sex and the City: Geographies of Prostitution in the Urban West*. Aldershot, Ashgate.

Hubbard, P. (2000) 'Desire/disgust: mapping the moral geographies of heterosexuality', *Progress in Human Geography*, **24**, 191–218.

Hubbard, P. (2002) 'Going out (of town): the contemporary geographies of British cinema', *Journal of Popular British Cinema*, **6**, forthcoming.

Hubbard, P. and Hall, T. (1998) 'The entrepreneurial city and the "new urban politics"', in T. Hall and P. Hubbard (eds), *The Entrepreneurial City: Geographies of Politics, Regime and Representation*. New York, John Wiley and Sons.

Hunter, T. (1993) 'Banks shutting their doors to the poor', *Guardian*, 18 September, 33.

Hussey, A. (2001) 'Spectacle, simulation and spectre: Debord, Baudrillard and the ghost of Marx', *Parallax*, **7**, 63–72.

Hutton, W. (1995) *The State We're In*. London, Vintage.

Imrie, R. (1996) 'Ableist geographers, disablist spaces: towards a reconstruction of Golledge's "Geography and the disabled"', *Transactions, Institute of British Geographers*, **21**(2), 397–403.

Ingham, G. (1994) 'States and markets in the production of world money: sterling and the dollar', in S. Corbridge, R. Martin and N. Thrift (eds), *Money, Power and Space*. Oxford, Blackwell.

Jackson, P. (1985) 'Urban ethnography', *Progress in Human Geography*, **9**, 157–76.

Jackson, P. (1987) 'The idea of "race" and the geography of racism', in P. Jackson (ed.), *Race and Racism*. London, Allen and Unwin.

Jackson, P. (1989) *Maps of Meaning*. London, Routledge.

Jackson, P. (1994) 'Social geography', in R. J. Johnston, D. Gregory and S. Smith (eds), *A Dictionary of Human Geography*. Oxford, Blackwell.

Jackson, P. (1999) 'Commodity cultures: the traffic in things', *Transactions, Institute of British Geographers*, **24**, 95–109.

Jackson, P. (2000) 'Re-materializing social and cultural geography', *Social and Cultural Geography*, **1**, 9–14.

Jackson, P. and Penrose, J. (eds) (1993) *Constructions of Race, Place and Nation*. London, UCL Press.

Jacobs, J. (1961) *The Death and Life of Great American Cities*. New York, Random House.

Jagose, A. (1996) *Queer Theory: An Introduction*. New York, New York University Press.

Jameson, F. (1984) 'Postmodernism or the cultural logic of late capitalism', *New Left Review*, **146**, 378–83.

Jameson, F. (1991) *Postmodernism, or the Cultural Logic of Late Capitalism*. London, Verso.

Janelle, D. (1969) 'Spatial reorganisation: a model and concept', *Annals, Association of American Geographers*, **59**, 6–348.

Jarosz, L. (1992) 'Constructing the dark continent: metaphor as geographic representation of Africa', *Geografiska Annaler*, **74B**, 105–15.

Jenkins, R. (1992) *Key Sociologists – Pierre Bourdieu*. London, Routledge.

Jervis, J. (1999) *Transgressing the Modern*. Oxford, Blackwell.

Jessop, B. (1994) 'Post-Fordism and the state', in A. Amin, *Post-Fordism: A Reader*. Oxford, Blackwell.

Jessop, B. (1995) 'The regulation approach, governance and post-Fordism: alternative perspectives on economic and political change?', *Economy and Society*, **24**(3), 307–33.

Jessop, B. (1997a) 'The entrepreneurial city: re-imagining localities, redesigning economic governance, or restructuring capital?', in N. Jewson and S. MacGregor (eds), *Transforming Cities: Contested Governance and New Spatial Divisions*. London, Routledge.

Jessop, B. (1997b) 'The governance of complexity and the complexity of governance: preliminary remarks on some problems and limits of economic guidance', in A. Amin and J. Hausner (eds), *Beyond Market and Hierarchy: Interactive Government and Social Complexity*. Cheltenham, Edward Elgar.

Jessop, B. (1997c) 'A neo-Gramscian approach to the regulation of urban regimes: accumulation strategies, hegemonic projects and governance', in M. Lauria (ed.), *Reconstructing Urban Regime Theory: Regulating Urban Politics in a Global Economy*. London, Sage.

Jessop, B. (1999) 'Globalisation and the nation state', in S. Aronowitz and P. Bratsis (eds), *Rethinking the State: Miliband, Poulatsas and State Theory*. Minneapolis, MN, University of Minnesota Press.

Johnson, N. (1996) 'Where geography and history meet: heritage tourism and the big house in Ireland', *Annals, Association of American Geographers*, **86**, 551–66.

Johnston, R. J. (1986) *Philosophy and Human Geography: An Introduction to Contemporary Approaches*. London, Arnold.

Johnston, R. J. (1991) *Geography and Geographers: Anglo-American Geography since 1945*, 4th edn. London, Edward Arnold.

Johnston, R. J. (2000) 'Authors, editors and authority in the postmodern academy', *Antipode*, **32**, 271–91.

Johnston, R. J., Taylor, P. J. and Watts, M. (eds) (1995) *Geographies of Global Change: Remapping the World in the Late Twentieth Century*. Oxford, Blackwell.

Jonas, A. and Wilson, D. (1999) *The Urban Growth Machine: Critical Perspectives Two Decades Later*. Albany, NY, State University of New York Press.

Jones, A. (1999) 'Dialectics and difference: against Harvey's dialectic post-Marxism', *Progress in Human Geography*, **23**, 529–55.

Jones, J. P., Nast, H. and Roberts, S. (eds) (1997) *Thresholds in Feminist Geography: Difference, Methodology, Representation*. Lanham, MA, Rowman and Littlefield.

Jones, J. P. and Natter, W. (1999) 'Space and representation', in A. Buttimer, S. D. Brunn and U. Wardenga (eds), *Text and Image: Social Construction of Regional Knowledges*. Leipzig, Institut für Länderkunde Leipzig.

Kaern, M., Phillips, B. S. and Cohen, R. S. (1990) *Georg Simmel and Contemporary Sociology*. Dordrecht, Kluwer Academic Publications.

Kearns, G. (1997) 'The imperial subject: geography and travel in the work of Mary Kingsley and Halford Mackinder', *Transactions, Institute of British Geographers*, **22**, 450–72.

Kearns, G. and Philo, C. (eds) (1993) *Selling Places: The City as Cultural Capital, Past and Present*. Oxford, Pergamon.

Keith, M. and Pile, S. (1993) (eds) *Place and the Politics of Identity*. London, Routledge.

Kendall, G. and Wickham, G. (1999) *Using Foucault's Methods*. London, Sage.

Kennedy, C. and Lukinbeal, C. (1998) 'Towards a holistic approach to geographic research on film', *Progress in Human Geography*, **21**, 33–50.

Kenney, J. (1995) 'Climate, race, and imperial authority: the symbolic landscape of the British hill station in India', *Annals, Association of American Geographers*, **85**, 694–714.

Kerr, D. (1965) 'Some aspects of the geography of finance in Canada', *Canadian Geographer*, **9**, 175–92.

Kinsman, P. (1995) 'Landscape, race and national identity: the photography of Ingrid Pollard', *Area*, **27**, 300–10.

Kirk, W. (1963) 'Problems of geography', *Geography*, **48**, 357–71.

Kitchin, R. M. (1996) 'Increasing the integrity of cognitive mapping research: appraising conceptual schemata of environment-behaviour interaction', *Progress in Human Geography*, **20**(1), 56–84.

Kitchin, R. M. (1998) *Cyberspace: The World in the Wires*. Chichester, John Wiley and Sons.

Kitchin, R. M. (1999) 'Ethics and morals in geographical studies of disability', in J. Proctor and D. Smith (eds), *Geography and Ethics: Journeys through a Moral Terrain*. London, Routledge, pp. 223–36.

Kitchin, R. and Kneale, J. (2002) *Lost in Space: Geographies of Science Fiction*. London, Continuum.

Kitchin, R. and Tate, N. (2000) *Conducting Research in Human Geography*. Harlow, Prentice Hall.

Kneale, J. (1999) 'The media', in P. Cloke, P. Crang and M. Goodwin (eds), *Introducing Human Geographies*. London, Arnold.

Knopp, L. (1995) 'Sexuality and urban space: a framework for analysis', in D. Bell and G. Valentine (eds), *Mapping Desire: Geographies of Sexuality*. London, Routledge.

Knox, P. (1991) 'The restless urban landscape', *Annals, Association of American Geographers*, **81**, 181–209.

Knox, P. (1993) *The Restless Urban Landscape*. Englewood Cliffs, Prentice Hall.

Knox, P. (1994) *Urban Social Geography*. Harlow, Longman.

Knox, P. (1995) 'World cities in a world system', in P. L. Knox and P. J. Taylor (eds), *World Cities in a World System*. Cambridge, Cambridge University Press.

Knox, P. (1996) 'Globalisation and the world city hypothesis', *Scottish Geographical Magazine*, **112** (2), 124–6.

Kong, L. (1993) 'Negotiating conceptions of sacred space', *Transactions, Institute of British Geographers*, **18**, 342–58.

Kresl, P. K. (1995) 'The determinants of urban competitiveness: a survey', in P. K. Kresl and G. Gaert (eds), *North American Cities and the Global Economy*. London, Sage, pp. 45–68.

Kristeva, J. (1982) *Powers of Horror*. Vancouver, Columbia University Press.

Krugman, P. (1991) *Geography and Trade*. Cambridge, MA, MIT Press.

Kuhn, T. (1970) *The Structure of Scientific Revolutions*. Chicago, Chicago University Press.

Kynaston, D. (1994) *The City of London: Volume One – A World of its Own 1815–1890*. London, Pimlico.

Kynaston, D. (2001) *The City of London: Volume Three 1945 Onwards*. London, Pimlico.

Laclau, E. and Mouffe, C. (1985) *Hegemony and Socialist Strategy: Towards a Radical Democratic Politics*. London, Verso.

Langer, M. M. (1989) *Merleau-Ponty's Phenomenology of Perception: A Guide and Commentary*. Basingstoke, Macmillan.

Lash, S. and Urry, J. (1994) *Economies of Signs and Space*. London, Sage.

Latour, B. (1987) *Science in Action: How to Follow Engineers in Society*. Milton Keynes, Open University Press.

Latour, B. (1993) *We Have Never Been Modern*. Hemel Hempstead, Harvester Wheatsheaf.

Lauria, M. (1997) *Reconstructing Urban Regime Theory: Regulating Urban Politics in a Global Economy*. London, Sage.

Laurie, N., Dwyer, C., Holloway, S. and Smith, F. (1999) *Geographies of New Femininities*. Harlow, Longman.

Laurier, E. (1999) 'Geographies of talk: Max left a message for you', *Area*, **31**, 36–45.

Law, J. (1992) 'Notes on the theory of the actor-network', *Systems Practice*, **5**, 379–93.

Law, J. and Mol, A. (1995) 'Notes on materiality and sociality', *Sociological Review*, **43**, 274–94.

Law, L. (1997) 'A matter of choice: discourses of prostitution in the Philippines', in L. Manderson and M. Jolly (eds), *Sites of Desire/Economies of Pleasure: Sexualities in Asia and the Pacific*. Chicago, University of Chicago Press.

Lee, R. (1996) 'Moral money? LETS and the social construction of local economic geographies in southeast England', *Environment and Planning A*, **28**(8), 1377–94.

Lee, R. (1999) 'Local money: geographies of autonomy and resistance?', in R. Martin (ed.), *Money and the Space Economy*. Chichester, John Wiley.

Lee, R., Leyshon, A. and Williams, C. (eds) (2002) *Alternative Economic Spaces: Rethinking the Economic in Economic Geography*. London, Sage.

Lee, R. and Wills, J. (eds) (1997) *Geographies of Economies*. London, Arnold.

Lees, L. (1996) 'In pursuit of difference: representations of gentrification', *Environment and Planning A*, **28**, 453–70.

Lees, L. (1997) 'Ageographica, heterotopia and Vancouver's new public library', *Environment and Planning D – Society and Space*, **15**, 321–47.

Lees, L. (2001) 'Towards a critical geography architecture: the case of an ersatz Colosseum', *Ecumene*, **8**, 51–86.

Lefebvre, H. (1991) *The Production of Space*. Oxford, Blackwell.

Leftwich, A. (1993) 'Governance, the state and the politics of development', *Third World Quarterly*, **14**, 363–83.

Le Galés, P. (1998) 'Regulations and governance in European cities', *International Journal of Urban and Regional Research*, **22**, 482–506.

Lévi-Strauss, C. (1969) *The Raw and the Cooked*. London, Nicholson.

Lewis, C. and Pile, S. (1996) 'Women, body, space: Rio carnival and the politics of performance', *Gender, Place and Culture*, **3**, 45–78.

Ley, D. (1983) *Urban Social Geography*. London, Unwin Hyman.

Ley, D. and Samuels, M. (1978) *Humanistic Geography*. London, Croom Helm.

Leyshon, A. (1995a) 'Annihilating space?: the speed-up of communications', in J. Allen and C. Hamnett (eds), *A Shrinking World: Global Unevenness and Inequality*. Oxford, Oxford University Press.

Leyshon, A. (1995b) 'Geographies of money and finance 1', *Progress in Human Geography*, **19**, 531–43.

Leyshon, A. (1995c) 'Missing words: whatever happened to the geography of poverty?', *Environment and Planning A*, **27**, 1021–8.

Leyshon, A. (1997a) 'Geographies of money and finance 2', *Progress in Human Geography*, **21**, 381–92.

Leyshon, A. (1997b) 'True stories? Global nightmares, global dreams and writing globalisation', in R. Lee and J. Wills (eds), *Geographies of Economies*. London, Arnold.

Leyshon, A. (1998) 'Geographies of money and finance 3', *Progress in Human Geography*, **22**, 433–46.

Leyshon, A. (2000) 'Money and finance, geography of', in R. J. Johnston, D. Gregory, G. Pratt and M. Watts (eds), *The Dictionary of Human Geography*. Oxford, Blackwell.

Leyshon, A., Matless, D. and Revill, G. (1998) *The Place of Music*. New York, Guilford.

Leyshon, A. and Thrift, N. (1993) 'The restructuring of the UK financial services industry in the 1990s: a reversal of fortune?', *Journal of Rural Studies*, **9**, 223–41.

Leyshon, A and Thrift, N (1995) 'Geographies of financial exclusion – financial abandonment in Britain and the United States', *Transactions, Institute of British Geographers*, **20**(3), 312–41.

Leyshon, A. and Thrift, N. (1996) 'Financial exclusion and the shifting boundaries of the financial system', *Environment and Planning A*, **28**, 1150–6.

Leyshon, A. and Thrift, N. (1997) *Money/Space: Geographies of Monetary Transformation*. London, Routledge.

Linehan, D. and Gruffudd, P. (2001) 'Bodies and souls: psycho-geographical collisions in the South Wales coalfield, 1926–1939', *Journal of Historical Geography*, **27**, 377–94.

Ling, T. (2000) 'Unpacking partnership: the case of health care', in J. Clarke, S. Gerwitz and E. McLaughlin, *New Managerialism, New Welfare?* London, Sage.

Livingstone, D. (1992a) *The Geographical Tradition: Episodes in the History of a Contested Enterprise*. Oxford, Blackwell.

Livingstone, D. (1992b) 'A brief history of geography', in A. Rogers, H. Viles and A. Goudie (eds), *The Student's Companion to Geography*. Oxford, Blackwell.

Logan, J. and Molotch, H. (1987) *Urban Fortunes*. Berkeley, University of California Press.

Logan, J., Whaley, R. B. and Crowder, K. (1997) 'The character and consequences of growth regimes: an assessment of 20 years of research', *Urban Affairs Review*, **32**, 603–30.

Longhurst, R. (2000a) 'Geography and gender: masculinities, male identity and men', *Progress in Human Geography*, **24**, 439–44.

Longhurst, R. (2000b) *Bodies: Exploring Fluid Boundaries*. London, Routledge.

Lösch, A. (1949) 'Theorie der Währung', *Weltwirtschaftliches Archive*, **LXII**, 35–88.

Lösch, A. (1954) *The Economics of Location*. New Haven, Yale University Press.

Lovering, J. (1995) 'Creating discourses rather than jobs: the crisis in the cities and the transition fantasies of intellectuals and policy makers', in P. Healey, S. Cameron, S. Davoudi, S. Graham and A. Madani-Pour (eds), *Managing Cities: The New Urban Context*. Chichester, John Wiley and Sons.

Low, M. (2001) 'States, citizenship and collective action', in P. Daniels, M. Bradshaw, D. Shaw and J. Sidaway (eds), *Human Geography: Issues for the 21st Century*. Harlow, Prentice Hall.

Lowenthal, D. (1961) 'Geography, experience and imagination: towards a geographical epistemology', *Annals, Association of American Geographers*, **51**, 241–60.

Lowenthal, D. (1991) 'British national identity and the English landscape', *Rural History*, **2**, 205–30.

Lowman, J. (1992) 'Street prostitution control: some Canadian reflections of the Finsbury Park experience', *British Journal of Criminology*, **32**, 1–16.

Luke, T. and O'Tuathail, G. (2000) 'Thinking geopolitical space: the spatiality of war, speed and vision', in M. Crang and N. Thrift (eds), *Thinking Space*. London, Routledge.

Lukinbeal, C. and Aitken, S. (1998) 'Sex, violence and the weather: male hysteria, scale and the fractal geographies of patriarchy', in H. J. Nast and S. Pile (eds), *Places Through the Body*. London, Routledge.

Lurie, A. (1992) *The Language of Clothes*. London, Bloomsbury.

Lynch, K. (1960) *The Image of the City*. Massachusetts, MIT Press.

Lyod, B. and Rowntree, L. (1978) 'Radical feminists and gay men in San Francisco: social space in dispersed communities', in D. Lanegran and R. Palm (eds), *An Invitation to Geography*. New York, McGraw-Hill.

Lyon, D. (1994). *Post-modernity*. Buckingham, Open University Press

Lyotard, J.-F. (1984) *The Postmodern Condition*. Manchester, Manchester University Press.

Lyotard, J.-F. (1993) *Libidinal Economy*. London, Athlone.

McCormack, D. (1999) 'Bodyshopping', *Gender, Place and Culture*, **6**, 155–177.

McDowell, L. (1983) 'Towards an understanding of the gender division of urban space', *Environment and Planning D – Society and Space*, **1**, 59–72.

McDowell, L. (1991) 'Life without father and Ford', *Transactions, Institute of British Geographers*, **16**, 400–18.

McDowell, L. (1995) 'Bodywork: heterosexual performance in city work', in D. Bell and G. Valentine (eds), *Mapping Desire: Geographies of Sexualities*. London, Routledge.

McDowell, L. (1997) *Capital Culture: Gender at Work in the City*. Oxford, Blackwell.

McDowell, L. (1999) *Gender, Identity and Place: Understanding Feminist Geographies*. Cambridge, Polity Press.

McDowell, L. (2000a) 'Acts of memory and millennial hopes and anxieties: the awkward relationship between the economic and the cultural', *Social and Cultural Geography*, **1**, 15–24.

McDowell, L. (2000b) 'Learning to serve? Employment aspirations and attitudes of young working class men in an era of labour market restructuring', *Gender, Place & Culture*, **7**, 389–416.

McDowell, L. and Sharp, J. (eds) (1997) *Space, Gender, Knowledge*. London, Arnold.

McDowell, L. and Sharp, J. (eds) (1999) *A Feminist Glossary of Human Geography*. London, Edward Arnold.

McEwan, C. (2001) 'Geography, culture and global change', in P. Daniels, M. Bradshaw, D. Shaw and J. Sidaway (eds), *Human Geography: Issues for the 21st Century*. Harlow, Prentice Hall.

McGuirk, P. (2000) 'Power and policy networks in urban governance: local government and property-led regeneration in Dublin', *Urban Studies*, **37**, 651–72.

MacHill, M. (1997) 'Beyond Foucault: towards a contemporary theory of surveillance', in C. Norris, J. Moran and G. Armstrong (eds), *Surveillance, CCTV and Social Control*. Aldershot, Ashgate.

McKay, G. (1996) *Senseless Acts of Beauty*. London, Verso.

MacKenzie, S. (1989) 'Women in the city', in R. Peet and N. Thrift (eds), *New Models in Geography*. London, Unwin Hyman.

Mackinder, H. (1887) 'On the scope and methods of geography', *Proceedings of the Royal Geographical Society*, **9**, 141–60.

McLuhan, M. (1964) *Understanding Media*. London, Routledge and Kegan Paul.

McLuhan, M. and Fiore, Q. (1967) *The Medium is the Message*. London, Allen Lane.

McRobbie, A. (1994) *Post-modernism and Popular Culture*. London, Routledge.

Maffesoli, M. (1996) *The Time of the Tribes*. London, Sage.

Mair, A. (1986) 'Thomas Kuhn and understanding geography', *Progress in Human Geography*, **10**, 34–369.

Malbon, B. (1998) *Clubbing*. London, Routledge.

Marcus, G. E. (2000) 'The twisting and turnings of geography and anthropology in winds of millennial transition', in I. Cook, D. Crouch, S. Naylor and J. Ryan (eds), *Cultural Turns/Geographical Turns*. Harlow, Prentice Hall.

Markus, T. (1993) *Buildings and Power*. London, Routledge.

Markusen, A. (1999) 'Fuzzy concepts, scanty evidence and policy distance: the case for rigour and policy relevance in critical regional studies', *Regional Studies*, **33**, 869–84.

Martin, G. J. and James, P. E. (1993) *All Possible Worlds: A History of Geographical Ideas*. New York, John Wiley and Sons.

Martin, R. (1999) *Money and the Space Economy*. Chichester, John Wiley.

Martin, R. and Sunley, P. (1997) 'The post-Keynesian state and the space economy', in R. Lee and J. Wills (eds), *Geographies of Economies*. London, Arnold.

Marx, K. (1977) *Capital*. London, Lawrence and Wishart.

Massey, D. (1973) 'Towards a critique of location theory', *Antipode*, **5**, 33–49.

Massey, D. (1984) *Spatial Divisions of Labour*. London, Macmillan.

Massey, D. (1991) 'A global sense of place', *Marxism Today*, 24–9 June.

Massey, D. (1993) 'Power geometry and a progressive sense of place', in J. Bird, B. Curtis, T. Putnam, G. Robertson and L. Tickner (eds), *Mapping the Futures*. London, Routledge.

Massey, D. (1994) *Space, Place and Gender*. London, Methuen.

Massey, D. (1995) 'The conceptualisation of place', in D. Massey and P. Jess (eds), *A Place in the World: Places, Cultures and Globalisation*. Buckingham, Open University Press.

Massey, D. (1997) 'The political place of locality studies', in L. McDowell (ed.), *Undoing Place? A Geographical Reader*. London, Arnold.

Massey, D. (1999a) 'Spaces of politics', in D. Massey, J. Allen and P. Sarre (eds), *Human Geography Today*. Cambridge, Polity.

Massey, D. (1999b) 'Space-time, science and the relationship between physical and human geography', *Transactions, Institute of British Geographers*, **24**, 261–76.

Massey, D. and Allen, J. (1984) *Geography Matters!* Cambridge, Cambridge University Press.

Matless, D. (1992) 'An occasion for geography: landscape, representation and Foucault's corpus', *Environment and Planning D – Society and Space*, **10**, 41–56.

Matless, D. (1995) 'The art of right living: landscape and citizenship 1918–1939', in S. Pile and N. Thrift (eds), *Mapping the Subject: Geographies of Cultural Transformation*. London, Routledge.

Matless, D. (1998) *Landscapes of Englishness*. London, Reaktion.

Matless, D. (2000) 'Five objects, geographical subjects', in I. Cook, D. Crouch, S. Naylor and J. Ryan (eds), *Cultural Turns/Geographical Turns*. Harlow, Prentice Hall.

May, T. (1997) *Social Research: Issues, Methods, Process*. Buckingham, Open University Press.

Mayer, M. (1995) 'Urban governance in the post-Fordist city', in P. Healey, S. Cameron, S. Davoudi, S. Graham and A. Madani-Pour (eds), *Managing Cities: The New Urban Context*. Chichester, John Wiley and Sons.

Mayhew R. J. (2001) 'The effacement of early modern geography (*c*.1600–1850): a historiographical essay', *Progress in Human Geography*, **25**, 383–401.

Meinig, D. (1983) *The Interpretation of Ordinary Landscapes*. Oxford, Oxford University Press.

Merleau-Ponty, M. (1940) [1962] *The Phenomenology of Perception*. London, Routledge and Kegan Paul.

Merrifield, A. (2000a) 'Flexible Marxism and the metropolis', in G. Bridge and S. Watson (eds), *A Companion to the City*. Oxford, Blackwell.

Merrifield, A. (2000b) 'Henri Lefebvre: a socialist in space', in M. Crang and N. Thrift (eds), *Thinking Space*. London, Routledge

Merrifield, A. (2000c) 'The dialectics of dystopia: disorder and Zero Tolerance in the city', *International Journal of Urban and Regional Research*, **24**, 473–89.

Merrifield, A. and Swyngedouw, E. (1996) *The Urbanisation of Injustice*. London, Lawrence and Wishart.

Michie, R. C. (1992) *The City of London: Continuity and Change*. London, Macmillan.

Milbourne, P. (1997) *Revealing Rural Others: Diverse Voices in the British Countryside*. London, Pinter Press.

Miller, D., Jackson, P., Thrift, N., Holbrook, B. and Rowlands, M. (1998) *Shopping, Place and Identity*. London, Routledge.

Mills, C. (1993) 'Myths and meanings of gentrification', in J. Duncan and D. Ley (eds), *Place/Culture/Representation*. London, Routledge.

Mitchell, D. (1995) 'There's no such thing as culture: towards a reconceptualisation of the idea of culture in geography', *Transactions, Institute of British Geographers*, **20**, 102–16.

Mitchell, D. (2000) *Cultural Geography: A Critical Introduction*. Oxford, Blackwell.

Mitchell, J. (1990) *Access to Basic Banking Services: The Problems of Low-income American Consumers*. Providence, RI, Rhode Island Consumers Council.

Mitchell, W. J. T. (1994) *Landscape and Power*. London, University of Chicago Press.

Mohan, J. (2000) 'Geographies of welfare and social exclusion', *Progress in Human Geography*, **24** (2), 291–300.

Monk, J. and Hanson, S. (1982) 'On not excluding half of the human in human geography', *Professional Geographer*, **34**, 11–23.

Moran, M. (1991) *The Politics of the Financial Services Revolution*. London, Macmillan.

Mordue, T. (1999) 'Heartbeat country: conflicting values, coinciding visions', *Environment and Planning D – Society and Space*, **31**, 629–46.

Mort, F. (1998) 'Cityscapes: consumption, masculinities and the mapping of London since 1850', *Urban Studies*, **35**, 889–907.

Moulaert, F. (2000) *Globalisation and Integrated Area Development in European Cities*. Oxford, Oxford University Press.

Mugerauer, R. (1994) *Interpretations on Behalf of Place: Environmental Displacements and Alternative Responses*. New York, SUNY Press.

Mulvey, L. (1989) *Visual and Other Pleasures*. Basingstoke, Macmillan.

Murdoch, J. (1995) 'Middle-class territory? Some remarks on the use of class analysis in rural studies', *Environment and Planning A*, **27**, 1213–30.

Murdoch, J. (1997) 'Towards a geography of heterogeneous associations', *Progress in Human Geography*, **21**, 321–7.

Murdoch, J. and Marsden, T. (1995) 'The spatialisation of politics: local and national actor spaces in environmental conflict', *Transactions, Institute of British Geographers*, **20**, 368–80.

Murdoch, J. and Pratt, A. (1993) 'Rural studies: modernism, post-modernism and the post-rural', *Journal of Rural Studies*, **8**, 429–36.

Myers, G. (1999) *Ad Worlds*. London, Arnold.

Myers, G. A. (1998) 'Intellectual of empire: Eric Dutton and hegemony in British Africa', *Annals, Association of American Geographers*, **88**, 1–17.

Myrdal, G. (1957) *Economic Theory and Underdeveloped Regions*. London, Gerald Duckworth.

Nash, C. (1993) 'Remapping and naming: new cartographies of identity, gender and landscape in Ireland', *Feminist Review*, **44**, 39–57.

Nash, C. (1999) 'Landscape', in P. Cloke, P. Crang and M. Goodwin (eds), *Introducing Human Geographies*. London, Arnold.

Nash, C. (2000) 'Performativity in practice: some recent work in cultural geography', *Progress in Human Geography*, **24**, 653–64.

Nast, H. (1998) 'Unsexy geographies', *Gender, Place and Culture*, **5**, 191–206.

Nast, H. (2000) 'Mapping the unconscious: racism and the Oedipal family', *Annals, Association of American Geographers*, **90**, 215–55.

Nast, H. and Pile, S. (1998a) 'Introduction: Making places bodies', in H. J. Nast and S. Pile (eds), *Places Through the Body*. London, Routledge.

Nast, H. and Pile, S. (1998b) (eds) *Places Through the Body*. London, Routledge.

Natter, W. (ed.) (1995) *Objectivity and Its Other*. New York, Guilford Press.

Nettleton, S. and Watson, J. (1998) *The Body in Everyday Life*. London, Routledge.

Neumann, R. (1995) 'Ways of seeing Africa: colonial recasting of African society and landscape in the Serengeti national park', *Ecumene*, **2**, 149–69.

Newlands, D. (1995) 'The economic role of regional governments in the European Community', in S. Hardy, M. Hart, L. Albrechts and A. Katos (eds), *An Enlarged Europe: Regions in Competition?* London, Jessica Kingsley.

Newman, P. and Thornley, A. (1996) *Urban Planning in Europe: International Competition, National Systems and Planning Projects*. New York, Routledge.

North, P. (1999) 'Explorations in heterotopia: Local Exchange Trading Schemes (LETS) and the micropolitics of money and livelihood', *Environment and Planning D*, **17**(1), 69–86.

Oatley, N. (ed.) (1998) 'Cities, economic competition and urban policy', in *Cities, Economic Competition and Urban Policy*. London, Paul Chapman.

O'Brien, R. (1991) *Global Financial Integration: The End of Geography*. London, Pinter.

Ogborn, M. (1995) 'Discipline, government and law: separate confinement in the prisons of England and Wales, 1830–1877', *Transactions, Institute of British Geographers*, **20**, 295–311.

Ohmae, K. (1990) *The Borderless World: Power and Strategy in the Global Marketplace*. London, Collins.

Ohmae, K. (1995) *The End of the Regional State: The Rise of the Regional Economies*. London, Collins.

Olds, K. (1995) 'Globalization and the production of new urban spaces: Pacific Rim mega-projects in the late twentieth century', *Environment and Planning A*, **27**, 1713–43.

Oliver, M. (1990) *The Politics of Disablement*. Basingstoke, Macmillan.

Olsson, G. (1980) *Birds in Egg: Eggs in Bird*. London, Pion.

O'Neill, M. (1996) 'Researching prostitution and violence: feminist praxis'. in L. Hester, L. Kelly and J. Radford (eds), *Women, Violence and Male Power*. Buckingham, Open University Press.

O'Neill, P. M. (1997) 'Bringing the qualitative state into economic geography', in R. Lee and J. Wills (eds), *Geographies of Economies*. London, Arnold.

Pacione, M. (1999) 'Applied geography: in pursuit of useful knowledge', *Applied Geography*, **19**, 1–12.

Painter, J. (1995) *Politics, Geography and Political Geography: A Critical Perspective*. London, Arnold.

Painter, J. (1997) 'Local politics, anti-essentialism and economic geography', in R. Lee and J. Wills (eds), *Geographies of Economies*. London, Arnold.

Painter, J. (1998) 'Entrepreneurs are made, not born: learning and urban regimes in the production of entrepreneurial cities', in T. Hall and P. Hubbard (eds), *The Entrepreneurial City: Geographies of Politics, Regime and Representation*. New York, John Wiley and Sons.

Painter, J. (2000a) 'Critical human geography', in R. J. Johnston, D. Gregory, G. Pratt and M. Watts (eds), *The Dictionary of Human Geography*. Oxford, Blackwell.

Painter, J. (2000b) 'Pierre Bourdieu', in M. Crang and N. Thrift (eds), *Thinking Space*. London, Routledge.

Parkinson, M. (1998) *Combating Social Exclusion: Lessons from Area-Based Programmes in Europe*. London, Policy Press.

Pateman, C. (1989) *The Disorder of Women: Democracy, Feminism and Political Theory*. Cambridge, Polity.

Peake, L. and Schein, R. (2000) 'Racing geography into the new millennium: studies of "race" and North American geographies', *Social and Cultural Geography*, **1**, 133–142.

Peck, J. (1995) 'Moving and shaking: business elites, state localism and urban privatism', *Progress in Human Geography*, **19**, 16–46.

Peck, J. (1996) 'Loose talk and tight fists', Manchester, *Guardian*, 17 August.

Peck, J. and Tickell, A. (1995) 'Business goes local: dissecting the business agenda in Manchester', *International Journal of Urban and Regional Research*, **19**, 55–78.

Peet, R. (1998) *Modern Geographic Thought*. Oxford, Blackwell.

Peet, R. and Thrift, N. (1989) *New Models in Geography*. Oxford, Blackwell.

Peterson, P. (1981) *City Limits*. Chicago, University of Chicago Press.

Phillips, M. (1998) 'The restructuring of social imaginations in rural geography', *Journal of Rural Studies*, **14**, 121–53.

Phillips, R. (1997) *Mapping Men and Empire: A Geography of Adventure*. London, Routledge.

Philo, C. (1987) ' "Fit localities for an asylum": the historical geography of the "mad-business" in England viewed through the pages of the Asylum Journal', *Journal of Historical Geography*, **13**, 398–415.

Philo, C. (1991) 'Introduction, acknowledgements and brief thoughts on older words and older worlds', in C. Philo (ed.), *New Words, New Worlds*. Lampeter, Social and Cultural Geography Study Group.

Philo, C. (1992) 'Neglected rural geographies: a review', *Journal of Rural Studies*, **8**, 193–208.

Philo, C. (1995) 'Where is poverty? The hidden geography of poverty in the United Kingdom', in C. Philo (ed.), *Off the Map: The Social Geography of Poverty in the UK*. London, Child Poverty Action Group.

Philo, C. (2000a) 'Foucault', in M. Crang and N. Thrift (eds), *Thinking Space*. London, Routledge.

Philo, C. (2000b) 'More words, more worlds: reflections on the "cultural turn" and human geography', in I. Cook, D. Crouch, S. Naylor and J. Ryan (eds), *Cultural Turns / Geographical Turns*. Harlow, Prentice Hall.

Philo, C. and Wilbert, C. (eds) (2000) *Animal Spaces, Beastly Places*. London, Routledge.

Pickles, J. (1995) *Ground Truth: The Social Implications of Geographic Information Systems*. New York, Guilford.

Pierson, C. (1998) *Beyond the Welfare State*, 2nd edn. London, Hutchinson.

Pieterse, J. N. (ed.) (2000) *Global Futures: Shaping Globalisation*. New York, Zed.

Pile, S. (1991) 'Practising interpretative human geography', *Transactions, Institute of British Geographers*, **18**, 122–39.

Pile, S. (1993) 'Human agency and human geography revisited: a critique of "new models" of the self', *Transactions, Institute of British Geographers*, **18**, 122–139.

Pile, S. (1996) *The Body and the City: Psychoanalysis, Space and Subjectivity*. London, Routledge.

Pile, S. and Thrift, N. (eds) (1995) *Mapping the Subject: Geographies of Cultural Transformation*. London, Routledge.

Pinch, P. (1995) 'Governing urban finance: changing budgetary strategies in British local government', *Environment and Planning A*, **27**, 965–83.

Ploszajska, T. (2000) 'Historiographies of geography and empire', in B. Graham and C. Nash (eds), *Modern Historical Geographies*. Harlow, Prentice Hall.

Plummer, K. (1983) *Documents of Life*. London, Unwin Hyman.

Pocock, D. (1981a) 'Place and the novelist', *Transactions, Institute of British Geographers*, **6**, 337–47.

Pocock, D. (1981b) *Literature and Geography*. London, Croom Helm.

Pollard, J. (2001) 'The global financial system: worlds of monies', in P. Daniels, M. Bradshaw, D. Shaw and J. Sidaway (eds), *Human Geography: Issues for the 21st Century*. Harlow, Prentice Hall.

Porteous, J. (1977) *Environment and Behaviour*. Harlow, Addison-Wesley.

Poster, M. (1990) *The Mode of Information: Post-structuralism and Social Context*. Cambridge, Polity.

Poster, M. (1995) *The Second Media Age*. Cambridge, Polity.

Pratt, A. (1995) 'Putting critical realism to work', *Progress in Human Geography*, **19**, 61–74.

Pratt, D. J. (1995) *Re-placing Money: The Evolution of Banking Systems in Britain and Germany*. PhD thesis, Department of Geography, University of Hull.

Pratt, G. (1992) 'Feminist geography', *Urban Geography*, **13**, 385–91.

Pred, A. (1977) 'The choreography of existence', *Economic Geography*, **53**, 207–21.

Pred, A. (1984) 'Place as a historically contingent process: structuration and the time geography of becoming places', *Annals, Association of American Geographers*, **74**, 279–97.

Preston, P. and Simpson-Housley, P. (1994) *Writing the City: Babylon and the New Jerusalem*. London, Routledge.

Prince, H. (1980) 'A review of humanistic geography', *Annals, Association of American Geographers*, **70**, 294–6.

Probyn, E. (1996) *Outsider Belongings*. London, Routledge.

Proctor, J. and Smith, D. (eds) (1999) *Geography and Ethics: Journeys in a Moral Terrain*. London, Routledge.

Pryke, M. (1991) 'An international city going global: spatial change in the City of London', *Environment and Planning D – Society and Space*, **9**, 197–222.

Pryke, M. and Allen, J. (2000) 'Monetized time-space: derivatives – money's "new imaginary"?', *Economy and Society*, **29**(2), 264–84.

Pulido, L. (1996) *Environmentalism and Economic Justice*. Tucson, University of Arizona Press.

Quiggin, M. A. (1949) *A Survey of Primitive Money: The Beginnings of Currency*. London, Methuen.

Radcliffe, S. (1999) 'Embodying national identities: *mesizo* men and white women in Ecuadorian racial-national identities', *Transactions, Institute of British Geographers*, **24**, 213–26.

Radcliffe, S. and Westwood, S. (1996) *Remaking the Nation: Place, Identity and Politics in Latin America*. London, Routledge.

Ragurman, K. (1994) 'Philosophical debates in human geography and their impact on graduate students', *Professional Geographer*, **46**, 242–9.

Ramsay, M. (1996) 'The local community: maker of culture and wealth', *Journal of Urban Affairs*, **18**, 95–118.

Reichert, D. (1992) 'On boundaries', *Environment and Planning D – Society and Space*, **10**, 87–98.

Reid, J. (1994) 'Money to burn?', *The Observer*, 25 September, Life Magazine.

Relph, E. (1976) *Place and Placelessness*. London, Pion.

Relph, E. (1987) *The Modern Urban Landscape*. London, Pion.

Rendell, J. (1998) 'Displaying sexuality', in N. Fyfe (ed.), *Images of the Streets*. London, Routledge.

Rhodes, R. A. W. (1997) *Understanding Governance: Policy Networks, Governance, Reflexivity and Account-ability*. Buckingham, Open University.

Rich, A. (1986) *Bread, Blood and Poetry: Selected Prose 1979–1985*. New York, W. W. Norton.

Richardson, H. W. (1972) *Regional Economics: Location, Theory, Urban Structure and Regional Change*. London, World University.

Richardson, H. W. (1973) *Regional Growth Theory*. London, Macmillan.

Ritzer, G. (1993) *The McDonaldization of Society*. Thousand Oaks, CA, Pine Forge Press.

Roberts, S. (1994) 'Fictitious capital, fictitious spaces: the geography of Offshore Financial Flows', in S. Corbridge, R. Martin and N. Thrift (eds), *Money, Power and Space*. Oxford, Blackwell.

Roberts, S. (1995) 'Global regulation and trans-state organisation', in R. J. Johnston, P. J. Taylor and M. Watts (eds), *Geographies of Global Change: Remapping the World in the Late Twentieth Century*. Oxford, Blackwell.

Roberts, S. (2000) 'Realizing critical geographies of the university', *Antipode*, **32**(3), 230–44.

Robins, K. (1995a) 'Global local times', in A. Anderson and M. Ricci (eds), *Society and Social Science: A Reader*, 2nd edn. Milton Keynes, Open University.

Robins, K. (1995b) 'The new spaces of global media', in R. J. Johnston, P. J. Taylor and M. Watts (eds), *Geographies of Global Change: Remapping the World in the Late Twentieth Century*. Oxford, Blackwell.

Robins, K. and Cornford, J. (1994) 'Local and regional broadcasting in the new media order', in A. Amin and N. Thrift (eds), *Globalisation, Institutions and Regional Development in Europe*. Oxford, Oxford University Press.

Robinson, G. (1998) *Methods and Techniques in Human Geography*. Chichester, John Wiley.

Robinson, J. (2000) 'Power as friendship: spatiality, femininity and noisy friendship', in J. Sharp, P. Routledge, C. Philo and R. Paddison (eds), *Entanglements of Power*. London, Routledge.

Rodaway, P. (1994) *Sensuous Geographies: Body, Sense and Place*. London, Routledge.

Rogers, A. (1992) 'The boundaries of reason: the world, the homeland and Edward Said', *Environment and Planning D – Society and Space*, **10**, 511–26.

Rogers, A. (1996) 'A chronology of geography 1859–1995', in J. Agnew, D. N. Livingstone and A. Rogers (eds), *Human Geography: An Essential Anthology*. Oxford, Blackwell.

Rojek, C. (1995) *Decentring Leisure*. London, Sage.

Room, G. (1995) 'Poverty and social exclusion: the new European agenda for policy and research', in G. Room, *Beyond the Threshold*. Bristol, Policy Press.

Rose, G. (1993) *Feminism and Geography*. Cambridge, Cambridge University Press.

Rose, G. (1995) 'Tradition and paternity: same difference?', *Transactions, Institute of British Geographers*, **20**, 414–16.

Rose, G. (1997) 'Situating knowledges: positionality, reflexivity and other tactics', *Progress in Human Geography*, **21**, 305–20.

Rose, G. (2000) *Visual Methodologies*. London, Sage.

Rose, N. (1996) 'The death of the social? Re-figuring the territory of government', *Economy and Society*, **25**, 327–56.

Rosenau, J. N. and Czempiel, E. (eds) (1992) *Governance without Government. Order and Change in World Politics*. Cambridge, Cambridge University Press.

Rosenau, P. M. (1992) *Postmodernism and the Social Sciences: Insights, Inroads and Intrusions*. Princeton, NJ, Princeton University Press.

Routledge, P (1995) 'Resisting and reshaping the modern', in R. Johnston, P. Taylor and M. Watts (eds), *Geographies of Global Change*. Oxford, Blackwell.

Routledge, P. (1997) 'Pollock Free State and the practice of postmodern politics', *Transactions, Institute of British Geographers*, **22**, 359–77.

Ryan, J. (1997) *Picturing Empire: Photography and Visualisation of the British Empire*. London, Reaktion.

Ryan, J. (2000) 'Introduction: cultural turns, geographical turns', in I. Cook, D. Crouch, S. Naylor and J. Ryan (eds), *Cultural Turns/Geographical Turns*. Harlow, Prentice Hall.

Said, E. (1978) *Orientalism*. New York, Vintage.

Said, E. (1990) 'Narrative, geography and interpretation', *New Left Review*, **180**, 81–97.

Said, E. (1994) *Culture and Imperialism*. New York, Vintage.

Said, E. (2001) 'Comment', *The Observer*, Sunday 16 September, 26.

Sassen, S. (1991) *The Global City: New York, London, Tokyo*. Princeton, NJ, Princeton University Press.

Sassen, S. (1994) *Cities in a World Economy*. Thousand Oaks, CA, Sage.

Sassen, S. (1996) *Losing Control: Sovereignty in an Age of Globalisation*. New York, Columbia University Press.

Sauer, C. [1925] (1963) 'The morphology of landscape', in J. Leighley (ed.), *Land and Life: Selections from the Writings of Carl Otwin Sauer*. Berkeley, University of California Press.

Saunders, H. and Stone, C. (1987) 'Development politics reconsidered', *Urban Affairs Quarterly*, **22**, 521–39.

Sayer, A. (1976) 'A critique of urban modelling', *Progress in Planning*, **6**, 187–254.

Sayer, A. (1992) *Method in Social Science: A Realist Approach*. London, Hutchinson.

Sayer, A. (2001) 'For a critical cultural political economy', *Antipode* **33**, 687–708.

Sayer, A. and Duncan, S. (1977) 'The new behavioural geography – a reply to Cullen', *Environment and Planning A*, **9**, 230–2.

Sayer, A. and Walker, R. (1992) *The New Social Economy: Reworking the Division of Labour*. Cambridge, Blackwell.

Schaefer, F. K. (1953) 'Exceptionalism in geography: a methodological examination', *Annals, Association of American Geographers*, **43**, 226–49.

Schivelbusch, W. (1986) *The Railway Journey: The Industrialisation and Perception of Time and Space in the Nineteenth Century*. Leamington Spa, Berg.

Schoenberger, E. (1996) *The Cultural Crisis of the Firm*. Oxford, Blackwell.

Scholte, J. A. (2000) *Globalisation: A Critical Introduction*. London, Macmillan.

Schutz, A. (1982) *Life Forms and Meaning Structures*. London, Routledge and Kegan Paul.

Seamon, D. (1979) *A Geography of the Lifeworld*. London, Croom Helm

Sennett, R. (1994) *The Flesh and the Stone: The Body and the City in Western Civilisation*. London, Faber and Faber.

Seymour, S. (2000) 'Historical geographies of landscape', in C. Nash and B. Graham (eds), *Modern Historical Geographies*. Harlow, Pearson.

Sharp, J. (1996) 'Hegemony, popular culture and geopolitics: Reader's Digest and the construction of danger', *Political Geography*, **12**, 491–503.

Sharp, J. P., Routledge, P., Philo, C. and Paddison, R. (2000) 'Entanglements of power: geographies of domination/resistance', in J. P. Sharp, P. Routledge, C. Philo and R. Paddison (eds), *Entanglements of Power*. London, Routledge.

Sheppard, E. (2001) 'Quantitative geography: representations, practices, and possibilities', *Environment and Planning D – Society and Space*,**19**, 535–54.

Sheridan, K. (1993) *Governing the Japanese Economy*. Cambridge, Polity Press.

Shields, R. (1991) *Places on the Margin*. London, Routledge.

Shields, R. (1997) 'Spatial stress and resistance: social meanings and spatialisation', in G. Benko and U. Strohmayer (eds), *Space and Social Theory*. Oxford, Blackwell.

Shields, R. (1998) *Lefebvre, Love and Struggle*. London, Routledge.

Short, J. R. (1991) *Imagined Country, Environment, Culture and Society*. London, Routledge.

Short, J. R. (1996) *The Urban Order*. Oxford, Blackwell.

Short, J. R. and Kim, Y.-H. (1999) *Globalisation and the City*. Harlow, Addison-Wesley Longman.

Shurmer-Smith, P. and Hannam, K. (1994) *Worlds of Desire, Realms of Power*. London, Arnold.

Sibley, D. (1990) 'Urban change and the exclusion of minority groups in British cities', *Geoforum*, **21**, 483–8.

Sibley, D. (1995) *Geographies of Exclusion: Society and Difference in the West*. London, Routledge.

Sibley, D. (2001) 'The binary city', *Urban Studies*, **38**, 239–50.

Sidaway, J. (1997) 'The production of British geography', *Transactions, Institute of British Geographers*, **22**, 488–504.

Silverstone, R. (1994) *Television and Everyday Life*. London, Routledge.

Simmel, G. (1971) *On Individuality and Social Forms*. Chicago, Chicago University Press.

Simmel, G. (1978) [1900] *The Philosophy of Money*, trans. T. Bottomore and D. Frisby. London, Routledge.

Sinclair, D. (2000) *The Pound: A Biography*. London, Arrow Books.

Skelton, T. and Valentine, G. (1998) *Cool Places: Geographies of Youth Cultures*. London, Routledge.

Sklair, L. (1991) *Sociology of the Global System: Social Change in Global Perspective*. London, Harvester Wheatsheaf.

Slater, D. (1998) 'Content analysis and semiotics', in C. Seale (ed.), *Researching Society and Culture*. London, Sage.

Slater, D. R. (1977) 'Geography and underdevelopment', *Antipode*, **5**, 21–33.

Slater, D. R. (1995) 'Trajectories of development theory: capitalism, socialism and beyond', in R. Johnston, P. Taylor and M. Watts (eds), *Geographies of Global Change*. Oxford, Blackwell.

Slater, D. R. (1999) 'Situating geopolitical representations: inside/outside and the crisis of national development', in D. Massey, J. Allen and P. Sarre (eds), *Human Geography Today*. Cambridge, Polity.

Slater, D. R. and Taylor, P. (eds) (1999) *The American Century*. Oxford, Blackwell.

Smart, B. (1996) *Post-modernism*. London, Routledge.

Smith, D. (2001) *Norbert Elias*. London, Sage.

Smith, D. A. and Timberlake, M. (1995) 'Cities in global matrices: toward mapping the world-system's city system', in P. L. Knox and P. J. Taylor (eds), *World Cities in a World System*. Cambridge, Cambridge University Press.

Smith, D. M. (1977) *Human Geography – A Welfare Approach*. London, Arnold.

Smith, D. M. (1994) *Geography and Social Justice*. Oxford, Blackwell.

Smith, D. M. (2000) *Moral Geographies*. Edinburgh, Edinburgh University Press.

Smith, M. J. (2000) *Culture: Reinventing the Social Sciences*. London, Sage.

Smith, N. (1984) *Urban Development: Nature, Capital and the Production of Space*. Oxford, Blackwell.

Smith, N. (1996) *The New Urban Frontier*. London, Routledge.

Smith, N. (1998) 'El Niño capitalism', *Progress in Human Geography*, **22**, 159–63.

Smith, N. (2000) 'Socializing culture, radicalizing the social', *Social and Cultural Geography*, **1**, 25–8.

Smith, R. G. (1997) 'The end of geography and radical politics in Baudrillard's philosophy', *Environment and Planning D – Society and Space*, **15**, 305–20.

Smith, S. (1989a) *The Politics of Race and Residence*. Cambridge, Polity.

Smith, S. (1989b) 'Society, space and citizenship: a human geography for the new times', *Transactions, Institute of British Geographers*, **14**, 144–56.

Social Exclusion Unit (1998) *Bringing Britain Together: A National Strategy for Neighbourhood Renewal*. London, HMSO.

Soja, E. (1985) 'The spatiality of social life: towards a transformative retheorisation', in D. Gregory and J. Urry (eds), *Social Relations and Spatial Structures*. Basingstoke, Macmillan.

Soja, E. (1986) 'Taking Los Angeles apart: some fragments of a critical human geography', *Environment and Planning D – Society and Space*, **4**, 255–72.

Soja, E. (1989) *Post-modern Geographies*. London, Verso.

Soja, E. (1996) *Thirdspace*. Oxford, Blackwell.

Sommers, J. (1998) 'Men at the margin: masculinity and space in downtown Vancouver 1950–86', *Urban Geography*, **19**, 287–310.

Sparke, M. (1996) 'Displacing the field in fieldwork: masculinity, metaphor and space', in N. Duncan (ed.) *Bodyspace: Destabilising Geographies of Gender and Sexuality*. London, Routledge.

Sparke, M. (1998) 'A map that roared and an original atlas', *Annals, Association of American Geographers*, **88**, 463–95.

Spivak, G. C. (1990) *The Post-colonial Critic: Interviews, Strategies, Dialogues*. London, Routledge.

Stoddart, D. (1986) *On Geography and its History*. Oxford, Blackwell.

Stoker, G. (1995) 'Regime theory and urban politics', in D. Judge, G. Stoker and H. Wolman (eds), *Theories of Urban Politics*. London, Sage.

Stoker, G. (1998) 'Public-private partnerships and urban governance', in J. Pierre (ed.), *Partnership in Urban Governance: European and American Experience*. New York, St Martin's Press.

Stone, C. (1989) *Regime Politics: Governing Atlanta*. Lawrence, KS, Kansas University Press.

Stone, C. (1993) 'Urban regimes and the capacity to govern: a political economy approach', *Journal of Urban Affairs*, **15**, 1–28.

Stone, C. (1996) 'Urban political machines: taking stock', *Political Science and Politics*, **29**(3), 446–50.

Stone, C., Orr, M. and Imbroscio, D. (1994) 'The re-shaping of urban leadership in U.S. cities: a regime analysis', in M. Gottdiener and C. Pickvance (eds), *Urban Life in Transition*. Beverly Hills, CA, Sage.

Stone, C. and Saunders, H. (1987) *The Politics of Urban Development*. Lawrence, KS, Kansas University Press.

Storey, J. (2001) *Cultural Theory and Popular Culture: An Introduction*. Harlow, Prentice Hall.

Storper, M. (1993) 'Regional worlds of production: learning and innovation in the technology districts of France, Italy and the USA', *Regional Studies*, **27**, 433–55.

Storper, M. (1997) *The Regional World: Territorial Development in a Global Economy*. Cambridge, MA, Harvard University Press.

Straussfogel, D. (1997) 'Redefining development as humane and sustainable', *Annals, Association of American Geographers*, **87**, 280–305.

Swyngedouw, E (1989) 'The heart of place: the resurrection of locality in an age of hyperspace', *Geografiska Annaler*, **71B**, 31–42.

Swyngedouw, E. (1992) 'The mammon quest. "Glocalisation", interspatial competition and the monetary order: the construction of new scale', in M. Dunford and G. Kafkala (eds), *Cities and Regions in the New Europe: The Global-Local Interplay and Spatial Development Strategies*. London, Belhaven.

Swyngedouw, E. (2000) 'Authoritarian governance, power and the politics of rescaling', *Environment and Planning D – Society and Space*, **18**, 63–76.

Taub, R. (1988) *Community Capitalism*. Boston, MA, Harvard Business School.

Taylor, P. (1991) 'The English and their Englishness: a curiously mysterious, elusive and little understood people', *Scottish Geographical Magazine*, **107**, 146–61.

Taylor, P. (1999a) '"So-called world cities": the evidential structure within a literature', *Environment and Planning A*, **31**, 1901–4.

Taylor, P. (1999b) *Modernities: A Geohistorical Analysis*. Cambridge, Polity.

Taylor, P. (1999c) 'Worlds of large cities: pondering Castells' space of flows', *Third World Planning Review*, **21**(3), 3–10.

Taylor, P. (2000) 'World cities and territorial states under conditions of contemporary globalization', *Political Geography*, **19**, 5–32.

Taylor, P. (2001) 'Urban hinterworlds: geographies of corporate service provision under conditions of contemporary globalization', *Geography*, **86**, 51–60.

Taylor, P., Catalano, G. and Walker. D. R. L. (2001) 'Measurement of the world city network', *GaWC Research Bulletin*, No. 43 (*www.lboro.ac.uk/gawc*).

Taylor, P. and Flint, C. (1999) *Political Geography: World-economy, Nation-state and Locality*, 4th edn. Harlow, Longman.

Teather, E. K. (ed.) (1999) *Embodied Geographies: Spaces, Bodies and Rites of Passage*. London, Routledge.

Thody, P. (1999) *Introducing Barthes*. Cambridge, Icon.

Thrift, N. (1977) *An Introduction to Time-geography: Concepts and Techniques in Modern Geography*. Norwich, Catmog 13.

Thrift, N. (1983) 'On the determination of social action in space and time', *Environment and Planning D – Society and Space*, **1**, 23–57.

Thrift, N. (1994a) 'Globalisation, regulation, urbanisation: the case of the Netherlands', *Urban Studies*, **31**, 365–80.

Thrift, N. (1994b) 'Money, geography of', in R. J. Johnston, D. Gregory and D. M. Smith (eds), *The Dictionary of Human Geography*, 3rd edn. Oxford, Blackwell.

Thrift, N. (1994c) 'On the social and cultural determinants of international financial centres: the case of the City of London', in S. Corbridge, N. Thrift and R. Martin (eds), *Money, Power and Space*. Oxford, Blackwell.

Thrift, N. (1995) 'A hyperactive world', in R. J. Johnston, P. J. Taylor and M. Watts (eds), *Geographies of Global Change: Remapping the World in the Late Twentieth Century*. Oxford, Blackwell.

Thrift, N. (1996) *Spatial Formations*. London, Sage.

Thrift, N. (1997) 'Cities without modernity, cities with magic', *Scottish Geographical Magazine*, **113**(2), 138–49.

Thrift, N. (1999) 'Steps toward an ecology of place', in D. Massey, J. Allen and P. Sarre (eds), *Human Geography Today*. Cambridge, Polity Press.

Thrift, N. (2000a) 'Not a straight line, but a curve', in D. Bell and A. Haddour (eds), *City Visions*. Harlow, Prentice Hall.

Thrift, N. (2000b) 'Performing cultures in the new economy', *Annals, Association of American Geographers*, **90**, 674–92.

Thrift, N. (2000c) 'Non-representational theory', in R. J. Johnston, D. Gregory, G. Pratt and M. Watts (eds), *The Dictionary of Human Geography*. Oxford, Blackwell.

Thrift, N. and Olds, K. (1996) 'Reconfiguring the economic in economic geography', *Progress in Human Geography*, **20**, 311–37.

Tickell, A. (1999) 'Money and finance', in P. Cloke, P. Crang and M. Goodwin (eds), *Introducing Human Geographies*. London, Arnold.

Tickell, A. and Peck, J. (1992) 'Accumulation, regulation and the geographies of post-Fordism: missing links in regulationist research', *Progress in Human Geography*, **16**, 190–218.

Tuan, Y.-F. (1974) 'Space and place: a humanistic perspective', *Progress in Geography*, **6**, 233–46 (excerpted in J. Agnew, D. Livingstone and A. Rogers (eds) (1996), *Human Geography: An Essential Anthology*. Oxford, Blackwell).

Tuan, Y.-F. (1975) 'Place: an experiential perspective', *Geographical Review*, **65**, 151–165.

Tuan, Y.-F. (1977) *Space and Place: The Perspective of Experience*. Minneapolis, University of Minnesota Press.

Tuan, Y.-F. (1978) *Landscapes of Fear*. Oxford, Blackwell.

Tuan, Y.-F. (1998a) *Escapism*. New York, John Hopkins University Press.

Tuan, Y.-F. (1998b) *A Life in Learning*. American Council of Science, Occasional Paper, No. 42.

Turner, B. (1988) *Status*. Buckingham, Open University.

Unwin, T. (1992) *The Place of Geography*. Harlow, Longman.

Unwin, T. (2000) 'A waste of space? Towards a critique of the social production of space', *Transactions, Institute of British Geographers*, **25**, 11–29.

Urry, J. (1994) *Consuming Places*. London, Routledge.

Urry, J. (2000a) 'Mobile sociology', *Sociology*, **51**(1), 185–203.

Urry, J. (2000b) *Sociology Beyond Societies: Mobilities for the Twenty-first Century*. London, Routledge.

Valentine, G. (1993) 'Hetero-sexing space: lesbian perceptions and experiences of everyday spaces', *Environment and Planning D – Society and Space*, **9**, 395–413.

Valentine, G. (1996) '(Re)negotiating the "heterosexual street": lesbian productions of space', in N. Duncan (ed.) *BodySpace*. London, Routledge.

Valentine, G. (1998) 'Sticks and stones may break my bones: a personal geography of harassment', *Antipode*, **30**, 305–32.

Valentine, G. (1999) 'A corporeal geography of consumption', *Environment and Planning D – Society and Space*, **17**, 329–51.

Valentine, G. (2001) *Social Geographies*. Harlow, Prentice Hall.

Veblen, T. (1934) *The Theory of the Leisure Class*. New York, Modern Library.

Virilio, P. (1991) *The Lost Dimension*. New York, Semiotext(e).

Virilio, P. (1999) *Polar Inertia*. London, Sage.

Wagner, P. and Mikesell, M. (1962) *Readings in Cultural Geography*. Chicago, University of Chicago Press.

Walby, S. (1990) *Theorising Patriarchy*. London, Blackwell.

Wall, M. (1997) 'Stereotyped constructions of Maori race in the media', *New Zealand Geographer*, **53**, 40–5.

Wallerstein, I. (1974) *The Modern World System*. New York, Academic Press.

Wallerstein, I. (1984) *The Politics of the World Economy*. Cambridge, Cambridge University Press.

Walmsley, D. J. and Lewis, G. (1993) *People and Environment: An Introduction to Behavioural Approaches*. Harlow, Longman.

Ward, K. (1996) 'Rereading urban regime theory: a sympathetic critique', *Geoforum*, **27**, 427–38.

Warf, B. (1994) 'Vicious circle: financial markets and commercial real estate in the United States', in S. Corbridge, R. Martin and N. Thrift (eds), *Money, Power and Space*. Oxford, Blackwell.

Waters, M. (2001) *Globalisation*. London, Routledge.

Watney, S. (1994) *Practices of Freedom: Selected Writings on HIV/AIDS*. London, Rivers Oram Press.

Watson, S. (1986) 'Housing the family', *International Journal of Urban and Regional Research*, **10**, 8–28.

Watts, M. (1983) *Silent Violence*. Berkeley, University of California Press.

Watts, M. (1997) 'Black gold, white heat: state violence, local resistance and the national question in Nigeria', in S. Pile and M. Keith (eds), *Geographies of Resistance*. London, Routledge.

Watts, M. (1999) 'Collective wish images: geographical imaginaries and the crisis of national development', in D. Massey, J. Allen and P. Sarre (eds), *Human Geography Today*. Cambridge, Polity, pp. 84–107

Watts, M. (2000) 'Political ecology', in R. Johnston, D. Gregory, G. Pratt and M. Watts (eds), *The Dictionary of Human Geography*, 4th edn. Oxford, Blackwell.

Weiss, L. and Hobson, J. (1995) *States and Economic Development: A Comparative Historical Analysis*. Cambridge, Polity Press.

Werlen, B. (1993) *Society, Action and Space: An Alternative Human Geography*. London, Routledge.

Whatmore, S. (1999) 'Hybrid geographies: rethinking the human in human geography', in D. Massey, J. Allen and P. Sarre (eds), *Human Geography Today*. Cambridge, Polity.

Whatmore, S. and Thorne, L. (1997) 'Nourishing networks: alternative geographies of food', in D. Goodman and M. Watts (eds), *Globalising Food: Agrarian Questions and Global Restructuring*. London, Routledge.

Whelan, R., Young, A. and Lauria, M. (1994) 'Urban regimes and racial politics in New Orleans', *Journal of Urban Affairs*, **16**, 1–21.

Whittle, S. (ed.) (1994) *The Margins of the City: Gay Men's Urban Lives*. Aldershot, Arena.

Williams, C. C. (1996) 'Local exchange and trading systems: a new source of work and credit for the poor and unemployed', *Environment and Planning A*, **28**, 1395–415.

Williams, C. C. and Windebank, J. (2000) 'Modes of goods acquisition in deprived neighbourhoods' *International Review of Retail, Distribution and Consumer Research*, **10**, 73–94.

Williams, R. (1973) *The Country and the City*. London, Chatto and Windus.

Williams, R. (1976) *Keywords*. London, Fontana.

Williams, S. and Bendelow, G. (1998) *The Lived Body: Sociological Themes, Embodied Issues*. London, Routledge.

Williamson, J. (1986) *The Meaning of Fashion*. London, Marion Byars.

Wilson, A. G. (1972) 'Theoretical geography', *Transactions, Institute of British Geographers*, **57**, 31–44.

Wilson, A. G. (1999) *Complex Urban Systems*. Harlow, Prentice Hall.

Wilson, E. (2001) *The Contradictions of Culture: Cities, Culture, Women*. London, Sage.

Wilton, R. D. (1998) 'The constitution of difference: space and psyche in landscapes of exclusion', *Geoforum*, **29**, 173–85.

Winchester, H. and White, P. (1988) 'The location of marginalised groups in the inner city', *Environment and Planning D – Society and Space*, **6**, 37–54.

Withers, C. (1996) 'Place, memory, monument: memorialising the past in contemporary Highland Scotland', *Ecumene*, **3**, 325–44.

Wittgenstein, L. (1921) [1974] *Tractatus Logico-Philosophicus*, trans. by D. F. Pears and B. F. McGuinness. London, Routledge.

Wolch, J. and Emel, J. (eds) (1997) *Animal Geographies*. New York, Verso.

Wolfreys, J. (ed.) (1998) *The Derrida Reader: Writing Performances*. Edinburgh, Edinburgh University Press.

Women and Geography Study Group (1984) *Geography and Gender: An Introduction to Feminist Geography*. London, Hutchinson.

Women and Geography Study Group (1997) *Feminist Geographies: Explorations in Diversity and Difference*. Harlow, Longman.

Wood, P. (1991) 'Flexible accumulation and the rise of business services', *Transactions, Institute of British Geographers*, **16**(2), 160–72.

Woodward, K. (1997) *Identity and Difference*. London, Sage.

Wright, J. K. (1947) 'Terrae incognitae: the place of imagination in geography', *Annals, Association of American Geographers*, **37**, 1–15.

Wylie, J. (2000) 'New and old worlds: *The Tempest* and early colonial discourse', *Social and Cultural Geography*, **1**, 45–64.

Yeates, M. (1968) *An Introduction to Quantitative Analysis in Economic Geography*. New York, McGraw-Hill.

Yeates, N. (2001) *Globalisation and Social Policy*. Thousand Oaks, CA, Sage.

Young, I. M. (1990) *Justice and the Politics of Difference*. Princeton, NJ, Princeton University Press.

Zelizer, V. (1989) 'The social meaning of money: special monies', *American Journal of Sociology*, **95**, 342–77.

Zelizer, V. (1994) *The Social Meaning of Money*. New York, Basic Books.

Žižek, S. (1999) *The Ticklish Subject*. London, Verso.

Zukin, S. (1992) *Landscapes of Power*. Berkeley, California University Press.

Index